JUSTICE

Crimes, Trials, and Punishments

Dominick Dunne

time
paperbacks

A *Time Warner* Paperback

First published in the United States of America by
Crown Publishers, New York in 2001
First published in Great Britain by Time Warner Paperbacks in 2002

Copyright © Dominick Dunne 2001

A CIP catalogue record for this book is available
from the British Library.

ISBN 0 7515 3260 6

Typeset in Bondini Book by
Palimpsest Book Production Limited,
Polmont, Stirlingshire

Printed and bound in Great Britain by
Clays Ltd, St Ives plc

Time Warner Paperbacks
An imprint of
Time Warner Books UK
Brettenham House
Lancaster Place
London WC2E 7EN

www.TimeWarnerBooks.co.uk

For my two great editors,
BETTY PRASHKER
of Crown,
who has guided me through my books,
and
WAYNE LAWSON
of *Vanity Fair,*
who has guided me through every article,
with love and thanks

CONTENTS

INTRODUCTION

I DIDN'T START WRITING until I was fifty years old although an observer's eye had been observing for forty of those fifty years, while trying out different areas of occupation. My career in television and movies in Hollywood had come to a permanent halt, and I had nowhere else to turn. The thought of writing had been lurking within me for some time, but I didn't actually begin until I finally removed myself from the glamorous world in which I no longer belonged to a one-room cabin in the Cascade Mountains of Oregon. There I began my second career as a writer and a recorder of the social history of the time. The plot of that first book had been played out in front of me the year before I left Hollywood. The gossip of the set in which I had once moved centered around the head of Columbia Studios, David Begelman, who, rumor had it, had forged a check for ten thousand dollars in the name of Cliff Robertson, an Academy Award-winning actor. Barely a word of the scandal appeared in the Los Angeles papers. Powerful people saw to that. The wagons closed in to protect one of their own. I was watching it firsthand as it was happening. I became obsessed with the story. As I was out of work, I had plenty of time to feed my obsession, and I gossiped about it nonstop on the telephone, trying to get the story into wider circulation. I knew all the players in it, and their wives, agents, secretaries, and mistresses.

By sheer happenstance, in the sort of coincidental meeting that is a signature of my life, a man I did not know recognized me in the Polo Lounge of the Beverly Hills Hotel. I was there having lunch with my agent, who was telling me I was all washed up, which I already knew. I was not remotely famous, so it was not that sort of recognition. It developed that one of my brothers had been in this man's class at Georgetown, and he recognized the family resemblance. He turned out to be a reporter from the *Washington Post*, and what he had been sent out to cover was the long-suppressed forgery story that was so gripping to me. He told me that the actress Dina Merrill, the then wife of Cliff Robertson, had gone to Kay Graham, then publisher of the *Washington Post*, and said that a cover-up of the forgery was going on. Mrs Graham sent out the reporter and a partner to check out the story. But no one would talk to them. Secretaries would not put through their calls. Doors would not open for him. They had not been able to gather anything of consequence to bear out Dina Merrill's version of the story. The enormity of the coincidence that this reporter and I should meet ultimately turned out to be a life-changing experience for me. I was like manna from heaven for him, and he was the release I needed for the story that was bursting inside of me to be made known. The Begelman story was the epitome of everything I had grown to hate about Hollywood. In all honesty, there was also a bit of revenge in my motive, because of my failure there. I knew a great deal of the information the reporter was seeking and I willingly shared it, including all the unlisted telephone numbers he needed. I spent a week with him and his partner, driving around with them, watching two investigative reporters research and then put together a story. It was they who broke the story nationally. It was thrilling for me to know that I had played a part in it. I felt a kind of excitement within myself that I hadn't felt about the movie industry for a long time. *I could do what these guys are doing*, I thought to myself. It took a while, but that's what happened, and that's what this book is: a collection of stories about the cases and trials that I have covered for *Vanity Fair* magazine. Incidentally, the studio head who forged the check only had to attend a few sessions with a psychologist popular in the Hollywood community as punishment for his theft. He then became the head of MGM and continued to be invited to parties and to give Sunday-night screenings in the projection room at his house of all the latest films for all the best people. On the other hand, the Academy Award-winning actor whose name he forged never got a role of any consequence in Hollywood again. Years later, Begelman shot himself to death in a room at the Century Plaza Towers. His widow sent me a straw hat of his that I once admired.

A tragic event in my personal life changed me forever.

In 1982, my only daughter, Dominique, was murdered by a former boyfriend, John Sweeney, who stalked her and strangled her. I had never attended a trial until that of the man who murdered my daughter. In fact, I had been a feather in the breeze until that cataclysmic event – here, there, everywhere, never sure of who I was or what I was supposed to be. What I witnessed in that courtroom enraged me and redirected me. The lies that are tolerated shocked me, as did the show-business aspect that has taken over the justice system. My daughter's killer was 'costumed' like a sacristan in a Catholic seminary. For a prop, he carried a Bible, which he read throughout the trial in a pious fashion. He was presented as a blue-collar boy who had fallen in love with a Beverly Hills society girl. How I hated his lawyer. I learned in that courtroom that the rights of the victim do not equate with the rights of the defendant. Anything can be said about the dead, and much was, but the killer's grave past offenses as a beater of women were kept from the jury. The testimony of another of his victims, who had been hospitalized as a result of his acts of violence, was, inexplicably, ruled inadmissable. The trial was a travesty. There has been a television documentary about it. The judge had a personal animosity toward the prosecutor. How I hated that judge. The jury fell for the Bible-reading act, and John Sweeney, who has subsequently changed his name, received a sentence of six years, which was automatically reduced to three. He was released from prison after two and a half. How I hated him, even as I knew that hate is not a state in which to linger. My rage needed a release from the persistent plan in my mind to hire someone to kill him, an obsession I had for months, which is not an uncommon reaction for the parent of a murdered child. But, unlike the killer, I would have ended up in prison for life. Instead, I wrote about the murder – not just about the facts of the story but about the emotional upheaval and permanent scars my wife, my sons, and I suffered during that terrible period. The first magazine article I ever wrote is the story of that trial. It appeared in *Vanity Fair* in March 1984. The affirmative reaction to the article, titled 'Justice', made me realize the power of the written word. It was read in some law schools to show just how badly a trial could go. I was proud of that. For the first time in my life, I felt that I was in step with my destiny. I became fascinated by trials. I attended a great many of the high profile trials of the last decade and a half, including the senatorial impeachment trial of President Clinton. I became repelled by the kind of defense attorney who would do anything – anything – to win an acquittal for a guilty person. 'They're just doing their job, Dominick,' other reporters would say to me, but I could never bring myself around to that way of thinking.

Somewhere along the line, most likely because I had had the experience myself, I began to get personally involved in the trials I was covering. During the Claus von Bülow trial in Providence, Rhode Island, I spent the night at Clarendon Court, the magnificent Newport estate of the comatose Sunny von Bülow, as the guest of her children Princess Ala von Auersperg and Prince Alexander von Auersperg. A friend of Sunny's who was a friend of mine had arranged the introductions. Ala and Alex showed me the bedroom where whatever happened between Claus and their mother happened, leading to the perpetual coma in which she remains twenty years later. Her Porthault sheets were still on the bed. Her Christmas presents from that year had never been unwrapped. I felt guilty for experiencing such excitement at the intimacy of the encounter. At that moment, I entered the story and became a part of it. 'Bad journalism,' journalists say. 'So what,' I say back. Things happen to me, and I let them happen and then write about them later. At a subsequent time in the von Bülow trial, during an Easter Sunday lunch party at Sunny von Bülow's grand Fifth Avenue apartment in New York, I sat on Sunny's bed with Claus's mistress, Andrea Reynolds, while she showed me that her jewels were equal to Sunny's. We ate off Sunny's beautiful dishes and drank from her glasses. The lobster salad was served by a Chinese butler in white gloves. It was surreal. I always say to myself, 'I can't believe I'm here watching what I'm watching.' The next day we were back in court in Providence, where von Bülow was on trial for attempted murder.

Trials can get boring, but the lives of the people involved in the trials are never boring to me. I had been friends with the Los Angeles socialites Alfred and Betsy Bloomingdale. After Alfred's death, I covered the trial of the madman who killed Vicki Morgan, Alfred's mistress, by beating her to death with a baseball bat. I became friendly with O. J. Simpson's sisters, fine ladies both, while writing each month that I believed Simpson was guilty. I was the first one to report that the young and handsome

Lyle Menendez wore a wig, an unknown fact until then that was passed on to me by Lyle's wig maker, who sought me out. From her debutante days in the '50s, I knew Lisa Dean Moseley, the du Pont heiress whose husband was on trial in Las Vegas for the murder-for-hire death of a drug-addicted prostitute with whom his stepson was in love. I was two years behind Michael Skakel's father at boarding school, and I had attended his aunt Ethel's wedding to Robert Kennedy in 1950.

On the day before the verdict at the O. J. Simpson trial, I stepped into an elevator in which the only other passenger was Simpson's son from his first marriage, Jason. He had been unfriendly and hostile for the nine months of the trial, and we had never spoken, but he spoke to me that day in the elevator. 'How was Norman Lear's dinner?' he asked me, referring to a celebrity dinner party I had attended a few evenings before at the home of the creator of *All in the Family*. 'How did you know I was at Norman Lear's dinner?' I asked, startled. He told me he had been the catering service chef in the kitchen while I had held court in the dining room discussing his father in a very derogatory manner. I thought, *My God, what are the odds that this could happen?* But things like that happen to me quite often. A young man appeared out of nowhere to hand me a secret report by a private detective agency hired by the father of Michael Skakel that led directly to the indictment and trial of Skakel for the murder of fifteen-year-old Martha Moxley twenty-five years earlier. After billionaire banker Edmund Safra was asphyxiated in his Monte Carlo penthouse on December 3, 1998, I had a chance encounter at the 21 Club in New York with a famous couple in the financial world that led me to the inner sanctum of Safra's mysterious life and even more mysterious death. While I was trying to make an early, unobtrusive exit from a New York party, a butler, helping me on with my coat, whispered to me, 'I have something to tell you.' He was talking about the case I was writing about. Another time, I was staying at the Brazilian Court in Palm Beach during the William Kennedy Smith trial. The telephone rang late at night, after I had gone to sleep. It was the woman who had brought the rape charge against Smith, Patricia Bowman, who became known as the girl behind the blue dot on television. 'I saw you in court today,' she said. She invited me to meet with her in her home. I got the only print interview she ever gave.

In my everyday life over the last fifty years, it has been my curious lot to move among the rich and famous and powerful, always as an outsider, always listening, watching, remembering. In many of the stories in this book, I have social relationships with the person on trial, or the victim, or their families and friends. I walk a very fine line. There are those I meet who despise me. The Kennedys. The Skakels. Claus von Bülow. O. J. Simpson, on and on. The list is long. At the William Kennedy Smith rape trial in Palm Beach, I sat right across the aisle from four of the female members of the Kennedy family, all of whom I knew. We never spoke. At the trial of the Menendez brothers in Los Angeles for the murder of their parents, I became the enemy of their defense attorney,

Leslie Abramson. Jose Menendez, the Hollywood corporate chief who was shotgunned to death by his two sons in their Beverly Hills mansion, was a tough and unlikable man, as well as an overdemanding father, but the lies told about him at the trial, reducing him to the lowest kind of pervert, revolted me. I am told by a reliable source who visits Lyle and Erik Menendez in the separate prisons where they are serving life without the possibility of parole, that the brothers, who never discuss the murders, regret that they participated in the defaming of their father. I long to visit them in prison myself one day to see if they will tell me what really happened that night. At the O. J. Simpson trial, at which I had a permanent seat courtesy of Judge Lance Ito, I received hate mail and death threats, and was booed by the crowds outside the courtroom because of my outspoken belief in Simpson's guilt. After the hearings for the Skakel–Moxley case in Stamford, Connecticut, Robert Kennedy, Jr, lashed out at me in print, but I lashed back pretty good. I have seen New York hostesses change place cards at the last minute, because the person I am seated next to doesn't want to sit next to me, because of a story I am working on. I never mind, really. It goes with the territory. Somehow, it always turns out there is a connection. Besides, I can always use it in one of my novels.

It is one of the curiosities of my life that its greatest tragedy turned me to an area of my writing career that is so rewarding to me. It's so wonderful to be able to say, 'I love my life,' and I do. When my daughter was about to be taken off the life-support system at Cedars-Sinai

Medical Center, we went in as a family and talked to her. Then we each went in alone to say good-bye to her privately. They had cut her beautiful hair off. She would have hated that. I kissed her on her bald head, and I said, 'Give me your talent.' She did. I believe with all my heart that she has guided me to the paths of justice.

JUSTICE:
A Father's Account of the Trial of His Daughter's Killer

I T WAS THE BEGINNING OF a long hot summer. I flew to Los Angeles on July 5, 1983, for an indefinite stay. Throughout the flight from New York I engaged in diligent conversation with the stranger next to me, postponing as long as possible facing the feelings of dread within me. My two sons, Griffin and Alex, had preceded me out from New York. Alex, the younger one, met me at the airport, and we drove into Beverly Hills to the house where my former wife, Ellen Griffin Dunne, called Lenny, lives. Griffin was already there. It is not the house we lived in as a family. It is smaller and on one level. Lenny has multiple sclerosis and is confined to a wheelchair. We were gathering, a family again, for a murder trial.

The first time I saw Lenny she was getting off a train at the railroad station in Hartford, Connecticut. She was ravishing, and I knew that instant that I would marry her if she would have me. We had a large wedding at her family's ranch in Nogales, Arizona, in 1954, and after living briefly in New York, we moved to Beverly Hills, where I worked for twenty-five years in television and films. We had five children, two of whom died when they were only a few days old. Long divorced, we have, rightly or wrongly, never become unmarried. Often I have felt through the years that our lives might have been better if we had just stuck out the difficult years of our marriage, but I do not know if she would agree with that. We never venture into the realm of what might have been. I refer to her in conversation as my wife, never my ex-wife, and there is not a day in which she does not occupy my thoughts for some period of time. We communicate regularly and mail each other clippings we cut out of newspapers, and I no longer resent, as I once did, addressing her as Mrs E. Griffin Dunne rather than as Mrs Dominick Dunne.

WHEN THE TELEPHONE in my New York apartment woke me at five o'clock in the morning on October 31, 1982, I sensed as I reached for the receiver that disaster loomed. Detective Harold Johnston of the Los Angeles Homicide Bureau told me that my twenty-two-year-old daughter, Dominique, was near death at Cedars-Sinai Medical Center. I asked him if he had notified my wife. He said he was calling from her home. Lenny got on the phone and said, 'I need you.'

'What happened?' I asked, afraid to hear.

'Sweeney,' she answered.

'I'll be on the first plane.'

I called Griffin, then twenty-seven, who lives two blocks away from me in New York, and within minutes he was at my door. He called TWA and reserved a seat on the next flight. Then he went to an automatic teller machine and got me money. As I threw clothes into a suitcase, I hesitated over my black suit and tie, thinking they might be bad luck, but I packed them. Before I got into the taxi, I hugged Griffin and kissed him. He was to go then to the apartment of my second son, Alex, and break the news to him. Uniquely individual, Alex chose to live with no telephone on Pitt Street in a relatively inaccessible part of New York. Only Alex, of the four of us, had voiced his dislike of John Sweeney when Dominique introduced him into our lives.

She had brought him to New York several months earlier for the boys and me to meet. Dominique was a successful young television actress, who had just made her first major feature film, *Poltergeist*. Sweeney was the head chef at Ma Maison, a West Hollywood restaurant so concerned with its fashionable image that it had an unlisted telephone number to discourage the *hoi polloi* from entering its portals. We watched an episode of the television series *Fame* in which Dominique was the guest star, and then went out to dinner. At one moment when the four of us were alone, the boys teased Dominique about marriage, and she said, oh no, she was not getting married, and I knew she meant it. I was relieved, for although I could see Sweeney was excessively devoted to her, there was something off-putting about him. That night I phoned her mother and said, 'He is much more in love with her than she is with him,' and Lenny said, 'You're absolutely right.'

The next morning Alex told me of an incident that had occurred in P. J. Clarke's after I left them. While Sweeney was in the men's room, a man at the bar recognized Dominique as the older sister in *Poltergeist* and called out one of her lines from the film: 'What's happening?' Dominique screams that line when evil spirits start to take over her home and cause frightening things to happen. A film clip of that scene has been shown so often on television that the line was familiar to people all over the country. There was no flirtation; it was the case of a slightly tipsy fan delighted to be in the presence of an actress he had seen in a film. But when Sweeney returned to the table and saw the man talking to Dominique, he became enraged. He picked up the man and shook him. Alex said that Sweeney's reaction was out of all proportion to the innocent scene going on. Alex said he was scary.

The following day I arrived a few minutes late at Lutèce, where I was meeting Dominique and Sweeney for lunch. They had not yet arrived, so I sat at a table in the bar to wait for them. I finished one Perrier and ordered another, and was beginning to think there had been a misunderstanding about either the time or the place when they entered the restaurant. It was a hot summer day, and Dominique looked marvelous in a starched white organdy dress, very California-looking. I was immediately aware that she had been crying, and that there was tension between them.

The chef made a great fuss over Sweeney. There was kissing on both cheeks, and they spoke together in French. At the chef's suggestion we ate the *spécialité* of the day, whatever it was, but the lunch was not a success. I found Sweeney ill at ease, nervous, difficult to talk to. It occurred to me that Dominique might have difficulty extricating herself from such a person, but I did not pursue the thought.

On the Fourth of July the three of us dined at the River Café under the Brooklyn Bridge. It was a lovely night, and we were at a window table where we could watch the fireworks. Sweeney told me he intended to leave Ma Maison. He said he had backing from a consortium of French and Japanese businessmen and was going to open his own restaurant in Melrose Park, a highly desirable location in Los Angeles. Never once did he speak affectionately of his employer, Patrick Terrail, a member of the French restaurant family that owns the Tour d'Argent in Paris. In fact, I suspected there were bad feelings between them.

ON THAT ENDLESS FLIGHT to Los Angeles I did not allow myself to consider the possibility of her death. She was making a pilot at Warner Bros for an NBC miniseries called *V*, and I remember thinking that they would have to shoot around her until she was on her feet again. Five weeks earlier she had broken up with John Sweeney, and he had moved out of the house they shared in West Hollywood. Her explanation to me at the time was, 'He's not in love with me, Dad. He's obsessed with me. It's driving me crazy.'

Two other daughters preceding Dominique died in

infancy from a lung disease once common in cesarean births known as hyaline membrane disease. Dominique was all three daughters in one to us, triply loved. She adored her older brothers and was always totally at ease in a sophisticated world without being sophisticated herself. She was a collector of stray animals; in her menagerie were a cat with a lobotomy and a large dog with stunted legs. She went to Westlake School in Los Angeles, then to Taft School in Connecticut, then to Fountain Valley School in Colorado. After that she spent a year in Florence, where she learned to speak Italian. Twice she and I took trips in Italy together. Extravagantly emotional, she was heartbroken when Lenny gave up the family home on Walden Drive because her worsening condition made it unmanageable. I was not surprised when Dominique announced her intention to become an actress. Griffin, who is an actor and a producer, later said jokingly that one day she decided to become an actress and the next week she was on a back lot making a movie, and that from then on she never stopped. It was very nearly true. She loved being an actress and was passionate about her career.

By the time I arrived in Los Angeles at noon that Sunday, the report that Dominique had been strangled outside her home by her former boyfriend and was in a coma at Cedars-Sinai Medical Center was on all the news channels and stations. Mart Crowley, the author of *The Boys in the Band*, the film version of which I had produced, met me at the airport and filled me in with what little information he had got from Lenny. Lenny's house on Crescent Drive was full of people when we got there. (It would stay that way from early morning until late at night for the next seven or eight days, during which relay teams of friends manned the telephones, screened the calls, handled the coffee detail, accepted the endless deliveries of flowers, made all the arrangements for our day-to-day living.) All the television sets and radios were on for news bulletins. In the midst of this confusion sat Lenny in her wheelchair. She was very calm. 'The news is not good,' she said to me. And within minutes I heard the words 'brain damage' being whispered around the house.

Lenny's mother, who had heard the news on the radio, was on her way from San Diego. Griffin and Alex's plane would be in in a few hours. My relatives in Hartford called, and, as the news spread, so did friends in New York and London. A doctor at the hospital telephoned for my permission to insert a bolt into Dominique's skull to relieve the pressure on her brain. Was it absolutely necessary? I asked. Yes, he replied. All right, I said. I asked him when we could go and see her. Not yet, he said.

The boys arrived, ashen-faced. When the time came to go to the hospital, we were full of dreadful apprehension. Some friends said to Lenny, 'You mustn't go. It would be a terrible mistake to look at her this way. You must remember her as she was.' They were, of course, thinking of Lenny's health; stress is the worst thing for multiple sclerosis victims. She replied, 'The mistake would be if I didn't see her. That is what I would have to live with.'

The four of us proceeded in silence through the maze of corridors leading to the intensive care unit on the fifth floor of Cedars-Sinai. One of us, I don't remember which, pushed Lenny's wheelchair, and the other two flanked her – a formation we would automatically fall into many times in the year that followed. Outside the double doors of the unit are printed instructions telling you to buzz and announce yourself. I did so: 'The family of Dominique Dunne is here.' We were told to wait, that someone would come out and get us.

Several people were standing there, among them the actor George Hamilton. We exchanged greetings. George said his brother was also in the ICU, and that he had been there the night before when Dominique was brought in. Another man introduced himself to us as Ken Johnson, the director of the pilot Dominique was working on. Waiting nearby was a young actor in the same film named David Packer, his eyes red from crying. Packer, we learned, had been in Dominique's house at the time of the attack and had called in the police, albeit too late. Later we also learned that Packer became so frightened by the struggle he heard outside on the lawn that he left a message on a friend's answering machine saying, 'If I die tonight, it was by John Sweeney.'

A nurse appeared and told us that after we had seen Dominique the doctors would want to talk with us. She said that no one but immediate family would be allowed in, and asked us to show identification. They were afraid the press would try to pass themselves off as members of the family. She warned us that it would be a shock to look at her, that we should be prepared.

I worried about Lenny and looked over at her. She

closed her eyes, bowed her head, and took a deep breath. I watched her will strength into herself, through some inner spiritual force, in a moment so intensely private that I dared not, even later, question her about it. Of the four of us, she was the strongest when we entered the room.

At first I did not realize that the person on the bed was Dominique. There were tubes in her everywhere, and the life-support system caused her to breathe in and out with a grotesque jerking movement that seemed a parody of life. Her eyes were open, massively enlarged, staring sightlessly up at the ceiling. Her beautiful hair had been shaved off. A large bolt had been screwed into her skull to relieve the pressure on her brain. Her neck was purpled and swollen; vividly visible on it were the marks of the massive hands of the man who had strangled her. It was nearly impossible to look at her, but also impossible to look away.

Lenny wheeled her chair to the bed, took Dominique's hand in hers, and spoke to her in a voice of complete calm. 'Hello, my darling, it's Mom. We're all here, Dominique. Dad and Griffin and Alex. We love you.'

Her words released us, and the boys and I stepped forward and surrounded the bed, each touching a different part of Dominique. The nurses had said that she could not hear us, but we felt she could, and took turns talking to her. We prayed for her to live even though we knew that it would be best for her to die.

There was a small conference room in the ICU where we met periodically over the next four days to discuss her ebbing life. Dr Edward Brettholz told us that the brain scan was even, meaning that it showed no life, but that it would be necessary to take three more scans so that, in the trial ahead, the defense could not claim that Cedars-Sinai had removed Dominique from the life-support system too soon. This was the first mention of a trial. In the shocked state in which we were operating, we had not yet started to deal with the fact that a murder had taken place.

On the fourth day Lenny said, quite unexpectedly, to the doctors, 'When Dominique dies, we would like her organs donated to the hospital.' The boys and I knew that was exactly what Dominique would have wanted, but it would not have occurred to us to say so at that moment. Lenny, ill herself with a disease for which there is no cure, understood. Dr Gray Elrod, with tears in his eyes, said two patients in the hospital were waiting for kidney transplants. We then went in and said good-bye to Dominique for the last time before they took her off the support system. She was wheeled to surgery for the removal of her kidneys, and transplant operations took place almost immediately. Her heart was sent to a hospital in San Francisco. Then her body was turned over to the coroner for an autopsy.

IN THE *LOS ANGELES TIMES* a day or so after the attack, Patrick Terrail, the owner of Ma Maison, described his chef, John Sweeney, as a 'very dependable young man' and said he would obtain the best legal representation for him. He made no comment about Dominique, whom he knew, as he knew us, and throughout the long ordeal that followed he did not call on us or write a letter of condolence. Since it was too early then to deal with the magnitude of my feelings for the killer of my daughter, Patrick Terrail became the interim object of my growing rage.

Obtaining the best legal representation for Sweeney took an economy turn when a public defender, Michael Adelson, was assigned to handle the case. We heard from Detective Johnston that Adelson was highly acclaimed and doggedly tough. Assisting the public defender, however, was Joseph Shapiro, the legal counsel for Ma Maison and a member of the prestigious law firm of Donovan, Leisure, Newton & Irvine. Although Shapiro's role on the defense team was later played down, he was an ever-present but elusive figure from the night following the murder, when he visited Sweeney in the Beverly Hills jail, right up until the day of the verdict, when he exulted in the courtroom.

At the time of the murder Dominique was consistently identified in the press as the niece of my brother and sister-in-law, John Gregory Dunne and Joan Didion, rather than as the daughter of Lenny and me. At first I was too stunned by the killing for this to matter, but as the days passed, it bothered me. I spoke to Lenny about it one morning in her bedroom. She said, 'Oh, what difference does it make?' with such despair in her voice that I felt ashamed to be concerned with such a trivial matter at such a crucial time.

In the room with us was my former mother-in-law, Beatriz Sandoval Griffin Goodwin, the widow of Lenny's father, Thomas Griffin, an Arizona cattle rancher, and of Lenny's stepfather, Ewart Goodwin, an insurance tycoon and rancher. She was a strong, uncompromising woman who has never not stated exactly what was on her mind in any given situation, a trait that has made her respected if not always endearing.

'Listen to what he's saying to you,' she said emphatically. 'It sounds as if Dominique was an orphan raised by her aunt and uncle.' Lenny looked up with a changed expression. '*And*', added her mother, to underscore the point, 'she had two brothers as well.'

'You handle it,' Lenny said to me. I called the publicist Rupert Allan, a family friend, and explained the situation to him. 'It's hurtful to us. It's as if we had not only lost her but been denied parentage as well,' I said. 'It'll be taken care of,' Rupert said, and it was.

ON THE MORNING OF November 4, while the autopsy was going on, I went to visit the elderly monsignor at the Church of the Good Shepherd in Beverly Hills to make the arrangements for Dominique's funeral. In years past this church was jokingly referred to as Our Lady of the Cadillacs for the affluence of its parishioners. The housekeeper at the rectory told me the monsignor was in the church saying mass. I waited in the front pew until he finished. Then I went back into the vestry with him and explained my reason for coming. He had read of the murder in the newspapers, and I thought I detected in him a slight hesitation over having the funeral of a murder victim in the Good Shepherd Church. I explained to him that we had once been members of the parish, that Dominique had been christened here by him twenty-two years earlier, and that he had come to our home afterward to the reception. The memory was dim to him, so I persisted. I said that Martin Manulis, the producer, who would be giving the eulogy at the funeral, was Dominique's godfather, but that evoked no remembrance either. I then said that Maria Cooper was Dominique's godmother, and at that he looked up. He remembered Maria well, he said, the beautiful daughter of Rocky and Gary Cooper. He told me he had given Gary Cooper the last rites when he died, and had performed the funeral mass. He said he had always hoped Maria would be a nun but that, alas, she had married a Jewish fella (the pianist Byron Janis). By now the church was a certainty. We discussed the music that I wanted played, and settled on eleven o'clock, Saturday, November 6, for the funeral.

On November 5 we discovered that the monsignor had also booked a wedding at eleven on Saturday morning. The mistake came to light when the groom-to-be read in one of Dominique's obituaries that her funeral was to be at the same time and in the same place as his wedding. He telephoned the church, and the church notified us.

Griffin, Alex, Martin Manulis, and I went to the rectory in the afternoon to try to straighten matters out. We waited endlessly, but the monsignor did not appear. The boys became impatient and began yelling up the stairs of the rectory. Finally a priest with a heavy Flemish accent came down, but he did not seem anxious to get mixed up in an error that was not of his making. When we pointed out to him that pandemonium was likely to occur the following morning unless steps were taken, he cooperated in figuring out a plan. As the wedding people refused to move their marriage up an hour, we agreed to have the funeral an hour later. It was too late to inform the newspapers, so we arranged for twelve ushers to be at the church at 10:30 to tell the people arriving for the funeral to come back an hour later.

'I cannot comprehend how such an error could have been made,' I said to the priest.

'It's even worse than you realize, Mr Dunne,' he replied.

'What do you mean?'

'The groom in the wedding is a friend of the man who murdered your daughter.'

That night on the news we watched John Sweeney being arraigned for Dominique's murder. He was accompanied by the defense team of Michael Adelson and Joseph Shapiro. As we watched, we all began to feel guilty for not having spoken out our true feelings about Sweeney when there was still time to save Dominique from him. In the days that followed, her friends began to tell us how terrified she was of him during the last weeks of her life. I found out for the first time that five weeks previously he had assaulted her and choked her, and that she had escaped from him and broken off her relationship with him. Fred Leopold, a family friend and the former mayor of Beverly Hills, told us during a condolence call that he had heard from a secretary in his law office that John Sweeney had severely beaten another woman a year or so earlier. We passed on this information to Detective Harold Johnston, who stayed close to our family during those days.

Later that night, the eve of the funeral, Dominique appeared on two television programs that had been previously scheduled. Also on television that night was a film I had produced, never before seen on television, and another film my brother had written, also being shown for the first time. We did not watch any of them.

The day of the funeral, November 6, was incredibly hot. Riding the few blocks from Lenny's house on Crescent Drive to the Good Shepherd Church at Santa Monica Boulevard and Bedford Drive, I noticed that the tinsel Christmas decorations were going up on the lampposts of Beverly Hills. As the limousine pulled up in front of the church, I was deeply touched to see Dr Brettholz from Cedars-Sinai in the crowd arriving for the service. Lenny, her mother, Griffin, Alex, and I were in the first car. When the chauffeur opened the door for us to get out, a hot gust of wind blew multicolored wedding confetti into the car.

The boys helped their grandmother out, and then we got the wheelchair out of the trunk and moved Lenny from the car into the chair.

'There's the mother,' we heard someone say, and a phalanx of photographers and television cameramen descended on us, coming within a foot of Lenny's face. Because there were so many steps in the front of the church, we decided to take the wheelchair around to the back, where there was a ramp entrance for handicapped people. The cameramen and photographers walked backward in front of us, shooting film. 'No matter what they do, don't say anything,' I said to the boys.

Lenny has extraordinary dignity. Dressed curiously for a funeral in a long lavender dress with pearls and a large straw hat, she made no attempt to turn away from the television cameramen. They seemed to respect her, and one by one they dropped away.

The church was filled to capacity, not with curiosity seekers attracted by the sensationalism of Dominique's death, but with people who knew her and loved her. During the service the boys read a poem by Yeats, and Martin Manulis, who had brought me to California twenty-six years earlier to work for him on *Playhouse 90*, delivered the eulogy. 'Every year of her life,' he said, 'we spent Christmas Eve together at a carol sing at our house. When she could barely talk, she stood between her brothers and sang what resembled "O Little Town of Bethlehem" and spoke a single line from the Gospel of Saint Luke, taught to her by her doting parents: "Because there is no room at the inn." And standing there with those huge grave eyes, she was, in life, an infanta by Goya, only more beautiful.'

A FEW NIGHTS after the funeral, Lenny and I sat in her bedroom, she in her bed, I on it, and watched Dominique in *Hill Street Blues*. The episode had been dedicated to her on the air by the producers. We did not talk. We did not cry. We simply stared at the set. She looked so incredibly young. She played a battered child. What we would not know until the trial was that the marks on her neck were real, from John Sweeney's assault on her five weeks before he killed her.

ON MY FIRST DAY BACK in New York after the funeral, I was mugged leaving the subway at twelve noon in Times Square. I thought I was the only person on the stairway I was ascending to the street, but suddenly I was grabbed from behind and pulled off balance. I heard the sound of a switch-blade opening, and a hand – which was all I ever saw of my assailant – reached around and held the knife in front of my face. From out of my mouth came a sound of rage that I did not know I was capable of making. It was more animal than human, and I was later told it had been heard a block away. Within seconds people came running from every direction. In his panic my assailant superficially slashed my chin with the blade of his knife, but I had beaten him. I had both my wallet and my life, and I realized that, uncourageous as I am about physical combat, I would have fought before giving in. Whoever that nameless, faceless man was, to me he was John Sweeney.

IF DOMINIQUE HAD BEEN KILLED in an automobile accident, horrible as that would have been, at least it would have been over, and mourning could have begun. A murder is an ongoing event until the day of sentencing, and mourning has to be postponed. After several trips west

for preliminary hearings, I returned to Los Angeles in July
for the trial.

For a while I drove Dominique's electric blue, convert-
ible Volkswagen. It had stood unused in the driveway of
Lenny's house since the murder, a reminder of her that
we neither wanted to look at nor could bear to get rid of.
I felt strange in the car; too old by far to be driving it, I
could always imagine her in it, young and pretty, driving
too fast, her beautiful long hair streaming out behind her.
In the glove compartment I found a pair of her sunglasses,
the ones she called her Annie Hall glasses. I had bought
them for her in Florence when I visited her in school there.
I took them out of the glove compartment and put them
in my briefcase. Throughout the trial, when the going got
rough, I would hold them in my hand, or touch them in
the inside pocket of my jacket next to my heart, as if I
could derive strength from her through them.

Alex was living on Crescent Drive with Lenny. Griffin
and his girlfriend, the actress Brooke Adams, had rented
a house in Malibu. I was staying at my old friend Tom
McDermott's house in Holmby Hills. On the Saturday
afternoon before the Monday morning when the jury selection was to start, Lenny rounded us up at her house. She
had received a call from a journalist friend of the family,
who said he wanted to meet with us to deliver a message
from Mike Adelson, the defense attorney representing
John Sweeney. We all had curious feelings about the meeting. Why should the lawyer of our daughter's murderer
be contacting us through a journalist rather than through
the district attorney? At that point in the proceedings our

relationship with the district attorney, Steven Barshop, was still very formal. We called him Mr Barshop, and he called us Mr and Mrs Dunne. We did not even have his home telephone number. We decided in advance that no matter what was said to us at the meeting we would listen to the message and make no comment.

The purpose of the journalist's visit was to offer us a plea bargain so that the case would not have to go to trial. He said that Sweeney was full of remorse and was willing to go to prison. Sweeney would plead guilty to a reduced charge of manslaughter and would serve seven and a half years, but he wanted the assault charge, based on his attack on Dominique five weeks before the murder, dropped. The journalist said that Adelson saw the case, not as a crime, but as a tragedy, of 'a blue-collar kid who got mixed up in Beverly Hills society and couldn't handle it.'

We had been down the plea-bargain road before. Five months earlier, in February, after the preliminary hearing on the assault charge, a plea bargain had been offered to us by Adelson through the district attorney. At that time we had accepted it, feeling that Lenny's health would be endangered by the trial. I had also seen at that hearing what a ruthless player Adelson was in the courtroom. Later, in May, Adelson had reneged on the plea bargain and opened up the whole matter of the trial, which we thought had been put to rest. Now, within two days of the beginning of jury selection, we were being offered, through a third party, another plea bargain, from which the district attorney had simply been excluded. I felt distrustful and manipulated. I despised the fact that we were supposed to be moved that Sweeney was remorseful and 'willing' to serve seven and a half years.

Although the journalist was only a messenger in the situation, the meeting became strained as he presented Adelson's viewpoints. Doubts were put in our mind about the ability of Steven Barshop. There was even a suggestion that Dominique was a participant in the crime. Neighbors would be called, we were told, who would testify that fights were commonplace between Dominique and Sweeney. The journalist said that if the two snitches who had come forward were put on the stand, Adelson would 'cut them off at the knees.' At that time I didn't know what snitches were; they were fellow prisoners who betray confidences of the cell for lessened sentences. (One prisoner reported that Sweeney had confessed to him that he thought he had the police believing he had not intended to kill Dominique, and another said that Sweeney had told him that Dominique was a snob, too ambitious, who deserved what she got.)

The journalist talked a great deal about a lawyer called Paul Fitzgerald. In the months ahead I was never to meet Fitzgerald, but he was often presented in conversation as a sage of the court system, with the detractors as vocal as his admirers. A former public defender, Fitzgerald was occasionally appointed as a conflict lawyer by Judge Burton S. Katz, in whose courtroom the case was being tried. A rumor persisted after the trial that he wrote Judge Katz's astonishing reversal speech on the day of the sentencing. He was also a close friend of Michael Adelson's. On that Saturday afternoon, before the jury selection had begun, Paul Fitzgerald was identified as the source of the information, reiterated again and again by the journalist who visited us, that Mike Adelson was a wonderful man.

It had not been my personal experience to find Mike Adelson a wonderful man. Twice during the February preliminary hearing he had addressed me in the corridor outside the courtroom as Mr Sweeney, as if mistaking me for the father of the killer rather than the father of the victim. A seasoned courtroom observer suggested to me that since I was a sympathetic figure in the courtroom, it had been Adelson's intention, by this obvious error, to incite me to make some kind of slur on him in public. During that same hearing, a young friend of Dominique's named Bryan Cook recounted a night on the town with his girlfriend, Denise Dennehy, and Dominique and Sweeney during which several bottles of champagne were consumed. Singling Dominique out from the quartet of celebrants, Adelson, in questioning Cook, asked several times, 'When Miss Dunne got in from the bars, how drunk was she?' The obvious intent of this ugly repetition was to give the impression in the courtroom that my actress daughter was an out-on-the-town drunkard. No amount of laudatory comment, after those preliminary hearings, would ever convince me that Mike Adelson was a wonderful man. Mustached and extremely short, his head topped with a full toupee, Adelson made me think of an angry, miniature bulldog.

The journalist's mission, though instigated with good intentions, only engendered bad feelings.

At nine o'clock on Monday morning, July 11, we gathered in Steven Barshop's office in the Santa Monica Courthouse. Alternately tough-talking and professional, the district attorney is about forty. He achieved public recognition for his prosecution of the killers of Sarai Ribicoff, the journalist niece of Senator Abraham Ribicoff. We felt lucky that Barshop had been assigned to our case by Robert Philibosian, the district attorney of the Los Angeles County, but we felt that he did not want any personal involvement with us. Although never discourteous, he was brusque, and he made it very clear that he was running the show and would not tolerate any interference.

Barshop was angered when we told him that a plea bargain had been offered to us by Adelson through a journalist. 'You didn't accept it, did you?' he asked. We said we had not. 'The matter is out of your hands,' he said. 'The state wishes to proceed with this trial.'

That day he gave us his home phone number, and for the first time we called each other by our first names.

THE CAST OF CHARACTERS was gathering. Down the corridor from the district attorney's office, several hundred potential jurors were milling about, waiting to be called for examination. Observing the scene from benches along the wall was a group known as the courthouse groupies, old people from Santa Monica who come to the courthouse every day to watch the murder trials. They know all the judges, all the lawyers, all the cases, and all the gossip. An old man in a blue polka-dot shirt and a base-ball hat with 'Hawaii' on it announced to the group that he was waiting to see Sweeney.

'Who's Sweeney?' asked an old woman with jet black, tightly permed hair.

'The guy who killed the movie star,' he answered.

'What movie star?'

'Dominique somebody.'

'Never heard of her.'

I asked a middle-aged woman in black slacks and a tan blouse who was carrying a small red suitcase and peering in the windows of the doors to Courtroom D where everyone was. She said they had broken for lunch. I asked what time they would be back, and she said at two o'clock. I thanked her. My son Alex told me the woman was Sweeney's mother, who had just arrived after a two-day bus trip from Hazelton, Pennsylvania. I had not thought of Sweeney in terms of family, although I knew he had divorced parents and was the oldest of six children, and that his mother had been a battered wife. It was a well-known fact among the people who knew John Sweeney that he had long since put distance between himself and his family. Alex said that he had been sitting next to Mrs Sweeney in the courtroom earlier, not knowing who she was, when Joseph Shapiro came over to her, addressed her by name, and said that he disliked being the one to give her the message, but her son did not wish to see her. Alex said her eyes filled with tears. For the next seven weeks we sat across the aisle from her every day, and though we never spoke, we felt compassion for her and knew that she in turn felt compassion for us in the dreadful situation that interlocked our families.

The jury selection took two weeks. Each side could eliminate, by way of peremptory challenge, twenty-six people from the main jury before arriving at the twelve, and six from the alternate jury before arriving at the six. People who had had violent crimes in their families were automatically excused. Women activists and people of obvious intelligence who asked pertinent questions were eliminated by the defense. 'What I'm looking for are twelve facists, and Adelson's looking for twelve bleeding-heart liberals or weirdos, and we'll arrive somewhere in between,' said Steven Barshop to me at one point. Adelson had announced that his defense would be based mostly on psychiatric findings. A writer-photographer who was being questioned said he would not accept the testimony of psychiatrists and psychologists as fact. He further said he found defense attorneys manipulative, to which Adelson replied, 'Suppose you don't like the way I comb my hair. Would that affect the way you listen to the testimony?' I found this an extraordinary image for a lawyer who wore a toupee to use, and then I realized that he must think that we thought that the quarter pound of hair taped to the top of his head was real. This would help me later to understand the total conviction with which he presented his client's version of the events surrounding the murder, which he knew to be untrue.

Presiding over the case was Judge Burton S. Katz. In his forties, Judge Katz gives the impression of a man greatly pleased with his good looks. He is expensively barbered, deeply tanned, and noticeably dressed in a manner associated more with Hollywood agents than with superior court judges. He has tinted aviator glasses, and on the first day he was wearing designer jeans, glossy white loafers, and no necktie beneath his judicial robes. Every seat in the courtroom was filled, and Judge Katz seemed to like playing to an audience. His explanations to the prospective jurors were concise and clear, and he made himself pleasing to them. He said funny things to make them laugh, but then was careful to warn them against levity.

The completed jury consisted of nine men and three women. The man who became the foreman ran a string of bowling alleys. One of the men was a postman, another a butcher. One worked for an airline and another for a computer company. One was a teacher. One had a juvenile delinquent son serving on a work team. Two of the men were black. One of the women was an Irish Catholic widow with six children, including a twenty-two-year-old daughter. Although we had hoped for more women, we were pleased with the makeup of the jury. On the instructions of the judge, not so much as a nod was ever exchanged between us, not even when we lunched in the same restaurant or met in the lavatory. However, I felt I grew to know them as the weeks passed, even though Steven Barshop often told me, 'Don't ever anticipate a jury. They'll fool you every time.'

Judge Katz's relationship with the jury bordered on the flirtatious, and they responded in kind. If the court was called for ten, Judge Katz invariably began around eleven, with elaborate and charming apologies to the jury. One

Monday morning he told them he had had a great week-end in Ensenada, that he had had the top down on his car both ways, and that he wished they had been with him. The ladies laughed delightedly, and the men grinned back at him.

Our family was never favored with Judge Katz's charms, not even to the point of simple courtesies. For seven weeks he mispronounced Dominique's name, insistently calling her by my name, Dominick. People wandered in and out of the courtroom; lawyers from other cases chatted with the clerk or used the bailiff's telephone. The microphone on the witness stand fell off its moorings innumerable times and either went dead or emitted a loud electronic screech, and it was never fixed.

It is the fashion among the criminal fraternity to find God, and Sweeney, the killer, was no exception. He arrived daily in the courtroom clutching a Bible, dressed in black, looking like a sacristan. The Bible was a prop; Sweeney never read it, he just rested his folded hands on it. He also wept regularly. One day the court had to be recessed because he claimed the other prisoners had been harass-ing him before he entered, and he needed time to cry in private. I could not believe that jurors would buy such a performance. 'You mark my words,' said Steven Barshop, watching him. 'Something weird is going to happen in this trial. I can feel it.'

ON JULY 20, Barshop called us to say that Adelson did not want Lenny at the trial because her presence in a wheelchair would create undue sympathy for her that would be prejudicial to Sweeney. She was to appear in court the following day so that the judge could hear what she had to say and decide if it was relevant to the trial.

We began to worry. It was becoming apparent that nearly everything Adelson requested was being granted. Adelson recognized Katz's enormous appetite for flattery and indulged it shamelessly. A camaraderie sprang up between the judge and the public defender, and the diminutive Adelson made himself a willing participant in a running series of 'short' jokes indulged in by the judge at his expense to the delight of the jury. It was becoming equally apparent that the district attorney, Steven Barshop, was ill-favored by the judge.

Lenny did not take the stand the following day. She was preceded by Lillian Pierce, who had been a girlfriend of John Sweeney's before my daughter. Detective Harold Johnston had tracked her down after receiving a telephone tip from Lynne Brennan, a Beverly Hills publicist, who had once been her friend and knew her story. Lillian Pierce appeared by subpoena issued by the prosecution and was known in advance to be a reluctant witness. Later we heard that she had sat in a car outside the church at Dominique's funeral and cried, feeling too guilty to go inside. At Adelson's request, her testimony was given out of the presence of the jury in order to determine its admissibility as evidence.

An attractive and well-dressed woman in her thirties, Lillian Pierce was very nervous and kept glancing over at Sweeney, who did not look at her. She had, she admitted, been in contact the day before with Joseph Shapiro, the Ma Maison lawyer. When the district attorney started to question her, her account of her relationship with John Sweeney was so shocking that it should have put to rest forever the defense stand that the strangulation death of Dominique Dunne at the hands of John Sweeney was an isolated incident. He was, it became perfectly apparent, a classic abuser of women, and his weapon was his hands.

Lillian Pierce said that on ten separate occasions during their two-year relationship he had beaten her. She had been hospitalized twice, once for six days, once for four. Sweeney had broken her nose, punctured her eardrum, collapsed her lung, thrown rocks at her when she tried to escape from him. She had seen him, she said, foam at the mouth when he lost control, and smash furniture and pictures. As she spoke, the courtroom was absolutely silent.

Adelson was incensed by the impact of Lillian Pierce's story, made more chilling by her quiet recital of all the acts of violence that she had survived. He became vicious with her. 'Were you not drunk?' he asked her. 'Were you not drugged?' His implication was that she had got what she deserved. He tried repeatedly to get her to veer from her story, but she remained steadfast.

'Let me remind you, Miss Pierce,' he said testily at one point, shuffling through a sheaf of papers, 'when you met with Mr Joe Shapiro and me for lunch on November third, you said . . .' I stopped following the sentence. My mind remained at the date November 3. On November 3, Dominique was still on the life-support system at Cedars-

Sinai. She was not pronounced legally dead until November 4. So even while Dominique lay dying, efforts were being made to free her killer by men who knew very well that this was not his first display of violence. Adelson knew, and sent a journalist to our house with the lachrymose message that he saw Dominique's death not as a crime but as a tragedy. Patrick Terrail had told Detective Johnston that he had seen Sweeney act violently only once, when he 'punched out' a telephone booth in the south of France. It is a fact of the legal system that all information gathered by the prosecution relevant to the case is available to the defense. The reverse is not true. If Detective Johnston had not learned about Lillian Pierce from a telephone tip, her existence would have been unknown to us. I felt hatred for Michael Adelson. His object was to win; nothing else mattered.

Steven Barshop cross-examined Lillian Pierce. 'Let me ask you, Miss Pierce, do you come from a well-to-do family?' Adelson objected. 'I am trying to establish a pattern,' Barshop told the judge.

At that moment – one of the most extraordinary I have ever experienced – we saw an enraged John Sweeney, his prop Bible flying, jump up from his seat at the counsel table and take off for the rear door of the courtroom which leads to the judge's chambers and the holding-cell area. Velma Smith, the court clerk, gave a startled cry. Lillian Pierce, on the stand, did the same. We heard someone shout, 'Get help!' Silent alarms were activated by Judge Katz and Velma Smith. The bailiff, Paul Turner, leaped to his feet in a pantherlike movement and made a lunge for Sweeney, grasping him around the chest from behind. Within seconds four armed guards rushed into the courtroom, nearly upsetting Lenny's wheelchair, and surrounded the melee. The bailiff and Sweeney crashed into a file cabinet. 'Don't hurt him!' screamed Adelson. Sweeney was wrestled to the floor and then handcuffed to the arms of his chair, where Adelson whispered frantically to him to get hold of himself.

Sobbing, Sweeney apologized to the court and said he had not been trying to escape. Judge Katz accepted his apology. 'We know what a strain you are under, Mr Sweeney,' he said. I was appalled at the lack of severity of the judge's admonishment. What we had witnessed had nothing to do with escape. It was an explosion of anger. It showed us how little it took to incite John Sweeney to active rage. Like most of the telling moments of the trial, however, it was not witnessed by the jury.

Mike Tipping, a reporter from the *Santa Monica Evening Outlook*, saw the episode and reported it in his paper. At the behest of Adelson, the court admonished Tipping for exaggerating the incident. The same day, a court gag order was issued to prevent anyone involved in the case from speaking to the press.

From then on, I felt, and continue to feel, that John Sweeney was sedated in the courtroom so that such an incident would never be repeated in front of the jury. He was asked under oath, not in the presence of the jury, if he was sedated, and he said he was not, except for some mild medicine for an upset stomach. The district attorney asked the court for either a blood test or a urine test to substantiate Sweeney's reply, but Judge Katz denied the request.

When Lenny took the stand the first time, the jury was again not present. Judge Katz had to decide on the admissibility of her testimony, but he wrote notes through most of it and scarcely looked in her direction. Lenny described an incident when Dominique came to her house at night after being beaten by Sweeney – the first of the three times he beat her. Dominique's terror was so abject, Lenny said, that she assumed a fetal position in the hallway. Sweeney had knocked her head on the floor and pulled out clumps of her hair. Adelson asked Lenny if she knew what the argument that precipitated the beating had been about. Lenny said she did not. He asked her if she knew that Dominique had had an abortion. She didn't. I didn't. The boys didn't. Her closest friend didn't. It remained throughout the trial an unsubstantiated charge that, to the defense, seemed to justify the beating. The look on Lenny's face was heartbreaking, as if she had been slapped in public. Judge Katz called her testimony hearsay and said he would make his decision as to its admissibility when the trial resumed on August 15 after a two-week hiatus.

DURING THIS PERIOD, our great friend Katie Manulis died of cancer. Our lives have been intricately involved with the Manuli, as we call them, for twenty-five years. Back at Martin's house after the funeral, I told Sammy Goldwyn that I had grave doubts about the judge. I cited his solicitousness toward Sweeney after his outburst in the courtroom, as well as his discourtesy with Lenny. Sammy said he was dining that evening with John Van de Kamp, the attorney general of the state of California, and he would get a rundown on the judge for me.

He reported back that Judge Katz went to law school at Loyola University and then served as a deputy district attorney for fourteen years. He had been unpopular in the district attorney's office, where he was considered a theatrical character. In 1970, he prosecuted members of the Charles Manson 'family' for the murders of Shorty Shea and Gary Hinman. In 1978, he was appointed to the municipal court by Governor Jerry Brown, and in 1981 he was appointed to the superior court. He was considered highly ambitious and was said to like cases with high media visibility, like this one.

JUDGE KATZ RULED that the prosecution could not use the testimony of Lillian Pierce to show the jury that John Sweeney had committed previous acts of violence against women. He said he would allow Miss Pierce to take the stand only in rebuttal if Adelson put expert witnesses, meaning psychiatrists, on the stand to testify that Sweeney was too mentally impaired by emotion to have formed the intent to kill. Once Judge Katz ruled that, Adelson threw out his psychiatric defense. Later in the trial, when the possibility of putting Lillian Pierce on the stand was raised again by Steven Barshop, Katz ruled that the 'prejudicial effect outweighed the probative value'. The jury would never know of Lillian Pierce's existence until after they had arrived at a verdict.

Judge Katz also ruled that Lenny's testimony about Dominique's coming to her in hysterics after Sweeney first beat her on August 27 could not be used by the prosecution during the main case. The judge once again agreed with Adelson that the prejudicial effect of the testimony outweighed its probative value; and he told Barshop not to mention the incident in his primary case. He said he would decide later in the trial whether her story could be used to rebut a mental-impairment defense for Sweeney.

Judge Katz agreed with Adelson that all statements made by Dominique to her agent, her fellow actors, and her friends regarding her fear of John Sweeney during the last five weeks of her life must be considered hearsay and ruled inadmissible as evidence.

It was not an auspicious opening to the trial. The loss of the Lillian Pierce testimony was a severe blow to Steven Barshop. Our hopes were buoyed by Barshop's opening argument in the case. He began with a description of the participants. Sweeney: twenty-seven, six foot one, 170 pounds. Dominique: twenty-two, five foot one, 112 pounds. He gave a rundown of the charges in the two incidents, the assault on Dominique on September 26 and the murder on the night of October 30. He described how Sweeney had walked out of Ma Maison restaurant at 8:30 that evening and proceeded on foot to the house, where he argued with Dominique and strangled her. He said that Dominique was brain-dead there at the scene of the strangulation, despite the fact that she was kept on the life-support system at Cedars-Sinai until November 4. He said that the coroner would testify that death by strangulation took between four and six minutes. Then he held up a watch with a second hand and said to the jury, 'Ladies and gentlemen, I am going to show you how long it took for Dominique Dunne to die.' For four minutes the courtroom sat in hushed silence. It was horrifying. I had never allowed myself to think how long she had struggled in his hands, thrashing for her life. A gunshot or a knife stab is over in an instant; a strangulation is an eternity. The only sound during the four minutes came from Michael Adelson and John Sweeney, who whispered together the whole time.

OUR DAILY PRESENCE in the courtroom annoyed Adelson throughout the trial. Defense lawyers in general don't like jurors to see the victim's family. Friends of ours had advised us to leave town until the trial was over. The organization known as Parents of Murdered Children advised us to attend every session. 'It's the last business of your daughter's life,' a father of a young girl stabbed to death by a former boyfriend said to me on the telephone one night. We sat in the front row behind the bailiff's desk in full view of the jury: Lenny in the aisle in her wheelchair, Alex, Griffin and his girlfriend, and I. We were within six feet of John Sweeney. As the weeks crept by, the boys became more and more silent. It seemed to me as if their youth were being stripped away from them.

In the row behind us sat representatives from Parents

of Murdered Children; some had been through their trials, others were awaiting theirs. Many of Dominique's friends came on a daily basis; so did friends of ours and friends of the boys. There were also representatives from Women Against Violence Against Women and from Victims for Victims, the group started by Theresa Saldana, an actress who was brutally stabbed a few years ago and survived.

'If any member of the Dunne family cries, cries out, rolls his eyes, exclaims in any way, he will be asked to leave the courtroom,' we were told by the judge at the behest of Adelson.

'Your honor, Alex Dunne had tears in his eyes,' Adelson called out one day. When Sweeney took the stand, Alex and Griffin changed their seats in order to be in his line of vision. Adelson tried to get them put out of the courtroom for this. We were intimidated but never searched. How easy it would have been to enter with a weapon and eradicate the killer if we had been of that mind. As the last week approached, Alex said one morning, 'I can't go back anymore. I can't be there where Sweeney is.'

Dominique's friends Bryan Cook and Denise Dennehy flew in from Lake Forest, Illinois, to testify about the time, five weeks before the murder, when Sweeney attempted to choke Dominique after their night on the town. She had escaped from her house that night by climbing through a bathroom window and driving her Volkswagen to the home of an artist friend named Norman Carby. (Lenny was in New York at the time.) Carby, appalled by the marks of attempted strangulation on her neck, had the presence of mind to take photographs. The pictures were the prosecution's prime exhibit of the seriousness of the assault. Adelson belittled the pictures. There was, he said, a third picture in the same series showing Dominique laughing. Carby explained that Dominique had a reading that morning for the role of a battered child on *Hill Street Blues*. Carby said he told her that at least she wouldn't have to wear any makeup for it, and that had made her laugh.

ONE OF THE SNITCHES appeared in the courtroom. He was the one who claimed Sweeney had said he thought he had the police believing that he had not intended to kill Dominique. He claimed further that Sweeney had asked him, 'Have you ever been with a girl who thought she was better than you?' Snitches are known to be unreliable witnesses, whom jurors usually dislike and distrust. This man's dossier, forwarded by his prison, depicted a disturbed troublemaker. His arms were tattooed from his shoulders to his wrists. Steven Barshop decided to dispense with his revelations. He was not put on the stand.

ON ONE OF THE COLOR PICTURES of the autopsy there was a bruise on Dominique's shoulder, which gave rise to disagreement. No one was quite sure if it had been incurred when she fell to the ground after being strangled, or if it had been caused by the life-support system, or if it was a result of the autopsy. Adelson was determined that the jury not see the photograph with the bruise, and the arguments went on endlessly while the jury waited in an adjoining room. Judge Katz solved the matter: with a pair of scissors provided by Velma Smith, the court clerk, he simply cut off the picture below the neck so that only the actual strangulation marks were visible to the jury.

Deputy Frank DeMilio, one of the first to arrive at the scene of the crime, testified on the stand that Sweeney had said to him, 'Man, I blew it. I killed her. I didn't think I choked her that hard, but I don't know, I just kept on choking her. I just lost my temper and blew it again.'

I wondered then and wonder still what the word *again* meant. Did it refer to one of the other times he attacked Dominique? Or Lillian Pierce? Or is there something else in this mysterious man's mysterious past that has not yet come to light? Sweeney had no car and no driver's license, an oddity for a young man in a city totally dependent on wheels. And although he had worked as head chef in one of the most prestigious restaurants in the city, he was nearly totally without funds. Furthermore, an informant at Ma Maison told Detective Johnston of another former girlfriend, then somewhere in France, against whom Sweeney had committed at least one act of violence.

AFTER STEVEN BARSHOP rested his case, Judge Katz delivered another devastating blow to the prosecution. He agreed with a request from Adelson that the jury be allowed to consider only charges of manslaughter and second-degree murder, thus acquitting Sweeney of first-degree murder.

In asking Katz to bar a first-degree murder verdict, Adelson argued, 'There is no premeditation or deliberation in this case,' and Katz agreed. Barshop argued that the jury should decide whether there was sufficient premeditation or deliberation. He said Sweeney had enough time to consider his actions during the period – up to six minutes, according to the coroner's testimony – that it took him to choke Dominique. Katz emphasized that Sweeney had arrived at Dominique's house without a murder weapon, although he knew that Sweeney's hands had nearly killed Lillian Pierce and that his hands had nearly strangled Dominique five weeks before he killed her. He also cited the fact that Sweeney had made no attempt to escape.

Rarely do twelve people on a jury agree: most verdicts are compromises. If this jury had had the option of first-degree murder and were in dispute, they could have compromised at second-degree. With first-degree ruled out, if there was a dispute, their only compromise was manslaughter.

Detective Harold Johnston was in the courtroom that day. He believed this was a case of first-degree murder, just as we did. Means of escape and means of method have nothing to do with premeditation, he told us. An informant at Ma Maison had told us that just before Sweeney left the restaurant to go to Dominique's house on the night he murdered her, he had ordered two martinis from the bar and drunk them. He felt that Sweeney must have decided that if he couldn't have Dominique, he wasn't going to let anyone else have her either.

Harold Johnston had become a friend over the year,

since the night that he rang the doorbell of Lenny's house on Crescent Drive at two in the morning to tell her that Dominique was near death in Cedars-Sinai. He had also questioned Sweeney on the night of the murder. He told me in the corridor outside the courtroom that day that the judge's ruling had made him lose faith in the system after twenty-six years on the force.

ONE DAY ADELSON'S WIFE and little boys came to the trial. As if to offset his unpleasant image in front of the jury, Adelson elaborately played father. 'Now don't you talk,' he admonished them, wagging his finger. Several times Judge Katz's mother and father also came to observe the proceedings. They were seated in special chairs set up inside the gate by the bailiff's desk and whispered incessantly. Invariably Katz showed off for their benefit. On one occasion, after both Barshop and Adelson had finished with the witness David Packer, the actor who was visiting Dominique at the time of the murder and who called the police, Judge Katz started an independent line of questioning, about eyeglasses, that had not been introduced by either the prosecution or the defense: Did David Packer wear them? Did he have them on the night he saw Sweeney standing over Dominique's body? The questions advanced nothing and muddied what had gone before.

A PHOTOGRAPHER FROM *People* magazine appeared in court one day, weighed down with equipment. I happened to

know him. He said he had been sent to take pictures of
our family for an article his magazine was doing on the
trial. Neither Griffin nor Alex wished to be photographed,
but the photographer stayed in the courtroom and took
pictures of the session with Sweeney and the lawyers. At
the lunch break, the judge signaled to the photographer
to see him in his chambers. Later, out in the parking lot,
I ran into the man. He told me he had thought the judge
was going to ask him not to shoot during the session.
Instead, the judge had said he wanted his eyes to show up
in the pictures and had tried on several different pairs of
glasses for the photographer's approval.

ADELSON HAD NEVER INTENDED to have Sweeney take the
stand. However, when he had to throw out his psychiatric
defense to keep the jurors from knowing about Sweeney's
previous acts of violence against Lillian Pierce, he had
no choice but to put the accused on. Sweeney was abjectly
courteous, addressing the lawyers and judge as sir. He
spoke very quietly, and often had to be told to raise his
voice so that the jurors could hear. Although he wept he
never once became flustered, and there was no sign of the
rage he exhibited on the day Lillian Pierce took the stand.
He painted his relationship with Dominique as nearly idyllic. He gave the names of all her animals – the bunny,
the kitten, the puppy. He refuted the testimony of Bryan
Cook and Denise Dennehy and denied that he had
attempted to choke Dominique after their night on the
town five weeks before the murder. He said he'd only tried

to restrain her from leaving the house. He admitted that they had separated after that, and that she had had the locks changed so that he could not get back in the house, but he insisted that she had promised to reconcile with him and that her refusal to do so was what brought on the final attack. He could not, he claimed, remember the events of the murder, which prompted Barshop to accuse him of having 'selective memory'. After the attack, Sweeney said, he had entered the house and attempted to commit suicide by swallowing two bottles of pills; however, no bottles were ever found, and if he had swallowed pills, they did not have any apparent effect on his system.

From the beginning we had been warned that the defense would slander Dominique. It is part of the defense premise that the victim is responsible for the crime. As Dr Willard Gaylin says in his book *The Killing of Bonnie Garland*, Bonnie Garland's killer, Richard Herrin, murdered Bonnie all over again in the courtroom. It is always the murder victim who is placed on trial. John Sweeney, who claimed to love Dominique, and whose defense was that this was a crime of passion, slandered her in court as viciously and cruelly as he had strangled her. It was agonizing for us to listen to him, led on by Adelson, besmirch Dominique's name. His violent past remained sacrosanct and inviolate, but her name was allowed to be trampled upon and kicked, with unsubstantiated charges, by the man who killed her.

'Look at her friends!' I wanted to scream at the judge and the jury. 'You have seen them both on the stand and in the courtroom: Bryan Cook, Denise Dennehy, Melinda Bittan, Kit McDonough, Erica Elliot, and the others who have been here every day – bright, clean-cut, successful young people. That is what Dominique Dunne was like. She wasn't at all the person whom John Sweeney is describing.' But I sat silent.

WHEN DOMINIQUE'S FRIENDS closed up her house after the funeral, her best friend, Melinda Bittan, came across a letter Dominique had written to Sweeney, which he may or may not have received. The letter had been filed away and forgotten. In the final days of the trial, Melinda remembered it one day when a group of us were having lunch together. Steven Barshop introduced it in his rebuttal, and as the court reporter, Sally Yerger, read it to the jury, it was as if Dominique was speaking from beyond the grave.

'Selfishness works both ways,' she wrote. *'You are just as selfish as I am. We have to be two individuals to work as a couple. I am not permitted to do enough things on my own. Why must you be a part of everything I do? Why do you want to come to my riding lessons and my acting classes? Why are you jealous of every scene partner I have?*

'Why must I recount word for word everything I spoke to Dr Black about? Why must I talk about every audition when you know it is bad luck for

me? Why do we have discussions at 3:00 A.M. all
the time, instead of during the day?

'Why must you know the name of every person
I come into contact with? You go crazy over my
rehearsals. You insist on going to work with me
when I have told you it makes me nervous. Your
paranoia is overboard . . . You do not love me. You
are obsessed with me. The person you think you love
is not me at all. It is someone you have made up
in your head. I'm the person who makes you angry,
who you fight with sometimes. I think we only fight
when images of me fade away and you are faced
with the real me. That's why arguments erupt out
of nowhere.

'The whole thing has made me realize how
scared I am of you, and I don't mean just physically. I'm afraid of the next time you are going to
have another mood swing . . . When we are good,
we are great. But when we are bad, we are horren-
dous. The bad outweighs the good.'

Throughout Steven Barshop's closing argument to the
jury, when he asked them to find Sweeney guilty of
murder in the second degree, the maximum verdict available to them, Judge Katz sat with a bottle of correction
fluid, brushing out lines on something he was preparing.
Later we learned it was his instructions to the jury. I
thought, if he isn't listening, or is only half listening,
what kind of subliminal signal is that sending to the jury?

During Adelson's final argument, on the other hand, he gave his full attention.

'THIS WILL BE the toughest day of the trial,' said Steven Barshop on the morning of Adelson's final argument. 'Today you will hear Adelson justify murder.' We had grown very close to Steven Barshop during the weeks of the trial and admired his integrity and honesty. 'You don't have to sit through it, you know,' he said. But we did, and he knew we would.

I lost count of how many times Adelson described Sweeney to the jury as an 'ordinarily reasonable person', as if this act of murder were an isolated instance in an otherwise serene life. Every time he said it he separated the three words – ordinarily reasonable person – and underscored them with a pointing gesture of his hand. We who had seen every moment of the trial knew of thirteen separate instances of violence, ten against Lillian Pierce and three against Dominique, but the jurors at this point were still not even aware of the existence of Lillian Pierce. Through an informant at Ma Maison, our family also knew of other acts of violence against women that had not been introduced into the case, but we sat in impassive silence as Adelson described the strangler as an ordinarily reasonable person.

He returned to his old theme: 'This was not a crime,' he told the jury. 'This was a tragedy.' It didn't matter that he knew it wasn't true. They didn't know it wasn't true, and he was concerned only with convincing them.

He talked about 'that old-fashioned thing: romantic love'. He made up dialogue and put it in the mouth of Dominique Dunne. 'I, Dominique, reject you, Sweeney,' he cried out. *'I lied to you, Sweeney!'*

We were sickened at his shamelessness. Leaving the courtroom during a break, I found myself next to him in the aisle. 'You piece of shit,' I said to him quietly so that only he could hear.

His eyes flashed in anger. 'Your Honor!' he called out. 'May I approach the bench?'

I continued out to the corridor, where I told Lenny what I had done.

'That was very stupid,' she said. 'Now you'll get kicked out of the courtroom.'

'No one heard me say it except Adelson,' I said. 'When the judge calls me up, I'll lie and say I didn't say it. Everybody else is lying. Why shouldn't I? It's his word against mine.'

Steven Barshop appeared.

'Is he going to kick me out?' I asked.

Barshop smiled. 'He can't kick the father of the victim out of the court on the last day of the trial with all the press present,' he said. Then he added, 'But don't do it again.'

JUDGE KATZ DRANK soft drinks from Styrofoam cups as he read instructions to the jury explaining second-degree murder, voluntary manslaughter, and involuntary manslaughter. Later, after the sentencing, the jury foreman, Paul Spiegel, would say on television that the judge's instructions were incomprehensible. During the eight days that the jury was out, deadlocked, they asked the judge four times for clarification of the instructions, and four times the judge told them that the answers to their questions were in the instructions.

I WAS NOW LIVING in the Bel Air home of Martin Manulis, who had returned east after Katie's death to complete postproduction work on a new miniseries. The jury had been out for over a week, and we knew they could not understand the instructions. Lenny, Griffin, Alex, and I were terribly edgy, and one evening we all went our separate ways. I paced restlessly from room to room in the Manulis house. I hadn't looked at television that summer except occasionally to see the news, but I suddenly picked up the remote-control unit and flicked the set on. I froze at the voice I heard.

There, on television, was Dominique screaming, 'What's happening?' I had not known that *Poltergeist* was scheduled on the cable channel, and the shock of seeing her was overwhelming. I felt as if she were sending me a message. 'I don't know what's happening, my darling,' I screamed back at the television set, and for the first time since the trial started, I sobbed. The next day the verdict came in.

THE WAITING WAS ENDLESS. Joseph Shapiro, the Ma Maison lawyer, regaled the reporters with an account of an African safari in the veldt where the native guides serving his party wore black tie. One of the courthouse groupies said that three buzzes to the clerk's desk meant that a verdict had been reached. Five minutes before the jury entered, we watched Judge Katz sentence a man who had robbed a flower shop in a nonviolent crime to five years in prison. Sweeney entered, clutching his Bible, and sat a few feet away from us. Mrs Sweeney sat across the aisle with Joseph Shapiro. The room was packed. A pool television camera, reporters, and photographers filled the aisles.

The jury entered, and the foreman, Paul Spiegel, delivered two envelopes to the bailiff to give to the judge. Katz opened first one envelope and then the other, milking his moment before the television camera like a starlet at the Golden Globes. Then, revealing nothing, he handed the two envelopes to his clerk, Velma Smith, who read the verdicts aloud to the court. The strangulation death of Dominique Dunne was voluntary manslaughter, and the earlier choking attack a misdemeanor assault. There was a gasp of disbelief in the courtroom. The maximum sentence for the two charges is six and a half years, and with good time and work time, the convict is paroled automatically when he has served half his sentence, without having to go through a parole hearing. Since the time spent in jail between the arrest and the sentencing counted as time served, Sweeney would be free in two and a half years.

'I am ecstatic!' cried Adelson. He embraced Sweeney, who laid his head on Adelson's shoulder. Shapiro clutched Mrs Sweeney's hand in a victorious salute, but Mrs Sweeney, of the lot of them, had the grace not to exult

publicly that her son had got away with murder. Then
Adelson and Shapiro clasped hands, acting as if they had
freed an innocent man from the gallows. Not content with
his victory, Adelson wanted more. 'Probation!' he cried.
As we sat there like whipped dogs and watched the spec-
tacle of justice at work, I felt a madness growing within
me.

Judge Katz excused the jury, telling them that even
though other people might agree or disagree with the
verdict, they must not doubt their decision. 'You were
there. You saw the evidence. You heard the witnesses.' He
knew, of course, that they would be hearing from the press
about Lillian Pierce in minutes.

He told them that justice had been served and thanked
them on behalf of the attorneys and both families. I could
not believe I had heard Judge Katz thank the jury on
behalf of my family for reducing the murder of my
daughter to manslaughter. Rage heated my blood. I felt
loathing for him. The weeks of sitting impassively through
the travesty that we had witnessed finally took their toll.
'Not for our family, Judge Katz!' I shouted. Friends behind
me put warning hands of caution on my shoulders, but
reason had deserted me.

Katz looked at me, aghast, as if he were above criticism in his own courtroom.

'You will have your chance to speak at the time of the
sentencing, Mr Dunne,' he said.

'It's too late then,' I answered.

'I will have to ask the bailiff to remove you from the
courtroom,' he said.

'No,' I answered. 'I'm leaving the courtroom. It's all over here.'

I took Lenny's wheelchair and pushed it up the aisle. The room was silent. At the double doors that opened onto the corridor, I turned back. My eyes locked with Judge Katz's, and I raised my hand and pointed at him. 'You have withheld important evidence from this jury about this man's history of violence against women.'

The jury foreman, when asked later by the press what finally broke the deadlock, replied on television, 'A few jurors were just hot and tired and wanted to give up.'

The trial was over. Sentencing was set for November 10.

THERE WAS AN UPROAR in the media over the verdict, and KABC radio ran an on-the-hour editorial blasting it. Letters of outrage filled the newspapers as stories of John Sweeney's history of violence against women became public knowledge. The *Herald-Examiner* published a front-page article about the case: 'Heat of Passion: Legitimate Defense or a Legal Loophole?' Judge Katz was severely criticized. In the weeks that followed, a local television station released the results of a poll of prosecutors and criminal defense lawyers in which he tied for fourth-worst judge in Los Angeles County.

SEVERAL DAYS AFTER the verdict I returned to the court-house to retrieve from the district attorney the photographs and letters and videotapes of television shows that Lenny

had lent him. The receptionist said I would find Steven
Barshop in one of the courtrooms. As I passed Courtroom
D, out of habit I looked in the window. At that instant
Judge Katz happened to look up. I moved on and entered
Courtroom C, where Barshop was busy with another
lawyer. The doors of the courtroom opened behind me,
and Judge Katz's bailiff, Paul Turner, who had wrestled
Sweeney to the ground several months earlier, asked me
to go out into the hall with him. 'What are you doing
here?' he asked me. He was stern and tough.

'What do you mean, what am I doing here?' I replied.

'Just what I said to you.'

'I don't have the right to be here?'

'There's been a lot of bad blood in this trial,' he said.
I realized that he thought, or the judge thought, that I
had come here to seek revenge. Then Steven Barshop came
out into the corridor, and the bailiff turned and left us.

IN THE MONTH between the verdict and the sentencing, we
tried to pick up the pieces of our lives, but the aftermath
of the trial continued. Joseph Shapiro appeared at the
wrap party given by 20th Century-Fox for the film *Johnny
Dangerously*, in which Griffin co-stars, and the producers
asked him to leave the lot.

According to Proposition 8, the victim's bill of rights,
the next of kin of murder victims have the right to take
the stand at the sentencing and plead with the judge for
the maximum sentence. We were told that Adelson
intended to cross-examine us if we did this. We were also

told that Adelson, in order to get Sweeney released on probation that day, intended to put on the stand psychiatrists and psychologists who would testify that Sweeney was nonviolent. And we were told that Adelson intended to show a videotape of Sweeney under hypnosis saying he could not remember the murder.

ON THE DAY of the sentencing, pickets protesting the verdict, the judge, and Ma Maison marched and sang on the courthouse steps in Santa Monica. Courtroom D was filled to capacity. Extra bailiffs stood in the aisles and among the standees at the rear of the room. A young man called Gavin DeBecker sat next to the bailiff's desk and made frequent trips back to the judge's chambers. DeBecker provides bodyguard service for political figures and public personalities.

Throughout the several hours of the proceedings John Sweeney remained hunched over, his face covered by his hands, so unobtrusive a figure that he seemed almost not to be there.

Two of Sweeney's sisters took the stand and asked for mercy for their brother. Mrs Sweeney described her life as a battered and beaten wife. Griffin took the stand and presented Judge Katz with a petition that had been circulated by Dominique's friends; it contained a thousand signatures of people protesting the verdict and asking for the maximum sentence. Lenny spoke, and I spoke.

We were not cross-examined by Adelson. No psychiatrists or psychologists took the stand. No videotape of

Sweeney saying he could not remember the murder was shown. But a whole new dynamic entered Courtroom D that day and dominated everything else: the outrage of Judge Burton S. Katz over the injustice of the verdict arrived at by the jury.

He mocked the argument that Sweeney had acted in the heat of passion. 'I will state on the record that I believe this is a murder. I believe that Sweeney is a murderer and not a manslaughterer . . . This is a killing with malice. This man held on to this young, vulnerable, beautiful, warm human being that had everything to live for, with his hands. He had to have known that as she was flailing to get oxygen, that the process of death was displacing the process of life.'

Judge Katz then addressed Sweeney: 'You knew of your capacity for uncontrolled violence. You knew you hurt Dominique badly with your own hands and that you nearly choked her into unconsciousness on September 26. You were in a rage because your fragile ego could not accept the final rejection.'

He said he was appalled by the jurors' decision over Sweeney's first attack: 'The jury came back – I don't understand it for the life of me – with simple assault, thus taking away the sentencing parameters that I might have on a felony assault.'

He called the punishment for the crime 'anemic and pathetically inadequate'. Having got the verdict we felt he had guided the jurors into giving, he was now blasting them for giving it.

He went on and on. It was as if he had suddenly become

a different human being. However, all his eloquence changed nothing. The verdict remained the same: manslaughter. The sentence remained the same: six and a half years, automatically out in two and a half.

Surrounded by four bailiffs, Sweeney rose, looking at no one, and walked out of the courtroom for the last time. He was sent to the minimum-security facility at Chino.

GAVIN DEBECKER PURSUED us down the hall. He said Judge Katz would like to see us in his chambers. Lenny declined, but I was curious, as was Griffin. DeBecker led us to Katz's chambers. 'Burt,' he said, tapping on the door, 'the Dunnes are here.'

Judge Katz was utterly charming. He called us by our first names. He talked at length about the injustice of the verdict and his own shock over it, as if all this was something in which he had played no part. He said his daughters had not spoken to him since the verdict came in.

He gave each of us his Superior Court card and wrote on it his unlisted telephone number at home and his private number in chambers so that we could call him direct. What, I thought to myself, would I ever have to call him about?

Back in the crowded corridor again, I was talking with friends as Michael Adelson made his exit. He caught my eye, and I sensed what he was going to do. In the manner of John McEnroe leaping over the net in a moment of largesse to exchange pleasantries with the vanquished, this defender of my daughter's killer made his way across the corridor to speak to me. I waited until he was very near, and as he was about to extend his hand I turned away from him.

WHEN MICHAEL ADELSON was asked in an NBC television interview if he thought Sweeney would pose a threat to society when released from prison in two and a half years, he pondered and replied, 'I think he will be safe if he gets the therapy he needs. His rage needs to be worked upon.' Judge Katz, when asked the same question by the same interviewer, answered, 'I wouldn't be comfortable with him in society.' Steven Barshop told a newspaper reporter, 'He'll be out in time to cook someone a nice dinner and kill someone else.' Paul Spiegel, the jury foreman, in a television interview, called the judge's criticism of the verdict a cheap shot. He said the judge was concerned over the criticism he himself had received since the trial and was trying to place the blame elsewhere. Spiegel said he felt that justice had not been served. He said the jury would certainly have found Sweeney guilty if they had heard all the evidence. 'If it were up to me,' he said, 'Sweeney would have spent the rest of his life in jail.'

Not one of us regrets having gone through the trial, or wishes that we had accepted the plea bargain, even though Sweeney would then have had to serve seven and a half years rather than two and a half. We chose to go to trial, and we did, and we saw into one another's souls in the process. We loved her, and we knew that she loved us back. Knowing that we did everything we could has been for us the beginning of the release from pain. We thought of revenge, the boys and I, but it was just a thought, no more than that, momentarily comforting. We believe in God and in ultimate justice, and the time came to let go of our obsession with the murder and proceed with life.

Alex decided to stay with his mother in California and finish his college education. Griffin had to return to New York to start a new film. Lenny became an active spokeswoman for Parents of Murdered Children. I returned to the novel I was writing, which I had put aside at the beginning of the trial.

IT WAS MY LAST DAY in Los Angeles. I had said my farewells to all, knowing I had experienced new dimensions of friendship and family love. I was waiting for the car to drive me to the airport. Outside it was raining for the first time in months. Through the windows I could see the gardeners of the house where I had been staying in Bel Air. They were watering the lawn as usual, wearing yellow slickers in the insistent downpour.

There was plenty of time. I told the driver to take me to Crescent Drive first. I wanted to say good-bye to Lenny again. I knew what an effort it had been for her to put herself through the ordeal of the trial. She was in bed watching *Good Morning America*. I sat in her wheelchair next to her bed and held her hand. 'I'm proud of you, Len,' I said to her. 'I'm proud of you too,' she said to me, but she kept looking at David Hartman on television.

On the way out I took a yellow rose from the hall table.

'I want to make one more stop,' I said to the driver.

We went out Whilshire Boulevard to Westwood. Past the Avco theater complex, the driver made a left turn into the Westwood Cemetery.

'I'll be just a few minutes,' I said.

Dominique is buried near two of her mother's close friends, the actresses Norma Crane and Natalie Wood. On her marker, under her name and dates, it says, 'Loved by All'. I knelt down and put the yellow rose on her grave.

'Good-bye, my darling daughter.'

John Sweeney, the murderer of my daughter, was released from prison after two and a half years. For a while, I hired the famous private detective Anthony Pellicano to follow him and track his movements, but after some time I decided that I didn't want to live in a state of revenge and desisted. Fourteen years later, when I mentioned John Sweeney's name in an article I wrote about Anthony Pellicano at the O. J. Simpson trial, a man in Florida contacted me to say that his daughter was engaged to be married to a man named John Sweeney. He was a chef in a top restaurant in Seattle. It was the same John Sweeney. He had not told his fiancée that he had ever been in prison, nor had he told her that he had killed a girl. The marriage did not take place. He claimed to fellow workers that I was harassing him. He changed his name. The most fervent wish of my life is that I never encounter him.

THE WOMAN WHO KNEW TOO LITTLE

S HE WAS A KEPT WOMAN on the skids, an actress-model
who neither acted nor modeled, living on the wrong
side of town in an apartment from which she was
about to be evicted for nonpayment of rent. Amid the
half-packed bags and unwatered plants, remnants of a past
life bespoke more affluent times: a luxurious white sofa,
a Chinese porcelain dish on a teakwood stand.

He was a homosexual-schizophrenic-alcoholic on the
fringes of show business, a collector of celebrities' telephone numbers, who basked for a while in the light of
the scarlet woman's illicit fame. They were old friends who
had met as patients in a mental hospital and who tolerated each other's transgressions and failures. After he
moved in, he found he was buying the groceries and even
making the monthly payments on a car she had totaled
when she was drunk. She treated him like her slave boy,
sending him out to get her bagels and cream cheese, to
walk her dog, to find her a new place to live. She spent
most of her time in bed, too paralyzed with fear at what

was happening to her to function. Her money and glamour gone, she felt that her options for ever recovering her former status had been exhausted. In the end she drove him to the breaking point, and he did for her what she could not do for herself: he killed her.

He waited until she went to sleep. He took her son's baseball bat, adjusted the lights, turned on the water so that the neighbors wouldn't hear anything through the paper-thin walls, and bludgeoned her with the bat until she was dead. She was lying under $500 gray-bordered Pratesi sheets embroidered with her initials, V. M. Next to her bed, on a Formica table, were an empty bottle of Soave wine and a paperback by Carlos Castaneda.

He drove to the North Hollywood police station and confessed. 'She wanted to die,' he said, and then he gave her credentials, as if seeking approval for the quality of life he had just extinguished. 'Don't you know who she is? Are you aware of her background? It was on the front page of every newspaper because Alfred Bloomingdale was on Ronald Reagan's kitchen cabinet . . .'

Everybody knew the story. Vicki Morgan established herself in tabloid history as the $18,000-a-month mistress of Alfred Bloomingdale, the department-store heir and founder of the Diners Club, when she filed a $5 million palimony suit against the dying millionaire, claiming he had reneged on a promise to provide her with lifetime support and a home of her own. The suit, which sent shock waves through the social world, was instigated after Bloomingdale's wife, Betsy, cut off the corporate checks Vicki had long been receiving. Mrs Bloomingdale, a leader

in Los Angeles and international society and a close friend
of Mrs Ronald Reagan's, refused to be intimidated by her
husband's mistress and held her ground throughout the
scandal.

The names came pouring out of the killer, a reveren-
tial litany of fame and power. People who had never heard
of Marvin Pancoast, for that was his name, were part of
his confession to the murder of Vicki Morgan.

Pancoast, who didn't usually command much attention, had the detective riveted. In jail two days later, he
told a reporter from the *Los Angeles Herald-Examiner*
that he expected to be sentenced to the gas chamber. But
that was before anyone had heard of the sex tapes. And
before he had a lawyer.

Vicki Morgan's fourteen-year-old son attended her
funeral at Forest Lawn Mortuary with his Mohawk-cut hair
dyed green. The service was sparsely attended, but even
as it was taking place, new headlines were in the making.
A Beverly Hills attorney announced to the press that he
had in his possession three videotape cassettes showing
high ranking members of the Reagan administration in
sexual frolics with Vicki and other women.

From Beverly Hills to Washington, in the months that
followed, rumors flourished. Wasn't it just too convenient
that this woman should end up dead? Broke and at breaking point, did Vicki Morgan threaten to sell the sex tapes
if she was not bought off? Surely, people speculated,
Marvin Pancoast had been planted in her house three
weeks before her death. Was Pancoast taking the rap for
a crime he did not commit – for which he would be found

insane, serve a short sentence, and be well remunerated? His clothes had not been blood-spattered after the murder. There were no fingerprints. And the drawers had been ransacked. Where were the tapes? Where was the tell-all memoir Vicki was supposed to be writing?

THE MURDER TRIAL of Marvin Pancoast got under way in June, eleven months after Vicki Morgan's death. When I arrived in Los Angeles, it had already been in the courtroom for three weeks, two weeks of jury selection and a week of prosecution testimony. But it appeared that there was a virtual news blackout on the story.

Although Pancoast had recanted his confession and his lawyers said they would prove that someone else killed Vicki Morgan because she was planning to use the sex tapes for purposes of blackmail, the story was rarely more prominently featured than on page 5 or 6 of the *Los Angeles Herald-Examiner*, with hardly a mention in the *LA Times* or newspapers around the country. Even the courtroom, in the city of Van Nuys, out in the San Fernando Valley, was never more than half-filled, often considerably less, and most of those people were court watchers. Was this because pressure had been brought to bear to downplay a story that might prove embarrassing to the Reagan administration? Or was it because the stars of the piece were dead and the leading players at the trial had been no more than bit players in the drama, hangers-on and acolytes of the discredited mistress of a disgraced multimillionaire?

Rumors die hard, though. Shortly after I arrived in Los Angeles, a friend of mine, a movie star, said to me, 'Oh, no, darling, Marvin's not guilty. We knew Marvin. He worked for my ex-husband. Nutty as a fruitcake, yes. A murderer, no. You check his mother's bank account after this whole thing is over, and you'll see she's been taken care of for life. They'll just put Marvin in the nuthouse for a few years. It's Marilyn all over again. Did you ever know that the CIA went into Marilyn's house afterward and cleaned out everything? I bet they did that at Vicki's too. That's where the tapes went.'

Even at his own trial Marvin Pancoast was not a dominant figure. He has an easily forgettable face, a West Hollywood mustache, and the kind of white skin that turns sunstroke scarlet after five minutes' exposure to the sun. He was always meticulously groomed. Every time he entered the courtroom, he waved to people he knew – his mother, his lawyer's wife, a friend with a ponytail, pierced ear, and turquoise rings on most of his fingers. At times he read *The Shining*, by Stephen King.

Pancoast met Vicki Morgan in 1979, when they were both patients at the Thalians Community Mental Health Center, in Los Angeles. Vicki was there, at Alfred Bloomingdale's expense, for depression following the collapse of her third marriage. Marvin, who had been in and out of such institutions for years, was also in for depression. At various times Marvin had been diagnosed as schizophrenic, manic-depressive, psychotic, and masochistic. They became friends.

He worked in subservient positions for such luminary

Hollywood institutions as Rogers & Cowan, the publicists, where he was a gofer, and William Morris, the talent agency, where he operated the Xerox machine. He bragged of knowing famous people in the film business, and his telephone book contained numbers of many celebrated individuals he had never met.

For thirteen months he worked in the office of Hollywood and Broadway producer Allan Carr. 'I remember him,' said Carr. 'He stole my Rolodex with all my celebrity phone numbers, and we couldn't get it back. Finally he sent us back the Rolodex frame, but all the cards were gone.'

I remarked to Virginia Peninger, a court watcher seated next to me, that Marvin seemed heavily sedated.

'Oh, he is,' she replied. 'Ask his mother. She'll tell you. He gets agitated if he doesn't get his medication.'

Pancoast had two lawyers defending him, Arthur Barens and Charles 'Ted' Mathews, who had been hired by Pancoast's mother and his grandmother. Barens was the star of the courtroom. Trim, handsome, and fashionably dressed, with gold jewelry glistening at each wrist, he drives a Jaguar with initialed license plates and lives on one of the best streets in Beverly Hills. His business card reads: 'Arthur Barens, Attorney at Law, A Professional Corporation'. This is his third murder trial. Before, he had been mainly a personal-injury lawyer, known as a P.I. He had also worked for years in real estate with Pancoast's mother. A curious twist in his background is that Vicki Morgan, at Pancoast's suggestion, went to ask him to handle her palimony suit after she fired the well-known lawyer Marvin Mitchelson. He admits to having met with her three times, but says he turned her down because he felt that 'she could not possibly win the suit'.

Ted Mathews is heavy bellied and wears suspenders. He made no secret of his revulsion for his client's lifestyle and sexual practices, but he kept pressing home the point that those things should not be brought into consideration when the jury was deciding the guilt or innocence of Marvin Pancoast. Barens and Mathews made an odd couple. In the corridor outside the courtroom, day after day, they titillated a handful of press and television reporters with promises that people who had viewed the sex tapes would appear, that presidential counselor Ed Meese had been subpoenaed, and that Marvin Pancoast would take the stand.

'This whole case is full of people who want nothing more than to have their faces on the six o'clock news,' said a disgusted witness as she made her way past the nightly sideshow.

'Have you ever represented Marvin before when he has been in trouble?' I asked Arthur Barens.

'Just fag stuff. Lewd conduct charges,' he said.

Representing the prosecution was Deputy District Attorney Stanley Weisberg. Wry, wise, probably witty in circumstances other than these, he was without flash, glamour, or fancy rhetoric. He stuck to the facts. While Barens and Mathews could talk about a police cover-up, the sex tapes, blackmail, hypnosis, drugs, and unnamed higher-ups in the administration, Weisberg had nothing more to go on than Marvin Pancoast's confession. As the days went by, Weisberg became the favorite of the court watchers.

Presiding over the court was forty-two-year-old Judge David Horowitz. Fair and unbiased, he never allowed his courtroom to turn into a circus. When evidence of the existence of sex tapes was not forthcoming, he disallowed the defense claim that Vicki Morgan was using the tapes for purposes of blackmail, and sustained all objections of the prosecution when the defense asked hearsay questions about the tapes.

One of the most fascinating aspects of the case was the colossal ineptitude of the police work. No fingerprints were taken at the scene of the crime. An officer lamely explained that since Marvin Pancoast had confessed, the police didn't see any point in taking prints. Nor did they seal the house afterward; therefore, anyone possessing a key had access to it in the days following the murder – a strange state of affairs in a case in which missing tapes, both audio and video, played such a large part. The coroner testified that when he arrived at the murder scene at seven o'clock in the morning, he was not able to examine the murder weapon, the baseball bat, for blood, skin, or hair, because the police had sealed it in a plastic bag. It is an almost elementary fact of police work that evidence containing blood, or any body fluid, is never wrapped in plastic, only paper or cloth, because plastic creates a humidity chamber in which bacteria grow and destroy such evidence as blood and tissue. 'If this is not an inept police investigation, then it's a deliberate cover-up,' said Ted Mathews.

* * *

FAR MORE REVEALING and potentially dangerous than any of Vicki's lurid testimony in the deposition for her palimony suit, in which she recounted in detail the sado-masochistic sexual practices of Alfred Bloomingdale, were her accounts of the personal conversations she had had with Bloomingdale. 'Alfred continuously confided in me by telling me his private opinions about influential and important people with whom he was intimately involved, such as Ronald and Nancy Reagan, and he would relate specific instances involving them; and he told me about his involvement in secret and delicate matters such as campaign contributions for Mr Reagan.'

In the second week of the trial, Pancoast's lawyers called a writer named Gordon Basichis to the stand. Basichis had been working with Vicki Morgan on *Alfred's Mistress*, her revenge memoir about her affair with Bloomingdale. Basichis had been introduced to her by a film producer for whom Basichis was writing a screenplay, and with whom Vicki Morgan had had an affair during her affair with Alfred Bloomingdale. Basichis is married to a television executive, has an eighteen-month-old son, and had been working with Vicki for eight months preceding her death. He is dark and intense, and on the stand was sweaty and nervous.

The contract drawn up by Morgan's lawyer, Michael Dave, provided that Basichis was to deliver to her the first chapter of the book plus an outline of the remaining chapter by August 1, 1983. If she disapproved of the material, she had no obligation to proceed with Basichis or compensate him.

Almost immediately after meeting, Basichis and Morgan began a love affair. Eight months after the contract between them was signed, despite nearly daily contact, the initial chapter and outline were still not written. There is some argument as to how many hours of microcassette audiotape were recorded. Vicki's mother, Connie Laney, and Marvin Pancoast, who moved in with Vicki three weeks before her death, recalled that there were many hours of recorded conversations. The tapes were kept in a safedeposit box to which both Vicki and Basichis had keys. After Vicki's death, when the tapes were ordered to be turned over to the estate, only six hours of tape were forthcoming. What happened to the other tapes, if there were others, has never come to light. Basichis says the six hours of tape he submitted were all that were recorded. What exactly he and Vicki did during the eight months of their collaboration remains a mystery.

One week before her death Vicki Morgan broke off her romantic relationship with Basichis and fired him as her collaborator. A fight occurred, and there were two versions of it. Basichis admitted to having pushed Morgan around. Vicki's mother said Vicki told her that Basichis had hit her and punched her in the face. There were black-and-blue marks on her face and body. In Marvin Pancoast's confession, he said about Basichis, whom he referred to as the writer, 'He beat the shit out of her.'

The police did not question Basichis until three months after the murder – and then only after prompted by a reporter – even though he was Vicki's known lover, her known collaborator, and thereby privy to the secrets of her life; even though it was a documented fact that she had fired him and that he had fought with her and struck her.

Basichis denied on the stand that he was responsible for the black-and-blue marks on Morgan's face and body. He denied feeding her Valium habit or buying her cocaine. He said that he and Vicki had made up on the night before her death and that he had spent the night with her. He said that on the following night, the night of the murder, he was home with his wife watching the All-Star Game on television, which his wife later corroborated on the stand.

'How often did you go to bed with her?' Barens asked him.

'I didn't keep count.'

When a break was called, Basichis stood up and walked across the courtroom to where I was sitting. 'Hello,' he said, and called me by my first name. I was stunned. Later he told me he had submitted a manuscript of one of his early books to me in 1976, when I was a film producer.

'They're trying to pin this murder on me,' Basichis said, talking rapidly into my ear. He kept jagging his finger into his shirt collar. 'I didn't kill her. I swear to you. I was deeply in love with her. I would never harm her.'

'Who do you think killed her?' I asked him.

'Marvin,' he answered, and then added, 'with help.'

'Help from whom?'

He shrugged and did not reply. His dislike of Arthur Barens and Ted Mathews was matched only by their dislike of him. Barens and Mathews said on television and to the press that Basichis was a definite suspect, a drug taker, and a drug supplier to Vicki, and that he might possibly have made a deal with 'someone' to turn over the missing audiotapes based on his eight months of conversations with Vicki. Basichis said that Barens's relationship with Vicki Morgan had involved more than just three office meetings.

That night Basichis called me at my hotel and asked if he could see me. He said he had things to tell me and offered to let me read *Alfred's Mistress*. I asked if we could talk on the telephone, and he said that the telephone might be tapped. He arrived more than an hour late, after his wife had called to say that he had lost his credit cards and money but that he would be there.

Basichis rarely completes a sentence. He begins, thinks of something else, switches to it. He talked nonstop for two hours. His nervous presence was compelling, a frightened man masquerading under a tough bluff, but when the tape of our meeting was transcribed, by a woman in Santa Monica who was so shocked by the profanity she left black spaces, page after page read like incoherent ramblings. He claimed there were no videotapes of Vicki Morgan cavorting with government officials. He said he would have known if there had been, because he and Vicki had spent so much time together. He said, 'She had a sense of vanity that went so deep she wasn't going to spread herself out among a whole bunch of those guys in their white fleur-de-lis boxer shorts.'

When he left my hotel room after midnight, I read *Alfred's Mistress*. It had, he told me, been turned down by his publisher because another writer, one of seven doing a book on the same subject, had told the publisher that Basichis was the murderer.

Basichis hadn't completed even the first chapter of *Alfred's Mistress* during the eight months of his collaboration with Vicki Morgan. He wrote the book sometime after her death in July 1983 and before Marvin Pancoast's trial for her murder in June 1984. When he showed it to me in June, it had already been rejected by ten publishers.

It is a curious book, told completely in the third person, as if the eight months of conversation, taping, and love-making between the author and the deceased has not taken place. Some of it is culled from the deposition that Vicki filed at the time of her palimony suit. Her meeting with Bloomingdale, their first assignation, his sadomasochistic tendencies, and the financial terms of their long affair were all things I had read about before. Some of the other facts in the book are inaccurate: a depiction of Mrs Bloomingdale as foul-mouthed is totally off the mark. Most important, none of the big administration names that had long been whispered as having connections with Vicki are mentioned; there is nothing in the book that would embarrass the administration.

It is Vicki Morgan's life story. It tells of her three marriages (her first ex-husband went to jail for dealing drugs in order to make enough money to win her back from Bloomingdale). It tells of her love affairs with the convicted financier Bernie Cornfeld, the King of Morocco, and a Saudi Arabian princess, as well as of a romance with Cary Grant.

Most compelling is the picture of Bloomingdale, caught in the grip of living a double life, too involved with each to let go of the other. A scene where Bloomingdale tells Vicki that he has cancer as he is leaving for England with his wife to attend the festivities connected with the royal wedding of Prince Charles and Lady Diana, and a scene where Bloomingdale is carried to Vicki's house by a male nurse for their final lunch, for which Vicki spent $1,000 on flowers and appointments for what she called her 'Betsy table', made crystal clear the complicated nature of their relationship.

'What about all this stuff she was supposed to have known concerning campaign contributions and personal things about people in the administration?' I asked Basichis.

He said her information was fragmented – pieces of a story, but not the whole story. Most of what she knew, he said, was more embarrassing than dangerous, gossip about the private and family lives of top figures.

The book tells her history, but it doesn't explain her. What did she have, this girl? What was her allure? Why did a king fly her to Rabat? Why did the princess charter a yacht to sail her to Honolulu? Why did a man who had everything risk it all on her? I once saw her at the Christmas party of a film-company business manager. 'That's Alfred Bloomingdale's girlfriend,' the daughter of one of Alfred Bloomingdale's friends told me. What I remember most about her were her eyes, taking in everything from the sidelines, meeting the looks of people who looked at her. Friendly-aloof. And pretty. But Hollywood parties are full of pretty girls who are somebody's girl-friend.

The moot point of the trial remained the celebrated sex tapes. There was not a person in the courtroom who had not heard that a certain member of the administration was supposed to be shown on them dallying with Vicki, with pink carnations in his pubic hair. But where were they? Do they exist? Did they ever exist? The main source of information about them was Marvin Pancoast, known to be pornography-mad. Could they have been a figment of his imagination? Vicki's close friend of fourteen years, Sally Talbert, said under oath that she had never heard Vicki mention the tapes. Even Gordon Basichis, everyone's enemy in this story, said Vicki never mentioned the tapes to him. The first public mention of the tapes was by Robert Steinberg, who was, for twenty-four hours, Marvin Pancoast's lawyer. Two days later, when asked for proof that the videotapes existed, Steinberg said that he had seen them, but that they had been stolen from his office. Later Steinberg was indicted for filing a false robbery report. When the defense called him to the stand during the Pancoast trial, he took the Fifth Amendment nine times because the misdemeanor charges for the robbery report were still pending.

A secretary from William Morris who knew Pancoast when he worked there said she had heard about the tapes a year and a half before Vicki died. This woman, who wished to remain anonymous, believes they did exist. She also believes that Pancoast definitely struck the fatal blows. 'Marvin's craving in life was to be famous. The people

Marvin had been in contact with all the time in the business have what Marvin has an absolute blood-lust for: they are famous. It goes beyond rich. I believe he's guilty. I have from the outset. Marvin's motive for killing Vicki was convoluted but to his mind very logical. She represented one of his closest links to the spotlight because of Bloomingdale. This made her a star to Marvin. When she no longer had the backing that made her a star, she began to lose value to him. That was reason enough for him to kill her, that she wasn't famous anymore.

'The last time I visited Marvin in jail,' she said, 'he had on his lap a file folder of all the newspaper front pages that he had been on, and he was stroking that folder and showing me, "Look, I'm on the front pages." If that folder had been a human being, it would have had the most incredible orgasm of its life. I thought to myself, I have now seen obscenity. I didn't go back to see him again. I couldn't.'

On July 5, after only four and a half hours of deliberation, the ten-woman, two-man jury returned a verdict of guilty of murder in the first degree. They believed the confession on the night of the murder, and the defense had not proved that the all-important tapes ever existed or that a conspiracy had taken place. The defense's contention that Gordon Basichis had held Vicki Morgan's Doberman pinscher while an unknown assailant delivered the fatal blows and then had hypnotized Pancoast into thinking that he had killed Vicki – this drew muted guffaws in the courtroom – apparently held no weight with the jury either.

Arthur Barens reported that Marvin Pancoast was devastated by the verdict. As he was led from the courtroom by bailiffs, Pancoast, who had sat through the trial in medicated silence, snapped at a photographer taking his picture, 'Fuck off, man. Leave me alone.'

From his cell in Los Angeles County Jail, Pancoast told a psychiatrist that he believes that Betsy Bloomingdale and Ronald Reagan are in a conspiracy against him and that he is being monitored by the FBI and the CIA through radios and television sets.

THE SAME DAY that Pancoast was convicted, a full-page color picture of Betsy Bloomingdale cutting roses in the garden of her Holmby Hills Palladian villa appeared on the cover of *W*. The article, about her widowhood, was called 'Betsy in Bloom'. Van Nuys, where the trial took place, on the other side of town, was farther away from her than New York or London or Paris. She is the survivor of this story.

Vicki Morgan was the victim twice over. She was only thirty when she died, and only seventeen when, according to her, the fifty-four-year-old Bloomingdale picked her up in a Los Angeles restaurant by pressing an $8,000 check into her hand. Their liaison lasted twelve years, starting the day Vicki joined Bloomingdale and several other women for a bout of sadomasochistic play and ending with his death, when she said of his wife, who had interred him privately without any announcement to the press, 'She buried him like a dog.'

Vicki Morgan was a mistress who led a mistress's life. She shopped and spent while a limousine waited with a driver to carry her packages. She worked on her tan, took social drugs, took acting lessons, and went to the same hairdresser that the wives of Bloomingdale's friends went to. She drove expensive cars, but she never had a pink slip of ownership. She lived in expensive houses in fashionable areas, but she never had the deed to a house. She heard secrets that could have made her solvent for life, but, sadly for her, she couldn't remember most of what she heard.

— ◆ —

For years I believed that other persons than Marvin Pancoast actually killed Vicki Morgan, while he was merely a bystander who took the rap for money. I always meant to visit him in prison, but he died there of AIDS before I could. I wrote a bestselling novel about this story called An Inconvenient Woman, *which was made into a highly rated television series. The book got me into a lot of trouble with prominent figures in Los Angeles society.*

FATAL CHARM:
The Social Web of Claus von Bülow

'THE PROBLEM WITH CLAUS', said one of Claus von Bülow's closest friends at a Park Avenue dinner party, 'is that he does not dwell in the Palace of Truth. You see, he's a fake. He's always been a fake. His name is a fake. His life is a fake. He has created a character that he plays. Claus is a *trompe l'oeil*.'

'Come in, come in,' said von Bülow expansively as he opened the front door to Helmut Newton, the photographer, who had just arrived from Monte Carlo for the session, and me. Von Bülow was standing in the marble-floored, green-walled, gilt-mirrored hallway of the Fifth Avenue apartment of his multimillionairess wife, whom he was accused of twice trying to kill. In the background a very old Chinese butler hovered, watching the master of the house usurp his duties. On that May Sunday of the seventh week of his second trial, the Danish society figure was dressed in tight blue jeans and a black leather jacket.

'This is the first time I've actually posed for a picture

since my front and side shots,' said von Bülow in his deep, resonant, English-school, international-set voice.

From the beginning, the von Bülow proceedings, legal and otherwise, had had an air of unreality about them. His once beautiful wife was one of the country's richest heiresses. His stepchildren were a prince and princess. His daughter was a disinherited teenager. His former mistress was a socialite actress. His current lady friend was a thrice-married Hungarian adventuress who was not the countess she was often described as being. The maid who testified against him had once worked for the Krupps. And lurking darkly in the background was a publicity-mad con man bent on destroying him.

The apartment of Sunny von Bülow, even by Fifth Avenue standards, is very grand. Located in one of the most exclusive buildings in New York, its current market value is estimated by one of the city's top Realtors at nearly $8 million. Although a sophisticated friend of von Bülow's complained that the forty-foot drawing room has 'far, far too many legs', it should be pointed out that the legs are by Chippendale and of museum quality, as is nearly every object in the fourteen-room apartment looking down on Central Park.

According to the terms of Sunny von Bülow's will, the apartment will go to von Bülow when she dies. So will Clarendon Court, the fabulous mansion set on ten acres overlooking the sea in Newport, Rhode Island, where her two comas took place during successive Christmas holidays, in 1979 and 1980. So will $14 million of her $75 million fortune. In the meantime the maintenance on the apartment is paid for by Sunny's estate, so in effect von Bülow and his self-proclaimed mistress, Andrea Reynolds, have been largely supported by his comatose wife since his conviction in 1982 for her attempted murder. That verdict was overturned on appeal because certain materials had been withheld from the defense and others had been improperly admitted as evidence.

'How is my old friend Bobby Moltke?' von Bülow asked Newton as he was setting up his photographic equipment. Then he added, 'Not well, I hear.' Newton resides in Monte Carlo, where Count Moltke lives part of the year, and the inquiry was distinctly perverse. Count Moltke is the father of Alexandra Isles, von Bülow's former mistress, for whom, in the opinion of many, he sought to be rid of his wife. That day her name was prominent in the newspapers because another former lover of hers, the theater critic John Simon, had given an interview to the *New York Post* saying that he was in almost daily contact with the missing actress and that she had no intention of returning to testify at the second trial. Furthermore, Count Moltke, a Danish aristocrat, is known to loathe his fellow countryman for having involved the count's daughter in a scandal that has haunted her for years.

When I admired the carpet in the drawing room, von Bülow said, 'I believe in building a room from the rug up. Did you ever know Billy Wallace in England? His father ordered this rug from Portugal before the war, and by the time it arrived the war had started, and it was put in storage and never used. I bought it from the family after the war.' As usual, his attitude and conversation totally belied the fact that he was at that very moment a candidate for a long sojourn in one of Rhode Island's adult correctional institutions.

While von Bülow posed for Newton in front of a portrait of himself painted in Paris when he was twenty-one, Mrs Reynolds, dressed in a white satin, lace-trimmed negligee, her eyes rimmed with black eyeliner, appeared and led me back to Sunny von Bülow's bedroom. On the bed Mrs Reynolds had laid out evening dresses and a black leather outfit that matched von Bülow's for the shoot. One of the many stories about Andrea Reynolds that circulated at the trial in Providence and in the Upper East Side dining rooms of New York was that she wore Mrs von Bülow's clothes and jewels, and that she had the clothes altered by a seamstress from the Yves Saint Laurent boutique on Madison Avenue.

'Not true!' Mrs Reynolds had exclaimed when I mentioned these allegations a few days earlier. 'I have far better jewels than Sunny von Bülow ever had. I've had fantastic jewels all my life. I wasn't even twenty when I had one of the biggest diamonds around. Be careful what you say about my jewels; I don't want to be robbed again.'

She suffered a million-dollar jewel heist at her villa in Saint-Tropez in the late sixties, and was quoted then by the French columnist Jacques Chazot as saying, 'They were only my *bijoux de plage*.' Another robbery occurred in her New York hotel suite while she was at the movies seeing *Deep Throat*, and once a pair of $80,000 earrings disappeared from a dressing room at Dior in Paris after she removed them to try on fur turbans. She suspects that

they were lifted by an American-born duchess of histor-
ical importance who used the dressing room after her. She
opened several velvet boxes on the bed, revealing a treas-
ure trove of emeralds, diamonds, and pearls. 'Mummy
sent me these,' she said.

During the final days of the first trial, Andrea Reynolds
and her third husband, television producer Sheldon
Reynolds, wrote a letter to von Bülow telling him they
believed he was innocent. Lonely and isolated, von Bülow
responded. They met in New York the day after his return
there from Newport following the guilty verdict, and a
warm friendship quickly developed. He spent weekends
at the couple's country house in Livingston Manor, New
York, and they stayed frequently at the von Bülow apartment. They made plans to have Reynolds be the agent for
von Bülow's proposed autobiography and the miniseries
based on it. (Von Bülow believes Robert Duvall should
play him if a film or miniseries *is* ever made.) These plans
fell apart when Reynolds, on a business trip in London,
read in a gossip column that his wife and von Bülow were
having an affair. A divorce is in progress. Mrs Reynolds
claims she was a neglected wife: 'We were both unhappy
when we met, Claus and I.'

'Look,' said one of von Bülow's swellest friends, who
doesn't see him anymore, 'six years ago, before all this
happened, Claus wouldn't have had time for Andrea
Reynolds.' Although she claims to have known von Bülow
for years, they did not travel in the same echelons of high
society. She has a history of taking up with men who are
at their low ebb and reviving them. A man just convicted

of twice attempting to murder his wife would not seem like much of a catch to most women, but to Andrea Reynolds, Claus von Bülow, sentenced to thirty years pending appeal, was the ticket to center stage that she had always craved.

They made one of their first public appearances together in New York at a party given by Lady Jeanne Campbell, a former wife of Norman Mailer and the daughter of the eleventh Duke of Argyll. It was a glittering gathering of social names, literary names, titles, and a few film stars, and when von Bülow and Mrs Reynolds entered late, after the theater, all conversation stopped. The occasion established Claus von Bülow's tremendous social celebrity; after that the couple maintained a high profile in the upper register of New York. They attended the opera regularly, on the smart night, and were frequent guests at the parties of such well-chronicled hostesses as von Bülow's old friend Mercedes Kellogg, the wife of Ambassador Francis Kellogg, and his new friend and staunch supporter Alice Mason, the New York Realtor. They were also regulars at Mortimer's, the Upper East Side restaurant that caters to Manhattan's people-you-love-to-read-about.

Von Bülow inspires feelings that range from detestation to zealotry. At one of Alice Mason's parties, the editor of a magazine, appalled to be in the same room with a man found guilty of attempting to murder his wife, said she would leave if she were seated at the same table with him. Another woman at the party remarked, 'He might look like the devil, but he's such a cozy old thing, and so amusing to sit next to at dinner. Have you seen him do his imitation of Queen Victoria?'

As a couple, they entertained frequently and elegantly at Sunny's Fifth Avenue apartment. 'Very good food and lots of waiters,' said man-about-town Johnny Galliher. One party was a *vernissage* for Andrea Reynolds's eyelift; the guest of honor was Dr Daniel Baker, the plastic surgeon who had performed the operation. Their frantic pace continued right up to the second trial, and included an eighteenth-birthday party for Claus and Sunny's daughter, Cosima, at Mortimer's, attended by such *bon vivants* of New York as John Richardson, Kenny Lane, and Reinaldo and Carolina Herrera, but not by a single person of Cosima's age. 'As long as they take Cosima with them when they go out, her trust pays the bill,' said an informed source. They spent their last evening in New York before the second trial at a party given by Cornelia Guest, the city's most highly publicized post-debutante, whose mother, C. Z. Guest, the noted horsewoman, gardener, and socialite, was prepared to give testimony in von Bülow's behalf at the trial and corroborate the allegations of the late Truman Capote and others that Sunny von Bülow was a drug addict and a drunk.

FOR THE FIRST SEVERAL WEEKS of the trial in Providence, my room at the Biltmore Plaza Hotel was on the same floor as the rooms von Bülow and Mrs Reynolds shared. For several years I had seen the two of them around New York. Although we had never spoken, we had often been at the same parties or in the same restaurants. The first day in the courtroom, von Bülow recognized me but did not acknowledge me. The second day he nodded to me in the men's room. When we met in the corridor on the fourteenth floor of the hotel, he struck up a conversation about a portable word processor I was carrying. At that moment the door to their suite opened, and Andrea Reynolds came out into the hall.

She said to von Bülow, 'I don't know Mr Dunne's first name.'

'Dominick,' I said.

Von Bülow, leaning toward her, said slowly and deliberately, 'And Mr Dunne is not friendly toward us.'

'I'm being friendly now,' I said.

They invited me into their room, which had a sitting area at one end of it. An open closet was crammed with Mrs Reynolds's clothes and at least twenty pairs of her shoes.

'We mustn't talk about the trial,' said von Bülow.

For a while we talked about Cosima von Bülow, who had that day been accepted at Brown University and would soon graduate from Brooks School in Massachusetts. Von Bülow spoke proudly and affectionately of her.

'Cosima has the best qualities of both her parents,' said Andrea Reynolds. 'She has the beauty and serenity of Sunny, and the intelligence and strength of Claus.' Von Bülow acknowledged to me later Mrs Reynolds's importance in Cosima's life. 'She had been the adult woman to whom Cosima would constantly turn with her little flirtations or whatever a young girl wants to talk about . . . No new woman in my life could have survived a lack of affinity with Cosima.'

'Senator Pell called this morning and wanted to have lunch with Claus in Providence,' said Andrea Reynolds, 'and you can print that.' She was referring to Senator Claiborne Pell of Rhode Island. 'He obviously doesn't think he's guilty.' Von Bülow remarked with the self-deprecatory kind of humor that had become a trademark with him, that he had declined the invitation because he didn't want to spoil the senator's chances of winning a sixth term by being seen with him in public.

That night I happened to fly back to New York on the same plane that Senator and Mrs Pell were on. I struck up a conversation with Mrs Pell and revealed that I was covering the von Bülow trial.

'I was with Claus von Bülow this afternoon and heard that the senator had called to ask him for lunch,' I said.

'Is that what you were told?' Mrs Pell asked. Nuala Pell is the daughter of Jo Hartford Bryce, the Great Atlantic & Pacific Tea Company heiress, and a Newport neighbor of the von Bülows.

'Yes,' I replied.

'Mr von Bülow called my husband. My husband didn't call Mr von Bülow,' she said.

EVERY FRIDAY AFTERNOON during the trial the von Bülow station wagon was packed and ready to depart the instant court adjourned. The doorman of the Biltmore Plaza Hotel held open the rear door, and the golden retriever,

Tiger Lily, bolted into her regular place, eager to be gone. As Mrs Reynolds, behind the wheel, waved gaily to photographers, von Bülow, wearing one of his handsomely cut cuffed-sleeved, foulard-lined tweed jackets, slipped into the front seat beside her, and they took off to New York. After the third week of the trial, they gave a christening party for Mrs Reynolds's granddaughter, Eliza McCarthy. Von Bülow was the godfather, and the infant wore the christening dress Cosima had worn. Mrs Reynolds, in a hat of red poppies with a veil and a blue high-fashion dress, nipped into Mortimer's for a celebratory drink between the religious service at St Jean Baptiste Church and the seated lunch for twenty at the apartment: cold poached salmon, cucumber salad, and champagne, served by three waiters in addition to Tai, the Chinese butler.

Mrs Reynolds interrupted von Bülow's toast to say, 'Claus, Ann-Mari Bismarck is calling from London.'

'Excuse me,' said the host, leaving the table to talk with Princess von Bismarck, one of his strongest supporters.

'He's innocent,' said the woman next to me. 'It's those awful drugged-out children who have brought all this on and framed him. I can't sleep nights worrying about Claus.'

A FEW DAYS BEFORE the christening, von Bülow had gone with the jury, the judge, and both teams of lawyers for a view of Clarendon Court, the Newport mansion he and Sunny and their children had shared during the marriage. Clarendon Court was the location of the two alleged murder attempts. The gates leading to the courtyard of the Georgian mansion were boarded up to discourage passersby from snooping. Entering the grounds of his former home through a service entrance in a side wall, von Bülow broke down and cried, wiping away his tears with a silk handkerchief. Skeptics were quick to note that he was directly in line with a television camera raised high on a cherry picker to film what went on behind the walls, where the media were denied access.

'Why did you cry?' I asked him.

'It was the dogs,' he replied, meaning three yellow Labradors that had belonged to him and Sunny and had often slept on their bed. 'I remembered the dogs as young and lean, and they had become old and fat. But they remembered me, and they jumped up on me and greeted me, and I felt like Ulysses returning. And I broke down.'

The only outward indication that Claus von Bülow was ever under severe strain was a habit he developed of stretching his neck and jutting out his chin at the same time, like a horse trying to throw the bit out of its mouth, or a man resisting a noose. Whatever one felt personally about the guilt or innocence of the man, one could not deny his charm, which was enormous, in a European, upper-class, courtly sort of way. One of the first calls he made after his arrest was to John Aspinall, his English gambler friend, to say that, alas, he would not be able to attend the ball Aspinall and his wife were giving that weekend in Kent.

The slightest incident would trigger an inexhaustible supply of heavy-furniture anecdotes about the titled, the famous, and the wealthy – his standard points of reference. He would regale you with the fact that Christian VII of Denmark, whose portrait hangs in his drawing room, died of syphilis and drink. Or that the marble of his dining table, as blue as malachite is green, is called azurite. 'I hate malachite, don't you?' he asked. 'It reminds me of the fellow who was so proud of his malachite cuff links until a Russian grand duke said to him, "Ah, yes, I used to have a staircase made of that."' Once when a waiter poured him wine, he sniffed it, sipped it, savored it, nodded his approval of it, and then continued with the anecdote he was telling about the Dowager Marchioness of Dufferin and Ava, concerning Sunny von Bülow's maid, Maria Schrallhammer, who testified against him in both trials. '"I know how difficult it is to get a good maid," Maureen said, "but this is ridiculous."'

He would cite as his Newport supporters Alan Pryce-Jones, Oatsie Charles, Mr and Mrs John Winslow, and especially Anne Brown, the septuagenarian dowager Mrs John Nicholas Brown, born a Kinsolving, who took the stand in von Bülow's behalf as a character witness at the first trial and became his most devoted champion in the deeply divided summer colony. At a dinner in Palm Beach last winter given by Mr and Mrs Walter Gubelmann, also of Newport, Mrs Brown announced that her faith in Claus von Bülow remained undiminished, and she asked the other guests to raise their glasses in a toast to him. No one rose to join her.

Von Bülow continued to wear the wedding ring from his marriage to Sunny, although he said any number of

times that they would have divorced if what happened had
not happened. The ring was in fact returned to him before
the first trial by Alexandra Isles, his former mistress,
whose appearance at that trial helped to convict him and
whose melodramatic appearance at the second trial again
turned sentiment against him. Mrs Isles had had the
wedding ring in her possession because it embarrassed her
to have him wear it during the course of their affair.

Sometimes he spoke of Sunny as if she were a beloved
late wife. 'That was one of Sunny's favorite books,' he said
one day when he saw me reading *The Raj Quartet* during
a break in the jury selection. Another time, at the apartment on Fifth Avenue, he saw me looking at a silver-framed
photograph of her, taken by Horst. 'God, she was beautiful,' he said quietly.

'Were you ever in love with Sunny?' I asked.

'Oh, yes. Very much so,' he replied in his dark bari-
tone. 'I'm really not letting out any secrets when I say
that Sunny and I were geographically apart, but in every
other sense together, for two years before we got married.'

WHO EXACTLY IS Claus von Bülow? For most of his life,
dark rumors have circulated about him: that he was a page
boy at Hermann Göring's wedding, that he is a necrophil-
iac, that he killed his mother and kept her body on ice,
that he was involved in international espionage. Von Bülow
either has a logical explanation for each rumor or shrugs
it off as ludicrous. The necrophilia story, he says, was
pinned on him in 1949, as a joke, on Capri, by Fiat owner

Gianni Agnelli and Prince Dado Ruspoli. 'Like dirt, it stuck,' he says.

He was born Claus Cecil Borberg on August 11, 1926, in Copenhagen to Jonna and Svend Borberg, who divorced when he was four. His mother was a beauty who throughout her life developed strong friendships with men in high places. His father was a drama critic who greatly admired the Germans, even after they occupied Denmark in World War II. 'He gave a good name to a bad cause,' says von Bülow about his father. 'He dined with the wrong people.' After the war he was arrested as a collaborator and sentenced to four years in prison. Von Bülow says that his father's conviction – like his own thirty-six years later – was thrown out on appeal, and he was released after eighteen months. However, when von Bülow returned to Denmark, he did not go to see his father, who died broken and ostracized a year after his release.

His mother was residing in England at the time of the German invasion of Denmark. Claus was spirited there via Sweden in the early years of the war through the efforts of both his parents. Claus took the name of his maternal grandfather, Frits Bülow, a former minister of justice, since the name Borberg had been besmirched. The *von* was added later.

When he was sixteen, he was accepted at Cambridge University, from which he graduated in 1946 with a law degree. Too young to take the bar, he spent a year in Paris auditing courses at the École des Sciences Politiques and introducing himself to the world of international high society. After working with Hambros bank in London, he joined the law offices of Quintin Hogg, later Lord Hailsham. An interesting fact that was not brought up in either trial is that during the fifties his law firm handled the first known case of murder by insulin injection.

Von Bülow and his mother, with whom he lived until her death, bought one of the grandest apartments in London, in Belgrave Square, which, von Bülow says, 'dined two hundred with ease and slept three with difficulty'. Before gambling became legal, he rented it out to his friend John Aspinall for private gambling parties. He also made friends with Lord Lucan who later murdered his children's nanny in the mistaken belief that she was his wife, and whose subsequent whereabouts have never been ascertained. Tall and handsome, with an eye for the right social contacts, von Bülow soon knew all the people who mattered. In Saint Moritz he had an affair with socialite Ann Woodward after she killed her husband.

In the early sixties, when he was thirty-three years old, von Bülow was hired as an administrative assistant to the legendary oil tycoon J. Paul Getty, who had recently moved his headquarters of the Los Angeles-based company to London. There has been much speculation as to exactly what von Bülow's importance was in the Getty empire, whether he was an errand boy or a figure of consequence. Getty hated to fly, so von Bülow frequently represented him at meetings and reported back to him. A woman friend of Getty's told me that von Bülow arranged parties in his apartment at which the old man could meet girls. What is certain is that his income from working for one of the richest men in the world was less than $20,000 a year. Von Bülow speaks of Mr Getty with enormous affection and says that one of the major mistakes of his life was leaving England and that job.

Margaret, Duchess of Argyll, was a great friend of Paul Getty's and often served as hostess at his parties. She remembers one occasion when she returned to London from Getty's estate in Surrey with von Bülow, whom she did not know well at the time. She was then involved in one of the most scandalous divorces in English history. Von Bülow asked her if she knew that her husband had taken a room at the Ritz in London that connected with the room of a certain Mrs So-and-so. She did not know. 'But, you can imagine, it was very important information for me to have at that time,' said the duchess, 'and Mr von Bülow didn't even know the duke.'

In 1966 von Bülow married the American Princess Martha 'Sunny' Crawford von Auersperg, thirteen months after her divorce from her first husband, Prince Alfie von Auersperg, on whom she had settled a million dollars and two houses. Tired of living in Austria, tired of her husband's philandering, tired of big-game hunting in Africa, Sunny wanted to bring up her two children from that marriage, Princess Annie-Laurie von Auersperg and Prince Alexander von Auersperg, aged seven and six, in the United States. Fifteen years later those same two children would charge their stepfather with attempting to murder her. The couple settled in New York in Sunny's apartment at 960 Fifth Avenue, the same apartment where von Bülow and Mrs Reynolds reside.

A year later, their only child, Cosima, was born. Prince

Otto von Bismarck, J. Paul Getty, the Marchioness of Londonderry, and Isabel Glover were her godparents.

'DID YOU SEE YOURSELF on Dan Rather last night?' I asked Andrea Reynolds the morning after CBS had run a long sequence of the trial, showing her watching Alexandra Isles, von Bülow's mistress before her, testify against him.

'No, darling, I didn't know it was on. But so many people have been filming me – can you imagine if I spent my days seeing if I can see myself on TV? How did I look?'

Clearly the star of the second trial was Mrs Reynolds, although she was, much to her chagrin, not allowed to sit in the courtroom. She was here, there, and everywhere else, though, known to every employee in the Biltmore Plaza Hotel, to all the cabdrivers of Providence, and to each member of the press. Forty-eight years old, she was born in Hungary and raised and educated in Switzerland. She speaks seven languages. Vivacious, curvaceous, and flirtatious, she seems a sort of latter-day Gabor, with a determination factor somewhere on the scale between Imelda Marcos and Leona Helmsley. She was openly loathed by Claus von Bülow's lawyers long before she told a reporter from *People* magazine that the jury didn't like Thomas Puccio: 'They draw away from him when he approaches the jury box.' Puccio, von Bülow's tough defense attorney, gained national recognition as the Abscam prosecutor. Friends claim Mrs Reynolds knew more about the first trial than the lawyers did. One reporter counted twenty-nine pages of Sunny von Bülow's medical records spread out on tables and chairs in her suite.

She was Claus von Bülow's most passionate defender, fighting to vindicate her man and at the same time establishing a name for herself. It was she, according to Sheldon Reynolds, who got most of the affidavits from prominent people saying that Sunny von Bülow was an alcoholic. Von Bülow said about her, 'I realize that that Hungarian hussar has, often to one's total exhaustion, whipped everybody, including me, into activity.' Nowhere was this more evident than in von Bülow's dealings with the media.

During the first trial, in Newport, von Bülow sometimes spoke to members of the press in the corridors of the courthouse during recesses, but he never socialized with them. During the second trial, in Providence, with Mrs Reynolds at the helm, he openly courted the media with masterly manipulation. They were on a first-name basis with most of the members, dined regularly with them in the various restaurants of Providence, and drove at least one reporter to New York in their station wagon for the weekend, dazzling them all, or so they thought, with their glamour, while always stipulating that anything they said was strictly off the record. Mrs Reynolds often telephoned reporters if she didn't like the way they reported on the trial, and occasionally went over their heads to their editors. When Tony Burton wrote in the *New York Daily News* that while the jury was sequestered in the Holiday Inn, cut off from family and friends, the defendant and his lady friend were dining nightly in the best restaurants in Providence, Mrs Reynolds called him a Commie pinko faggot. Eventually reporters grew sick of the off-the-record quotes fed to them by the pair. One journalist baited Mrs Reynolds by asking her, 'Come on, Andrea, what kind of fuck is Claus?' She replied, without a second's hesitation, 'How can you expect me to answer that? If I tell you he's good, there will be even more women after him than there already are, and if I tell you he's no good, how does that make me look?'

Barred from the courtroom, Mrs Reynolds watched the trial in the truck of Cable News Network, which carried the proceedings live, gavel to gavel. There she was able to see exactly what went on in the courtroom, without all the commercials and cutaways. To the dismay of the CNN personnel, she slowly began to take over the small booth. When Alexander von Auersperg's lawyer entered one day, he was met by Mrs Reynolds. When Judge Corinne Grande called the booth, Mrs Reynolds answered the telephone. Mrs Reynolds was then asked not to return. She begged to be readmitted for just one more day in order to watch a hearing for one of several mistrials requested by the defense, but CNN declined. 'Even a maid gets two weeks' notice,' snapped Mrs Reynolds.

Mrs Reynolds's style was a curious mixture of femininity and rough language. Her stories about the von Auersperg children, whom she had never met, were scurrilous. 'Everyone who ever went to Xenon knows all about them,' she said. On a secret tape submitted to the producers of *60 Minutes*, she referred to Alexander as an asshole.

One day I asked her, 'Is it true that you shot your first husband?'

'Absolutely not.'

'That's a pretty well-circulated story about you, Andrea.'

'It wasn't my first husband. It was my second husband,' she said. 'And I didn't shoot him. He shot himself. When I left him. I'm the one who saved him. Not the one who shot him.'

Andrea Reynolds was born Andrea Milos. Her family was described to me by a Hungarian who knew them as noble without a title. She and her mother fled Hungary for Switzerland when the Russians arrived, but her father, a banker, was forced to stay behind. Eventually he escaped to Morocco with the family jewels, sewn, according to Mrs Reynolds, into the seams of his lederhosen. In Casablanca, he opened a dry-cleaning establishment called Mille Fleurs, and his fortune started to flourish again after he secured the business of the United States Army base in Casablanca. After her parents divorced, her mother married Sir Oliver Duncan, an immensely rich Englishman with pro-German leanings who sat out the war in Switzerland. Older by far than his new wife and suffering from Parkinson's disease, he was an heir to the Pfizer pharmaceutical company. The facts of his death are murky, but nearly all sources agree that he was kidnapped from Switzerland and hidden in a convent in Rome. At some point during his incarceration, he was carried to

Monte Carlo and forced to sign away his fortune to his abductors. Some Europeans familiar with the story told me his body had never been found, but Mrs Reynolds said she knew exactly where her stepfather was buried and that his funeral was attended by hundreds of prominent people. Her mother, the widowed Lady Duncan, now lives in Brazil. 'During all these topsy-turvy things, I always went to the best schools,' said Mrs Reynolds.

Her first husband was a French-Italian named Ellis Giorgini. They had, according to Mrs Reynolds, 'a beautiful wedding in Paris'. But the marriage was short-lived: 'He drank a bit too much.' Her second husband, Pierre Frottier-Duche, a Frenchman, is the father of her only child, Caroline, who is a student of veterinary medicine at the University of Pennsylvania and the mother of Eliza McCarthy. They lived in a house in Paris that had once belonged to Anatole France, and had a villa in Saint-Tropez. At one time very rich, Frottier suffered severe financial reverses. When he later went bankrupt, Mrs Reynolds gave him back all the jewels he had given her. 'I'm a gentleman,' she said. Asked to comment on the story that Frottier had been forced to become a taxi driver after he went broke, she replied, 'No, no, no, a limousine driver, and he would pick up people like Henry Ford, whom he knew from before, and Henry would sit up in the front seat with him when he realized it was Pierre.'

Her conversation is peppered with fashionable names. The late Florence Gould, daughter-in-law of robber baron Jay Gould, was the godmother of her daughter, Caroline. The late Babe Paley was the matron of honor at her third marriage, to film producer Sheldon Reynolds. When pressed, she admitted, 'Well, actually, Babe was sick on the day of the wedding, with a toothache, and someone else had to stand in, but I think of her as my matron of honor.'

She claims to be on excellent terms with all her husbands, but at least one did not share this opinion. 'If Claus has to marry Andrea,' said Sheldon Reynolds, 'he will wish he'd been convicted.'

One night the telephone rang in my hotel room in Providence. It was Mrs Reynolds. She asked me not to mention something she had told me about her first husband, and I agreed not to.

'I talk too much when I'm with you,' she said. 'I'm going to have to arrange for you to have a little accident.'

We both laughed and hung up.

A RICH PERSON on trial is very different from an ordinary person on trial. The powerful defense team assembled by von Bülow for the second trial so outshone the prosecution that the trial often seemed like a football game between the New York Jets and Providence High. Outsiders versed in legal costs estimated that the second trial alone cost von Bülow somewhere in the neighborhood of a million dollars. Besides Thomas Puccio and Alan Dershowitz, the Harvard law professor who won the appeal, four other lawyers, two of them from New York, attended the trial daily. Von Bülow even hired his own court stenographer, because the court-appointed one could not turn out transcripts fast enough to suit the defense. That cost alone, combined with printing, binding, and messenger fees, was probably close to $1,500 a day. Where the money for this extravagant operation came from was anyone's guess. Von Bülow's personal income is $120,000 a year, the interest on a $2 million trust Sunny von Bülow donated to the Metropolitan Opera with the stipulation that the income should go to von Bülow for life. Some said he sold art objects. Others said he had a loan of $900,000 from the Getty Oil Company. Still others said Mrs Reynolds controlled the backers who provided the money.

'Are you in love with Andrea?' I asked von Bülow one Sunday morning late in the trial, when we were sitting on a bench in Central Park.

His eyes were closed. He was catching the warm May rays of the sun on his face. 'I love Andrea,' he replied slowly, measuring his words. 'I find this very hard. Being *in* love is very different from loving somebody. There has to be the right timing and the right climate . . . The climate and timing are wrong. I just don't have enough left for the enthusiasm and recklessness and carefreeness that are inherent in falling in love. I'm a man with a noose around my neck.'

DAVID MARRIOTT WAS meticulously suited and vested in beige gabardine, with an *M* monogrammed on his French cuffs. Tall, slender, twenty-seven years old, he had arrived for our meeting, as he arrived for all of his public appearances, in a limousine. His chauffeur-bodyguard sat with us in the cocktail lounge of the Biltmore Plaza, munching peanuts.

'Would you describe the color of your glasses as grape?'

'No, rose. The press always calls them rose. Call them rose. Not grape,' insisted David Marriott.

One of the most bizarre and unresolved aspects of the complicated von Bülow story was this mysterious young man from Wakefield, Massachusetts, where he lived with his mother. David Marriott had a voracious appetite for publicity and a deep hatred of Claus von Bülow and Andrea Reynolds. He surfaced after the first trial and was, for some time, embraced by von Bülow, Mrs Reynolds, and Alan Dershowitz. Because of Marriott, von Bülow announced that he had discovered dramatic new evidence which he claimed would establish his innocence. At the urging of a later discredited Catholic priest, Father Philip Magaldi, Marriott swore that he had delivered packages containing hypodermic needles, bags of white powder, syringes, vials of Demerol, and pills to Alexander von Auersperg, who had told him that some of the material was for his mother, 'to keep her off my back'.

This evidence was a direct contradiction of the state's claim that the only person in the von Bülow household who had access to, or familiarity with, drugs and paraphernalia was Claus von Bülow. Affidavits signed by both Marriott and Father Magaldi were therefore important to von Bülow for his appeal.

Marriott paid visits to von Bülow's Fifth Avenue apartment and to the Reynoldses' country house in Livingston

Manor, had lunches and dinners in fashionable restaurants, and took several trips to Puerto Rico, paid for by von Bülow. But then a falling-out occurred. By the start of the second trial, Marriott had recanted his original confession, and was claiming instead that his story had been concocted by von Bülow and that the drugs and needles he had delivered 'didn't go to Sunny and Alex, they went to Claus'. Marriott further revealed that he had secreted a tape recorder in his Jockey shorts and taped von Bülow, Mrs Reynolds, Father Magaldi, and Alan Dershowitz in compromising conversations. He invited members of the press to his house in Wakefield to listen to them. Although the voices of von Bülow, Mrs Reynolds, and Father Magaldi were distinguishable, the content of their talk, while suspicious in nature, was not incriminating. That left Marriott unwanted by either side.

Marriott was variously described by the media as an undertaker, a male prostitute, and a drug dealer. He claimed to me to be none of these, although he said that von Bülow had once offered to send him to mortician's school, and his remarks about von Bülow were filled with homosexual innuendo. Von Bülow said he had never heard of David Marriott before he came forward with his story of having sold drugs at Clarendon Court. Marriott, on the other hand, said he had known von Bülow for seven or eight years, having met him through a now deceased twenty-three-year-old drug dealer and hustler named Gilbert Jackson, who was, in Marriott's words, 'bound up in elastic cord and strangled and stabbed many, many times on August 28, 1978'. Two vagrants are serving time for that murder. When I asked Andrea Reynolds whether von Bülow ever knew Gilbert Jackson, she said, 'Darling, one doesn't know people like that.'

In a move of desperation to achieve the notoriety that was eluding him, Marriott passed out defamatory leaflets about his onetime cohort, Father Magaldi, during mass at St Anthony Church in North Providence, but the local television stations, alerted by Marriott of his intentions to make scandalous allegations about the priest, ignored the stunt.

When I called Marriott to double-check his version of how he had met von Bülow, he said, 'I'm not telling you this unless I get paid for it. I'm saving that for my book.'

'Listen, it doesn't matter, I'm running short of space anyway. I don't need to use you at all.'

'It's all right. You can use it. I met him through Gilbert Jackson in 1978.'

During the seventh week of the trial, David Marriott was severely beaten up. His nose was broken and his eyes were blackened. No explanation was given for the assault.

After the jury retired to deliberate, Father Magaldi was indicted for perjury and conspiring to obstruct justice by lying on behalf of Claus von Bülow.

Our mother, as you know, has been in an irreversible coma for four years: she cannot see, hear or speak. She is a victim in every sense. Our mother gave us unfailing love and devotion. She taught us the very big difference between right and wrong. We carry her sensitivities and her teachings as, perhaps, only

*children can . . . She was not there to tell what
had happened to her. She was not there to speak
for herself when her character was assaulted.
Lying in a deep coma, our mother became a non-
person.*

That is a portion of a letter written by Alexander von
Auersperg and Annie-Laurie Kneissl that appeared in the
newsletter of an organization known as Justice for
Surviving Victims, Inc. Alexander and Annie-Laurie, who
is known as Ala, remained remote figures throughout most
of the second trial, but then they emerged in a blaze of
worldwide publicity at a press conference in which they
begged their stepfather's former mistress, Alexandra Isles,
who had fled the country, to come forward and provide
critical testimony. 'We realize that coming forward the last
time was an act of courage on your part. We ask that you
summon the same courage again.'

Sunny's children by her first marriage, backed by their
maternal grandmother, Annie Laurie Aitken, who died
last year, undertook the original investigation of their stepfather and hired former New York District Attorney
Richard Kuh to confirm their suspicions. Jonathan
Houston, executive director of Justice Assistance in
Providence, brought me together with Ala Kneissl early
in the trial. We met for the first time in the New York
apartment of Pamela Combemale, a close friend of Sunny
von Bülow's and the cousin of another ill-fated heiress,
Barbara Hutton.

Married to an Austrian, the beautiful Ala Kneissl was

pregnant with her second child when we met. Her brother, who is equally good-looking, graduated from Brown University in 1983 and works in the retirement division of E. F. Hutton. Deeply devoted to their mother, they acknowledged that she and von Bülow were happy for many years, and that they themselves had had affection for him. They had called him Uncle Claus or Ducky. Why Ducky? In those days, while his hair transplant was growing in, he wore a toupee, and when he swam he held his head far out of the water like a duck. Their mother, they said, preferred home life to social life, and they reminisced about family meals and going to films together and lying on their mother's bed watching television.

While the jury was out deliberating, Ala and Alexander invited me to Newport to spend the night at Clarendon Court. We dined across Bellevue Avenue at the home of the Countess Elizabeth de Ramel, an American friend of Ala's titled by a former marriage, whose Newport antecedents, the Prince and Wood-Prince families, date back for generations. There were a dozen guests. Despite attempts at joviality, the conversation throughout dinner never strayed far from the trial and the looming verdict. Ala and Alexander, who were dubbed 'the kids' by the press during the trial, are remarkably unspoiled for young people who have grown up amid a kind of wealth and opulence that is almost incomprehensible.

Clarendon Court faces Bellevue Avenue on one side and the Atlantic Ocean on the other. In 1956 it was used as the setting for Grace Kelly's home in the film *High Society*. Another page of its colorful history concerns a young man named Paul Molitor, who was hired by Claus von Bülow in 1979 from the China Trade Museum in Massachusetts to work for the Newport Preservation Society, of which von Bülow was then an officer. Molitor beat out 120 other applicants for the job. Shortly after his arrival in Newport, von Bülow invited him to move into the carriage house on the grounds of Clarendon Court. Extremely personable, he soon became a popular extra man at dinner parties. He was in residence at the time of Sunny von Bülow's second coma, and his Newport friends recall that he was extremely fearful of having to testify at the first trial. He was not called to the stand, but one night six months later, he jumped off the Newport Bridge. A persistent rumor in the resort colony is that he was pushed. He was wearing a dinner jacket. An early report in the *Providence Journal*, later denied, said that his feet were bound with chicken wire.

Clarendon Court is a house where you walk through huge rooms to get to other huge rooms. Outside, between the terrace and the sea, is the mammoth swimming pool built by Sunny when she acquired the house after her second marriage; two fountains in the pool shoot water twenty feet into the air. She gave her last great party here, a twenty-first-birthday celebration for Alexander, at which all the guests wore white and played croquet on the sweeping lawns as the mist rolled in from the ocean.

'That was Claus's,' said Ala, with a shudder of distaste, pointing to a cast-iron jardiniere held up by three mythological figures with erect penises. Some of the furniture in the house belongs to von Bülow, from his Belgrave

Square apartment. At the end of the first trial, when he put in a list of the pieces of furniture that were his, he claimed a partners' desk. Later it was discovered in an old photograph that the desk had been in Sunny's house in Kitzbühel during her marriage to Alfie von Auersperg. The furniture in von Bülow's study has a different feeling entirely from the rest of the house; exotic formula-laden pieces crowd the room, and opium pipes hang on the wall. It was here that he left the note containing the phrase 'metal box', which led to the discovery of the infamous black bag that contained the syringe and insulin that were at the heart and soul of the case.

In a world of people who call their mother Mummy, Ala and Alexander call theirs Mom. As I walked through the house with them, they said things like 'This was my mom's favorite color,' pointing to the coral-painted walls of an upstairs sitting room, or 'You should have seen my mom arrange flowers.'

Their mother's bedroom remains exactly the way it was on the night of the second coma. Her elegantly canopied bed consists of two beds pushed together, made up separately with Porthault sheets and monogrammed blanket covers. On von Bülow's side of the bed is an old, silver-framed photograph of him in a striking, almost noble pose. I opened a handsome box on his bed table. It was filled with cartridge shells. Under the shells was a used syringe. In one of Sunny's closets, next to her evening dresses, are unopened gifts from that last Christmas of 1980 – one from her lifelong friend Isabel Glover, another from her now deceased mother. Their festive wrappings are faded and limp.

On the day that Alexandra Isles returned to the United States to testify against von Bülow, Cosima graduated from Brooks School. She was the only member of the graduating class with no relatives present, but her classmates rallied behind her and cheered loudly when she received her diploma.

The estrangement from her half-brother and half-sister was over Clarendon Court. Although she was welcome to use the house at any time, Ala and Alexander would not vacate the place for her. When I told von Bülow that Ala and Alexander still cared for Cosima, he replied, 'I just think they have to put their money where their mouth is. I am not impressed with constant repetitions of love and holding on to her money. I'd much rather hear them say they hate the brat and that's why they're holding on to her money.'

Both von Bülow and Mrs Reynolds were obsessed with the fact that Cosima had been cut out of the $110 million estate of her grandmother, Annie-Laurie Aitken, for siding with her father. 'She's out twenty-five million,' Mrs Reynolds said to me one day after Cosima and her boyfriend had left the table at Mortimer's.

One of the most poignant moments of the trial occurred on the last day, when all three of Sunny von Bülow's children appeared in the courthouse. It was the first time Ala and Cosima had seen each other since a chance encounter on the street three years earlier. As the divided family passed in the corridor, they looked straight ahead and did not speak. 'She's gotten so beautiful,' Ala said to me later of Cosima. 'My mother would be very proud of her.'

NO ONE ELSE in the trial came near to the sheer dramatic power of Alexandra Isles. Often described in the media as a soap-opera actress, the patrician Mrs Isles attended the same schools as Sunny von Bülow: Chapin and St Timothy's. Her mother, the Countess Mab Moltke, was born into the Wilson family of San Francisco, whose fortune, diminished now, traces its roots back to the Comstock Lode. Mrs Isles is divorced from Philip Isles, a member of the wealthy Lehman banking family; his father changed his name from Ickelheimer in the fifties. Following their divorce, Isles married the former wife of Dr Richard Raskind, who changed his name to Renée Richards when he became a woman.

Deeply wounded by the hostile reaction she received at the end of the first trial, von Bülow's former mistress fled the country rather than testify again, believing, she said, that a videotape of her testimony in the first trial could be used in the second. At a New York party, Mrs Isles's friend John Simon told me that under no condition would she return. He claimed, and later repeated to the press, that she did not want her son, Adam, fifteen, a student at Groton, to suffer the embarrassment of having his mother on the stand as the mistress and motive of the defendant in an attempted murder trial; that her mother was ill and had begged her not to take the stand; that she was terrified of being cross-examined by Thomas Puccio because she knew von Bülow's lawyer would expose her private life; and that she had received threatening letters from von Bülow warning her not to testify. Von Bülow vehemently and angrily denied this, claiming he had not been in touch with her since the first trial.

Mrs Isles, who was reported to be hiding out at Forest Mere, an exclusive fat farm in England, flew from Frankfurt, Germany, the day after the von Auersperg children made their plea for her to return. After conferring with the prosecution team in Boston, she spent the night under an assumed name in the Ritz-Carlton Hotel, watching a Celtics game with her son. The next morning she testified that von Bülow had called her at her mother's house in Ireland after the first coma to say that he had lain on the bed next to his wife for hours waiting for her to die, but that at the last minute he had not been able to go through with it and had called the doctor. Feisty and unwavering, she withstood the pummeling of Thomas Puccio. When he asked her to explain how she could have continued an affair with a man she suspected of trying to kill his wife, she shouted, 'Have you ever been in love?' Then she added, 'I doubt it.'

Mrs Reynolds was openly contemptuous of Mrs Isles. Speaking of the jury, she said to me, 'They have been told Claus was consumed by so much passion he was willing to kill his wife and get her money so that he could marry Alexandra Isles. In real life, two days after the end of the first trial, he and I fell in love with each other.' Later the press said that she bared her claws and declared that Alexandra Isles had had two or three men at a time. Mrs Isles had no comment to make about Mrs Reynolds.

Meanwhile, the subject, or object, of all this conflict, Sunny von Bülow, lies in the sixth year of her coma on the tenth floor of the Harkness Pavilion in the Columbia-Presbyterian Medical Center in New York City. She is not, as many believe, on a life-support system, nor is she the total vegetable she is often described as being. I was told that the yearly cost of maintaining her is considerably in excess of half a million dollars. Her $725-a-day room is guarded around the clock by a special security force, and private nurses and a maid look after her at all times. A maze of curtained screens further protects her from the remote possibility that an outsider should gain entry to her room. A current photograph of the comatose woman would be worth a fortune.

Dr Richard Stock, who has been her physician for twenty-nine years, as he was her mother's and grandmother's, visits her several times a week. She is fed through a tube in her nose. She receives physical therapy and dental care, and her hair is washed and set twice a week. Her own skin creams are used on her hands and face. She wears her own nightgowns and bed jackets and sleeps on Porthault sheets. Music plays in the room, and there are always highly scented flowers on her bedside table.

Ala and Alexander visit her regularly. Sometimes Ala brings her two-year-old daughter, also called Sunny, so that her mother can know she has a grandchild. They talk to her. They touch her. They tell her about things.

In a bizarre twist of fate, their father, Prince Alfie von Auersperg, is also in an irreversible coma, in Salzburg, the result of an automobile accident two years ago, when he was driving with Alexander. Their father's sister, Princess Hetty von Auersperg von Bohlen, the wife of Arndt von Bohlen and Halbach, the Krupp munitions heir, has found a healer in Europe who specializes in comas. She plans to bring the healer to New York to minister to her former sister-in-law. There are those who say that when Alfie von Auersperg and Sunny von Bülow stood side by side in the receiving line at their daughter's marriage to Franz Kneissl, he asked her to divorce Claus von Bülow and remarry him.

Maria Schrallhammer, the German maid so devoted to her mistress that she refused to divulge to two sets of defense attorneys the fact that Sunny von Bülow had had a face-lift because she had promised her she would never tell, also visits regularly, as does G. Morris Gurley, the Chemical Bank trust officer for Sunny's estate. Old friends are occasionally admitted, and one of them told me, 'She has a personality just like you or I do. She reacts differently to different people. Some days you have a termagant on your hands. You try to brush her hair and you will have hell to pay. Other times, if the shades aren't open, she still looks beautiful in the half-light, although her hair has gone completely gray.'

Cosima von Bülow has not been to the hospital since December 1981. Nor has Claus von Bülow.

In the three years that preceded Sunny von Bülow's second coma, most of her friends did not see her, or saw her only rarely. Some of them claim that von Bülow isolated her, answered the telephone for her, took messages that they felt she never received.

One of Sunny's last public appearances in New York was at the funeral of her childhood friend Peggy Bedford, a Standard Oil heiress with an inheritance comparable to Sunny's, although she was reputed to have gone through most of it by the time of her death in an automobile accident. Married first to Thomas Bancroft, she had later become the Princess d'Arenberg and then the Duchess d'Uzes. Friends say they spoke with Sunny on the steps of St James Church following the service and found her warm and friendly and eager to make plans to see them. Then von Bülow appeared at her side, took hold of her elbow, and led her off to their waiting limousine. One old friend, Diego Del Vayo, remembers that she waved a gloved hand to him out of the car window.

FOR THE EIGHT WEEKS that the trial mesmerized the country, a related development of the strange case ran its parallel course. Nowhere was the scent of rot more pervasive than in the minimally publicized story of a Providence parish priest, Father Philip Magaldi, and his onetime companion David Marriott, an unemployed mystery man who drove around in limousines and who was happy to show anyone who cared to look Xeroxed copies of his hotel bills from Puerto Rican resorts, which he claimed were paid for by Claus von Bülow. Why, people wondered, if von Bülow was innocent, would he have involved himself in such an unsavory atmosphere?

Let us backtrack.

On July 21, 1983, Father Magaldi, on the stationery of Saint Anthony Church, 5 Gibbs Street, North Providence, Rhode Island, wrote and signed the following statement in the presence of a notary:

TO WHOM IT MAY CONCERN:

. . . I wish to state that I am ready to testify, if necessary, and under oath, that DAVID MARRIOTT did in fact discuss with me in professional consultation, his delivering to Mr Claus von Bülow's stepson, Alexander [von Auersperg], packages which he thought contained drapery materials from his friend Gilbert [Jackson] in Boston, but on one occasion a package which he opened contained drugs which were delivered to the Newport mansion and accepted by Mrs Sunny von Bülow who stated Alexander was not home but she had been expecting the package.

My reason for writing this affidavit is that in the event of accident or death, I wish to leave testimony as to the veracity of the statements made to me by DAVID MARRIOTT and also that as his counselor in spiritual matters, I advised him to inform Mr Claus von Bülow and his lawyers as to what he knew concerning drug involvement by Alexander. I intend to speak to Mr Roberts, the Attorney General of the State of Rhode Island, concerning these matters in August.

Five days later, on white watermarked stationery bearing the engraved address 960 Fifth Avenue, New York, Claus von Bülow wrote Father Magaldi a letter that was quoted in the *New York Post* by gossip columnist Cindy Adams at the conclusion of the second trial. It reads in part:

> *Dear Father Magaldi:*
>
> *I want to thank you for your kindness and courage in braving the storm and the airport delays, and then coming to meet me in New York. Had I been able to contact you in Boston I would gladly have faced those problems myself.*
>
> *We were however rewarded with a very enjoyable evening, and I am grateful to you.*
>
> *I want to repeat my wish to consult with you in finding an acceptable charity for donating the royalties of my book. The total profits, including film rights, could be anything between $500,000 and $1,000,000 . . . I will be happy to meet with you in Providence, Boston, or New York at your convenience.*

On September 30, 1983, Father Magaldi, in a document notarized by his attorney, William A. Dimitri, Jr (who later became the attorney for von Bülow's mistress, Andrea Reynolds), made the following statement:

> *In addition to my affidavit I wish to state something which I feel is too delicate a matter to come before the media and public at this time.*

> *I refer to pictures shown me by David Marriott*
> *in which Alexander is engaged in homosexual*
> *activity with an unidentified male whom David*
> *told me was Gilbert Jackson.*
>
> *Because these pictures in my estimation served*
> *no purpose and were patently pornographic, I*
> *destroyed them. However I can state that I recog-*
> *nized Alexander in the picture but cannot verify*
> *that the other was Gilbert Jackson since I have never*
> *seen him.*

In actuality, Father Magaldi had never met Alexander von Auersperg, and Alexander von Auersperg had never met Gilbert Jackson, who was murdered in 1978, and therefore no such pornographic pictures ever existed for Father Magaldi to destroy. In other, more exotic areas of his life, Father Magaldi traveled in the netherland of Boston under the alias Paul Marino. It was in this role that he met David Marriott, in the Greyhound bus terminal in 1977, and not in the spiritual capacity he claimed in his affidavit. David Marriott told me that he did not know his benefactor was a Catholic priest until Magaldi was in a minor automobile accident several years after their friendship began and his true identity came out.

Marriott, who participated in preparing these and other affidavits besmirching the names of Claus von Bülow's wife, Sunny, and his stepson, Alexander von Auersperg, later claimed that they were all lies and that he had been paid by von Bülow for his part in the deception. Furthermore, Marriott had secretly tape-recorded conversations with

Father Magaldi, von Bülow, and Andrea Reynolds to attempt to support his claim. On one tape that I listened to, Father Magaldi and Marriott discuss von Bülow's alleged offer to help the priest be elevated to bishop. On another there is talk about getting the late Raymond Patriarca, the Mafia chieftain of Providence, to get a drug dealer serving time in jail to say that Alexander von Auersperg had been one of his customers.

This murky matter played no part in Claus von Bülow's second trial in Providence. However, there were frequent rumors that Father Magaldi, who is a popular priest in the city, was about to be indicted for lying in a sworn statement he had given in 1983 to help von Bülow get a new trial, and that may have been the principal reason why Judge Corinne Grande insisted that the jury be sequestered for the eight weeks of the trial, especially since several of the members were acquainted with Father Magaldi. The priest was not indicted until after the jury had retired to deliberate, and the contents of the sealed indictment were not made known.

On the day before the jury returned its verdict, Claus von Bülow and Father Magaldi met – perhaps by accident, perhaps by design – in the lobby of the Biltmore Plaza Hotel. The encounter took place at seven o'clock on a Sunday morning and was witnessed by one of the bell-men, who used to serve as an altar boy for Father Magaldi. The priest, the bellman told me, had made the fifteen-minute drive from North Providence to buy the Sunday papers at the newsstand in the lobby of the hotel. Just as he arrived, the elevator doors opened and von Bülow emerged to walk Mrs Reynolds's golden retriever, Tiger Lily. The encounter between the two men was brief, but the bellman was sure they had exchanged a few words.

That night, twelve members of the media who had covered the trial gathered for a farewell dinner in a Providence restaurant. Their conversation never strayed far from the subject that had held them together for nearly nine weeks – the trial. They discussed the fact that once again Claus von Bülow had not taken the stand, and they felt that it had been a foregone conclusion in the defense strategy from the start that he was never going to. The defense was aware that the prosecution was in possession of an exhaustive report by a European private-detective agency on the life of von Bülow before his marriage to Sunny, and a clever prosecutor, given the opportunity to examine the defendant directly, would have been able to ask many potentially embarrassing questions. Another topic of conversation was Judge Corinne Grande, whose frequent rulings favorable to the defense raised questions of her impartiality. In what was certainly the most controversial ruling of the trial, Judge Grande had agreed with von Bülow's lawyers that the testimony of G. Morris Gurley, Sunny's banker at the Chemical Bank in New York, should be barred. Gurley would certainly have testified that, according to a prenuptial agreement, von Bülow would receive nothing from his wife in a divorce. However, according to her will, he would inherit $14 million if she died.

I repeated a story I had heard that afternoon from someone who had been present at an exchange between Mr Gurley and Alexandra Isles in the witness room. Mrs

Isles had just completed her testimony when Gurley was informed that he would not be called to the stand. Gurley was stunned. So was Mrs Isles. 'I can't believe they're not letting you testify,' she told him. 'I wasn't the motive, Morris. The money was the motive. He had me for free.'

Late in the evening someone came up with the idea, since there were twelve of us, of pretending to be a jury and voting a verdict, not as we anticipated the jury would vote, but as we would vote if we were members of the jury and knew everything we knew rather than what Judge Grande had selected for us to know. The waitress brought a pad and pencils, and each person cast his vote. Our verdict, we all agreed, would remain our secret.

DURING THE FOUR DAYS the jury was out deliberating, Claus von Bülow wandered up and down the crowded corridors of the courthouse, chain-smoking Vantage cigarettes and behaving like a genial host at a liquorless cocktail party, moving from one group of reporters to another with his endless supply of anecdotes. He even took time to call his most consistently loyal friend, the art historian John Richardson, to ask when he planned to leave for London. Monday week, he was told. He asked Richardson if he would take twelve large bags of potato chips to Paul Getty, Jr, who loved potato chips, but only the American kind.

On Monday morning, June 10, 1985, while waiting for the jury to reappear, von Bülow was tense and withdrawn. In the minutes before the jury entered, Barbara Nevins, a popular CBS reporter, leaned over from the press box and asked him if he had any final words before the verdict was delivered. In an uncharacteristic gesture, von Bülow raised the middle finger of his left hand to her.

'Is that for me, Mr von Bülow, or for the press in general?' asked Miss Nevins. Thinking better of his gesture, he pretended that he had meant to scratch his forehead. At that moment the jury entered.

The proceedings were swift. The verdict was, predictably, 'Not Guilty' on both charges. Von Bülow bowed his head for an instant and blinked back a tear. Then he and his lawyer Thomas Puccio nodded to each other without emotion. The courtroom was strangely mute despite a few cheers from elderly Clausettes in the back of the room. Very little of the ecstasy that accompanies a vindication was present, except in the histrionics of Mrs Reynolds, whose moment had finally come, and she played it to the hilt. Flanked by two of her favorite reporters and directly in line with the television camera, she raised her diamond-ringed fingers to her diamond-earringed ears and wept.

In his moment of victory, von Bülow bypassed the embrace and kiss offered him by Mrs Reynolds, who was wearing the same blue party dress she had worn at her granddaughter's christening, and gave her a peck on the cheek. Then he raced to a telephone to call Cosima.

During the triumphant press conference after the trial, von Bülow, surrounded by seven lawyers glowing with the flush of victory, returned to his old arrogance as he fielded questions from media representatives he no longer needed to court. Following a champagne visit with the jury that had acquitted him, he and Mrs Reynolds returned to New

York. Even in his moment of victory, dramatic rumors preceded his arrival. At Mortimer's restaurant, a French visitor said that if Claus had been found guilty, there was a plan to spirit him out of the country on the private jet of a vastly rich Texan.

'IF I TOOK YOU down to our beach and you started asking people, the two hundred of us who have dinner and swim and play golf together, you would find nearly everybody will say he did it,' Mrs John Slocum, a member of Newport society whose pedigree goes back twelve generations, told a reporter a week before von Bülow was acquitted. 'And I'll tell you something else,' she added, 'people are afraid of Claus.'

A few days after the trial, I went to Newport to check out the scene, and found that the battle lines between the pro- and anti-von Bülow factions remained drawn, and seemed possibly even fiercer than ever. On the front page of the *Newport Daily News*, Mrs Slocum crossed swords with Mrs John Nicholas Brown, who had been von Bülow's staunchest defender in Newport society from the beginning, in their respective damnation and praise of Judge Grande and the verdict. In the same article Mrs Claiborne Pell, the wife of Senator Pell of Rhode Island, said she was 'delighted' that von Bülow had walked from the courthouse a free man, while Hugh D. Auchincloss, the stepbrother of Jacqueline Kennedy Onassis, who had once written a letter on von Bülow's behalf to help him gain membership in the Knickerbocker Club, had harsh words for the verdict, the judge, and his former friend.

At the exclusive Clambake Club, Russell Aitken, the widower of Sunny von Bülow's mother, Annie-Laurie Aitken, stared ahead stone-faced as Mr and Mrs John Winslow, who had once said that the Aitkens would not be welcome at Bailey's Beach if Claus were acquitted, were seated nearby with their party. The Winslows were equally stone-faced.

RUSSELL AITKEN'S DISLIKE of his stepson-in-law is ferocious, and it predates the two charges of attempted murder by insulin injection. Standing on the terrace of Champs Soleil, the Bellevue Avenue estate he inherited from his late wife, which rivals, perhaps even surpasses, Clarendon Court in splendor, Mr Aitken recalled for me the first time he and his wife ever met Claus von Bülow. It was in 1966 in London, in the lounge of Claridge's Hotel, when von Bülow was a suitor for Sunny, who had just divorced Prince Alfie von Auersperg. Von Bülow arrived for the meeting with Sunny's parents with his head covered in bandages, explaining that he had been in an automobile accident. Later Mr and Mrs Aitken heard from Sunny that the truth was rather different: his head was bandaged because he had just had his first hair-transplant operation.

Behind Russell Aitken, on the rolling lawns of the French manor house, a new croquet court was under construction, which promises to be the handsomest croquet court on the Eastern Seaboard. A respected sculptor, he had had one of his own artworks installed on a wall overlooking the new court. Mr Aitken interrupted his tour to continue our conversation about his stepson-in-law. 'He is an extremely dangerous man,' he said, 'because he's a Cambridge-educated con man with legal training. He is totally amoral, greedy as a wolverine, cold-blooded as a snake. And I apologize to the snake.'

'May I quote you saying that, Mr Aitken?' I asked.

'Oh, yes, indeed,' he replied.

WHILE VON BÜLOW saved himself for an exclusive interview with Barbara Walters on *20/20*, his mistress did a saturation booking on the television shows. Back in Providence, Judge Grande defended herself against a barrage of criticism that she had let a guilty man walk free. 'I DIDN'T HELP CLAUS BEAT RAP', went one headline. Out in Seattle, Jennie Bülow, the elderly widow of Frits Bülow, Claus von Bülow's long-dead maternal grandfather, from whom he acquired his name when he changed it from Borberg, made no secret of her dissatisfaction with both the judge and the verdict.

In New York, von Bülow announced that he would visit Sunny at Columbia-Presbyterian Medical Center for the first time in four years as a gesture of his continuing love for her. Later, seated in the library of his wife's Fifth Avenue apartment, he met with Barbara Walters, as he had met with her at the conclusion of his first trial. He talked about his desire to go back to work. 'I was never going to divorce Sunny because of any other woman,' he told her. 'I was going to divorce Sunny because she didn't tolerate my work.' At the end of the interview, Miss Walters announced that von Bülow would soon be leaving for England to begin work for Paul Getty, Jr, the son of his former boss.

Getty, who was very possibly the donor of both von Bülow's bail money and his defense fund, is fifty-two years old and makes his home in England. He recently gave $63 million to the National Gallery in London. In 1984, according to *Fortune* magazine, he had an income from the Getty trust of $110 million. A virtual recluse, Getty is said to be a registered drug addict in England. His second wife, Talitha Pol, a popular member of the jet set, died in her husband's penthouse apartment in Rome of a massive overdose of heroin in 1971. To this day many of her friends insist that the fatal injection was not self-administered. The oldest of Getty's five children, John Paul III, lost an ear during his kidnapping in Italy in 1973. He later suffered a methadone-induced stroke that left him blind and crippled. Getty's youngest child, Tara Gabriel Galaxy Gramaphone Getty, seventeen, the son of Talitha, is at present engaged in legal proceedings against the $4 billion Getty trust.

IN THE ONGOING CONTROVERSY that constantly surrounds him, von Bülow for some reason denied to reporter Ellen Fleysher during a news conference an item in Liz Smith's syndicated column saying that he and Mrs Reynolds had posed for *Vanity Fair* magazine and photographer Helmut Newton dressed in black leather. 'No, I think you've got the wrong case,' he told the reporter. Liz Smith, quick to respond, printed in her column two days later, 'Once you see Claus inside the magazine in his black leather jacket, I want you to tell me how we can believe anything he says.'

The same day that Liz Smith questioned von Bülow's veracity, the *New York Times* reported that the indictment against Father Magaldi in Providence had been unsealed and that the priest was charged with perjury and conspiring to obstruct justice to affect the outcome of Claus von Bülow's appeal. Early that morning the telephone rang in my New York apartment. It was Mrs Reynolds. Displeased with the latest developments in the media, she accused me of planting the story in Liz Smith's column to attract publicity for my article in *Vanity Fair*.

'Do you have any fear of being subpoenaed in the Father Magaldi case?' I asked her.

'They wouldn't subpoena me over their dead bodies,' replied Mrs Reynolds.

'Why?'

'I can totally demolish Mr Marriott,' she said. There was ice in her voice.

I asked her if it was true that she and von Bülow were only waiting for the return of his passport so that they could get out of the country before they were subpoenaed. She angrily denied to me that they had played any part in the false affidavits.

Von Bülow now got on the line, and his anger equaled that of Mrs Reynolds. 'I suggest you talk with Professor Dershowitz at Harvard,' he told me sternly.

'Let me give you his telephone number,' snapped Mrs

Reynolds, 'to save you the seventy-five cents it will cost you to dial information.'

THE BURNING QUESTION WAS, would Claus von Bülow's acquittal give him automatic use of his comatose wife's $3.5 million annual income, minus, of course, the half-million dollars a year it costs to maintain her in Columbia-Presbyterian Medical Center? If so, his access to the money was not immediate, and civil litigation loomed that could tie up Sunny's fortune for years. In the meantime, unless Sunny dies and von Bülow inherits the $14 million that he is guaranteed in her will, he will have to make do with the interest on the $2 million trust his wife gave to the Metropolitan Opera, which amounts to $120,000 a year before taxes. There was talk in the first week of his freedom that money was debt.

Despite the wide coverage of von Bülow's acquittal across the country, the accolades of victory were spare in New York. The jewelry designer Kenneth Jay Lane entertained von Bülow and Mrs Reynolds at a lunch in their honor – cold curried chicken, pasta salad, raspberries and blueberries with crème fraîche – and the guest list included John Richardson; Giorgio co-owner Gale Hayman; the English film star Rachel Ward; her husband, Australian actor Bryan Brown; and her mother, Claire Ward, long-time companion of von Bülow's great friend Lord Lambton, a former parliamentary undersecretary for the Royal Air Force who was forced to resign after his involvement in a government sex scandal. The lunch coincided with the announcement in the *New York Times* of Father Magaldi's indictment, and one guest reported that the atmosphere was subdued.

While von Bülow waited for his passport to be returned, he and Mrs Reynolds became – for them, at least – almost socially invisible. They lunched quietly at Le Cirque, with their staunch ally Alice Mason, the New York Realtor and hostess. On another occasion Mrs Reynolds entertained two members of the press at lunch at the Four Seasons. They attended a coming-out party given in honor of two daughters of the family with whom Cosima had lived during the first trial. For some reason they did not once venture into Mortimer's, the Upper East Side restaurant that had become their favorite haunt between trials.

Mrs Reynolds told friends she was writing a miniseries based on the trial. Von Bülow made plans with his publisher for his autobiography and according to one friend, made arrangements for a face-lift. Together they visited the Livingston Manor house of Mrs Reynolds's about-to-be-former husband, Sheldon Reynolds, to look at trees she had planted and pick up clothes she had left there. A witness to the scene reported that von Bülow's attitude to Mrs Reynolds was chilly.

ALEXANDRA ISLES DECLINED to be interviewed at the end of the trial. 'We all have our own ways of surviving,' she wrote me. 'Mine is to try to put it out of my head and get on with other things. I know you will understand that an interview somehow keeps it all "unfinished business", but here is a bit of irony you are welcome to use: It was my father who, in the Danish underground, got little Claus Borberg (in his boy scout uniform!) out of Denmark.'

THE PARTICIPANTS BEGAN to scatter. Maria Schrallhammer, after twenty-eight years of service with Sunny Crawford von Auersperg von Bülow and her children, retired and returned to Germany the day after the verdict. Cosima von Bülow, eighteen, threw herself into the hectic whirl of a summer of debutante parties. Alexander von Auersperg returned to his job in the retirement division of E. F. Hutton. Ala Kneissl, pregnant with her second child, began work on a documentary film about victims of homicide. Together Ala and Alexander, through the Chemical Bank, which handles the fortunes of their mother and grandmother, are in the process of establishing two major foundations. One will provide funds for the solace of the families of homicide victims and for changes in legislation to allow victims' rights to equate with the rights of criminals. A second foundation, commemorating both their parents, will be for medical research in the field of comas. G. Morris Gurley, the bank officer who was not allowed to testify at the trial, is in charge of overseeing the foundations.

Von Bülow did not visit his wife at Columbia-Presbyterian Medical Center. Two weeks after the acquittal, his passport was returned to him, and for the first time in five years he was free to travel abroad. The next day he and Mrs Reynolds left New York. They did not fly first class. He stopped in London to visit friends. Mrs Reynolds, after a one-day stopover in London, went on to Geneva to visit her father. A few days later they rendezvoused at the Grand Hotel & de la Pace in the Italian spa of Montecatini Terme.

THE THIRD ACT of the von Bülow affair is still to be played. Will Father Magaldi be tried for lying in a sworn statement he gave to help von Bülow get a new trial? Will David Marriott, who once said and later recanted that he had delivered drugs, needles, and a hypodermic syringe to Clarendon Court, testify against his former friend and benefactor? Will Claus von Bülow and Mrs Reynolds be called to testify at Father Magaldi's trial? Will the relationship of von Bülow and Mrs Reynolds sustain the serenity of his acquittal, with or without Sunny's income of $3.5 million a year? Will New York and London society receive the couple back into the charmed circle at the top?

The drama seems a long way from the final curtain, although Claus von Bülow's dark and spacious place in social history has been assured.

━━━ ◄━

The romance of Claus von Bülow and Andrea Reynolds did not endure long after his acquittal. A civil case that followed the criminal case was settled out of court. Cosima von Bülow was reestablished in her grandmother's will. Von Bülow and Cosima moved to London, where he still lives. Cosima has married. Claus has reestablished himself in society there. The von Auersperg children, Ala and

Alexander, are both married. They are the founders of the National Victim Center, a national umbrella organization that helps victims of crime. I am a member of the Board of Directors of the organization. Andrea Reynolds married an English aristocrat, the Hon. Sean Plunkett, and runs a bed-and-breakfast in the Catskills. Sunny von Bülow is still alive as of this writing and still in the coma from which she has never awakened.

NIGHTMARE ON ELM DRIVE

O N A RECENT New York-to-Los Angeles trip on
MGM Grand Air, that most luxurious of all coast-
to-coast flights, I was chilled to the bone marrow
during a brief encounter with a fellow passenger, a boy
of perhaps fourteen, or fifteen, or maybe even sixteen,
who lounged restlessly in a sprawled-out fashion, arms and
legs akimbo, avidly reading racing-car magazines, chew-
ing gum, and beating time to the music on his Walkman.
Although I rarely engage in conversations with strangers
on airplanes, I always have a certain curiosity to know who
everyone is on MGM Grand Air, which I imagine is a bit
like the Orient Express in its heyday. The young traveler
in the swivel chair was returning to California after a
sojourn in Europe. There were signals of affluence in his
chat; the Concorde was mentioned. His carry-on luggage
was expensive, filled with audiotapes, playing cards, and
more magazines. During the meal, we talked. A week
before, two rich and privileged young men named Lyle
and Erik Menendez had been arrested for the brutal slay-

ing of their parents in the family's $5 million mansion on Elm Drive, a sedate tree-lined street that is considered one of the most prestigious addresses in Beverly Hills. The tale in all its gory grimness was the cover story that week in *People* magazine, many copies of which were being read on the plane.

'Do you live in Beverly Hills?' I asked.

'Yes.'

'Where?'

He told me the name of his street, which was every bit as prestigious as Elm Drive. I once lived in Beverly Hills and knew the terrain well. His home was in the same general area as the house where Kitty and Jose Menendez had been gunned down several months earlier in a fusillade of fourteen twelve-gauge shotgun blasts – five to the head and body of the father, nine to the face and body of the mother – that left them virtually unrecognizable as human beings, according to eyewitness reports. The slaying was so violent that it was assumed at first to have been of Mafia origins – a hit, or Mob rubout, as it was called, even in the *Wall Street Journal*. The arrest of the two handsome, athletic Menendez sons after so many months of investigation had shocked an unshockable community.

'Did you ever know the Menendez brothers?' I asked the teenager.

'No,' he replied. They had gone to different schools. They were older. Lyle was twenty-two, Erik nineteen. In that age group, a few years makes an enormous difference.

'A terrible thing,' I said.

'Yeah,' he replied, 'But I heard the father was pretty rough on those kids.'

With that, our conversation was concluded.

Patricide is not an altogether new crime in the second echelon of Southland society. Nor is matricide. On March 24, 1983, twenty-year-old Michael Miller, the son of President Reagan's personal lawyer, Roy Miller, raped and clubbed to death his mother, Marguerite. In a minimally publicized trial, from which the media was barred, Miller was found guilty of first-degree murder but was acquitted of the rape charge, presumably on the technicality that the rape had occurred after his mother was dead. The judge then ruled that young Miller, who had been diagnosed as schizophrenic, was legally innocent of murder by reason of insanity. 'Hallelujah,' muttered Michael Miller after the verdict. He was sent to Patton State Hospital, a mental institution in California.

On July 22, 1983, in a Sunset Boulevard mansion in Bel Air, twenty-year-old Ricky Kyle shot his father, millionaire Henry Harrison Kyle, the president of Four Star International, a television-and-movie-production firm, in the back after awakening him in the middle of the night to tell him there was a prowler in the house. Several witnesses testified that Ricky had confided in them about a longstanding desire to kill his father, who was alleged to have been physically and mentally abusive to his son. The prosecution argued that Ricky was consumed with hatred for his father and greed for his fortune, and that, fearing that he was about to be disinherited, he plotted the ruse of the prowler. With the extraordinary leniency of the Southern California courts for first-time murderers, young Kyle was sentenced to five years for the slaying. Expressing dismay with the verdict, Ricky's mother told reporters she had hoped her son would be spared a prison term. 'I think he has suffered enough,' she said. Ricky agreed. 'I feel like I don't deserve to go to prison,' he said.

And then there were the Woodman brothers, Stewart and Neil, accused of hiring two assassins to gun down their rich parents in Brentwood. Tried separately, Stewart was convicted of first-degree murder. To escape the death penalty, he incriminated his brother. Neil's trial is about to start.

Further elaboration is not necessary: the point has been made. One other case, however, on a lesser social stratum but of equal importance, under the circumstances, should be mentioned: the Salvatierra murder, which received international attention. In 1986, Oscar Salvatierra, the Los Angeles-based executive of a newspaper called *Philippine News*, was shot while he was asleep in bed, after having received a death threat that was at first believed to be tied to the newspaper's opposition to former Philippine president Ferdinand Marcos. Later, Arnel Salvatierra, his seventeen-year-old son, admitted sending the letter and killing his father. In court, Arnel Salvatierra's lawyer convinced the jury that Arnel was the victim of a lifetime of physical and psychological abuse by his father. The lawyer, Leslie Abramson, who is considered to be the most brilliant Los Angeles defense lawyer for death-row cases, compared Arnel Salvatierra to the tragic Lisa Steinberg of New York, whose father, Joel Steinberg, had been convicted of murdering her after relentlessly abusing her. 'What happens if the Lisa Steinbergs don't die?' Abramson asked the jury. 'What happens if they get older, and if the cumulative effect of all these years of abuse finally drives them over the edge, and Lisa Steinberg pulls out a gun and kills Joel Steinberg?' Arnel Salvatierra, who had been charged with first-degree murder, was convicted of voluntary manslaughter and placed on probation.

This story is relevant to the Menendez case in that the same Leslie Abramson is one-half the team defending the affluent Menendez brothers. Her client is Erik Menendez, the younger brother. Gerald Chaleff, with whom she frequently teams, is representing Lyle. On an earlier burglary case involving the brother, Chaleff, who gained prominence in criminal law as the defender of the Hillside Strangler, represented Erik. It is rumored that Abramson and Chaleff are each being paid $700,000. Psychological abuse is a constant theme in articles written about the brothers, and will probably be the basis of the defense strategy when the case comes to trial. There are even whispers – shocker of shockers – of sexual abuse in the Menendez family.

JOSE ENRIQUE MENENDEZ was an American success story. A Cuban émigré, he was sent to the United States by his parents in 1960 at age fifteen to escape from Castro's Cuba. His father, a onetime soccer star, and his mother, a former champion swimmer, stayed behind until their last properties were seized by Castro. Young Jose, who excelled in swimming, basketball, and soccer, won a swimming scholarship to Southern Illinois University, but he gave it up when he married Mary Louise Andersen, known as Kitty, at the age of nineteen and moved to New York. He earned a degree in accounting at Queens College in Flushing, New York, while working part-time as a dishwasher at the swank '21' Club in Manhattan, where, later, successful and prosperous, he would often dine. Then began a career of astonishing ascendancy which took him through Hertz, where he was in charge of car and commercial leasing, to the record division of RCA, where he signed such high-earning acts as Menudo, the Eurythmics, and Duran Duran. By this time he and Kitty had had two sons and settled down to a graceful life on a million-dollar estate in Princeton, New Jersey. The boys attended the exclusive Princeton Day School and, urged on by their father, began developing into first-rate tennis and soccer players. Their mother attended every match and game they played. When Jose clashed with a senior executive at RCA in 1986, after having been passed over for the executive vice presidency of RCA Records, he uprooted his family, much to the distress of Kitty, who loved her life and house in Princeton, and moved to Los Angeles. There he leapfrogged to IVE, International Video Entertainment, a video distributor which eventually became Live Entertainment, a division of the hugely successful Carolco Pictures, the company that produced the Rambo films of Sylvester Stallone as well as some of Arnold Schwarzenegger's action films. Jose Menendez's success at Live Entertainment was dazzling. In 1986 the company lost $20 million; a year later, under Menendez, Live earned $8 million and in 1988 doubled that. 'He was the perfect corporate executive,' I was told by one of his lieutenants. 'He had an incredible dedication to business. He was focused, specific about what he wanted from the business, very much in control. He believed that whatever had to be done should be done – with no heart, if necessary.'

The family lived at first in Calabasas, an upper-middle-class suburb of Los Angeles, inland beyond Malibu, where they occupied one house while building a more spectacular one on thirteen acres with mountaintop views. Then unexpectedly, almost overnight, the family abandoned Calabasas and moved to Beverly Hills, where Jose bought the house on Elm Drive, a six-bedroom Mediterranean-style house with a red tile roof, a courtyard, a swimming pool, a tennis court, and a guesthouse. Built in 1927, rebuilt in 1974, the house had good credentials. It had previously been rented to Elton John. And Prince. And Hal Prince. And a Saudi prince, for $35,000 a month. Erik Menendez, the younger son, transferred from Calabasas High to Beverly Hills High, probably the most snobbish public school in America. Lyle was a student at Princeton University, fulfilling one of the many American dreams of his immigrant father.

They were the ideal family; everyone said so. 'They were extraordinarily close-knit,' an executive of Live Entertainment told me. 'It was one big happy family,' said John E. Mason, a friend and Live Entertainment director. They did things together. They almost always had dinner

together, which, in a community where most parents go
to parties or screenings every night and leave their children to their own devices, is a rare thing. They talked
about world events, as well as about what was happening
in Jose's business. On the day before the catastrophic
event, a Saturday, they chartered a boat called *Motion
Picture Marine* in Marina del Rey and spent the day
together shark-fishing, just the four of them.

ON THE EVENING of the following day, August 20, 1989,
the seemingly idyllic world that Jose Menendez had
created was shattered. With their kids at the movies in
Century City, Jose and Kitty settled in for a comfortable
evening of television and videos in the television room at
the rear of their house. Jose was in shorts and a sweatshirt; Kitty was in a sweatshirt, jogging pants, and sneak-
ers. They had dishes of strawberries and ice cream on the
table in front of the sofa where they were sitting. Later,
after everything happened, a neighbor would report hearing sounds like firecrackers coming from the house at
about ten o'clock, but he took no notice. It wasn't until
a hysterical 911 call came in to the Beverly Hills police
station around midnight that there was any indication that
the sounds had not been made by firecrackers. The sons
of the house, Lyle and Erik, having returned from the
movies, where they said they saw *Batman* again after they
couldn't get into *License to Kill* because of the lines,
drove in the gate at 722 North Elm Drive, parked their
car in the courtyard, entered the house by the front door,

and found their parents dead, sprawled on the floor and couch in the television room. In shock at the grisly sight, Lyle telephoned for help. 'They shot and killed my parents!' he shrieked into the instrument. 'I don't know . . . I didn't hear anything . . . I just came home. Erik! Shut up! Get away from them!'

Another neighbor said on television that she had seen one of the Menendez boys curled up in a ball on the lawn in front of their house and screaming in grief. 'I have heard of very few murders that were more savage,' said Beverly Hills police chief Marvin Iannone. Dan Stewart, a retired police detective hired by the family to investigate the murders, gave the most graphic description of the sight in the television room. 'I've seen a lot of homicides, but nothing quite that brutal. Blood, flesh, skulls. It would be hard to describe, especially Jose, as resembling a human that you would recognize. That's how bad it was.' According to the autopsy report, one blast caused 'explosive decapitation with evisceration of the brain' and 'deformity of the face' to Jose Menendez. The first round of shots apparently struck Kitty in her chest, right arm, left hip, and left leg. Her murderers then reloaded and fired into her face, causing 'multiple lacerations of the brain'. Her face was an unrecognizable pulp.

The prevalent theory in the days following the murders was that it had been a Mob hit. Erik Menendez went so far as to point the finger at Noel Bloom, a distributor of pornographic films and a former associate of the Bonanno organized-crime family, as a possible suspect. Erik told police and early reporters on the story that Bloom and his father had despised each other after a business deal turned sour. (When questioned, Bloom denied any involvement whatsoever.) Expressing fear that the Mob might be after them as well, the brothers moved from hotel to hotel in the aftermath of the murders. Marlene Mizzy, the front-desk supervisor at the Beverly Hills Hotel, said that Lyle arrived at the hotel without a reservation two days after the murders and asked for a two-bedroom suite. Not liking the suites that were available on such short notice, he went to another hotel.

Seven months later, after the boys were arrested, I visited the house on Elm Drive. It is deceptive in size, far larger than one would imagine from the outside. You enter a spacious hallway with a white marble floor and a skylight above. Ahead, to the right, is a stairway carpeted in pale green. Off the hallway on one side is an immense drawing room, forty feet in length. The lone piece of sheet music on the grand piano was 'American Pie', by Don McLean. On the other side are a small paneled sitting room and a large dining room. At the far end of the hallway, in full view of the front door, is the television room, where Kitty and Jose spent their last evening together. On the back wall is a floor-to-ceiling bookcase, filled with books, many of them paperbacks, including all the American-history novels of Gore Vidal, Jose's favorite author. On the top shelf of the bookcase were sixty tennis trophies – all first place – that had been won over the years by Lyle and Erik.

Like a lot of houses of the movie nouveaux riches still in their social and business rise, the grand exterior is not matched by a grand interior. When the Menendez family bought the house, it was handsomely furnished, and they could have bought the furniture from the former owner for an extra $350,000, but they declined. With the exception of some reproduction Chippendale chairs in the dining room, the house is appallingly furnished with second-rate pieces; either the purchase price left nothing for interior decoration or there was just a lack of interest. In any case, your attention, once you are in the house, is not on the furniture. You are drawn, like a magnet, to the television room.

Trying to imagine what happened that night, I found it unlikely that the boys – if indeed it was the boys, and there is a very vocal contingent who believe it was not – would have come down the stairs with the guns, turned right, and entered the television room, facing their parents. Since Jose was hit point-blank in the back of the head, it seems far more likely that the killers entered the television room through the terrace doors behind the sofa on which Kitty and Jose were sitting, their backs to the doors, facing the television set. The killers would probably have unlocked the doors in advance. In every account of the murders, Kitty was said to have run toward the kitchen. This would suggest, assuming she was running away from her assailants, that they had entered from behind.

Every person who saw the death scene has described the blood, the guts, and the carnage in sick-making detail. The furniture I saw in that room was replacement furniture, rented after the murders from Antiquarian Traders in West Hollywood. The original blood-drenched furniture and Oriental carpet had been hauled away, never to be sat on or walked on again. It is not farfetched to imagine that splatterings of blood and guts found their way onto the clothes and shoes of the killers, which would have necessitated a change of clothing and possibly a shower. There is no way the killers could have gone up the stairs, however; the blood on their shoes would have left tracks on the pale green stair carpet. The lavatory beneath the stairs and adjacent to the television room does not have a shower. What probably happened is that the killers retreated out the same terrace doors they had entered, and went back to the guesthouse to shower and change into clothes they had left there. The guesthouse is a separate, two-story unit beyond the swimming pool and adjacent to the tennis court, with a sitting room, a bedroom, a full bath, and a two-car garage opening onto an alley.

There is also the possibility that the killers, knowing the carnage twelve-guage-shotgun blasts would cause, wore boots, gloves, and overalls. In that event, they would have only had to discard the clothes and boots into a large garbage bag and make a dash for it. One of the most interesting aspects of the case is that the fourteen shell casings were picked up and removed. I have been told that such fastidiousness is out of character in a Mafia hit, where a speedy getaway is essential. There is a sense of leisurely time here, of people not in a hurry, not expecting anyone, when they delay their departure from a massacre to pick the shell casings out of the bloody remains of their victims' bodies. They almost certainly wore rubber gloves to do it.

Then they had to get rid of the guns. The guns, as of this writing, have still not been found. We will come back to the guns. The car the killers left in was probably parked in the guesthouse garage; from there they could make their exit unobserved down the alley behind the house. Had they left out the front gate on Elm Drive, they would have risked being observed by neighbors or passersby. Between the time the killers left the house and the time the boys made the call to the police, the bloody clothes were probably disposed of.

ON THE DAY BEFORE the fishing trip on the *Motion Picture Marine*, Erik Menendez allegedly drove south to San Diego and purchased two Mossberg twelve-gauge shotguns in a Big 5 sporting-goods store, using for identification the stolen driver's license of a young man named Donovan Goodreau. Under federal law, to purchase a weapon, an individual must fill out a 4473 form, which requires the buyer to provide his name, address, and signature, as well as an identification card with picture. Donovan Goodreau had subsequently said on television that he can prove he was in New York at the time of the gun purchase in San Diego. Goodreau had once roomed with Jamie Pisarcik, who was, and still is, Lyle Menendez's girlfriend and stalwart supporter, visiting him daily in jail and attending his every court session. When Goodreau stopped rooming with Jamie, he moved into Lyle's room at Princeton, which was against the rules, since he was not a student at the university. But then, Lyle had once kept a puppy in his room at Princeton, and having animals in the rooms was against the rules too.

What has emerged most significantly in the year since the murders is that all was not what it seemed in the seemingly perfect Menendez household. There are people who will tell you that Jose was well liked. There are more people by far who will tell you that he was greatly disliked. Even despised. He had made enemies all along the way in his rise to the high middle of the entertainment industry, but everyone agrees that had he lived he would have gone right to the top. He did not have many personal friends, and he and Kitty were not involved in the party circuit of Beverly Hills. His life was family and business. I was told that at the memorial service in Los Angeles, which preceded the funeral in Princeton, most of the two hundred people who attended had a business rather than a personal relationship with him. Stung by the allegations that Jose had Mob connections in his business dealings at Live Entertainment, allegations that surfaced immediately after the murders, the company hired Warren Cowan, the famed public-relations man, to arrange the memorial service. His idea was to present Menendez as Jose the family man. He suggested starting a Jose Menendez scholarship fund, a suggestion that never came to fruition. It was also his idea to hold the memorial service in an auditorium at the Directors' Guild in Hollywood, in order to show that Jose was a member of the entertainment community, although it is doubtful that Jose had ever been there. Two

people from Live Entertainment gave flowing eulogies.
Brian Andersen, Kitty's brother, spoke lovingly about
Kitty, and each son spoke reverently about his parents.
One person leaving the service was heard to say, 'The only
word not used to describe Jose was "prick."'

Although Jose spoke with a very slight accent, a business cohort described him to me as 'very non-Hispanic'.
He was once offended when he received a letter of congrat-
ulations for having achieved such a high place in the business world 'for a Hispanic'. 'He hated anyone who knew
anything about his heritage,' the colleague said. On the
other hand, there was a part of Jose Menendez that secretly
wanted to run for the US Senate from Florida in order to
free Cuba from the tyranny of Fidel Castro and make it
a US territory.

Kitty Menendez was another matter. You never hear a
bad word about Kitty. Back in Princeton, people remember her on the tennis courts with affection. Those who
knew her in the later years of her life felt affection too,
but they also felt sorry for her. She was a deeply unhappy
woman, and was becoming a pathetic one. Her husband
was flagrantly unfaithful to her, and she was devastated
by his infidelity. There has been much talk since the
killings of Jose's having had a mistress, but that mistress
was by no means his first, although he was said to have
had 'fidelity in his infidelity' in that particular relationship. Kitty fought hard to hold her marriage together, but
it is unlikely that Jose would ever have divorced her. An
employee of Live Entertainment said, 'Kitty called Jose
at his office every thirty minutes, sometimes just to tell

him what kind of pizza to bring home for supper. She was a dependent person. She wanted to go on his business trips with him. She had June Allyson looks. Very warm. She also had a history of drinking and pills.' Another business associate of Jose's at Live said, 'I knew Kitty at company dinners and cocktail parties. They used to say about Kitty that she was Jose with a wig. She was always very much at his side, part of his vision, dedicated to the cause, whatever the cause was.'

A more intimate picture of Kitty comes from Karen Lamm, one of the most highly publicized secondary characters in the Menendez saga. A beautiful former actress and model who was once wed to the late Dennis Wilson of the Beach Boys, Lamm is now a television producer, and she and her partner, Zev Braun, are developing a mini-series based on the Menendez case. Lamm is often presented as Kitty's closest friend and confidante. However, friends of Erik and Lyle decry her claims of friendship with Kitty, asserting that the boys did not know her, and asking how she could have been such a great friend of Kitty's if she was totally unknown to the sons.

Most newspaper accounts say that Karen Lamm and Kitty Menendez met in an aerobics class, but Lamm, who says she dislikes exercise classes, gave a different account of the beginning of their friendship. About a year before the murders, she was living with a film executive named Stuart Benjamin, who was a business acquaintance of Jose Menendez. Benjamin was a partner of the film director Taylor Hackford in a production company called New Visions Pictures, which Menendez was interested in acquiring as a subsidiary for Live Entertainment. During the negotiation period, Benjamin, with Lamm as his date, attended a dinner party at the Menendez house on Elm Drive. Lamm, who is an effusive and witty conversationalist, and Kitty spent much of the evening talking together. It was the beginning of a friendship that would blossom. Lamm described Kitty to me as being deeply unhappy over her husband's philandering. She claims that Kitty had tried suicide on three occasions, the kind of at-home suicide attempts that are more cries for help than a longing for death. Kitty had once won a beauty contest and could still be pretty on occasion, but she had let her looks go, grown fat (her autopsy report described her as 'fairly well-nourished' and gave her weight as 165), and dyed her hair an unbecoming blond color that did not suit her. Lamm suggested that she get back into shape, and took her to aerobics classes, as well as offering her advice on a darker hair color. During the year that followed, the two women became intimate friends, and Kitty confided in Lamm, not only about Jose's infidelity but also about the many problems they were having with their sons.

Lamm said she met the boys three times, but never talked to them in the house on Elm Drive. She told me, 'Those kids watched their mother become a doormat for their father. Jose lived through Lyle. Jose made Lyle white bread. He sent him to Princeton. He gave him all the things that were not available to him as an immigrant.' Lamm finally talked with Kitty's sons at the memorial service at the Directors' Guild. She was introduced to Lyle, who, in turn, introduced her to Erik as 'Mom's friend'. She said that Lyle had become Jose overnight. He radiated confidence and showed no emotion, 'unless it was a convenient moment'. Erik, on the other hand, fell apart.

Over the previous two years, the handsome, athletic, and gifted Menendez sons had been getting into trouble. Although a great friend of the boys dismissed their scrapes as merely 'rich kids' sick jokes', two events occurred in Calabasas, where the family lived before the move to Beverly Hills, that were to have momentous consequences for all the members of the family. The brothers got involved in two very serious criminal offenses, a burglary at the home of Michael Warren Ginsberg in Calabasas and grand theft at the home of John Richard List in Hidden Hills. In total, more than $100,000 in money and jewels was taken from the two houses – not an insignificant sum.

Jose dealt with his sons' transgressions the way he would deal with any prickly business problem, said a business associate, by 'minimizing the damage and going forward, fixing something that was broken without actually dealing with the problem'. He simply took over and solved it. The money and jewels were returned, and $11,000 in damages was paid. Since Erik was underage, it was decided that he would take the fall for both brothers, thereby safeguarding Jose's dream of having Lyle study at Princeton. Jose hired the criminal lawyer Gerald Chaleff to represent Erik – the same Gerald Chaleff who is now representing Lyle on the charge of murdering the man who once hired him to represent Erik on the burglary charge. Everything was solved to perfection. Erik got probation, no more. And compulsory counseling. And for that, Kitty asked her psychologist, Les Summerfield, to recommend someone her son could go to for the required number of hours ordered by the judge. Les Summerfield recommended a Beverly Hills psychologist named Jerome Oziel, who, like Gerald Chaleff, continues his role in the Menendez saga right up to the present.

Prior to the thefts, Erik had made a friend at Calabasas High School who would also play a continuing part in the story. Craig Cignarelli, the son of a prominent executive in the television industry, is a Tom Cruise look-alike currently studying at the University of California in Santa Barbara. Craig was the captain of the Calabasas High School tennis team, and Erik, who had recently trans- ferred from Princeton Day, was the number-one singles player on the team. One day, while playing a match together, they were taunted by two students from El Camino High School, a rival school in a less affluent neigh- borhood. Menendez and Cignarelli went out to the street to face their adversaries, and a fight started. Suddenly, a whole group of El Camino boys jumped out of cars and joined the fray. Erik and Craig were both badly beaten up. Erik's jaw was broken, and Craig received severe damage to his ribs. The incident sparked a close friend- ship between the two, which would culminate in the co- writing of a movie script called *Friends*, in which a young man named Hamilton Cromwell murders his extremely rich parents for his inheritance. One of the most quoted passages from this screenplay comes from the mouth of Hamilton Cromwell, speaking about his father:

'Sometimes he would tell me that I was not worthy to be his son. When he did that, it would make me strive harder . . . just so I could hear the words "I love you, son" . . . And I never heard those words.' To add to the awful irony, Kitty, the loving mother who could not do enough for her sons, typed the screenplay in which her own demise seems to have been predicted. In the embarrassing aftermath of the burglaries, the family moved to the house on Elm Drive in Beverly Hills. Jose told people at Live Entertainment that he was upset by the drug activity in Calabasas and that the tires of his car had been slashed, but it is quite possible that these stories were a diversionary tactic, or smoke screen, created to cover the disgrace of his son's criminal record.

A further setback for the family, also partly covered up, had occurred the previous winter, when Lyle was suspended from Princeton after one semester for cheating in Psychology 101. Taken before a disciplinary committee, he was told he could leave the university voluntarily or be expelled. He chose to leave. This was a grave blow to Jose, who loved to tell people that he had a son at Princeton. Again taking over, he tried to talk the authorities at Princeton into reinstating his son, but this time the pressure he applied did not work. The suspension lasted a year. In a typical reaction, Jose became more angry at the school than he was at his son. He urged Lyle to stay on in Princeton rather than return to Beverly Hills, so that he would not have to admit to anyone that Lyle had been kicked out.

But Lyle did return, and worked briefly at Live

Entertainment, where he showed all the worst qualities of the spoiled rich boy holding down a grace-and-favor job in his father's company. He was consistently late for work. His attention span was brief. He worked short hours, leaving in the afternoon to play tennis. He was unpopular with the career-oriented staff. 'The kids had a sense of being young royalty,' said an employee of the company. 'They could be nasty, arrogant, and self-centered.' But, the same person said, Jose had a blind spot about his sons. And tennis held the family together. Once, Jose took the Concorde to Europe just to watch Lyle play in a tennis tournament, and then came right back. However, for all the seeming closeness of the family, the sons were proving to be disappointments, even failures, in the eyes of their perfection-demanding father. Jose had apparently come to the end of financing his recalcitrant sons' rebellion, and there are indications that he planned to revise his will.

After the Calabasas debacle, Erik transferred to Beverly Hills High School for his senior year. His classmates remember him chiefly as a loner, walking around in tennis shorts, always carrying his tennis racket.

'A girl I was going out with lusted after him,' a student told me. 'She said he had good legs.'

'Was he spoiled?'

'Everyone at Beverly High is spoiled.'

Like his father, Lyle is said to have been a great ladies' man, which pleased Jose, but several of Lyle's girlfriends, mostly older than he, were not considered to be suitable by his parents, and clashes occurred. When Jose forbade Lyle to go to Europe with an older girlfriend, Lyle went anyway. A person extremely close to the family told me that another of Lyle's girlfriends – not Jamie Pisarcik, who has been so loyal to him during his incarceration – was 'manipulating him', which I took to mean manipulating him into marriage. This girl became pregnant. Jose, in his usual method of dealing with his sons' problems, moved in and paid off the girl to abort the child. The manner of Jose's interference in so personal a matter – not allowing Lyle to deal with his own problem – is said to have infuriated Lyle and caused a deep rift between father and son. Lyle moved out of the main house into the guesthouse at the back of the property. He was still living there at the time of the murders, although Erik continued to live in the main house.

Karen Lamm told me that in her final conversation with Kitty, three days before the killing and one day before the purchase of the guns in San Diego, Kitty told her that Lyle had been verbally abusive to her in a long, late-night call from the guesthouse to the main house.

FROM THE BEGINNING, the police were disinclined to buy the highly publicized Mafia-hit story, on the grounds that Mafia hits are rarely done in the home, that the victim is usually executed with a single shot to the back of the head, and that the wife is not usually killed also. The hit, if hit it was, looked more like a Colombian drug-lord hit, like the bloody massacre carried out by Al Pacino in the film *Scarface*, which, incidentally, was one of Lyle's favorite movies.

Months later, after the arrests, the Beverly Hills police claimed to have been suspicious of the Menendez brothers from the beginning, even from the first night. One detective at the scene asked the boys if they had the ticket stubs from the film they said they had just seen in Century City. 'When both parents are hit, our feeling is usually that the kids did it,' said a Beverly Hills police officer. Another officer declared, two days after the event, 'These kids fried their parents. They cooked them.' But there was no proof, nothing to go on, merely gut reactions.

Inadvertently, the boys brought suspicion upon themselves. In the aftermath of the terrible event, close observers noted the extraordinary calm the boys exhibited, almost as if the murders had happened to another family. They were seen renting furniture at Antiquarian Traders to replace the furniture that had been removed from the television room. And, as new heirs, they embarked on a spending spree that even the merriest widow, who had married for money, would have refrained from going on – for propriety's sake, if nothing else – in the first flush of her mourning period. They bought and bought and bought. Estimates of their spending have gone as high as $700,000. Lyle bought a $60,000 Porsche 911 Carrera to replace the Alfa Romeo his father had given him. Erik turned in his Ford Mustang 5.0 hardtop and bought a tan Jeep Wrangler, which his girlfriend, Noelle Terelsky, is now driving. Lyle bought $40,000 worth of clothes and a $15,000 Rolex watch. Erik hired a $50,000-a-year tennis coach. Lyle decided to go into the restaurant business, and paid a reported $550,000 for a cafeteria-style eatery in Princeton, which he renamed Mr Buffalo's, flying back and forth coast to coast on MGM Grand Air. 'It was one of my mother's delights that I pursue a small restaurant chain and serve healthy food with friendly service,' he said in an interview with *The Daily Princetonian*, the campus newspaper. Erik, less successful as an entrepreneur than Lyle, put up $40,000 for a rock concert at the Palladium, but got ripped off by a conman partner and lost the entire amount. Erik decided not to attend UCLA, which had been his father's plan for him, but to pursue a career in tennis instead. After moving from hotel to hotel to elude the Mafia, who they claimed were watching them, the brothers leased adjoining condos in the tony Marina City Club Towers. 'They liked high-tech surrounds, and they wanted to get out of the house,' one of their friends said to me. Then there was the ghoulish sense of humor another of their friends spoke about: Sitting with a gang of pals one night, deciding what videos to rent for the evening, Erik suggested *Dad* and *Parenthood*. Even as close a friend as Glenn Stevens, who was in the car with Lyle when he was arrested, later told the *Los Angeles Times* that two days after the murders, when he asked Lyle how he was holding up emotionally, his friend replied, 'I've been waiting so long to be in this position that the transition came easy.' The police were also aware that Lyle Menendez had hired a computer expert who eradicated from the hard disk of the family computer a revised will that Jose had been working on. Most remarkable of all was that, unlike the families of most homicide victims, the sons of Jose and Kitty Menendez did not have the obsessive interest in the police search for the killers of their parents that usually supersedes all else in the wake of such a tragedy.

AS THE CEO of Live Entertainment, Jose Menendez earned a base pay of $500,000 a year, with a maximum bonus of $850,000 based on the company's yearly earnings. On top of that, there were life-insurance policies. An interesting sidebar to the story concerns two policies that were thought to have been taken out on Menendez by Live Entertainment. The bigger of the two was a $15 million keyman policy; $10 million of which was with Bankers Trust and $5 million with Crédit Lyonnais. Taking out a keyman life-insurance policy on a top executive is common practice in business, with the company being named as beneficiary. Live Entertainment was also required to maintain a second policy on Menendez in the amount of $5 million, with the beneficiary to be named by him. Given the family's much-talked-about closeness, it is not unlikely that Kitty and the boys were aware of this policy. Presumably, the beneficiary of the insurance policy would have been the same as the beneficiary of Jose's will. In the will, it was stated that if Kitty died first everything would go to Jose, and if Jose died first everything would go to Kitty. In the event that both died, everything would go to the boys.

The murders happened on a Sunday night. On the afternoon of the following Tuesday, Lyle and Erik, accompanied by two uncles, Kitty's brother Brian Andersen and

Jose's brother-in-law Carlos Baralt, who was the executor
of Jose's will, met with officials of Live Entertainment at
the company's headquarters to go over Jose's financial
situation. At that meeting, it became the difficult duty of
Jose's successor to inform the heirs that the $5 million
policy with beneficiaries named by Jose had not gone into
effect, because Jose had failed to take the required physical examination, believing that the one he had taken for
the $15 million policy applied to both policies. It did not.
A person present at that meeting told me of the resound-
ing silence that followed the reception of that information. To expect $5 million, payable upon death, and to
find that it was not forthcoming, would be a crushing
disappointment. Finally, Erik Menedez spoke. His voice
was cold. 'And the $15 million policy in favor of the
company? Was that in order?' he asked. It was. Jose had
apparently been told that he would have to take another
physical for the second policy, but he had postponed it.
As an officer of the company said to me, 'That anything
could ever happen to Jose never occurred to Jose.'

The news that the policy was invalid caused bad blood
between the family and the company, especially since the
immediate payment of the $15 million keyman policy gave
Carolco one of its biggest quarters since the inception of
the company. One of Jose's former employees in New
York, who was close enough to the family to warrant having
a limousine sent to take him from a suburb of New York
to the funeral in Princeton, said to me, 'The grandmother?
Did you talk to her? Did she tell you her theory? Did she
tell you the company had Jose taken care of for the $15

million insurance policy?' The grandmother had not told me this, but it is a theory that the dwindling group of people who believe in the innocence of the Menendez boys cling to with passion. The same former employee continued, 'Jose must have made a lot of money in California. I don't know where all that money came from that I've been hearing about and reading about.'

Further bad feelings between the family and Live Entertainment have arisen over the house on Elm Drive, which, like the house in Calabasas, is heavily mortgaged: Approximately $2 million is still owed on the Elm Drive house, with estimated payments of $225,000 a year, plus $40,000 a year in taxes and approximately $40,000 in maintenance. In addition, the house in Calabasas has been on the market for some time and remains unsold; $1.5 million is still owed on it. So, in effect, the expenses on the two houses are approximately $500,000 a year, a staggering amount for the two sons to have dealt with before their arrest. During the meeting on the Tuesday after the murders, when the boys were told that the $5 million life insurance policy had not gone into effect, it was suggested that Live Entertainment might buy the house on Elm Drive from the estate, thereby removing the financial burden from the boys while the house was waiting to be resold. Furthermore, Live Entertainment was prepared to take less for the house than Jose had paid for it, knowing that houses where murders have taken place are hard sells, even in as inflated a real estate market as Beverly Hills.

Ads have run in the real estate section of the *Los Angeles Times* for the Elm Drive house. The asking price is \$5.95 million. Surprisingly, a buyer did come along. The unidentified person offered only \$4.5 million, a bargain for a house on that street, and the offer was hastily accepted. Later, however, the deal fell through. The purchaser was said to have been intimidated by the event that occurred there, and worried about the reaction neighborhood children would have to his own children for living in the house.

The arrangement for Live Entertainment to purchase the property from the estate failed to go into effect, once the police investigation pointed more and more toward the boys, and so the estate has had to assume the immense cost of maintaining the properties. Recently, the Elm Drive house has been leased to a member of the Saudi royal family – not the same prince who rented it before – for \$50,000 a month to allay expenses.

Carolco, wishing to stifle rumors that Live Entertainment had Mob connections because of its acquisition of companies like Strawberries, an audio-video retailing chain, from Morris Levy, who allegedly has Genovese crime-family connections, and its bitter battle with Noel Bloom, hired the prestigious New York firm of Kaye, Scholer, Fierman, Hays & Handler to investigate the company for underworld ties. The 220-page report, which cynics in the industry mock as a whitewash, exonerated the company of any such involvement. The report was read at a board meeting on March 8, and the conclusion made clear that the Beverly Hills police, in their investigation of the Menendez murders, were increasingly focusing on their sons, not the Mob. An ironic bit of drama came at precisely that moment, when a vice president of the company burst in on the meeting with the news that Lyle Menendez had just been arrested.

CONCURRENTLY, IN ANOTHER, less fashionable area of the city known as Carthay Circle, an attractive thirty-seven-year-old woman named Judalon Rose Smyth, pronounced Smith, was living out her own drama in a complicated love affair. Judalon Smyth's lover was a Beverly Hills psychologist named Jerome Oziel, whom she called Jerry. Dr Oziel was the same Dr Oziel whom Kitty Menendez's psychologist, Les Summerfield, had recommended to her a year earlier as the doctor for her troubled son, after the judge in the burglary case in Calabasas had ruled that Erik must have counseling while he was on probation. During that brief period of court-ordered therapy, Jerome Oziel had met the entire Menendez family. Judalon Smyth, however, was as unknown to Lyle and Erik as they were to her, and yet, seven months from the time of the double murder, she would be responsible for their arrest on the charge of killing their parents.

On March 8, Lyle Menendez was flagged down by more than a dozen heavily armed Beverly Hills policemen as he was leaving the house on Elm Drive in his brother's Jeep Wrangler, accompanied by his former Princeton classmate Glenn Stevens. Lyle was made to lie on the street, in full view of his neighbors, while the police, with drawn guns, manacled his hands behind his back before taking him to the police station to book him for suspicion of murder.

The arrest came as a complete surprise to Lyle, who had been playing chess, a game at which he excelled, until two the night before at the home of a friend in Beverly Hills.

Three days earlier, Judalon Smyth had contacted the police in Beverly Hills and told them of the existence of audiotapes in the Bedford Drive office of Dr Oziel on which the Menendez brothers had allegedly confessed to the murders of their parents. She also told police that the brothers had threatened to kill Oziel if he reported them. Lastly, she told them that the two twelve-gauge shotguns had been purchased at a sporting-goods store in San Diego. All of this information was unknown to the Beverly Hills police, after seven months of investigation. They obtained a subpoena to search all of Oziel's locations. The tapes were found in a safe-deposit box in a bank on Ventura Boulevard.

Lyle's arrest was reported almost immediately on the local Los Angeles newscasts. Among those who heard the news was Noel Nedli, a tennis-team friend from Beverly Hills High who was Erik Menendez's roommate in a condominium that Erik was leasing for six months at the Marina City Club Towers, next to the condominium that his brother had leased with his girlfriend, Jamie Pisarcik. Erik was playing in a tennis tournament in Israel, where he had been for two weeks, accompanied by Mark Heffernan, his $50,000-a-year tennis coach. By a curious coincidence, Erik happened to telephone Nedli at almost the same moment Nedli was listening to the report of Lyle's arrest on the radio. It was merely a routine checking-up-on-everything call, and Nedli realized at once that Erik did not know about Lyle's arrest. He is reported to have said to Erik, 'I hope you're sitting down.' Then he said, 'Lyle was just arrested.'

'Erik became hysterical. He was crying, the whole nine yards,' said a friend of Nedli's who had heard the story from him. This friend went on to say that the immediate problem for Erik was to get out of Israel before he was arrested there. Accompanied by Heffernan, who was not aware of the seriousness of the situation, the two got on a plane without incident, bound for London. There they split up. Heffernan returned to Los Angeles. Erik flew to Miami, where several members of the Menendez side of the family reside. An aunt advised him to return to Los Angeles and turn himself in. Erik notified police of his travel plans and gave himself up at Los Angeles International Airport, where he was taken into custody by four detectives. He was later booked at the Los Angeles County Men's Central Jail on suspicion of murder and held without bond.

According to Judalon Smyth, and the California Court of Appeals decision, she had stood outside the door of Dr Oziel's office and, unbeknownst to the Menendez brothers, listened to their confession and threats. Dr Oziel has denied this.

APPROXIMATELY A YEAR BEFORE any of the above happened, Judalon Smyth told me, she telephoned Jerome Oziel's clinic, the Phobia Institute of Beverly Hills, after having heard a series of tapes called *Through the Briar*

Patch, which had impressed her. She was then thirty-six, had been married twice, and was desirous of having a relationship and a family, but she tended to choose the wrong kind of men, men who were controlling. The *Briar Patch* tapes told her she could break the pattern of picking the wrong kind of men in five minutes.

She says Oziel began telephoning her, and she found him very nice on the phone. She felt he seemed genuinely interested in her. After Oziel's third call, she sent him a tape of love poems she had written and called *Love Tears*. She also told him she was in the tape-duplicating business. She found his calls were like therapy, and she began to tell him intimate things about herself, like the fact that she had been going to a professional matchmaker she had seen on television. 'I was falling in love over the phone,' she said. 'You don't think someone's married when he calls you from home at night.'

Eventually, he came to her house with two enormous bouquets.

'The minute I opened the door I was relieved,' she said. 'I wasn't attracted to him. He was shorter than me, blond, balding, with a round face.' She told me she was attracted to men who looked like the actor Ken Wahl or Tom Cruise. Oziel was forty-two at the time. 'He kept trying to get physical right away. I said, "Look, you're not my type. I'm not attracted to you." He said he just wanted a hug. I said, "Just because you know all this intimate stuff about me doesn't mean . . ."

'Finally I gave in. It was the worst sex I ever had in my life. To have good sex you either have to be in love or in lust. I wasn't either. It was also awful the second time. The third time was better. I broke off with him four or five times between September and October. Then Erik Menendez came.'

ALTHOUGH DR OZIEL had not seen any members of the Menendez family since Erik's counseling had ended, when news of the murders was announced in August 1989, according to Smyth, he became consumed with excitement at his proximity to the tragedy. 'Right away, he called the boys and offered his help.' At the time, the boys were hiding out in hotels, saying they thought the Mafia was after them. 'Jerry would go to where the boys were. He was advising them about attorneys for the will, etc. He had an I'll-be-your-father attitude.'

At the end of October, Smyth told me, Oziel got a call from Erik, who said he needed to talk with him. Erik came at four in the afternoon of Halloween, October 31, to the office at 435 North Bedford Drive. There is a small waiting room outside the office, with a table for magazines and several places to sit, but there is no receptionist. An arriving patient pushes a button with the name of the doctor he is there to see, and a light goes on in the inner office to let the doctor know that his next patient has arrived. Off the waiting room is a doorway that opens into a small inner hallway off which are three small offices. Oziel shares the space with several other doctors, one of them his wife, Dr Laurel Oziel, the mother of his two daughters.

Once there, Erik did not want to talk in the office, so he and Oziel went for a walk. On the walk, according to Smyth, Erik confessed that he and his brother had killed their parents. Lyle, who was at the Elm Drive house at the time, did not know that Erik was seeing Oziel for that purpose. Lyle did not know either that Erik had apparently also confessed to his good friend Craig Cignarelli, with whom he had written the screenplay called *Friends*.

When Smyth arrived at the office, Erik and Oziel had returned from their walk and were in the inner office. According to Smyth, Oziel wanted Erik to tell Lyle that he had confessed to him. Erik did not want to do that. He said that he and Lyle were soon going to the Caribbean to get rid of the guns and that he would tell him then. The plan, according to Erik, Judalon Smyth told me, was to break down the guns, put them into suitcases, and dump the bags in the Caribbean. On the night of the murders, the boys had hidden the two shotguns in the trunk of one of their parents' cars in the garage. The police had searched only the cars in the courtyard in front of the house, not the cars in the garage. Subsequently, the boys had buried the guns on Mulholland Drive. Smyth says Dr Oziel convinced Erik that the boys would certainly be caught if they were carrying guns in their luggage. He also persuaded him to call Lyle and ask him to come to the office immediately.

It took ten minutes for Lyle to get to the office from the house on Elm Drive. Smyth says he did not know before he got there that Erik had confessed. When he walked into the waiting room, he picked up a magazine and chatted briefly with Smyth, assuming that she was another patient. 'Been waiting long?' he asked her. He also pushed the button to indicate to Oziel that he had arrived. Oziel came out and asked Lyle to come in.

According to the California Court of Appeals decision, Smyth says she listened through the door to the doctor's meeting with the boys and heard Lyle become furious with Erik for having confessed. She told me he made threats to Oziel that they were going to kill him. 'I never thought I believed in evil, but when I heard those boys speak, I did,' she said.

The particulars of the murders she is not allowed to discuss, because of an agreement with the Beverly Hills police, but occasionally, in our conversation, things would creep in. 'They did go to the theater to buy the tickets,' she said one time. Or, 'The mother kept moving, which is why she was hit more.' Or, 'If they just killed the father, the mother would have inherited the money. So they had to kill her too.' Or, 'Lyle said he thought he committed the perfect murder, that his father would have had to congratulate him – for once, he couldn't put him down.'

Judalon went on to say, and it is in the opinion of the California Court of Appeals, that she was frightened that she might be caught listening if the boys came out of the office. She went back to the waiting room. Almost immediately, the door opened. 'Erik came running out, crying. Then Lyle and Jerry came out. At the elevator, I heard Jerry ask if Lyle was threatening him. Erik had already gone down. Lyle and Jerry followed.' From a window in the office, Smyth could see Lyle and Oziel talking to Erik, who was in his Jeep on Bedford Drive.

According to Smyth, Erik knew, from his period of therapy with Oziel after the burglaries, where the doctor lived in Sherman Oaks, a suburb of Los Angeles in the San Fernando Valley. Fearing the boys might come after him, Oziel called his wife and told her to get the children and move out of the house. 'Laurel and the kids went to stay with friends,' said Smyth. Oziel then moved into Smyth's apartment, the ground floor of a two-family house in the Carthay Circle area of Los Angeles.

In the days that followed, Smyth told several people what she had heard. She has her own business, an audio-video duplicating service called Judalon Sound and Light, in the Fairfax section of Los Angeles. Behind her shop, in which she also sells crystals, quartz, and greeting cards, there is a small office which she rents to two friends, Bruce and Grant, who also have a video-duplicating service. As self-protection, she told them that the Menendez boys had killed their parents. She also told her mother and father and her best friend, Donna.

Then Oziel set up another meeting with the boys. He told them on the second visit that everything they had told him was taped. According to Smyth, the original confession, on October 31, was not taped. What was taped was Oziel's documentation of everything that happened in that session and subsequent sessions with the boys, giving times and dates, telling about the confession and the threat on his life, 'a log of what was happening during the time his life was in danger'. Smyth further contends that, as time went on, the relationship between the doctor and the boys grew more stable, and the doctor no longer felt threatened.

She said that Oziel convinced the boys 'he was their only ally – that if they were arrested he would be their only ally. He was the only one who knew they were abused children, who knew how horrible their home life was, who knew that Jose was a monster father, who knew that Kitty was an abused wife. He convinced them that if they had any hope of ever getting off, they needed him.'

Meanwhile, the personal relationship between Smyth and Oziel deteriorated. In a lawsuit filed in the Superior Court of the State of California by Judalon Rose Smyth against L. Jerome Oziel, PhD, on May 31, three months after the arrest of the Menendez brothers, it is charged that while Smyth was receiving psychiatric and psychological counseling from defendant Oziel he 'improperly maintained Smyth on large doses of drugs and, during said time periods, manipulated and took advantage of Smyth, controlled Smyth, and limited Smyth's ability to care for herself . . . creating a belief in Smyth that she could not handle her affairs without the guidance of Oziel, and convincing Smyth that no other therapist could provide the insight and benefit to her life that Oziel could.' In the second cause of action in the suit, Smyth charges that on or about February 16, 1990, defendant Oziel 'placed his hands around her throat attempting to choke her, and pulled her hair with great force. Subsequently, on the same day, defendant Oziel forced Smyth to engage in an act of forcible and unconsented sexual intercourse.'

According to the California Court of Appeals decision, approximately three weeks after the alleged attack, Smyth contacted the police in Beverly Hills to inform them about the confession she said the Menendez brothers had made to Oziel.

Oziel's lawyer, Bradley Brunon, called Smyth's allegations 'completely untrue', and characterized her behavior as 'an unfortunate real-life enactment of the scenario in *Fatal Attraction* . . . She has twisted reality to the point where it is unrecognizable.'

'THE BOYS ARE *ADORABLE*. They're like two foundlings. You want to take them home with you,' said the defense attorney Leslie Abramson, who has saved a dozen people from death row. She was talking about the Menendez brothers. Leslie Abramson is Erik's lawyer. Gerald Chaleff is Lyle's.

'Leslie will fight to the grave for her clients,' I heard from reporters in Los Angeles who have followed her career. 'When there is a murder rap, Leslie is the best in town.'

Abramson and Chaleff have worked together before. 'We're fifty-fifty, but she's in charge,' Chaleff said in an interview. They like each other, and are friends in private life. Abramson met her present husband, Tim Rutten, an editorial writer for the *Los Angeles Times*, at a dinner party at Chaleff's home.

During the arraignment in the Beverly Hills courthouse, I was struck by the glamour of the young Menendez brothers, whom I was seeing face-to-face for the first time. They entered the courtroom, heads held high, like leading actors in a television series. They walked like colts. Their clothes, if not by Armani himself, were by a designer heavily influenced by Armani, probably purchased in the brief period of their independent affluence, between the murders and their arrest. Their demeanor seemed remarkably lighthearted for people in the kind of trouble they were in, as they smiled dimpled smiles and laughed at the steady stream of Abramson's jocular banter. Their two girlfriends, Jamie Pisarcik and Noelle Terelsky, were in the front row next to Erik's tennis coach, Mark Heffernan. Everyone waved. Maria Menendez, the loyal grandmother, was also in the front row, and aunts and uncles and a probate lawyer were in the same section of the courtroom. Several times the boys turned around and flashed smiles at their pretty girlfriends.

They were told to rise. The judge, Judith Stein, spoke in a lugubrious, knell-like voice. The brothers smiled, almost smirked, as she read the charges. 'You have been charged with multiple murder for financial gain, while lying in wait, with a loaded firearm, for which, if convicted, you could receive the death penalty. How do you plead?'

'Not guilty, Your Honor,' said Erik.

'Not guilty,' said Lyle.

Later I asked a friend of theirs who believes in their innocence why they were smiling.

'At the judge's voice,' she replied.

Leslie Abramson's curly blond hair bounces, Orphan

Annie style, when she walks and talks. She is funny. She is fearless. And she is tough. Oh, is she tough. She walked down the entire corridor of the Beverly Hills courthouse giving the middle finger to an NBC cameraman. 'This what you want? You want that?' she said with an angry sneer into the camera, thrusting the finger at the lens, a shot that appeared on the NBC special *Exposé*, narrated by Tom Brokaw. Her passion for the welfare of the accused murderers she defends is legendary. She is considered one of the most merciless cross-examiners in the legal business, with a remarkable ability to degrade and confuse prosecution witnesses. 'She loves to intimidate people,' I was told. 'She thrives on it. She knows when she has you. She can twist and turn a witness's memory like no one else can.' John Gregory Dunne, in his 1987 novel *The Red White and Blue*, based the character Leah Kaye, a left-leaning criminal-defense attorney, on Leslie Abramson.

'Why did you give the finger to the cameraman?' I asked her.

'I'll tell you why,' she answered, bristling at the memory. 'Because I was talking privately to a member of the Menendez family, and NBC turned the camera on, one inch from my face. I said, "Take that fucker out of my face." These people think they own the courthouse. They will go to any sleazoid end these days. So I said, "Is this what you want?" That's when I gave them the finger. Imagine, Tom Brokaw on a show like that.

'I do not understand the publicity of the case,' she continued, although of course she understood perfectly. 'I mean, the president of the United States wasn't shot.'

Before I could reply with such words as 'patricide', 'matricide', 'wealth', 'Beverly Hills', she had thought over what she had said. 'Well, I rate murder cases different from the public.' Most of her cases are from less swell circumstances. In the Bob's Big Boy case, the only death-penalty case she has ever lost, her clients herded nine employees and two customers into the restaurant's walk-in freezer and fired shotguns into their bodies at close range. Three died and four were maimed. One of those who lived had part of her brain removed. Another lost an eye.

'What's the mood of the boys?' I asked.

'I can't comment on my clients,' she said. 'All I can say is, they're among the very best clients I've ever had, as far as relating. Both of them. It's nonsense, all this talk that there's a good brother and a bad brother. Lyle is wonderful. They're both adorable.'

IN THE AVALANCHE of media blitz that followed the arrest of the Menendez brothers, no one close to Lyle and Erik was the object of more intense fascination and scrutiny than Craig Cignarelli, Erik's tennis partner, with whom he had written the screenplay *Friends*. A family spokesperson told me that in one day alone Craig Cignarelli received thirty-two calls from the media, including 'one from Dan Rather, *A Current Affair*, *Hard Copy*, etc., etc. I can't remember them all. We had to hire an attorney to field calls.' The spokesperson said that 'from the beginning it was presumed that Craig knew something'.

Craig, clearly enjoying his moments of stardom following the arrests of his best friend and best friend's brother, talked freely to the press and was, by all accounts of other friends of the brothers, too talkative by far. In articles by Ron Soble and John Johnson in the *Los Angeles Times*, Craig said he was attracted to Erik by a shared sense that they were special. He recalled how they would drive out to Malibu late at night, park on a hilltop overlooking the ocean, and talk about their hopes for the future, about how much smarter they were than everyone else, and about how to commit the perfect crime. They had nicknames for each other: Craig was 'King', and Erik was 'Shepherd'. 'People really looked up to us. We have an aura of superiority,' he said.

As the months passed, it was whispered that Erik had confessed the murders to Craig. This was borne out to me by Judalon Smyth. But he confessed them in an elliptical manner, according to Smyth, in a suppose-it-happened-like-this way, as if planning another screenplay. It was further said that Craig told the police about the confession, but there were not the hard facts on which to make an arrest, such as came later from Judalon Smyth.

Craig's loquaciousness gave rise to many rumors about the two boys, as well as about the possibility that a second screenplay by them exists, one that parallels the murders even more closely. Craig has since been requested by the police not to speak to the press.

At one point, Cignarelli was presumed to be in danger because of what he knew, and was sent away by his family to a place known only to them. An ongoing story is that a relation of the Menendez brothers threatened Craig after hearing that he had gone to the police. The spokesperson for Craig wanted me to make it clear that, contrary to rumors, Craig 'never approached the police. The police approached Craig. At a point Craig decided to tell them what he knew.' When I asked this same spokesperson about the possibility of a second screenplay written by Craig and Erik, he said he had never seen one. He also said that the deputy district attorney, Elliott Alhadeff, was satisfied that all the information on the confession tapes was known to Craig, so in the event that the tapes were ruled inadmissible by the court he would be able to supply the information on the stand.

Sometime last January, two months before the arrests, the friendship between the two boys cooled. That may have been because Erik suspected that Craig had talked to the police.

Earlier that month, during a New Year's skiing vacation at Lake Tahoe, Erik had met and fallen in love with Noelle Terelsky, a pretty blond student at the University of California in Santa Barbara from Cincinnati. The romance was instantaneous. 'Erik's not a hard guy to fall for,' said a friend of Noelle. 'He's very sweet, very sexy, has a great body, and is an all-around great guy.' Noelle, together with Jamie Pisarcik, Lyle's girlfriend, visits the brothers in jail every day, and has been present at every court appearance of the brothers since their arrest. Until recently, when the house on Elm Drive was rented to the member of the Saudi royal family, the two girls lived in the guesthouse, as the guests of Maria Menendez, the proud and passionate grandmother of Lyle and Erik, who believes completely in the innocence of her grandsons. Maria Menendez, Noelle, and Jamie are now living in the Menendezes' Calabasas house, which has still not been sold.

FIVE MONTHS HAD PASSED since the arrest. Five months of hearings and deliberations to see whether the audiotapes of Dr Jerome Oziel were admissible in the murder trial of Lyle and Erik Menendez. Police seizure of therapy tapes is rare, because ordinarily conversations between patients and therapists are secret. But there are occasional exceptions to the secrecy rule, one being that the therapist believes the patient is a serious threat to himself or others. Only the defense attorneys, who did not want the tapes to be heard, had been allowed to participate in the hearings. The prosecution, which did want them to be heard, was barred. Oziel had been on the stand in private hearings from which the family, the media, and the public were barred. Judalon Smyth had also been on the stand for two days in private sessions, being grilled by Leslie Abramson. The day of the decision had arrived.

There was great tension in the courtroom. Noelle and Jamie, the girlfriends, were there. And Maria, the grandmother. And an aunt from Miami. And a cousin. And the probate lawyer. And others.

Then the Menendez brothers walked in. The swagger, the smirks, the smiles were all gone. And the glamour. So were the Armani-type suits. Their ever-loyal grandmother had arrived with their clothes in suit bags, but the bags were returned to her by the bailiff. They appeared in V-necked, short-sleeved jailhouse blues with T-shirts underneath. Their tennis tans had long since faded. It was impossible not to notice the deterioration in the appearance of the boys, especially Erik. His eyes looked tormented, tortured, haunted. At his neck was a tiny gold cross. He nodded to Noelle Terelsky. He nodded to his grandmother. There were no smiles that day.

Leslie Abramson and Gerald Chaleff went to Judge James Albracht's chambers to hear his ruling on the admissibility of the tapes before it was read to the court. The brothers sat alone at the defense table, stripped of their support system. 'Everybody's staring at us,' said Erik to the bailiff in a pleading voice, as if the bailiff could do something about it, but there was nothing the bailiff could do. Everybody did stare at them. Lyle leaned forward and whispered something to his brother.

The fierce demeanor of Leslie Abramson when she returned to the courtroom left no doubt that the judge's ruling had not gone in favor of the defense. As the judge read his ruling to the crowded courtroom, Abramson, with her back to the judge, kept up a nonstop commentary in Erik Menendez's ear.

'I have ruled that none of the communications are privileged,' said the judge. There was an audible sound of dismay from the Menendez family members. The tapes would be admissible. The judge found that psychologist Jerome Oziel had reasonable cause to believe that Lyle and Erik Menendez 'constituted a threat, and it was necessary to disclose the communications to prevent a danger'.

There was no doubt that this was a serious setback to the defense.

Abramson and Chaleff immediately announced at a news conference that they would appeal the judge's ruling. Abramson called Oziel 'a gossip, a liar, and less than credible'. Neither Judalon Smyth's name nor her role in the proceedings was ever mentioned.

A mere eight days later, in a stunning reversal of Judge Albracht's ruling, the 2nd District Court of Appeals blocked the release of the tapes, to the undisguised delight of Abramson and Chaleff. Prosecutors were then given a date by which to file opposing arguments. Another complication occurred when Erik Menendez, from jail, refused to provide the prosecution with a handwriting sample to compare with the handwriting found on forms for the purchase of two shotguns in San Diego, despite a warning by the court that his refusal to do so could be used as evidence against him. In a further surprise, Deputy District Attorney Elliott Alhadeff, who won the original court ruling that the tapes would be admissible, was abruptly replaced on the notorious case by Deputy District Attorney Pamela Ferrero.

SINCE THEIR ARREST in March, Lyle and Erik Menendez have dwelt in the Los Angeles County Men's Central Jail, in the section reserved for prisoners awaiting trial in heavily publicized cases. The brothers' cells are not side by side. They order reading material from Book Soup, the trendy Sunset Strip bookshop. Erik has been sent *The*

Dead Zone, by Stephen King, and a book on chess. They have frequent visits from family members, and talk with one friend almost daily by telephone. That friend told me that they have to pay for protection in jail. 'Other prisoners, who are tough, hate them – who they are, what they've been accused of. They've been threatened.' He also told me they feel they have lost every one of their friends. Late in August, when three razor blades were reportedly found in Erik's possession, he was put in solitary confinement, deprived of visitors, books except for the Bible, telephone calls, and exercise. That same week, Lyle suddenly shaved his head.

LOS ANGELES DISTRICT ATTORNEY IRA REINER stated on television that one motive for the murders was greed. Certainly it is possible for a child to kill his parents for money, to wish to continue the easy life on easy street without the encumbrance of parental restrictions. But is it really possible for a child to kill, for merely financial gain, in the manner Kitty and Jose Menendez were killed? To blast holes into one's parents? To deface them? To obliterate them? In the fatal, *coup de grâce* shot, the barrel of one shot-gun touched the cheek of Kitty Menendez. You wonder if her eyes met the eyes of her killer in the last second of her life. In this case, we have two children who allegedly participated in the killing of each parent, not in the heat of rage but in a carefully orchestrated scenario after a long gestation period. There is more than money involved here. There is a deep, deep hatred, a hatred that goes beyond hate.

The closest friend of the Menendez brothers, with whom I talked at length on the condition of anonymity, kept saying to me over and over, 'It's only the tip of the iceberg.' No amount of persuasion on my part could make him explain what the iceberg was. Months earlier, however, a person close to the situation mouthed but did not speak the word 'incest' to me. Subsequently, a rich woman in Los Angeles told me that her bodyguard, a former cop, had heard from a friend of his on the Beverly Hills police force that Kitty Menendez had been shot in the vagina. At a Malibu barbecue, a film star said to me, 'I heard the mother was shot up the wazoo.' There is, however, no indication of such a penetration in the autopsy report, which carefully delineates each of the ten wounds from the nine shots fired into Kitty Menendez's body. But the subject continues to surface. Could it be possible that these boys were puppets of their father's dark side? 'They had sexual hatred for their parents,' one of the friends told me. This same person went on to say, 'The tapes will show that Jose molested Lyle at a very young age.'

Is this true? Only the boys know. If it is, it could be the defense argument that will return them to their tennis court, swimming pool, and chess set, as inheritors of a $14 million estate that they could not have inherited if they had been found guilty. Karen Lamm, however, does not believe such a story, although it is unlikely that Kitty would have revealed to her a secret of that dimension. Judalon Smyth was also skeptical of this information when I brought up the subject of sexual abuse. She said she

had heard nothing of the kind on the Halloween afternoon when, according to the California Court of Appeals
decision, she listened outside Dr Oziel's office door as Lyle
and Erik talked about the murders. She said that last
December, almost two months after the October 31 confession to Oziel, which was not taped, the boys, feeling that
the police were beginning to suspect them, voluntarily
made a tape in which they confessed to the crime. In it,
they spoke of their remorse. In it, apparently, they told
of psychological abuse. But sexual abuse? Judalon Smyth
did not hear this tape, and by that time Dr Oziel was no
longer confiding in her.

——▶ ◀——

*I became deeply and personally involved in this story. The trial
went on for months. Erik and Lyle Menendez, the young killers,
became romantic figures in the televised proceedings. In cases of
high crime, I've never made any attempt to present a balanced
picture. This was no exception. I was appalled by the lies I heard
defense attorneys tell in the courtroom. I became despised by Leslie
Abramson, the lead defense attorney. I couldn't have cared less. The
trial ended in a hung jury, which was considered a victory for the
defense. Their luck did not hold for the second trial. They are both
doing life without the possibility of parole in separate prisons in
California.*

LA IN THE AGE OF O. J.

WHEN I RETURNED to New York last February, after seven months here covering the first Menendez trial, it never occurred to me that another cataclysmic event, another double homicide in high circles, would bring this city to a halt again so soon. But it has, and I'm back, and there's quite a lot going on, even though neither trial has started yet.

The Menendez brothers, who held the city of Los Angeles in their thrall for four years, have ceased to fascinate the town, so overwhelming is the interest in O. J. Simpson. Simpson is the most famous American to be charged with a violent crime since Fatty Arbuckle was tried for manslaughter back in the '20s, amid rumors that he had inserted a Coca-Cola bottle into a young woman's vagina during an orgy at the St Francis Hotel in San Francisco, thereby causing her death. Arbuckle was acquitted after three trials, but his reputation and career were ruined. In the wake of the killings of Nicole Simpson and Ronald Goldman last June, O. J. has superseded all others in history as the town's top topic, a topic that will continue to captivate until the jury arrives at a verdict, if it does arrive at a verdict. The cynicism of the citizenry about the possibility of a conviction, after the two non-verdicts in the Menendez trial, makes 'hung jury' and 'acquittal' the most often repeated words in the community.

The late unlamented Jose Menendez, about whom a decent word was scarcely uttered during the six-month murder trial of the two sons who had shotgunned him and his wife, Kitty, to death, was once a top-ranking executive at Hertz car rental. At the time, O. J. Simpson was doing his extremely popular commercials for Hertz. The story goes that Lyle and Erik Menendez, then preteenagers, were fans of the football star, so one night Jose and Kitty invited O. J. to dinner with them and their sons, and the evening was a great success. The Menendez brothers and O. J. Simpson did not meet again until they were all in the celebrity section of the Los Angeles County Jail, all three charged with double murder. O. J. was briefly in the cell next to Erik's; then Erik was moved to another cellblock. Subsequently Simpson was put in an area by himself, where he has an exercise machine and a private room for his visitors. Even in jail, the Menendez brothers have been upstaged by the star quality of O. J. Simpson.

The Simpson case is like a great trash novel come to life, a mammoth fireworks display of interracial marriage, love, lust, lies, hate, fame, wealth, beauty, obsession, spousal abuse, stalking, brokenhearted children, the bloodiest of bloody knife-slashing homicides, and all the justice that money can buy. With Kato Kaelin, Al

Cowlings, Faye Resnick, Denise Brown, and Detective Mark Fuhrman in key supporting roles, there's not a vanilla character in the whole story. Even the lawyers on both sides are bigger than life. By now, who doesn't know who Robert Shapiro and Johnnie Cochran Jr are? Or Marcia Clark? At dinner parties and in restaurants, whole evenings are spent discussing the case. Everyone has a tidbit of information. Everyone has a theory about what happened. Even those people who affect weariness with the subject, who say things like 'I'm sick, sick, sick to *death* of O. J.', lean in and listen intently when a new nugget is brought forth. A great many people I have encountered were friends, or friends of friends, of O. J.'s or Nicole's before the knifings. Everyone has a topper to everyone else's piece of information. 'I saw Nicole jogging in Brentwood just the day before,' said a man at a screening, to which another man immediately replied, 'Craig Baumgarten played golf with O. J. that Sunday morning at Riviera.'

The parties and private screenings go on and on, and so does the chatter after dinner. Sometimes people talk right through the film. 'This piece of shit cost $60 million,' said a Hollywood mogul the other night about a film we were watching at someone's house, where the screen came out of the ceiling and the Picassos went up at the push of a button to reveal the windows of the projection booth. The comment signaled that conversation could begin. There's always a lot to say about Paula Barbieri, who was O. J.'s last girlfriend before the slayings.

> *'Paula Barbieri visits O. J. in jail.'*
>
> *'Bob Evans knows Paula Barbieri.'*
>
> *'I heard that Paula Barbieri was with Michael Bolton at the Mirage in Vegas on the night of the murder.'*
>
> *'If Paula had been there, I bet Nicole would never have been killed that night. He didn't have anyplace to go.'*

ALTHOUGH I ONCE lived here for many years, I have never before been so aware of what a small town the Hollywood community really is. Everyone knows everything about everyone else. It's like an update of Thornton Wilder's *Our Town*, except in this version everyone drives a Ferrari or a Rolls-Royce, and the Stage Manager has been – but may not be much longer – Robert Shapiro, one of LA's best-known defense lawyers. Shapiro, who is an acknowledged spin doctor and master of media manipulation, has been heading O. J.'s defense team. 'He only had $60 on him,' Shapiro said on-camera to offset the belief that O. J., with Al Cowlings at the wheel of the white Bronco, was escaping to Mexico five days after the killings. Actually, according to all reports, O. J. had something like $8,000 with him at the time, but, as they keep saying out here, Shapiro was just doing his job. We live in the age of the defense attorney as superstar. Witness Shapiro's daily arrival at the downtown Los Angeles courthouse, surrounded by television cameras, with microphones stuck in his face and reporters yelling questions at him. This is a man experiencing Nirvana. Shapiro has even hired the lawyer-agent Ed Hookstratten to field book offers and to discuss possibilities for his own television talk show.

Everyone seems to know Shapiro. He's a bona fide member of the film colony, as well as a personable and jovial fellow to meet. He's here, he's there, he's everywhere – the most ubiquitous figure in movieland society, and everyone in town is talking about him.

> *'Bob was Tina Sinatra's lawyer in her stalking suit against Jimmy Farentino.'*
>
> *'Bob was Bob Evans's lawyer at the* Cotton Club *murder trial.'*
>
> *'I heard Bob got an out-of-state death threat, but he denied it.'*
>
> *'I bet you didn't know that Bob was the lawyer for the guy who shot Marcia Clark's first husband.'*

'NICOLE KNEW HOW to push O. J.'s buttons,' said a woman who knew the Simpsons as a couple, at lunch at Le Dôme. 'When she didn't save a seat for O. J. at their daughter's dance recital that last afternoon, she knew how crazy that was going to make him, having to walk up and down the aisle looking for a place to sit. She knew that was the equivalent of giving him the middle finger. Once she found out he was still seeing Paula Barbieri, after they were supposed to be reconciling, she said, *Over, out!* Fuck you, Charlie.' The lady paused. 'Mind if I smoke? You see, Nicole stayed too long in that relationship. You're supposed to get *out* of an abusive relationship, not stay in it. Even after they were divorced, they were involved.

You know what happens? It becomes a dance of death. That's what they were in.

'You won't quote me, will you? I mean, you can tell the story, but don't attach my name to it. Is that a deal?' Many people who know things about the Simpsons do not want to take any chances going public, in case O. J. is acquitted.

IN THE MIDST of all this, the Prince of Wales came to town, shortly after his I-never-loved-her-my-father-made-me-marry-her declaration about the mother of his sons. What a flat tire that trip was. I can remember a time out here when the visit of any member of the British royal family was the social event of the season. Years ago Sharman Douglas, the daughter of the late Lewis Douglas, the American ambassador to the Court of St James's, gave a dinner dance at the Bistro in Beverly Hills in honor of her old friend Princess Margaret. That party was considered to be the beginning of the A group and the B group in the movieland society set, so humiliating was it not to be invited to dine with the princess, who danced that night with Paul Newman. How things have changed. The city was most certainly not gripped with royal fever during the visit of the heir to the British throne. The beleaguered Prince was simply not a hot ticket. There was a great deal of behind-the-scenes telephoning to beg people to show up at certain of the charity events. The stars did not turn out. There was no hostility toward the Prince, merely indifference.

*   *   *

ROBERT SHAPIRO WAS one of the most photographed superstars at Barbara and Marvin Davis's Carousel of Hope Ball in October, right along with Hillary Clinton, Barbra Streisand, Warren Beatty and Annette Bening, Dustin Hoffman, Goldie Hawn and Kurt Russell, Arnold Schwarzenegger and Maria Shriver, and Fergie, the Duchess of York. One of the hottest items bid on at the silent auction preceding the ball was lunch with Shapiro after the trial; it went for $2,000. All eyes in the ballroom were focused on Shapiro for his reactions as Jay Leno, the master of ceremonies, told a round of O. J. jokes. 'One of O. J.'s lawyers only handles clients with one glove,' said Leno, referring to Johnnie Cochran, who represented Michael Jackson in the child-molestation suit in 1993, as well as to the bloody glove found on the Simpson estate.

> 'I saw Bob last night at Eclipse. He's one of the backers.'
>
> 'My wife sat next to Shapiro at Jackie Collins's party last night.'
>
> 'When the camera panned around the Rose Bowl at the Rolling Stones concert, Bob got more applause than any star there.'
>
> 'I wish you could have seen Bob at this Halloween costume party we were at last night at Chasen's. He came as a prizefighter, in black satin shorts and a white satin robe with SHAPIRO embroidered on the back. He and Linell won first prize for best costume. Linell was in a very short white leather mini, like a ring girl announcing the rounds.

> *Jo-Ellan Dimitrius, the defense jury consultant on the case, came as Carmen Miranda. And Kardashian (do you know Bob Kardashian? His ex-wife's married to Bruce Jenner) came as Count Dracula.'*

IT WAS FROM Robert Kardashian's house in the San Fernando Valley that O. J., with a gun, a lot of cash, a passport, a fake beard, and Al Cowlings at the wheel, departed on his famous bolt for Mexico, or his bolt for Nicole Simpson's freshly dug grave to commit suicide, depending on which version of the story you believe. Shapiro and Kardashian claimed that they had been upstairs in a conference room and didn't know O. J. and Cowlings were leaving. Kardashian, with Shapiro at his side, read O. J.'s cover-every-base 'suicide' note at a press conference. As for the fake beard, Shapiro's spin was that O. J. had been planning on taking his children to Disneyland, an interpretation which might work for Michael Jackson but which seems improbable for Simpson, who was not having problems being mobbed by fans, particularly kids, prior to the slayings in June. Again, as they say out here, Shapiro was just doing his job.

ROBERT SHAPIRO APPEARED at Michael Jackson's 2,700-acre Neverland ranch last August to attend the wedding and reception of Jackson's bodyguard Miko Brando, a son of Marlon Brando's. His co-counsel Johnnie Cochran, who had represented Jackson during his alleged-child-abuse woes, did not attend the wedding. Neither did Marlon Brando. Shapiro had been defense attorney for Miko's half-brother Christian Brando, who in May 1990 left his father's house, took his half-sister Cheyenne to dinner, drove to his girl-friend's house to get a gun, and then returned to his father's house, where he shot and killed Cheyenne's boyfriend, Dag Drollet, whose child she was carrying. Christian Brando is now doing ten years in San Luis Obispo (which means he will probably serve only five, because most California sentences have been cut in half), following a plea bargain arranged by Shapiro. High drama is a constant in the lives of these people. Michael Jackson had to leave Miko's wedding reception when he got word that Delores Jackson, his ex-sister-in-law, had drowned in her boyfriend's swim-ming pool. An investigation is now under way since the coroner discovered suspicious marks on the body.

> *'This is the only town I ever heard of where the husband keeps the mansion in a divorce and the wife and kids move to a condo.'*
> *'Nicole was used to having her laundry done, and after the divorce she was pushing the cart up and down the aisles of the supermarket.'*

NICOLE PULVERS, A LAWYER from Robert Shapiro's office, is in charge of O. J.'s visitors list. Some of O. J.'s pals, such as the producer Craig Baumgarten and NBC's West Coast president, Don Ohlmeyer, are also on O. J.'s material witness list and, as witnesses, have regular access to his private visiting room, where sounds of party-like hilarity have been reported. Other prisoners in the LA County Jail, including the once rich Menendez brothers, usually receive their guests in large visiting areas supervised by deputies, and have to speak to them over telephones through glass partitions. Four nights a week, O. J. receives visitors in a room where he can speak to them directly without telephones. There is only a lawyer present, usually Nicole Pulvers.

THERE ARE MORE ATTORNEYS here than I have ever seen before on a homicide case. The prosecution has a squad of eleven. Every time I look at the huge defense team, I wonder how much this is costing Simpson. Besides the famous names – Shapiro, Cochran, Dershowitz, Bailey, and Uelmen – there is a battery of up-and-coming young lawyers on the defense staff. One day the big legal guns on both sides retired to Judge Ito's chambers for an in camera hearing. Whatever they were discussing went on and on. As time passed, the atmosphere relaxed, and general conversation took place. Some of the lawyers began to gravitate to O. J. and sat down at the defense end of the table. Within minutes, the scene had the curious look of a dinner party, where Simpson was the host, holding court. The young lawyers often laughed too loudly at things he said, the way people who are not used to being in the orbit of a celebrity do.

THE TIDE OF SYMPATHY for the man people used to call a

hero has turned. When the 911 tape of Nicole calling the police was played on television, it marked the beginning of the turn. More recently, the extraordinary television appearances of an enraged Denise Brown, Nicole's sister, have had their effect on the public. Whatever spin the defense puts on the 911 tape in the trial, if it is ruled admissible, there can be no doubt in anyone's mind that we were listening to a terrified woman who was not unused to the situation she was in. If the DNA results are anywhere near as overwhelming as they are whispered to be, it will be difficult for even the most die-hard loyalist to remain loyal. Rarely, very rarely, someone says that he thinks O. J. is innocent. It happened at a dinner I attended one night.

'I don't think O. J. did it,' said one guest, who was a friend of Simpson's. He used to go to the house on Rockingham. He liked O. J. a lot and said so.

There were oh-come-on-get-real groans from some people at the table.

'I mean it. He couldn't have killed two people in that amount of time.'

'Just ignore John on this topic, thank you very much,' said the hostess. 'Otherwise, he's charming.'

'I don't know Faye Resnick. I've never met her. She came into Nicole's life in the last couple of years, but she covered it all in her book. It's heartbreakingly true. I could have done without the blow-job story, but it was her life. Nicole was a woman with her own life.'

'The newspapers keep calling Faye Resnick a

socialite. I've never seen her anywhere, have you?'
'Faye Resnick's hiding out at Michael Viner and
Deborah Raffin's house in Stowe, Vermont. She and
Mike Walker wrote the book in three weeks.'

Michael Viner, the president of Dove Books, is Resnick's publisher. He also brought out her book on tape, which Resnick reads herself. Mike Walker is a gossip columnist for the *National Enquirer*. Whether Resnick's book would have reached its dizzying heights of success without Judge Ito's ire over its publication and his exhortation to prospective jurors to avoid bookstores is open to speculation.

THE DEFENSE TEAM, especially Robert Shapiro and Johnnie Cochran, schmooze with the media in the corridor outside the courtroom, know the names of all the regular reporters, and laugh and joke with them. The prosecution team all smile a greeting but move on, almost never stopping to chat.

Out of the courtroom, Marcia Clark, the prosecutor with William Hodgman, has a friendly manner and a feisty wit. Her background story, which I know of only through the *National Enquirer*, is movie material in itself. *The Enquirer*, which is the tabloid every reporter and journalist covering the case reads faithfully every Monday morning, must not be dismissed for inaccuracy in its reporting. Clark was once a dancer. After she divorced her first husband, Gaby Horowitz, a backgammon gambler who played for high stakes with such fanatics of the game as Lucille Ball and John Wayne, he was accidentally shot in the head by his best friend, Bruce Roman, who was represented by Robert Shapiro. Horowitz survived, but is severely handicapped. Clark has two very young children by her second marriage, to Gordon Clark, from whom she filed for divorce three days before Nicole Simpson and Ron Goldman were killed.

'My boyfriend went to the birthday party for Justin Simpson the other day. Arnelle, O. J.'s daughter, arrived in Nicole's jeep. Al Cowlings was there.'

'Al Cowlings was backstage in the Rolling Stones' inner sanctum after their concert at the Rose Bowl.'

'Actually, Al's a nice guy. He really loved Nicole and the kids.'

IN 1989 the Menendez brothers appeared to be the inheritors of their parents' $14 million estate. That was before they were caught and charged with double murder, after suggesting to the police that the Mafia might have committed the crime. The Beverly Hills house where the killings took place has been sold. The bank accounts of their parents, which paid for their defense in the first trial, are empty. Leslie Abramson has continued to represent Erik, at a greatly reduced fee, which is paid this time by the county of Los Angeles. Lyle's lawyer Jill Lansing left the case after the first trial. The court assigned a public defender to represent Lyle in the second trial. At a recent court hearing I attended, Judge Stanley Weisberg referred to Lyle Menendez, the former rich kid, as an indigent defendant.

Lyle is not happy with William Weiss, the public defender assigned to him by the court, and wants Jill Lansing back on the case. The greatly underpraised Lansing changed the course of the first trial when she expertly guided Lyle Menendez step-by-step through his tearful testimony, proving concretely the staggering power of male tears on a female jury. David Conn and Carol Najera, the new prosecution team assigned to the case by Los Angeles district attorney Gil Garcetti, may effectively block Lansing's return by calling her as a witness in the second trial.

Conn was the prosecutor in the *Cotton Club* murder case, in which film producer Robert Evans, with his attorney, Robert Shapiro, at his side, took the Fifth. Conn got life sentences without parole for the two hired killers and for Lanie Greenberger, the mastermind of the hit, in which Roy Radin, an aspiring film producer, was shot to death in gangland fashion. In that trial, Marcia Morrissey, who is now the co-defense counsel with Leslie Abramson, was one of Greenberger's lawyers.

The second Menendez trial is going to be very different from the first. Leslie Abramson has long wanted the trials to be separate, with Erik's going first. The prosecution wants the brothers tried together, as before. The general belief is that Erik will turn on Lyle. As of now, Judge Weisberg has indicated that there will be only one jury this time, not two. The defense will be two separate camps, rather than one cohesive unit dominated by Abramson.

'*I went to Whoopi Goldberg's wedding to that union guy. Richard Pryor was there. Richard knew O. J. All anybody talked about at the wedding was O. J. Did you know that Whoopi had FUCK YOU painted on the roof of her house on the day of her wedding to keep the helicopters away?*'

IN THE OLD grab-it-while-you're-hot Hollywood syndrome, several lawyers in high-profile cases are taking advantage of their newfound celebrity status to ensure a continuation of their fame beyond their trials. Since Leslie Abramson's spectacular sexual-molestation defense of Erik Menendez, which resulted in hung juries for both Erik and Lyle Menendez, she has won an acquittal for another client, Roman Luisi, who was also charged with double murder. Fame and recognition have come her way. Abramson describes herself as a proponent of a line of defense that seeks justice for victimized people who kill their victimizers, which, roughly translated, means the abuse excuse.

Abramson, like Robert Shapiro, now moves in the orbit of celebrity. Barbara Walters on ABC picked her as one of the ten most fascinating personalities of 1994. Liz Smith devoted an entire column to her in *New York Newsday*, in which she stated that things were cooking for a possible future career in television. Abramson attended the International Press Freedom Awards dinner at the Grand Hyatt in New York accompanied by ABC anchorman Peter Jennings. She made the rounds of the New York publishing houses with her literary agent,

Kathy Robbins, to pitch a book proposal, and got a $500,000 deal with Simon & Schuster for a book entitled *My Life in Crime*. Part of that fee will be split with her co-author, Richard Flaste. 'The book I am thinking of writing is a typical lawyer's autobiography. I would probably not even mention Erik and Lyle in it,' she confided to Liz Smith.

At Princeton University on November 11, Leslie Abramson gave a luncheon talk at a seminar called 'The Appearance of Justice: Juries, Judges, and the Media'. The event was co-sponsored by the Woodrow Wilson School of Public and International Affairs at Princeton and the Annenberg Washington Program of Northwestern University. Abramson was accompanied by Hazel Thornton, an Erik Menendez juror who has appeared with her on television since the first trial. Hazel Thornton has written a book called *Hung Jury: The Diary of a Menendez Juror*, about her experiences in the jury room of the Menendez trial, which has yet to find a publisher. Abramson spent several minutes of her speech blasting me. She called me a liar and said that I had made up facts in my coverage of the Menendez case. I subscribe to the theory that name-callers project onto others what they most dislike in themselves. In a BBC *Omnibus* documentary called 'The Trials of Dominick Dunne', which was aired in November, Abramson snarled into the camera and said, 'He's trying very hard to be Truman Capote . . . He doesn't have . . . Truman Capote's talent.' About that at least, she was correct.

Abramson has signed with ABC to be a commentator at the O. J. Simpson trial. The scuttlebutt in television-news circles is that she will receive $4,000 a day, which could, if the trial is as sensational as people expect it to be, net her as much as $20,000 a week. In her book proposal, Abramson wrote, 'Rick [Flaste] and I will spend the months before Menendez resumes in the spring going over my career and combing through transcripts, an incredibly rich source for a book like this. Much of this work will have to be done while the Simpson trial is in progress, and I expect that I will be called on again for extensive work as a commentator for ABC News. (The plan is to turn my television experience into a chapter, too – behind the scenes at the media circus.)'

'The dirty D word that is not being mentioned in the Simpson case is drugs.'

O. J. SIMPSON, whatever his private torments may be, puts on a front that is as audacious as his absolutely-100-percent-not-guilty reply to the guilty-or-not-guilty query. He enters the courtroom each time looking like a star. Shapiro and Cochran often precede him out the door of the holding room, where O. J.'s manacles are removed and he changes from his jailhouse blues into his own, beautifully cut suits. They often enter laughing, as if they have just heard a wonderful joke. Shapiro sometimes turns back to O. J. to whisper some final thing. They are all aware that the camera is on them, and behave accordingly. By contrast, the Menendez brothers, their luster dimmed, schlepped into the courtroom in Van Nuys, looking like

TV actors whose series had been canceled. The ranks of their groupies had greatly diminished. Those who were there wore yellow ribbons of the free-the-hostages variety.

'I think the women on the jury will be sympathetic to Nicole because she was abused.'
'I don't think that at all. There are eight women on that jury. Mostly black. Nicole is everything they hate in life.'

LYLE MENENDEZ, the indigent defendant, was wearing a new, $2,500 toupee, by Don Kovakovich, of Fresno, California, who made and then gave the piece to Lyle. Kovakovich is a bit of a celebrity himself in the world of false hair, having recently appeared, rather controversially, on the Jenny Jones television show in Chicago, where he discussed the hair problems of Lyle Menendez and O. J. Simpson in the Los Angeles County Jail. He said that Lyle wears his toupee and O. J. uses his hair-restorative treatment every day.

'O. J. is in total, complete denial.'

THE SIMPSON DREAM TEAM put together by the defense is not so dreamy these days. From all reports, there is disharmony in the ranks. People seeing Robert Shapiro out and about on the party circuit have begun to ask, 'When does he work?' Friends of Shapiro's have urged him to cut down on his overactive social life, even to quit the case, saying he's gotten all he can out of it. Nowadays, Shapiro is constantly denying that he is leaving. Johnnie Cochran is moving more and more toward center stage, however, and will probably lead the actual trial.

One of the arguments is whether or not O. J. will take the stand. There are two schools of thought. Some feel that his attractiveness and charm can win over the jury. However, there are others on the defense who feel that O. J. is incapable of answering a question simply. When he talks, he talks too much. It is the complicated answer that can trip up a defendant in a cross-examination. At a bail hearing, when Cochran asked Judge Ito if the defendant could make a statement, Simpson went into a long harangue, saying that prosecutor Clark thought he was trying to escape in the white Bronco when all he was doing was making a phone call to his father-in-law and heading home. If O. J. were to talk like that on the stand, Marcia Clark, in cross-examination, would make mincemeat of him. He also has a short fuse. He has a tendency to roll his eyes if someone says something he doesn't like, and he has had to be admonished by Judge Ito because of unauthorized audible statements he has made during jury selection. An angry O. J. outburst on the stand might be one of the most exciting moments ever seen on television, but it would also be a disaster for the defense.

'If only the Akita could talk. That dog saw the whole thing.'

'They should bring the Akita into the courtroom and see how he reacts to O. J.'

Yes, if only dogs could talk. Nicole Simpson's Akita, named Kato after Kato Kaelin, who lived in O. J.'s guest-house, was, as far as anyone knows, the only witness to the crime. It had blood on its paws. It led someone back to the crime scene. It knows everything. The Akita is a watchdog, bred to defend its human family. But Nicole Simpson's Akita did not come to its mistress's aid. Janet Ross, who has raised Akitas for twenty years, told a writer for *Newsday*, 'I was at an event last weekend where there must have been forty Akita people and not one of them thought [Simpson or Goldman] had been killed by a stranger.' The Akita is now in the possession of Jason Simpson, O. J.'s son by his first wife, who has reportedly changed the dog's name from Kato to Satchmo. Kato Kaelin, who will appear as a prosecution witness, is appar-ently out of favor. So is Paula Barbieri. Jason kicked her out of his father's mansion, where she had been living. As for Jason himself, he has been charged with two mis-demeanor counts, driving with a suspended license and leaving the scene of an accident.

NICOLE SIMPSON'S OUTSPOKEN SISTER Denise Brown, who has become something of a loose cannon with her comments, is a constant vexation to the defense. 'If O. J. is so innocent, why are they trying to suppress all the evidence?' she demanded. Shapiro responded that that is what lawyers are supposed to do. Recently, Brown, who bears an uncanny resemblance to her slain sister, and Ron Goldman's father have gone public with their rage against

Shapiro and Cochran. 'O. J. did it,' Brown told Geraldo Rivera. 'He murdered my sister.' Cochran railed against them in court, calling their assertions of O. J.'s guilt in the double murder part of an organized media blitz. That was just before the *Star* published Nicole Simpson's letter to her family, foretelling her death and detailing the incidents of abuse she had sustained from her husband during their relationship. Although her father later denied the authenticity of the letter, it shook people here to their roots.

IF O. J. DIDN'T kill his wife and Ron Goldman, who did? It is the question that everyone asks. Are the police looking for other suspects? I don't think so. The defense floated a story that the perpetrator was a Colombian or Mafia drug dealer. The story went that the slashed voice box was the clue, that people who talk too much about their drug dealer meet their end that way. That story got laughs. The poor Mafia. Everyone blames it for everything.

THE DEFENSE ATTACK on Detective Mark Fuhrman was a brilliant tactic. Even if Fuhrman's record is ruled inadmissible in the trial, there is probably not a single juror or alternate juror who has not heard about it. Fuhrman, who discovered the bloody glove on the grounds of the Simpson estate that matched the bloody glove at the crime scene, is going into the trial under a cloud of allegations that he is a racist who tried to frame Simpson by planting the bloody glove near the guesthouse where Kato Kaelin was staying on O. J.'s estate.

WHOEVER SAID CRIME DOESN'T PAY was nuts. Some people are getting rich on the Menendez and Simpson cases. The most extraordinary story to me, which will be denied but which is true, is that O. J. Simpson, represented by a major talent agency, is in negotiation for a pay-per-view interview provided he is acquitted – similar to the handling of certain major sports events. No Barbara Walters, no Diane Sawyer, no Connie Chung for him. It is estimated that the gig would net O. J. $10 million, which should be enough to pay off his defense attorneys, settle all his bills, and allow him to start out a new life someplace else.

'My condo is three blocks from Nicole's condo.'
'O. J.'s dentist is my dentist.'

MEANWHILE, DOWN THE HALLWAY from Judge Lance Ito's courtroom on the ninth floor of the Los Angeles courthouse, the pandering trial of Heidi Fleiss, the so-called Hollywood Madam, who monopolized the headlines for quite some time last year after her arrest, an arrest that scared the daylights out of some of the film industry's most notable names, was drawing to a close. Poor Fleiss has become a ho-hum media figure. She scarcely gets her picture taken, so lukewarm is the press's interest in her compared with O. J. Seats were always available in her courtroom. Yet, as one cynic observed, 'Heidi Fleiss will probably do more time than O. J. *or* the

Menendez brothers.' There are stories that Frank Sinatra Jr is going to marry Heidi Fleiss when she is free. Big Frank is said not to be delirious with happiness over his son's intended nuptials.

Among Fleiss's courtroom observers were Al Goldstein, the publisher of *Screw* magazine; Sydney Biddle Barrows, the former Mayflower Madam, who was elegantly dressed in what appeared to be a dark-blue Chanel suit; and Norma Jean Almodovar, who has documented her police and prostitution experiences in a steamy book entitled *Cop to Call Girl*. Later, Goldstein sat in on a Simpson hearing relating to Captain Margaret York, the highest-ranking female in the Los Angeles Police Department, who, incidentally, is the wife of Judge Lance Ito. The defense wanted to question York about any role she may have played in investigating the controversial Detective Mark Fuhrman during a sexual-harassment inquiry. Some thought putting Captain York on the stand was a way of making Judge Ito recuse himself, because of a conflict of interest, in order to put a new judge on the bench. If that happened, the entire legal process might have had to start over. In reality, no one actually wanted Ito to go, even though at that moment a great portion of the media was gloating over the public roasting the judge had been getting for having appeared on a heavily advertised five-segment television interview with Tritia Toyota on KCBS during November sweeps. Ito's public disdain for the media, as well as for those on the case who used the media for self-aggrandizement, brought on some of the most blistering attacks in recent memory on a judge, even though Ito discussed only his personal life, not the case. On one day alone, the *Los Angeles Times* had three separate articles on Ito's interview with Tritia Toyota, including an unfavorable review by the paper's television critic Howard Rosenberg.

Anyway, back to Al Goldstein; he is a regular court watcher at the bigtime trials. Once, during the Menendez trial in Van Nuys, he slept outside on the court steps all night so that he would be assured of the first place in line to get into the trial the next morning. Goldstein was accompanied by his good friend Ron Jeremy, a porn star, who, according to Goldstein, has appeared in 1,100 hard-core films.

Perhaps this is an appropriate moment to say that the night maids at the hotel where I am staying leave a condom in a gold wrapper, looking like a piece of chocolate, on my pillow every night. Very flattering. To paraphrase Cindy Adams's standard closing line in the *New York Post*, 'Only in LA, folks. Only in LA.'

ALTHOUGH I AM in a minority, I still am not ruling out the possibility of a last-minute plea bargain. Plea bargains are the special province of Robert Shapiro. If he should bring such a thing about, he would re-emerge from his current shaky position to the national eminence he craves.

With a plea bargain comes an admission of guilt, which Simpson would probably be loath to make especially after his absolutely-100-percent-not-guilty plea and his insistence, according to an insider, to his lawyers, when they tried to talk turkey to him, that he didn't do it. In a plea bargain for a case of this nature, the defense might ask for a manslaughter conviction, and the prosecution might counter with one count of murder in the first degree and one of murder in the second degree. An agreement, if reached, might fall somewhere between. Granted, it would be a national disappointment. The country has been looking forward to this trial. We are all a part of an entertainment classic in the making, onstage and backstage. As the rapper Dr Dre, whose new video, 'Natural Born Killaz', performed with Ice Cube, shows a re-enactment of the murders of Nicole Simpson and Ron Goldman, said in a television interview on *Hard Copy* recently, 'Murder sells. Sex sells, but is not as popular as murder.' I wonder if O. J. would still earn $10 million on pay-per-view if he plea-bargained.

THE TWO MRS SIMPSONS

*What did it matter where you lay once you were
dead? . . . You just slept the big sleep, not caring
about the nastiness of how you died or where you
fell. Me, I was part of the nastiness now.*
—RAYMOND CHANDLER, *The Big Sleep.*

FOR SIXTY YEARS, whenever the name 'Mrs Simpson'
was mentioned, it belonged, irrevocably, to Wallis
Warfield Simpson, the lady from Baltimore for
whom King Edward VIII gave up his throne in 1936 and
shook the British monarchy to its roots. No longer. Now
the name belongs, irrevocably, to the tragic and beautiful
Nicole Brown Simpson of Brentwood, California, whose
dreadful death on the night of Sunday, June 12, 1994,
along with that of her friend Ron Goldman, has riveted
this country for nine months. The nastiness of how she
died and where she fell is the reason the gaze of the country is focused on a courtroom in downtown Los Angeles.

O. J. and Nicole Simpson were constantly photographed

in happy poses, belying the truth of their real relationship. Has there ever been a murder case where there were more photographs and videotapes of the victim and the alleged killer? New images appear almost daily in tabloids and magazines. In them, their lives look so enviable, so glamorous. They are always at wonderful parties in wonderful clothes, smiling and waving, or on wonderful trips, or at wonderful beaches, or gazing into each other's eyes, or kissing each other, exuding sexuality. How perfect it looked. How rotten it was.

SOME OF THE GREAT crime and trial reporters in the country are walking down the terrazzo corridors of the courthouse. Some just drop in. Some stay. Linda Deutsch of the Associated Press, who has covered every important trial since the Charles Manson case, has a front-row seat. Jimmy Breslin, Michael Daly, Art Spiegelman, and Mike McAlary have been spotted. In a different journalistic vein altogether, Jackie Mason and Raoul Felder, the comic and the New York divorce lawyer, have wandered through the media room in their capacity as commentators on the trial for the BBC. The writer and performance artist Anna Deavere Smith and the famed attorney and CNN commentator Gerry Spence are regular courtroom visitors. From the Old Guard reporters you hear snippets of conversation about participants in past trials they have covered. Roy Black, who successfully defended William Kennedy Smith against rape charges in West Palm Beach, is married, maybe, to Lea Haller, the juror who kissed him

at Bradley's saloon on the night of Smith's acquittal. Lea
Black recently reported a major burglary at their home
in Coral Gables. Marvin Pancoast, who killed the society
mistress Vicki Morgan, died in prison of AIDS. Lanie
Greenberger, of the *Cotton Club* murder case, who is
doing life without parole for the kidnapping and the hiring
of hit men to kill the producer Roy Radin, is in the Central
California Women's Facility in Chowchilla. Claus von
Bülow, who was acquitted of attempting to kill his heiress
wife, lives in London and has become a Catholic. Sunny
von Bülow is still in a coma at Columbia-Presbyterian
hospital in New York. Von Bülow's mistress at the time
of the second trial, Andrea Reynolds, has married into
the British aristocracy and is running a bed-and-breakfast
in the Catskills.

The competition among reporters is fierce. At no time
did that become more noticeable than when Judge Lance
Ito's seating list for the media was announced on the court
day before the opening statements were to begin. To my
surprise, I received a front-row seat, but I thereby became
the instant enemy of several members of the media who
didn't care for their seat assignments. I was raked over
the coals in a rather mocking fashion in the *Los Angeles
Times* by a reporter named Bob Pool. I've been interviewed enough times in my life to recognize the false-
friendly smile that masks the sneak attack Pool had in
mind when he spoke to me. He wrote indignantly that I
was unapologetic about the seat that had been assigned to
me. No one was more vocal in the article than Paul Pringle,
bureau chief of the Copley News Service, who called me

'Judith Krantz in pants'. From what I gather from people on the courthouse staff who have had prior dealings with Pringle, 'beloved' is a word that will never be used to describe him.

In celebrity trials, visiting celebrities are treated like celebrities, with all the perks that accompany fame. We members of the media, whom Judge Ito calls jackals when he is displeased with us, enter the courtroom by the front door when the bailiffs tell us we can enter, after first going through a metal detector and then having our press passes checked. There is nothing lax about Judge Ito's court-room. There are rules to be observed, and they'd better be observed or else. One day during a court session, we looked up from our seats and saw Larry King standing in the doorway that leads to the judge's chambers. He had obviously come in by some special arrangement through an entry not available to us. King waved. The writer Joe McGinniss, whom I was sitting next to, thought he was waving at him. I thought he was waving at me. We both waved back. Then Judge Ito ordered a ten-minute break, and we repaired to the corridor. The ten-minute break escalated to nearly forty minutes. Then the lawyers re-entered, after which we were let back in. King was still there, chatting and laughing with Johnnie Cochran and F. Lee Bailey. As we all watched, the door to the holding room opened and Simpson entered the courtroom with Robert Shapiro. Simpson and King looked at each other. 'O. J.,' said King, greeting the defendant. Each put out his hand for the other to shake, but a court officer stepped in and said, 'Please don't do this.' She said it twice more, adding, 'He is a defendant. You can't shake hands in this courtroom.' Rebuffed, King gave a hang-in-there gesture to Simpson. Then Suzanne Childs, the director of communications for the district attorney's office, took King to the other side of the courtroom and introduced him to Marcia Clark and William Hodgman. One reporter turned to me and said, 'I can't believe what I'm watching here.' Leaving as Judge Ito was about to enter, King by mistake started to exit through the door leading to Simpson's holding room. The defendant was heard to say, 'He doesn't want to go in there.' King then redirected himself to the door to the judge's chambers. Two nights later at the Palm, McGinniss and I ran into King and reminded him of the incident. King said, 'Did you hear what O. J. said to me?' We hadn't heard. 'He said, "Thank you for being so supportive."'

THE RAINS CAME. Last year at this time there was the earthquake. Now the skies unleashed their torrents on the city.

It was bound to happen, with all the big egos involved, but it happened at a highly inappropriate time, just before the start of the opening statements. And it didn't make O. J. Simpson's dream team look very good, hanging their dirty linen out for all to see at the very moment their client was about to go on trial for the murder of two people. For some time the backstairs gossip was that the long and solid friendship of Robert Shapiro and F. Lee Bailey had deteriorated into sheer hatred. The breakdown of the friendship had to do with leaks to the press. Shapiro thought Bailey was doing him in. Mike McAlary's January 4 column in the New York *Daily News* brought the matter to a head. It was about Shapiro's Christmas vacation in Hawaii, taken while the rest of the dream team were getting ready for the trial. The piece was funny, but it was guaranteed to cause trouble, and trouble it caused. Shapiro's reaction was like another earthquake. As I understand it, Johnnie Cochran, fearful that the story of dissension in the ranks would leak, gave orders that if the media picked up on the rift the participants were to deny it or say 'No comment.' But Shapiro unloaded to David Margolick of *The New York Times* and said some very hurtful things, the kind of things that cause wounds that don't heal overnight, such as 'his presence before this particular jury adds nothing that can't be done by Johnnie and others on the team' – that sort of thing. Somebody I know with pretty good ins in that group told me that O. J., outraged, said, '"Whose trial is this anyway, mine or those guys'?"' or words to that effect. He was right. He was being upstaged at his own trial. Many of the lawyers critiquing the trial on television predicted that one or the other, Shapiro or Bailey, would have to go.

But these guys are not spin doctors for nothing. They know how to clean up a mess fast. Roosevelt Grier was pulled into the fray again for his second important moment in the role of preacher and spiritual adviser. According to Johnnie Cochran's account at a lunchtime press conference on the main floor of the courthouse, after Rev. Grier conducted a prayer meeting with Simpson's lawyers, all personal difficulties were put aside, and they were once again a solid team, dedicated to obtaining their innocent client's freedom. Ah, the power of prayer. Thereafter came an instantaneous healing of bruised feelings and battered egos. Bailey and Shapiro, performers both, were seen walking arm in arm and laughing like friends again.

And then the trial began.

Heading the teams in the opening statements were two new casts of characters. Of the faces we had been looking at for months during the hearings – Gerald Uelmen, Robert Shapiro, William Hodgman, and Marcia Clark – only Clark was part of the opening. Three of the four major starting players were black: Cochran and his lieutenant, Carl Douglas, for the defense, and Christopher Darden for the prosecution, alongside Marcia Clark. William Hodgman, with whom Clark had worked so closely for so long that they could almost read each other's minds, was rushed to the hospital for what was first reported to be a heart attack but was later down-graded to stress. Two weeks later he returned to the team in a new capacity, as the case manager, but he would no longer appear in court.

Christopher Darden, thirty-eight, a late addition to the prosecution team, is, for my money, the man to watch in this trial. His addition to the team was vigorously protested by the defense, supposedly because he had supervised the grand-jury investigation of Al Cowlings, but the protest probably had more to do with the fact that he is black and brilliant, and that the largely black jury would have him as a counterbalance to Cochran. Like an understudy who has stepped into the star's role, Darden became more effective daily as he hammered home to the jury the litany of spousal abuse in the Simpson marriage. As a black prosecutor trying to convict a black football hero he once worshipped in front of a mostly black jury, he is in a virtually untenable position.

For the defense, Johnnie Cochran, as long predicted, has moved to the head of the team. He is now the man in charge. Cochran is experienced and charismatic, a smooth character, a charmer, a rich and successful man as well as a popular figure in the city. He is also a superb lawyer, highly respected, who possesses the ability to seduce a jury. I am told that juries find him so persuasive that they cast their votes for *him* more than for the clients he represents. From the time he gets off the elevator every morning until he gets back on that elevator at the end of the day, at about five, it's hard to keep your eyes off him. He has style and wit and something to say to everyone who stops him for a comment. He obviously gives thought to his wardrobe each day. Personally, I have never liked brown, pale-blue, or mustard-colored suits, or ties with horizontal stripes, but when he wears them, they work. Behind his trendy glasses, he has very intense eyes, which can crinkle with kindness just as easily as they can freeze you like ice. Carl Douglas, with whom Cochran has had a long association, has also suddenly emerged as a courtroom presence, seeming to outrank the veterans Shapiro and Bailey. And Douglas is right up there with the best of them when it comes to understanding where the camera's pointing.

So is Marcia Clark, when it comes to understanding a theatrical moment. When a sealed box was delivered to her in court, Judge Ito provided her with his own Swiss Army Knife to cut through the tape. Clark held up her hands and put on a pair of surgical gloves as if they were white kid opera gloves before she reached into the box and gently brought forth the dark-blue knitted watch cap found at the crime scene, as well as the famed bloody glove that is one of the central pieces of evidence in the case. At that goose-bump instant, the court broke for a three-day weekend.

EVERY DAY THERE ARE new and provocative stories about the principals in the case, which seem to appear with almost choreographed timing. On January 29, in a story on Johnnie Cochran in the *Los Angeles Times Magazine*, it was revealed, very deep in the article, that Cochran's first wife, Barbara, twice accused him of assaulting her, in 1967 and 1977. The 1967 declaration for a restraining order read, 'My husband violently pushed me against the wall, held me there and grabbed me by the chin. He has slapped me in the past, torn a dress off me, [and] threatened on numerous occasions to beat me up.' With the prosecution opening their case on the issue of domestic violence, the timing could not have been worse. The first wife refused to deny the charges, as Cochran had said she would, but she said that she was happy for Johnnie's success. Subsequently she announced that she is writing a tell-all book about their stormy marriage. Then it appeared elsewhere, in Cindy Adams's *New York Post* column and on one of Geraldo Rivera's television shows, that Cochran had a hitherto unreported twenty-one-year-old son from an affair he had with a Caucasian woman during the time he was married to his first wife.

In one of the great tacky episodes of all time, Cochran's first wife and his white mistress, who goes by the name of Patricia Cochran, joined forces on *Geraldo* to let Cochran have it on the day after he tried to convince the jury that important evidence at the crime scene had been moved or contaminated by the Los Angeles Police Department. Patricia told Geraldo, 'Before they selected the jury I asked him, "Johnnie, what are you going to do?" And he said, "Sweetheart . . . just give me one black person on that jury – that's all I ask, one," and he could get a hung jury.'

Cochran's daughter, Tiffany, from his first marriage, a television news anchor in Myrtle Beach, South Carolina, and his handsome and popular current wife, Dale, to whom he has been married for nearly ten years, have been solid courtroom supports for him.

In Cochran's opening statement, which he delivered with theatrical bravura, he named witnesses his team had failed to make known to the prosecution – a violation of the California reciprocal-discovery law. The prosecution's objections were loud and clear. Judge Ito chastised Cochran by telling the jury to disregard his statements about these witnesses and by allowing Marcia Clark ten minutes to reopen her opening statement – a California first – to refute Cochran. Clark, on target, took only six minutes to make her point.

One of Cochran's witnesses, Mary Anne Gerchas, who claims that she saw four men, none of them Simpson, near the murder scene on the night of the murders, was subsequently arrested on charges of grand theft, credit-card fraud, and defrauding a hotel. Another, Rosa Lopez, a maid at the house next door to Simpson's, who said she had seen Simpson's white Bronco there at the time of the murders, left her job and vanished, apparently, to El Salvador. Later, she was found hiding out in Los Angeles, afraid to appear at the trial. During all this, Cochran hosted a big party for 300 at his Wilshire Boulevard offices to launch his new business-affairs and entertainment divisions.

RON SHIPP IS the former Los Angeles policeman who was a friend of O. J.'s for twenty years, in one of those unequal run-my-errands-for-me sort of friendships that many famous people have. Shipp understood his role perfectly. He knew it was a you-can-use-my-tennis-court-but-you're-not-invited-to-my-party kind of friendship, and he accepted that. On the stand, he was clearly a tortured man, haunted by a death that he believed he might have prevented had he intervened in the domestic violence that he knew had occurred in the Simpson marriage, especially since he had taught about domestic violence at a police academy. In Sheila Weller's book *Raging Heart* and on the stand, he gave his account of what happened on the night after the murders, when he was a visitor in O. J.'s house along with O. J.'s sisters and mother and a few close friends. Shipp said he went upstairs with his friend and stayed with him until he went to bed. It was the conversation before sleep that was the crux of his testimony, when O. J. allegedly asked him how long it would take for the results of the DNA testing to come back from the lab. I'd be suspicious too if someone asked me that the day after a murder. According to Shipp, O. J. also said 'with a chuckle' that he had had dreams about killing Nicole. Shipp, who had sat in on a dozen polygraph tests during his years as a police officer, knew that that sort of statement was often a pre-set alibi for failing a polygraph test. Judge Ito had ruled inadmissible any discussion of Simpson's taking a polygraph, which he allegedly had told Shipp he didn't want to do. Shipp worshiped his friend but believed he was guilty.

I think that I have never seen a meaner face than Carl Douglas's when he went after Shipp in his cross-examination. His eyes bulged almost out of their sockets as he directed a Bela Lugosi gaze on his prey. From a show-biz point of view, it was a great scene, brilliantly acted. Legally, it was less than great. Douglas's attack went on much too long, and it allowed the prosecution to ask Shipp for more and more details about family life in the Simpson household, which in no manner enhanced O. J.'s already tarnished image. Before Shipp's testimony, I hadn't known that O. J. had a life-size statue of himself in his garden, which his son Jason, from his first marriage, once tried to destroy with a baseball bat. (I wonder if that's the same baseball bat that O. J. used when he smashed the windshield of Nicole's Mercedes.) Nor had I known that Jason had a seizure after taking some cocaine when he was sixteen, and that O. J. asked Shipp to find out who the dealer was. If the defense risked going that far with Shipp, imagine their plans for Detective Mark Fuhrman.

SOMETIMES I DON'T UNDERSTAND why the defense team tells us the things they tell us. Take Simpson's book, *I Want to Tell You*, for example, which has become a publishing hit. In it, Simpson discusses his innocence, his children, the media, the judicial system, and racism, in response to letters from the public he has received in jail. According to *USA Today*, the defense team didn't know about his million-dollar book deal until one or two days before Little, Brown announced it. But isn't it a bit disingenuous – to borrow a word from Robert Shapiro, who once used it in court to describe Judge Ito, thereby incurring the judge's wrath and being forced to make an apology – of the defense team to think that we believe they had no idea that the book was being published? Simpson's co-author, Larry Schiller, said on *Larry King Live* that he had visited Simpson in jail about fifteen times. He even taped Simpson in jail. The place for these meetings was a special room made available to Simpson. Schiller, by the way, was on Simpson's material-witness list, so he had access to that room. Although there did not have to be a deputy in the room, there did have to be a lawyer.

Robert Kardashian, from whose house O. J. and Al Cowlings took off in the white Bronco prior to their famous low-speed freeway chase, brokered the book deal

with Little, Brown, along with Leroy 'Skip' Taft, who is
O. J.'s personal lawyer. Kardashian is a rather mysterious but constant presence in the courtroom. Early on,
there was a news shot of him carrying a garment bag
from O. J.'s home on the day after the murders. Later,
it was he who read the famous 'suicide' note on television. Three days after the Bronco chase, Kardashian, a
non-practicing attorney, reactivated his license, which had
expired January 1, 1991. Kardashian sits directly in front
of me with Sara Caplan, a lawyer with Shapiro's office,
and Jo-Ellan Dimitrius, the defense jury consultant.
During those moments when O. J.'s lawyers temporarily
abandon him at the defense table for a sidebar conference,
Kardashian, who has a white streak in his black hair, moves
up next to his great friend and keeps him occupied in
conversation. Kardashian, whose former wife is now
married to Bruce Jenner, is engaged to Denice Halicki,
who frequently sits with the Simpson family. Halicki
herself is involved in litigation concerning the estate of
her late husband, a millionaire stuntman and film-maker
killed three months after their marriage.

On a Friday when no court session was scheduled, I
had lunch at the Grill in Beverly Hills, which is an industry kind of place. Everyone had something to say about
the trial. 'Why aren't you home writing?' I heard someone ask as I passed a table. It was Kardashian, with whom
I had never spoken before. He was smiling, and held out
his hand. We chatted a bit. He's an affable fellow. He was
wearing a mustard-colored jacket, black trousers, and a
black turtleneck. He said the same line that everyone says

who has anything to do with this case: 'Have you ever seen anything like this?' The answer to that one is always the same: 'No.' Columnist Cindy Adams, who seems to have sources in Kardashian's social set, reported that he is a bit of a cutup at parties. She wrote that at one Kardashian played a party joke: a manila envelope which he was carrying suddenly came open and a stiletto knife fell out, bringing down the house with screams of laughter. At another, in his own house, he quieted the room of 100 guests and asked, 'Want to see how O. J. took off on his famous drive? Look to the back of the room.' When the mob turned around there was Al Cowlings, who 'smiled, waved, rose on cue and toddled out the door', according to Cindy Adams. He got into a white Bronco and drove off, again to screams of laughter. I don't get asked to those parties.

Speaking of Al Cowlings, Joe McGinniss recently observed him on an American Airlines flight from Los Angeles. Cowlings was in first class with a bodyguard to keep the curious from talking to him. When the plane landed in New York, he was escorted off the plane as if he were a head of state. What I want to know is who makes such VIP arrangements for Al Cowlings, who is famous mainly for driving O. J. Simpson, with a gun and a passport and something like $8,000 and a disguise, in the white Bronco when he was heading for wherever he was heading in the direction of Mexico on June 17, the day he was supposed to turn himself in to the police? Not to be outdone in the book department, Cowlings reportedly hoped to cash in on his friendship with Simpson by peddling a proposal of *his* version of the story – which denigrated Nicole – for big bucks. A wag in the media room suggested a title for Cowling's book: *I Want to Drive You*. There were no major takers, however, and within a day Cowlings's lawyer announced on CNN that Cowlings had no intention of publishing such a book. Instead, Cowlings announced at a press conference that he was taking a 900 number to give callers his thoughts and feelings about his friendship with O. J. for $2.99 a minute.

So that we won't be short of books on O. J., his sister, Shirley Simpson Baker, is co-authoring the only authorized biography on the Simpson family's life.

THE MAKEUP OF the jury keeps changing. Three jurors have gone, replaced by alternates. A sixty-three-year-old white woman was replaced by a fifty-four-year-old black man after she allegedly became involved in a shoving match with another juror, and accused several black jurors of being pro-O. J. Despite subsequent denials by the court and the white juror concerning the event, the daily admonishment of Judge Ito to the jury not to discuss the case among themselves seems not to be very effective. The resulting jury consists of nine blacks, one white, one Hispanic, and one person of mixed race.

We see things in the courtroom that the camera can't show. Juries are endlessly fascinating to watch. Quite soon, you begin to pick up little traits and characteristics about them. You begin to learn which one has a sense of humor and which one never laughs. You know which ones take notes and which ones don't. You know which one takes a little snooze in his seat in the session after lunch. For some reason, this jury is particularly well dressed. Thus far at least, each has made an effort at grooming, the way people do for an important event. Some days, a male juror wears a perfectly tailored tomato-red gabardine suit, with red shoes and a red tie. It is an eye-catcher. Before the jury was seated, this juror allegedly bet a week's salary with a co-worker that O. J. would be acquitted. Many of them bring books to read during the hours they spend when not in court. There is a man in the front row who carries a book entitled *Makes Me Wanna Holler*, by Nathan McCall, which *The Philadelphia Inquirer* said is 'required reading for anyone interested in American race relations'. There are two alternate jurors with the most elaborate hairdos I've ever seen. They have cascades of intricately intertwined curls falling to their shoulders, sometimes topped off with a bow. They must have to get up at five every morning to prepare themselves for the nine o'clock start of the trial. I wonder what it must be like to live in a hotel with twenty strangers the way they are doing, for months. They can have family visits, but most of the time they are with one another. They are allowed to look at the *Los Angeles Times* only after every reference to Simpson and the trial has been excised by one of Judge Ito's staff. They can watch certain television shows that have been approved, but a deputy has to change the channels. One day in court the judge told them that they were going to have a video of the film *The Flintstones* that night, as though that were a big deal.

When the jurors visited the crime scene at Nicole Simpson's condominium on South Bundy Drive in Brentwood, not only had all vestiges of the gruesome murders long been removed but so had all evidence that she or her children had ever lived there. It is now an empty shell, stripped bare, up for sale. By contrast, at the sumptuous Simpson estate, the beautiful house was dressed like a set. There were fresh flowers, fires burning in two fireplaces, and a Bible lying on a table. Despite prosecutorial objections to the shrine-like atmosphere, Judge Ito allowed most of the props to remain. However, he ordered that a photograph of Simpson's mother be removed from his bedside table, because it had not been there before, and that the homey fires be put out.

DRAI'S ON LA CIENEGA was the place to be for Saturday-night dinner. Like everywhere else, it was abuzz with O. J. By the time my companions and I left, people had come to our table to tell us that the *National Enquirer* was about to publish a picture of Marcia Clark topless, and that the guy who had reported seeing a white Bronco with the first three digits of Al Cowlings's license-plate number near the crime scene on the night of the murders allegedly received a death threat fingered in the dust on his car. O. J., O. J., O. J. He remains the town's main topic of conversation.

Another night, at Eclipse, Fredi Friedman of Little, Brown, which published Simpson's bestseller, *I Want to Tell You*, sat at the table next to that of Michael Viner of Dove Books, which published Faye Resnick's bestseller, *Nicole Brown Simpson: The Private Diary of a Life Interrupted*. Even at staid Chasen's, which has been mobbed since the announcement that it is going to close in April, the Reagan kitchen cabinet, all dining together at one large table, were talking about O. J. At Fiona Lewis's launch party for her new book, *Between Men*, at the West Beach Café in Venice, Sean Penn, Dennis Hopper, and Val Kilmer were all talking about O. J. Everyone has a different perspective. A Beverly Hills butler said that he was disappointed with O. J.'s body in the stripped-to-his-Jockey-shorts photographs shown at the trial to prove that he hadn't been hit by Ron Goldman, whose bruised hands indicated that he may have struck someone before he died.

People at smart dinner parties talk about their fear that the racial issue will be fanned into flame, while being waited on by black waiters and maids. The local joke is about the Beverly Hills woman who asks her maid if she'd kill her if the riots came. The maid replies, 'No, ma'am, but the maid next door might.'

I wonder if it was ever possible for race not to play a part in this story. Certainly it did not fit into the relationship of O. J. and Nicole Simpson. Listen carefully to those tapes. As angry and fearful as their voices were, neither ever hurled a racial slur at the other.

Outside the courthouse, street-corner orators make speeches claiming that the Los Angeles Police Department planted evidence to frame Simpson. It became clear to me during Ron Shipp's testimony that the African-

American and Caucasian members of the media interpreted his testimony in very different ways.

THE THREE FAMILIES involved in the Simpson case, the
Simpsons, the Browns, and the Goldmans, all have assigned
seats. On some days the Browns sit in the front row. On
others, the Goldmans sit there. The Simpsons sit across
the aisle in the front row. For several days in the beginning, Eunice Simpson, O. J.'s mother, was wheeled in. She's
a distinguished-looking lady of seventy-two who carries a
prayer book. One morning, Simpson turned to her from
his seat at the defense table and said, 'Hi, Mom.' He has
a friendly rapport with his two sisters, Shirley and
Carmelita, who are there almost every day. What is very
apparent is that there is a deep bond between Simpson
and his daughter Arnelle, a beautiful young woman of
twenty-six. The relationship of Simpson and his son Jason,
twenty-four, is more complicated. Sometimes Simpson
doesn't seem to get through to him when he looks over.
Jason nods his head in reply, but often does not smile
back.

In a moment of what I thought was real class, two of
Nicole's sisters, Dominique and Tanya, rose from their
seats and went over to speak to Eunice Simpson in her
wheelchair. They then turned and spoke to Jason and
Arnelle. It was an awkward moment, but it was gracefully
performed by all involved. They had, after all, known one
another for seventeen years. When we broke for lunch that
day, Juditha Brown, Nicole's mother, who must have been

a knockout in her day, very briefly touched Eunice Simpson's hand on the arm of her wheelchair as she left the courtroom. I thought to myself, These are all nice people. This was confirmed the next day, when I watched from a distance as Mrs Brown showed Mrs Simpson some snapshots of Justin Simpson's sixth-birthday party. The photos were in an album, and Mrs Brown turned the pages, pointing out to Mrs Simpson who various people were. Then she said to her about their mutual grandson, 'He has the loveliest eyes.' The chasm between the two families will be so great by the end of this trial that none of them will probably ever see one another again. I felt that those two women, who are carrying such tragedy within them, both knew that, and that they were saying good-bye.

ALL O. J., ALL THE TIME

PEOPLE ASK ME every day, 'Don't you get sick of it? Being in there all day every day?' They're talking about the O. J. Simpson trial, which they claim they're sick to death of. O. J. has taken over my life. I start thinking about O. J. before six o'clock every morning, when room service brings me my o. j. and coffee. By that time I'm usually halfway through *The New York Times*, where I read David Margolick on the O. J. Simpson case before I read anything else; then I switch over to the *Los Angeles Times*, where I read Andrea Ford and Jim Newton on the O. J. Simpson case before I read anything else, even though I already know what they're all writing about, because I was sitting in court the day before as it was happening, and watched it on television on the early *and* late news, as well as on *Larry King Live* or any other show that had special coverage. Once I have showered and shaved, it's seven o'clock, time to turn on the television set to see whom Katie Couric and Paula Zahn and Joan Lunden may be interviewing about the case. Then I hear the fax machine making sounds in the other room, and I know it's my office in New York sending me the tabs, the weeklies, Liz Smith, Cindy Adams, Richard Johnson and what *they* have to say about the case today. At 7:35, I'm in my rental car, barreling down Beverly Boulevard as I switch radio stations to hear the latest on the case until I arrive at the downtown Criminal Courts Building on West Temple Street in Los Angeles. Then we in the media line up to get our daily badges, all the while talking about the latest rumors in the O. J. case, or saying things to each other such as 'You were good on *Larry King* last night.' At nine o'clock we walk into the courtroom and take our places in our assigned seats, and then the door to the holding room opens and in comes O. J. Simpson himself, usually surrounded by Johnnie Cochran, Robert Shapiro, and Carl Douglas. We all stare at O. J. to see what kind of mood he's in or to which lawyer he's talking, and we watch him say good morning to members of his family. When Judge Lance Ito comes in, we do not rise, but we do rise on the bailiff's order to do so as the jury enters. Then the trial begins again, and all day long we watch it, except for our lunch break, when we talk about it, saying things such as 'Did you notice if O. J. looked when they showed the picture of Nicole lying in the blood?' The other night, after watching a segment of *Hard Copy* devoted to O. J. and a drug dealer, I went to a friend's house for dinner. I had hardly gotten inside the front door when I was confronted by people who wanted to know what had happened in court that day. I had hoped for a little respite from the topic. I wanted to talk about something else for a change, and volunteered that Ethan Hawke was in the room across the hall from me at the Chateau Marmont, and that Keanu Reeves was in the room next to me, and that I had just seen Johnny Depp being interviewed in the lobby. But nobody cared. Polite nods were the most my movie-star name-dropping got. They all wanted to talk about nothing but O. J. Simpson.

Lady Thatcher would love to hear about the trial.
—Introduction at a dinner for Margaret
Thatcher at Chasen's.

I THINK IT'S SAFE to say that at this moment in time O. J. Simpson is the most famous, the most discussed person in the world. Lady Thatcher was here. She wanted to know about O. J. Mrs Michael York, the wife of the actor, told me that at an ashram in India the guru had said, 'Tell me about O. J.' In the projects, growing up poor with his sisters and brother, brought up by their mother after their father left to pursue another lifestyle, when O. J. Simpson dreamed of being Someone, Someday, he could never have imagined – for it is unimaginable – the extent of the fame that would one day be his. He has become an epic figure, albeit one with an imaginary hunchback. From certain angles, you don't see the hunchback, and he is magnificent, kinglike, beyond Othello even, his handsome face marred only by the sullen arrogance of his expression. But the hunchback is there, the repository for the rage within him toward the woman he is on trial for killing, along with a friend of hers who happened by at an inconvenient moment. Why does he fascinate us so?

> *'You must remember, darling, O. J.'s innocent until proven guilty.'*
> *'Bullshit.'*
> *'Don't mind Polly, darling. She's a great friend of Bob and Linell Shapiro's.'*
>> —POLLY BERGEN, ME, AND JOLENE
>> SCHLATTER at dinner at Drai's.

The O. J. of the trial is a more muted presence in the courtroom than the O. J. of the hearings, when he allowed his exasperation to show through grimaces, eye rolls, and, on occasion, audible comments or angry gestures. No more. Now he's like a trained Thoroughbred, behaving perfectly almost all the time, presumably on instructions from Johnnie Cochran, his slick lead lawyer, who dominates the courtroom. In this passive role Simpson is playing, his inner light has dimmed. Sometimes I feel that he needs verification that his power still exists, outside of the defense team whom he is paying. Recently, by chance, our eyes met. After all this time, it was our first contact, and we held it. The look in his eye was wary at first, as if he was unsure of my sentiments – was I friend or foe? – but then, for a fraction of a second, his expression softened. I saw and felt that famous devastating charm his friends have told me about. If he were not the defendant in a double-murder trial, he would have had me in the palm of his hand.

Apparently, though, Simpson's passivity is only for public consumption. A person close to the defense team told me that he went ballistic when his lawyers were caught out in what seemed an obvious lie over the tape of the interview with the maid Rosa Lopez conducted by defense investigator William Pavelic, which Carl Douglas had told Judge Ito did not exist. After the jury, the spectators, and the media had left the courtroom for the day, Simpson asked to see the whole defense team. His holding room was not big enough for all of them, so they gathered around the defense table in the courtroom. By this time, O. J. had had to change from his trial clothes back into his jailhouse blues. His leg shackles had not been put on yet, but there were cuffs on his wrists, which he kept under the table as he read the riot act to his counsel.

If Rosa's as lousy a housekeeper as she is a liar, I'd hate to see what the Salingers' house looks like inside.
> —MART CROWLEY, playwright, about Rosa Lopez.

Dear Rosa: We love you. We believe you.
> —Banner hanging outside the courthouse on Rosa Lopez's last day on the stand.

One day, O. J.'s neighbors Wolfgang Salinger and his wife, who had employed Rosa Lopez — who lied on the stand but continues to be O. J.'s key alibi witness — came to court. The Salingers and Simpsons had lived side by side in beautiful houses behind gates protected by private security, with landscaped gardens and trees set in beds of ivy. Their maids had been friends. When O. J. waved to the Salingers from the defense table, he looked embarrassed to be in the position they were seeing him in. Another day, he turned around in his seat with a little wave and smiled with that expert manner that stars give photographers at premiers. Then he did it again. And again, as if on cue, I looked back to see to whom he was being so effusively gracious. There was Annie Leibovitz, in the back of the courtroom, her camera to her eye, focusing directly on him. It seems that a signal had been arranged by Leibovitz and Robert Shapiro, who was seated to O. J.'s left. When Leibovitz gave the signal, Shapiro tapped Simpson, who turned and smiled each time.

6–12–1994, the date of the murders. Add up the digits and they come to 32, which was O. J. Simpson's number on his football jersey.
      —Current LA factoid.

The loyalty of the Simpson family is extraordinarily touching. His mother, daughter, son, and nieces, his brother-in-law, his first wife and her current husband, and others have attended the trial, but none have been as stalwart as his two sisters, Shirley Baker and Carmelita Durio. Both San Franciscans, they and Shirley's husband, Benny, are staying in O. J.'s house on Rockingham Avenue. Carmelita attends the trial Monday through Thursday and then goes home to San Francisco for a three-day weekend.

Shirley attends Tuesday through Friday, so one or the other or both are always present in the courtroom for their brother. Most nights they visit him in jail, where Simpson is still a participant in family affairs outside of the case. 'I go back up to San Francisco to make sure my job is still there, and my husband is still there, and my child is still there,' Carmelita told me. At times, talking with her family in the corridor during breaks, Carmelita has a wry twinkle in her eye, and it is easy to imagine that in any other circumstances she would be the life of the party. Shirley Baker has three daughters. On June 12, 1994, two of them, Toni and Tracy, had a double christening in San Francisco for their babies, a boy and a girl, respectively, who were born four months apart. The next day Toni told people at work that she had had a perfect day. Then she heard the news from Los Angeles.

There was a bomb scare one day during lunch, and we couldn't get back into the courthouse for an hour or more. In the scheme of things having to do with this trial, a bomb scare seemed a relatively normal occurrence. This was the third or fourth since the trial had begun. I wandered into Camp O. J., across the street from the courthouse, where all the television stations have their trailers. A friend in the Channel 9 trailer told me I could wait in there until the trial resumed. It turned out that Carmelita Durio was also sitting in the trailer, and we watched David Goldstein on one of the monitors talking about the bomb scare from inside the courthouse. For a while we said nothing as pictures of O. J. appeared on almost all the monitors and that morning's trial news was recapped.

'What's it like for you to be going through all this?' I asked her.

She didn't answer at first, and I thought that maybe she wouldn't answer at all. She looked at me and then looked away. She was wearing dark glasses, but her shoulders told what her eyes didn't. Then she said very slowly, 'I feel like I'm in someone else's nightmare, and one day I'll wake up and everything will be normal again, but it probably never will be.'

> *They are obviously very desperate to engage in such*
> *obvious tactics.*
> —Prosecutor MARCIA CLARK on the
>   defense's failure to hand over notes from
>   a Rosa Lopez interview.

When F. Lee Bailey was asked during a press conference on March 9 whether his cross-examination of Detective Mark Fuhrman would be a character assassination, he replied, 'Hopefully.' The old gladiator, who gained his reputation in the '60s with such celebrated cases as those of Dr Sam Sheppard and Albert DeSalvo, known as the Boston Strangler, and then nearly demolished it when he lost the Patty Hearst case in 1976 and the kidnapped heiress was sent to prison, had been salivating in anticipation of conducting the cross-examination of Detective Fuhrman, about whom the defense had spread the story that he removed a bloody glove from the murder scene at South Bundy Drive and planted it behind Kato Kaelin's room on the Simpson estate in order to frame O. J., because he hated blacks, called them 'niggers', and recoiled at the thought of interracial couples. The defects of Fuhrman's personality were like gold coins for the defense, and Bailey, champing at the bit for his return to the big-time arena, had been preparing his performance for months. 'Any lawyer in his right mind who would not be looking forward to cross-examining Mark Fuhrman is an idiot,' Bailey declared.

Bailey is an old hand at putting cops on trial. In his 1982 drunken-driving trial in San Francisco, one of the longest DWI trials in California history, at which he was represented by his used-to-be-friend Robert Shapiro, Bailey put the police officer who had arrested him on trial, using as witnesses other people who had seen the officer making arrests, all of whom had horror stories to tell about him. Bailey, who had refused to take a blood-alcohol test, was acquitted.

Mark's gonna do just fine, as long as he doesn't lose his temper. I told him he doesn't gain anything by attacking. He has to sit back and take the fire.
   —ANTHONY PELLICANO, private investigator
      for Mark Fuhrman.

Fuhrman's entrance into the courtroom was electric. For eight months he had been portrayed by the defense as the arch-villain of the Simpson case. Stories of his alleged racism had been brilliantly fed to the media by Simpson's lawyers, and had first appeared in an article by Jeffrey Toobin in the July 25 issue of *The New Yorker*, thereby gaining such notoriety and credibility that there was probably not a juror in the box who had not heard them. A similar tactic had been used by the defense in the William Kennedy Smith case in Palm Beach in 1991, when a piece attacking Patricia Bowman, who had brought rape charges against Smith, appeared in *The New York Times*; the two defense teams even employed at least one of the same investigators. The racist profile and the Simpson frame-up have become part and parcel of the persona of Mark Fuhrman. Anticipating his appearance on the stand was like waiting for the late arrival of a television star at a party. People kept looking toward the door. The lawyers kept walking back and forth. Outside the courtroom, bailiffs barked orders for people to step back behind taped lines on the floor, just as they do when the sequestered jury arrives and leaves. When Fuhrman appeared, surrounded by four Los Angeles police officers serving in the role of bodyguards, he looked like nothing so much as the handsome lead in a cop series.

Fuhrman is to the Simpson case what Dr L. Jerome Oziel was to the Menendez case: a major participant with a flawed record of his own, a person on whom hate can be heaped in righteous tones. As Oziel's deplorable ethics distracted jurors from the killer Menendez brothers, so the alleged racism of Fuhrman was meant to distract jurors from O. J. Simpson. Even though the accusations of his having framed Simpson are fanciful, without proof of any sort, the allegations about Fuhrman's life made him fair game to be portrayed by the defense as a man whose deeds are as hateful as the murders Simpson is accused of committing.

But, in this round at least, Fuhrman outfoxed Bailey all the way by remaining cool, calm, and sometimes even witty. It was Bailey – not Fuhrman – who used the ugly n-word twelve times in court. The introduction of racism brought about the most intense and personal fight in the trial, when Marcia Clark called Bailey a liar and Bailey responded in kind. Subsequently, Judge Ito asked for, and received, public apologies from both sides.

Marcia Clark is becoming very Rosalind Russell.
—GORE VIDAL at a Sue Mengers dinner party.

Both the prosecution and the defense have a strong sense of drama. Johnnie Cochran's colorful news bites as he leaves the courthouse most evenings are matched many Friday afternoons by the prosecution's habit of introducing a new cliff-hanger piece of evidence just before the jurors are dismissed for the weekend, which gives them something goose-bumpy to think about until Monday morning, since they are not supposed to discuss the case among themselves. On one such Friday, we saw Mark Fuhrman hold up a heavy-gauge clear plastic bag found in the cargo area of O. J.'s white Bronco, a bag big enough to hold Nicole Simpson's body. The dramatic effect was somewhat diminished when the bag turned out to be standard equipment for holding the Bronco's spare tire. More recently, Detective Philip Vannatter identified a close-up of a cut on the knuckle of the second finger of O. J. Simpson's left hand, which prosecutors believe was the source of blood drops found at both Nicole's condo and Simpson's estate.

This is the first trial I have ever attended where the public sends bouquets of flowers to the participants. One day there were so many arrangements around the desk of Court Clerk Deirdre Robertson that the courtroom had the appearance of a gangster's wake. That day Johnnie Cochran balanced his heart-shaped wreath on the top of his video monitor. Even Simpson's great friend Robert Kardashian received one, and it was reported that a bouquet sent to Chris Darden, whom the *New York Post* referred to as Mister Prosecutie, cost $300. Marcia Clark receives so many bouquets, especially from working mothers, for whom she has become a heroine since her husband went public with his child-custody suit. Clark, however, does not receive her floral tributes in the courtroom; she has them sent up to her office on the 18th floor of the building, and later donates them to Los Angeles's Children's Hospital.

In the circles in which I travel, Marcia Clark is perhaps the most admired member of the legal teams, but her role in this case is a difficult one, made even more difficult by the fact that Gordon Clark, her estranged husband, is seeking primary custody of their two sons, claiming that his wife is never home during this single most important moment of her career. I have found in covering trials that juries tend to dislike female prosecutors, especially if the defendant is male, good-looking, rich, famous, or young, all of which categories Simpson falls into except the last. They have little sympathy for a woman who is trying so hard to send a man to prison, perhaps for life. Sexist? Yes, of course. The jury disliked Moira Lasch, the prosecutor in the Palm Beach rape trial of Willie Smith. The jury disliked Pamela Bozanich in the Van Nuys murder trial of the Menendez brothers. This dislike is unrelated to intelligence or ability; it is simply the nature of the beast. Conversely, the female defense attorney does not have this problem, even though she may be trying to win an acquittal for a guilty defendant. Very often she comes off as a lioness trying to protect her cub.

> *Another life shredded in the name of justice.*
> —MICHAEL FLEEMAN, of the Associated
> Press, about Rosa Lopez.

> *It is hard to laugh at the need for beauty and romance, no matter how tasteless, even horrible, the results of that need are. But it is easy to sigh. Few things are sadder than the truly monstrous.*
> —NATHANAEL WEST, *The Day of the Locust.*

A MANUSCRIPT EXISTS, not yet published, by an undisclosed author from another city, who says about himself that he has written several crime novels. Somehow, through someone who knew someone who knew someone, the book proposal and part of the manuscript fell into my hands. The book deals with the Simpson defense case. It uses real names: Carl Douglas, Johnnie Cochran, Robert Shapiro, and other, lesser players in the ongoing real-life drama. It presents as fact that Detective Fuhrman moved the bloody glove from one location to another, and suggests that he smeared blood from the glove on the inside of Simpson's

Bronco. It also indicates that Fuhrman got hold of the vial of O. J. Simpson's blood drawn by the police, extracted some of it with a syringe, and sprinkled it around the scene of the crime. It describes dark deeds of doctoring evidence in the DNA labs. The book reeks of conspiracy. It is a tract against corruption in the Los Angeles Police Department. It is, in short, quite amazing. When I asked my source, '*Where* did this come from?' I got no answer. It's the old which-came-first-the-chicken-or-the-egg story. Did someone hire a writer to come up with all this? Or did someone possibly feed the writer what to write? Either way, it's a mystery. And there's more to come on this story.

Speaking of sensational books, I took Norma Novelli to dinner at Le Dôme on the Sunset Strip. Norma has four grown children, lives over in Toluca Lake, where she owns a service called Grime Blasters, which removes oil and greasy patches from driveways. I met her at the Menendez trial. Novelli has written a book of astonishing nerve, which Dove Books is bringing out before the second Menendez trial and which has the Menendez defense team up in arms. Perhaps 'written' isn't the right word. 'Conceived of' fits the bill better, since it includes transcripts of Novelli's taped phone conversations with Lyle Menendez. This is her memoir of her four-year fascination and friendship with the young killer. Novelli has played me some of the tapes, and there's only one word to describe them: riveting.

Watching her, before I knew her, I took her to be a lady-in-waiting to Lyle Menendez. Her attachment to him was extraordinary, and she also became a friend of Maria

Menendez, his grandmother. She visited Lyle in jail. She
took him treats. She did the most menial favors for him.
She disrupted her life for him. She knew every one of his
moods, from his best to his worst. She talked to him for
hours on end, from her home to his cellblock. She coun-
seled him on his romances. And she always believed he
was guilty, and she never believed the defense's contention
that the brothers had been abused by their parents, a fact
she shared with Lyle.

Before we left Le Dôme, she asked for her leftovers in
a doggie bag. 'When your book comes out,' I told her,
'you won't have to do *that* anymore.'

*Where I come from, a Chrysler is just like a
limousine.*
—Prosecutor CHRIS DARDEN.

*I'd like you to meet Buddy Monasch. He's Kato
Kaelin's lawyer.*
—JOANNA CARSON at L'Orangerie.

If ever a city cried out for a daily tabloid newspaper,
it's Los Angeles now. The Simpson case has so many fascinating subplots, which are either glossed over or disdained
by the *Los Angeles Times*, but which have a bearing on
the lives of some of the principal figures in the trial.
There's a story of J. R., a rather notorious drug dealer in
West Los Angeles who caters to the famous. 'I almost died
when I heard you mention J. R. on television last night.
We all know who J. R. is,' a well-connected woman once

married to a prominent figure in the film world told me. J. R. claims – and has taken a lie-detector test administered by forensic psychophysiologist Edward I. Gelb to verify his claim – that he received a call on his beeper from Kato Kaelin, whom he calls a regular client, at 8:30 P.M. on the night of the murders; that he met Kato and O. J. Simpson ten minutes later in the parking lot of a Burger King; and that he got into the backseat of O. J.'s Bentley and sold the two men $100 worth of crystal methamphetamine, known as crystal meth. He further claims that he saw Kato do a couple of lines on a mirror in the car, that he then went into Burger King with a twenty that Kato had given him to pick up a couple of Whoppers because O. J. didn't want to ingest in front of him, and that when he returned they told him the stuff was 'dynamite'. There's the story of Patricia Cochran, a former mistress of Johnnie Cochran and the mother of his only son, who is suing him for palimony. She is represented by the celebrity divorce attorney Raoul Felder, and Cochran has hired Larry Feldman, a past president of the Los Angeles County bar, who represented the boy who made sexual-molestation charges against Cochran's client Michael Jackson and won a multimillion-dollar settlement, to represent him in the suit. There is the story of the brother of prosecutor Chris Darden, who is a crack addict with a criminal record, so alienated from his parents and siblings that his mother sometimes leaves food for him on the front porch of the family home in Richmond, California. There is the story of Denise Brown, Nicole's sister, and her alleged romance with Anthony Fiato, identified as a former mobster turned

FBI informant. Even Judge Ito has made it into the tabloids.
A college roommate remembers the judge running naked
through the halls of their dormitory at UCLA on the
anniversary of the bombing of Pearl Harbor yelling,
'*Banzai! Banzai!*' One way or another, everybody's famous
in this story, but revelations such as these about their
personal lives rarely make it into the local papers.

> *My involvement in this case is an accident of
> geography.*
> > —PABLO FENJVES, screenwriter, who heard
> > Nicole Simpson's Akita bark – indicating
> > the likely time of the murders – and
> > described the sounds as a plaintive wail.

> *People who say things get hurt. You're dead,
> motherfucker. You are dead.*
> > —Messages left on Pablo Fenjves's answering
> > machine.

'Have you ever heard of something called a Colombian
necklace?' asked Johnnie Cochran.

'I believe so,' replied Detective Tom Lange.

A Colombian necklace is a throat slit from ear to ear.
A Colombian necktie is a throat slit from ear to ear with
the tongue pulled out through the slit and flopped over
the chest. It is a payback to one who talks.

The hardest telephone number in town to get is Faye
Resnick's, but I know somebody who knows her, so I called
him to ask her to call me, and she did within fifteen

minutes. It was on the day that Johnnie Cochran suggested that Resnick, one of Nicole Simpson's best friends, who wrote the hit book about her, may have been the cause of her death. I wanted to know how Resnick reacted when Cochran suggested to Lange that the killers' target was really Faye Resnick, because she had been freebasing cocaine in Nicole's condominium and hadn't been able to pay her drug bills.

'Were you watching?' I asked Resnick.

'I was, but I couldn't continue watching that travesty of justice. Cochran wants Detective Lange to look like an asshole.'

'Does it worry you, having this tossed in your lap?'

The fact is, Faye Resnick hates O. J., and O. J. hates her. The irony of ironies is that Resnick could end up being O. J.'s salvation if Cochran ever gets the jury to believe the preposterous theory that a Colombian drug cartel had two people slashed to death over a woman with what she says was a $30-a-day habit.

'I am so nervous for my child,' Resnick told me. 'They feed those kooks out there with false information. This is typical O. J. behavior. Nicole always said he would do every-thing in his power to get away with it, but even I didn't know he had *this* much power.'

I went back in the house and woke up the children and got them dressed and the girl opened the garage door for us.

> —Officer ROBERT RISKE, the first police officer at the crime scene on South Bundy Drive.

The Browns have been less frequent courtroom visitors of late. Kim Goldman, the sister of Ron Goldman, and Patti Goldman, his stepmother, are there every day. They are extremely popular with the media. The Goldmans and the Simpsons do not interact at all, but the Browns and the Simpsons do. I have seen Lou Brown, Nicole Simpson's father, kiss Carmelita Durio and speak in a friendly manner to Shirley Baker. I have seen Jason Simpson, O. J.'s son by his first marriage, talk in a friendly manner to Denise Brown. I learned from Larry Schiller, who is the co-author of O. J.'s book, *I Want to Tell You*, that Jason frequently goes to visit his half-brother and -sister, Justin and Sydney Simpson, who now live with Lou and Juditha Brown in Dana Point in Orange County, seventy miles from Los Angeles.

Of the Brown family, Denise is the most accessible. One day during a break, we were sitting on the same bench in the corridor. It was a couple of days after Robert Riske had been on the stand. I said to her, 'I am haunted by what Officer Riske said about waking up Sydney and Justin in the middle of the night. What terror those kids must have felt, being told to get dressed by a cop in a uniform.'

If Denise likes you, she is very forthcoming on any subject. Once, she said to me in the courtroom, with her hand cupping her mouth. 'This trial of the century is turning into the biggest joke of the century, and you can quote me on that.' Her emotions are right out there. She cries, she laughs, she snorts with derision, she smiles with approval. She likes or she doesn't like. There are no blurs with her. You know just where you stand at all times. Now she told me, 'Sydney said that she knew something had happened to her mother. She said that to Justin in the police car on the way to the station.' Carl Douglas walked by as we were talking. She motioned her head in his direction. 'They want to put her on the stand.'

'Who?'

'Sydney.'

'Why?'

'She told them at the police station that her mother was crying on the telephone with a friend.'

I looked at her. In this trial of daily dramatic surprises, I was trying to visualize the courtroom appearance of the beautiful nine-year-old Sydney Simpson, who would be seeing her father for the first time since he held her hand at her slain mother's funeral.

But Denise put a stop to that thought. 'Over my dead body,' she said, walking away.

THE LADY VANISHES

When he gets this crazed, I get scared . . . He gets a very animalistic look in him. All his veins pop out. His eyes are black, just black, I mean cold, like an animal.

— NICOLE SIMPSON to police who responded to her 911 call after O. J. Simpson kicked in her door.

I T IS A FACT OF LIFE that victims get lost in murder trials as the focus of attention shifts to the defendant in the courtroom. No issue – not even the holes made by a stapler in a police-department form – is too insignificant to tie up a trial and distract jurors from what they are there to hear. In the trial of Lyle and Erik Menendez, days at a time would go by without a mention of the brutally slain victims, Kitty and Jose Menendez, while the defense concentrated on the tacky private life of the psychologist to whom the brothers had confessed their guilt – as if discrediting him lessened the seriousness of the killings the defendants were on trial for. The victims are, after all, dead, and the shock of their deaths has long since been absorbed, except by their families and close friends.

It is also a fact that the defendant becomes a sympathetic figure in many people's eyes. We are experiencing that increasingly in Department 103 of the Criminal Courts Building in Los Angeles. The charismatic star O. J. Simpson dominates the proceedings from the moment he makes his entrance into the courtroom each morning, totally aware of the effect his presence makes. His cadre of lawyers, as well as one of the deputies assigned to guard him, are deferential to him. His every reaction, from his frequent exasperation to his occasional laughter, captivates the attention of the room. When photographs of the slashed victims, Nicole Brown Simpson and Ron Goldman, lying in grotesque positions in gallons of blood, are flashed on the large screen in the courtroom, observers no longer recoil in horror. We have become used to them.

Kato Kaelin, to whom Simpson gave a free room in the guest quarters of his Brentwood estate, amused the defendant when he was on the stand. Simpson's obvious pleasure at Kaelin's antics enraged the family of Ron Goldman, who were sitting next to me. Their anger was so intense that I thought I could feel the heat from it. They stared at Simpson as if willing him to turn and look in their direction so that he could see their hatred. But O. J. knows where not to look in the courtroom. He knows where the friendly faces are. The deputy mentioned above, who sometimes jokes with Simpson, berated a cousin of

Goldman's one day when she giggled at an audible stomach growl coming from Patti Goldman, Ron's stepmother. 'If you do that one more time, you'll have to leave the courtroom,' he told the terrified young woman.

You can convict $10 million.
   —Hollywood screenwriter IVAN MOFFAT at a
   dinner party at Mrs Jerry Wald's.

The two juries in the Menendez trial could not arrive at verdicts even though the used-to-be-rich killers admitted firing all those shots into their parents' faces, heads, and bodies, and the resulting nonverdicts continue to bewilder a great portion of this city. The fact that the same prospect exists again in the double-murder trial of O. J. Simpson has caused further bewilderment, if not rage, here in Los Angeles, brought on by the revelations of the most recently dismissed juror, Jeanette Harris, who had failed to remember to include on her juror's questionnaire that she had claimed in the past to have experienced domestic abuse, which is a cornerstone of the prosecution's case. Apparently angered by her dismissal, the disgruntled Harris rushed to anchorperson Pat Harvey of LA's Channel 9 – they share a dentist, who arranged the meeting – to secure the instant fame available to anyone involved in this trial. Barbara Walters got her next. Larry King got her after that. Harris pooh-poohed her past domestic-abuse claim against her husband, which she said she had forgotten; accused a Caucasian juror of kicking her; said that the prosecution was spinning its wheels, and

at the same time lauded defense attorney Johnnie
Cochran; told of her admiration for the way O. J. was
handling himself in court, 'whether he did it or not'; and
stated that sheriff's deputies guarding the jury were creating racial tensions by showing favoritism to the three white
female panelists when the jury shopped, watched videos,
or used the gym. Most important, she predicted that the
trial would end with a hung jury. It was not an original
thought; others have believed that, even while hoping that
it would not be so. Harris dispelled that hope. The *Los
Angeles Times* published a cartoon by Mike Luckovich in
which the jury foreperson says, 'Judge Ito, we the jury
regret we are unable to reach a verdict,' to which a sweat-
ing, harried Judge Ito replies, 'YOU'RE NOT SUPPOSED
TO BE DELIBERATING YET!'

MANY PEOPLE feel that Johnnie Cochran won the case the
day the jury was seated. The prosecution made a serious
miscalculation during jury selection in thinking that black
women would be sympathetic to the prosecution because
of the issue of domestic abuse. Nicole Simpson's cries on
the 911 tapes were not as shocking to black people as they
were to whites. An African-American woman married to
a Caucasian wrote me, 'I believe O. J. isn't guilty; my
husband believes he is. In our eight years of marriage,
this is the only disagreement we've had on an issue related
to race. I feel that you, like my husband, are unable to
understand a black man's rage the way that blacks themselves understand it. In us, a black man's shouts do not

produce the same shock that they do in the white community. Sometimes these shouts accompany physical abuse, but very often they do not. Rarely do they accompany murder. So to black people, evidence of O. J.'s rage doesn't translate to a belief in his guilt.'

NO ONE DENIES that the life of sequestered jurors in a long trial is a difficult one. They live in isolation from their families, friends, and jobs, and are admonished several times each day not to talk about the only topic that they all have in common. Their pre-taped television is monitored by deputies, and their newspapers are stripped of all mention of the trial. For the Simpson jurors, Judge Ito has gone out of his way to arrange special treats. Roger Williams has entertained them with a concert. Richard Koshalek, the director of LA's Museum of Contemporary Art, has arranged a private tour for the group. Mr Blackwell, the fashion maven who brings out an annual Worst-Dressed Women list, has lectured to them. Shirley Jones is scheduled to sing for them, and Jay Leno and the Tonight Show Band have given them a private performance, minus his nightly O. J. jokes and the five Dancing Itos.

On April 20, the jury was in jeopardy one more time: a female juror wanted to depart the diminishing panel. A very pretty African-American flight attendant of twenty-five, she told Judge Ito she couldn't take it anymore. 'It's either them or me,' she said about certain deputies assigned to the jury. Apparently not wanting to lose her, the judge replaced the deputies. It turned out to be a rash decision and caused a furor, both from the head of the sheriff's department and, more surprisingly, from thirteen of the jurors, both black and white, who wanted them to stay. In what is said to be a legal first, the jurors revolted and would not sit in the jury box. When they arrived in the courthouse, thirteen of the eighteen were dressed in black, as a protest. They marched in single file down the corridor, looking neither left nor right, as in a funeral procession. Maybe it would have been better to let the juror who wanted to leave go, even though that would have reduced the number of alternates to five. She sits with her eyes cast downward most of the time, hardly ever taking in the action or writing any notes. But Judge Ito saved the day. After private meetings with individual jurors, the rebellion was quashed, harmony was restored, and the trial shakily resumed on April 25.

'THE POLICE NEVER READ *Crime and Punishment*,' said Josh Greenfeld, the screenwriter and author of *A Place for Noah*, about his autistic son. Greenfeld has nothing to do with the trial, except as an observer. That day we had met by accident in the courthouse and listened to Johnnie Cochran's press conference after the dismissal of juror Jeanette Harris. Cochran said that he feared that the prosecutors were having his witnesses followed. It was ominous. Mistrial was in the air. Greenfeld invited me out to lunch, where he talked about O. J. and Dostoyevsky in the same breath. 'They arrested O. J. too quick. They should have let him dangle for five or six months, like Raskolnikov. They should have kept bringing him in, talking to him, asking him questions. If he ran, they'd know where he went. If he committed suicide, there wouldn't have to be a trial. Maybe he'd break. Maybe he'd confess. The cops moved too quick.'

'DESPAIR' WAS THE OPERATIVE WORD for the prosecution team as they watched criminalist Dennis Fung squirm under the relentless cross-examination of Barry Scheck, whose courtroom expertise surpassed that of every other member of the defense team thus far. During the five days that the attack went on, the prospect of defeat was written in the slump of the shoulders of Marcia Clark, Christopher Darden, and Hank Goldberg. Fung, who wilted more each day, was unprepared for the superbly crafted onslaught aimed at destroying his credibility and competence. Scheck, who possesses the requisite mean streak and unpleasantly curled lip of the successful defense attorney, was not satisfied with mere victory in felling Fung for his failure to collect evidence properly at the crime scene. In a cross-examination sometimes painful to watch – especially with Johnnie Cochran, looking like the cat that ate the canary, beaming his approval from the defense table – Scheck verbally kicked and humiliated his victim with the insistent implication that if Fung was so inept in gathering evidence, O. J. Simpson was therefore innocent.

In the corridor during a break, defense-camp jubilation was in the air. Johnnie Cochran sang, 'We're having

Fung, we're having Fung', on his way to the men's room. Inside the courtroom, Robert Shapiro handed out fortune cookies to some of the reporters, saying, 'These are from Hang Fung Restaurant.' My fortune cookie read, 'Give time and thought to all that you do.' I think Shapiro should have gotten that one, because once the story of the fortune cookies hit the wire services, he was in Dutch with the Asian-American community. Privately, he asked Fung to accept his apology, which Fung reportedly declined, and then made a public apology to the court and to his 'friends in the Asian-American community' prior to a scheduled courthouse news conference and protest by Asian-Americans.

Meanwhile, Dennis Fung – beaten, bothered, and bewildered – stood by, waiting for more of the same punishment. During the break, he reportedly went up to Scheck and asked, 'Are you going to buy me a beer when this is all over?' Scheck smiled but did not reply. An anonymous person sent Fung flowers with a card that read, 'Stay strong. It'll be over soon.'

Then Barry Scheck went too far. Not willing to quit when he was ahead, he got greedy. And by going for more he diminished the brilliant impact he had made. His attempt to tie Fung into a conspiracy/cover-up with Detectives Fuhrman, Vannatter, and Lange to frame O. J. Simpson for the double murder was as patently absurd as the defense's other preposterous theory, that Nicole Simpson and Ron Goldman were slashed to death by Colombian drug dealers who really meant to kill Faye Resnick. Watching Scheck, I wondered how he could keep a straight face. At one moment, the defense was saying that the Los Angeles police were so hopelessly incompetent that they had contaminated all the evidence at the crime scene. The very next moment, it was accusing the same hopelessly incompetent officers of masterminding a brilliant frame-up of Simpson, complete with planted blood and glove, all conceived of on the spot.

In the end, the mood in the courtroom changed. Sympathy shifted to the beleaguered Fung, who took his punishment like a man. As he departed the courtroom after nine days on the stand, Johnnie Cochran rose to shake his hand. Shapiro gave him a half-embrace. Even Simpson, whom no one is supposed to touch, gave him a dazzling smile and shook his hand. Curious gestures all, directed toward a man they had just implied was a co-conspirator.

This story has ruined fiction. No one would believe it.
    —CALLIE KHOURI, Academy Award-winning screenwriter for *Thelma & Louise.*

Such strange things happen on a daily basis here. One night when I returned to the hotel, there was a message from someone named Mary, who didn't leave her last name. 'John Gotti at the Marion prison in Illinois put a contract out on O. J. Sorry I couldn't call you in person, but I'm traveling.' I took it to be a hoax, but I couldn't think of a single Mary I know who has that kind of sense of humor. The message refused to be dismissed from my mind. Suppose, I thought to myself, just suppose it *wasn't* a hoax. Such things do happen in the prison system. So I faxed the message to Judge Ito. So far, no word back from His Honor.

It doesn't seem strange at all in this trial that the coroner reportedly waved a gun in his workplace and told people he wanted to kill nine or ten lawyers. Or that the mother of Allan Park, the limousine driver who was such a good witness for the prosecution, was the lawyer for Patricia Krenwinkel of the Manson gang, who has served twenty-five years so far for her part in the murders of Sharon Tate and her friends, during Krenwinkel's most recent parole hearing. Or that a man wearing a dress, earrings, and pearls caused a disruption in the courtroom and was dragged out by a couple of bailiffs. Or that the prosecution suggested that the defense might want Nobel Prize winner Dr Kary Mullis, one of their DNA experts, to go into detox before testifying because of his use of LSD.

> *'I think I'll go back to New York for a week during DNA,'* I said to my friend Richie Berlin, an ardent follower of the trial on television, who lives in Beverly Hills.
> *'Chrissie's going to get her face lifted during DNA,'* she replied.

Those close to Simpson tell me that he wants to take the stand, and F. Lee Bailey said on David Frost's show that he and Cochran will probably recommend that he do so. If he does, all of America will stop work to watch. 'It is in his nature,' said one person. He's a showman. He's used to the cheers of the crowd. He understands the art of dazzling, whether it's making an eighty-yard run, or talking a police officer out of giving him a ticket, or hitting on the prettiest girl at the party. It's a scene he would play directly to the twelve people who count.

Whether Simpson takes the stand or not, it has occurred to me and many others that the possibility that he could walk exists, a possibility I considered highly unlikely at the start. During a lunch in the Japanese garden of the New Otani Hotel, near the courthouse, I remarked to two writer friends that I couldn't imagine what Simpson's life would be like if he went free, other than that it would be very different from the life he had lived prior to the murders. We agreed that he would no longer have commercial endorsements, and that he would not be starring in any television series. I said that the doors of the elite country-club world, in which he once moved so gracefully, would be closed to him. One of my companions, it turned out, was actually quite up on O. J.'s plans should he get off. Some months ago, I reported that in such an event there was a pay-per-view deal in the works that could net him $10 million, a sum that would pay off his lawyers and leave him with more than enough to resume a life of luxury. The program is still very much a possibility, and I now learn that it could net him $20 million. It would not be done until ten days after his release. It would feature his children from both marriages, his family and friends, and his lawyers, and the interviewer

– not yet picked – would be Barbara Walters or someone
of comparable stature. After that, he would drop out of
the spotlight for two years, raise his children on a ranch,
and then return slowly to Los Angeles to restart his life.
It sounds so logical, so planned. But I couldn't help thinking to myself, What about Nicole? What about Ron? Do
we just forget about them?

*A lady who attended the Pediatric AIDS Foundation
benefit told me it was the last time she saw O. J.
before the murders. That was the benefit Kato
talked about on the stand, to which O. J. had taken
Sydney and Justin, and Kato had taken his own
daughter, Tiffany. The lady told me that O. J. had
said to her, 'If you see two white-looking kids,
they're mine.'*

'What do you think of Kato?' For days, during Kato
Kaelin's time on the witness stand, everywhere I went
people asked me that. Kaelin struck a nerve in a certain
group in this town, the group involved with fame and
celebrity, for he represents a type well known in that
community. A lot of stars have Katos around. They have
an above-servant-below-family status in a household, and
most of them are content to bask in other people's glory.
From here on in, 'Kato' will be the word used to describe
a hanger-on who is looking for fame himself, if it should
happen to come his way through the association with his
benefactor, but who is not working very hard to make it
happen. Kato Kaelin is the quintessential example of that

type. He is Eve Harrington in grunge.

Nicole Simpson's murder brought about Kaelin's rendezvous with fame. Nicole had introduced him into the family fold. She and Faye Resnick met him and his friend Grant Cramer in Aspen. Cramer is the son of socialite Stuart Cramer and fifties film star Terry Moore, who claims to have been married to Howard Hughes. Nicole had a guesthouse for rent, and Kato was looking for a place to live. He didn't have enough money to pay the $450 a month she was asking, so they worked out an arrangement whereby he could make up the difference by performing baby-sitting chores. Nicole wanted a guy around the house. She told her friends that she was nervous. She thought O. J. had people looking in her windows at her.

For a while, it was great for Kato too. His daughter, Tiffany, could visit him on weekends, and Nicole's kids, Sydney and Justin, liked him so much that they named their dog after him. It was Kato the dog's incessant, plaintive wails, heard by a neighbor, the screenwriter Pablo Fenjves, that helped establish the likely time of the murders. It was Kato the dog that walked through a pool of Nicole Simpson's blood and went looking for someone to discover her body before her children did.

One thing you have to say about the guy: for an actor going out on the biggest audition in the history of show business, a public performance in front of the nation, with every casting director in Hollywood tuned in to watch him, he didn't go out of his way to make an impression in the hair-and-clothes department. But he had charm, and there was an easy, likable quality about him. When he was walking up to the stand, he said 'Oh, hi!' in the friendliest manner to several of the people he had seen covering the trial on television, such as Cynthia McFadden of ABC. When he was on the stand, he said a few funny things. There is a juror in the back row who seems angry at the world. 'Grim' is the word for her. Even she laughed at Kato, in her first and only laugh at the trial thus far. Ultimately, though, he wasn't all that charming. Marcia Clark turned on him and had him declared a hostile witness, suggesting that he knew more than he was saying. What he said on the stand and what the prosecution believed he had told his old friend Grant Cramer, with whom he stayed briefly after the murders, were inconsistent. I find it interesting that O. J.'s first lawyer, Howard Weitzman, his secretary, Cathy Randa, and O. J. himself all spoke with Kato within twenty-four hours of the murders. I don't suppose we're ever going to find out what those telephone calls were about.

Kato soon passed into a new phase of his fame. Donna Shalala, the secretary of health and human services, got his autograph at a Radio and Television Correspondents dinner in Washington. Barbara Walters dined with him at Drai's and interviewed him on television. He was on Larry King's show. There were other television offers. And people in Hollywood were amazed that there were no Kato Kaelin jokes at the Academy Awards. That's fame. Not everyone finds Kato a perfect darling, though. One who doesn't is Juditha Brown, Nicole Simpson's mother. She shook her head as we were leaving the courtroom for a morning break one day when he was on the stand. 'If only he'd tell the truth,' she said. When I asked her in the corridor what she thought of him, she was cautious.

'He's a nice guy,' she said, but her voice didn't carry much enthusiasm. 'The kids loved him. Sometimes I thought he played too hard with the kids. He got them too worked up, and I couldn't get them to calm down to go to bed. I have nothing against him, except that he didn't move with Nicole but went with O. J. instead. Nicole was very hurt when he did that. When Nicole was moving to Bundy, he helped her. He came over to hug me,' she added, 'but I wouldn't, because I thought he had betrayed Nicole.'

Predictably, Kato quickly blew it. Although he told Marcia Clark under oath that he was not writing a book, it turned out that he had sat for sixteen hours of taped interviews for a book with co-author Mark Eliot, saying things, according to Eliot, that contradicted what he said on the stand. Eliot accused Kaelin of perjuring himself, and turned the tapes over to Marcia Clark. Prosecutor Chris Darden in a sidebar suggested the possibility of impeachment.

ANOTHER NONFAN OF KATO'S is Cici Shahian, who was a great friend of Nicole's. She thinks Kato is an opportunist who moved on from Nicole when he got a better offer. The offer came from O. J., who didn't want Kato living under the same roof as Nicole, so he invited him to live free in his guesthouse. He'd have a pool, a tennis court, a basketball court, and a Jacuzzi. And he could say he lived at O. J. Simpson's house – very important in Kato's crowd.

Shahian is a first cousin of O. J.'s friend Robert Kardashian, who was videotaped walking off the Simpson estate on Rockingham with O. J.'s Louis Vuitton bag the day after the murders, and who later read O. J.'s 'suicide' note on national television, after O. J. had taken off from Kardashian's house for the famous freeway chase with Al Cowlings at the wheel of the white Bronco. Shahian and Kardashian are very definitely on opposite sides in this case.

Cici Shahian told me a story: One day, shortly before the end, when she and Nicole were jogging on the green of San Vicente Boulevard in Brentwood, they passed Kato. Nicole wouldn't speak to him. She called him a turncoat for walking out on her and moving in with O. J. She also said that nothing in life is free when it comes to O. J. She said that she would go out someplace and Kato would be there. She thought that O. J. had sent him to report on whom she was with. O. J. sent people to spy on her. She said she saw Kato in the clubs too often 'for a guy who didn't have a dollar'. She knew O. J.'s tactics, his MO. 'He's got me followed again,' she said. 'He knows every-thing.'

Nicole told Cici, 'I'm afraid my friends are going to be bought. Like before, in the divorce, he tried to buy my friends. He's going to kill me and get away with it, and charm the world, because he's O. J. Simpson.'

Shahian told me, 'That's what Nicole said to me one

week before she was killed. She knew. She foresaw what was going to happen. She just didn't know what day it was going to happen . . . She had her will in order. She documented her beatings.'

A MAN WHO had seen me on television contacted me, identifying himself as Ron X, the lookout for J. R., the drug dealer to the stars who claims he sold crystal methamphetamine to O. J. and Kato in the parking lot of a Burger King on the night of the murders. 'J. R. dresses up. I masquerade as a homeless guy, but I graduated from college and have an IQ of 160. How many homeless people have you met who make $200,000 a year?' The $100 bill that he and J. R. say O. J. paid for the crystal meth with has, according to Ron X, been turned over to the prosecution. He alleges that there are fingerprints of O. J.'s and crystal-meth residue on the bill. 'This drug is more dangerous than any other. A good two lines would keep you up for three days. I got out of it for that reason. I don't sell it anymore.'

A girlfriend of mine had a three-way with O. J.
       —Start of a conversation with a stranger at
          artist Paul Jasmin's birthday party.

F. Lee Bailey, who reintroduced the word 'nigger' into our lives with his marathon name-drop of the same during his cross-examination of Detective Mark Fuhrman – which he told Cynthia McFadden on *20/20* was a great success, approved by both O. J. and Johnnie Cochran – celebrated with a St Patrick's Day dinner at the Beverly Hills home and gallery of Barbara DeVorzon, a prominent Los Angeles art dealer. It was a fancy affair. Approximately thirty for dinner. Place cards. Corned beef and cabbage on the menu. The entire defense team was invited, except for Robert and Linell Shapiro. No one need be reminded that Shapiro and Bailey are not the presidents of each other's fan club. Their mutual loathing was not lessened when Shapiro – on-camera of course – distanced himself from his colleague's introduction of race into the Fuhrman cross-examination and turned up wearing a police pin on his lapel. At the last minute, Johnnie Cochran and his wife, Dale, backed out of Bailey's party. Cochran, I am told, thought his presence might make it look as if he were taking sides in the fray. But the Cochrans' place cards were not removed from the table. Recently, Bailey, who is known around the trial as Flee, has remained out of sight much of the time. Has Flee fled? No. Wendy Stark saw him having lunch at the Bistro Garden in Beverly Hills with Lee Iacocca just a couple of days before Iacocca and Kirk Kerkorian made their $22.8 billion bid for Chrysler.

CICI SHAHIAN HAS two great friends, who were also great friends of Nicole's, Robin Greer and the famous Faye Resnick, who wrote *Nicole Brown Simpson: The Private Diary of a Life Interrupted*, the memoir that became a bestseller, although the Brown family has steadfastly withheld its endorsement of it. One night Shahian invited me to have dinner with the three of them at her new apartment in a building in Beverly Hills where I lived in the '70s. It was a strange feeling to look across the courtyard into my old apartment. Michael Viner, the president of Dove Audio/Books, was also there, but he left early, saying he was meeting Jack Nicholson at the producer Robert Evans's house, where they were going to run *Muriel's Wedding*. Viner published Resnick's book, and Shahian works for him at Dove.

It was Shahian's first dinner party in the new apartment, and she had hostess jitters, because she didn't think her new stove was working properly. It worked fine. The lasagne was great. There was a fire in the fireplace, candles on the table, and candles on the mantel. We had a wonderful time.

I told them that I had heard from Art Harris of CNN that there was going to be a show on the next night which would deal with O. J.'s cocaine use, in which several people, including a cousin of Nicole's named Rolf Baur and a chauffeur named Mark Burris, who once drove for O. J., would tell of taking cocaine with Simpson. Drugs, which many people feel played a part in what happened on the fatal Sunday night of June 12, 1994, have been a subject avoided thus far in the trial. For reasons unknown, the prosecution appears reluctant to introduce it into the case. When we got down to some serious talking, Faye Resnick, who was in rehab on the night of the murders, opened up on O. J. and drugs. 'I used to do coke with him . . . I believe he was high on crystal meth that night. The man used to do everything,' she said. 'But he was a periodic. He could stop for a few months, have three days of binge-ing, and then go off and drink.'

All three ladies really loved Nicole. She was their friend, and they miss her. They laughed talking about her. They cried talking about her. They said that she always felt that she was unimportant, that she lived in O. J.'s shadow. He was always the star, the center of the universe. 'If he walked into a restaurant and was not noticed, he would raise the volume of his voice so people would look at him,' said Resnick. 'He didn't like Europe, because he wasn't recognized there. He took Nicole on the Orient Express. He loved the Express, but he hated Europe.'

Sometimes they forgot I was there and just talked among themselves, all speaking at the same time in louder and louder voices, understanding one another in the way that friends do. Nicole, who had seemed elusive to me – a beautiful face with wary eyes in a vast array of photo-graphs – began to emerge as a person. They said she used to say 'Hi, guys' every time she would meet up with them. All of them mimicked the sound of her voice and the wave of her hand as she said that. They all said that Nicole knew that O. J. was going to kill her. She had told each one of them. It is a fact that haunts them all.

'Kato's fame came about through the death of Nicole, who didn't even like him,' said Robin Greer, dismissing the very thought of the man. 'I've known O. J. for seven-teen years, since I was fifteen,' she said. She had been a school friend of the sister of O. J.'s first wife, Marguerite. Greer, an actress, is the niece of Jane Greer, a cool and

sophisticated leading lady at RKO during the '40s and
'50s, when she played opposite Robert Mitchum in the
film noir classics *Out of the Past* and *The Big Steal.*
Tall, blonde, handsome, funny, sad, Robin Greer was once
married to real-estate mogul Mark Slotkin, who later sold
their Beverly Hills house on Elm Drive to Jose and Kitty
Menendez, who were killed there a year or so later by their
two sons. Slotkin took the stand during the first Menendez
trial and may possibly take the stand during the Simpson
trial. Greer said she wanted to move away from Los
Angeles. 'A lot of people who used to be really nice to me
don't even speak to me now,' she said. All three women
feel an isolation from former friends who have sided with
O. J. That feeling began on the day of the funeral.

'We walked up to pay our respects to the family,' said
Shahian. 'O. J. was right there. We all knew in our hearts
that he had done it, but we all hugged him. He gave each
of us a different message. He said to Faye, "You know, I
loved her too much." He said to me, 'Please help Arnelle
take care of the children" . . . At the funeral, I sat down,
Cora Fischman sat next to me, then Faye and Kris Jenner.
Who sits next to me on the other side but Kato. He never
looked at me. I said, "Kato, what happened?" He never
looked me in the eye. I told Cora, "This guy knows something. He won't look at me."'

THERE WAS A VIEWING of Nicole's body in an open casket
on the day before the funeral. Robin Greer told me, 'She
didn't look anything like herself. She looked old and

unhappy. It wasn't like looking at Nicole.' Greer said that
Robert Shapiro showed up with O. J. Shapiro said to
Juditha Brown, Nicole's mother, 'Are you sure the phone
call was at a quarter to eleven?' Juditha had initially made
a mistake remembering the time of her call to her daughter to tell her she had left her glasses at the Mezzaluna
restaurant. If it had been at 10:45, that would mean that
O. J. couldn't have committed the murders. Juditha, they
told me, wanted to believe that O. J. didn't do it.

'Nicole was secretive,' said Greer, who begged her not
to return to O. J. 'She told me about his abuse, but she
didn't tell me she was seeing O. J. again.'

'Nicole was somewhat of an enigma,' agreed Resnick.

'Nicole felt that O. J.'s abusiveness to women had something to do with his father being gay,' said Greer. 'Nicole
called O. J.'s mother after one of the beatings to ask her
if she had been beaten by her husband. She wanted to
know if it ran in the family.'

Shahian said, 'Nicole didn't want the kids to know she
was fighting with O. J. on the phone. She would say, "It's
my friend." I'll tell you one thing, that fight wasn't with
Faye.' She was talking about the fight Nicole allegedly had
on the telephone the night she was killed. They are posi-
tive that the fight was with O. J. 'Nicole used to say, "You
don't get it. He doesn't love me. He's obsessed with me,"'
said Shahian.

'Why did she go back to him then?' I asked.

'Nicole could not be happy being alone,' said Greer.
'She had to have a man. She had to have someone else
with her. Every guy she went out with let her down,

so she always went back to O. J.'

When I mentioned that a lot of people don't think that he did it, Resnick snapped impatiently, 'The kind of people who think O. J. didn't do it are not the kind of people he's interested in. If they release him, they're releasing a dangerous man. He's not sorry for what he did. He's sorry he got caught.'

Resnick added, 'I am so tired of people going on television and talking about me. I'm getting attacked by people I don't even know who say they know me. Some guy said on TV he had nude pictures of me. There are no nude pictures of me. They're talking about a different person. It's not me. People I don't know say they did drugs with me.'

'Do you think the defense will put you on the stand?' I asked.

'I doubt it. I'm full of ammunition on O. J. I'm one of the very few people who isn't intimidated by him. He knows full well I'll be another Ron Shipp up there.' Then she said, 'Chris Darden thinks they'll tear me down without calling me.'

'She almost got out of it. She came this close,' said Robin Greer suddenly. She put her thumb and first finger together to indicate how close Nicole had come to freeing herself of her former husband. With that she broke down and sobbed. 'She helped me through so many hard times,' she said as she tried to pull herself together. Then she repeated, 'She almost got out of it.'

FOLLOW THE BLOOD

THE OPENING NIGHT of the opera is a great social event in any city, and Los Angeles on May 6 was no exception. All the swells and all the music buffs turned out. Black tie. Big dresses. Big jewels. Big stars. That kind of night. Baroness Di Portanova of Houston, the Countess of Dudley of London, and Nan Kempner of New York added a touch of out-of-town glamour to the already glamorous occasion. The Founders Room was packed to the rafters during intermission. Champagne flowed. The candlelit grand promenade was the scene of the party afterward.

The opera was Verdi's *Otello*. Placido Domingo sang Otello, the dark-skinned hero, and June Anderson was Desdemona, his fair, blonde wife. Sometime during the second act, husbands began to turn to wives, and wives to husbands, and whisper, 'O. J. and Nicole.' The scene onstage and the tragic dénouement seemed eerily reminiscent of the terrible events that had occurred in Brentwood a year before. Obsession. Jealousy. Suspicion. Spousal abuse. Rage.

Violence. Otello's hands. Desdemona's throat. Murder.

'The jury should see this,' said Mrs Marvin Davis, the wife of the billionaire oil-and-real-estate tycoon.

Although jurors and the media start off each day like a group of Bambis, gamely making their way through the forest of DNA evidence, they end each day looking like deer in the headlights of the Encyclopedia Britannica.

—Dr Mark Goulston, UCLA psychiatrist and observer for the prosecution, in the corridor outside the courtroom.

The April 19 terrorist bombing in Oklahoma City put the O. J. Simpson trial back in perspective. A serious tone has returned to the trial. There haven't been any more men in drag disturbing the proceedings since the one who was removed in April, although one day a religious zealot rose from her seat and approached the well of the courtroom as if it were the high altar of a cathedral. She fell to her knees and loudly prayed, 'Father, in Jesus's name, I ask you to open the heavens to give peace and strength to this court.' We paid little attention as the bailiffs led her away. The Felliniesque period – the days when Rosa Lopez, the maid from next door to the Simpson house on Rockingham Avenue, who lied on the stand, could announce to the court that she was tired, didn't want to answer any more questions, and wanted to go home, and the court would defer to her wishes – is at an end. These days, the stricter, sterner

Judge Lance A. Ito would probably toss Lopez in jail for the night if she gave him any of that sass. He recently threw a couple of visitors out for whispering to each other. He threatened to have everyone in court searched when a woman whose cellular phone went off in her bag didn't come forward right away and identify herself. And, in a very angry moment over the bickering of defense attorney Peter Neufeld and prosecution lawyer George 'Woody' Clarke, he loudly slapped his two hands hard on the top of his desk, bringing the entire courtroom to a stunned silence. He then waved the jury out, sanctioned the two lawyers, and fined them $250 each, to be paid immediately to the court clerk, Deirdre Robertson. He even specified that Neufeld could not bill his fine to Simpson, to which Simpson said politely, 'Thank you.' The judge is in no mood for any temperament from *anybody*. On May 18 he banned Court TV reporter Kristin Jeannette-Meyers and Gale Holland, of *USA Today*, for the duration of the trial after two jurors complained that they had been talking in the courtroom. The frequent sidebars of the early months have practically stopped. Judge Ito is focused on the desire of the sequestered jury – who became restless, then rebellious, over the slow pace of the trial – for him to speed things up.

Now we're back to a murder trial, with victims and blood. Blood is the key word these days. We saw new pictures of Nicole's hands drenched with her own blood. Horrifying. O. J. studiously looked away, but he must have peeked, because he covered his eyes. It was reported in the papers that he cried. He did not. We're into the DNA evidence, on which the prosecution must rest its case, as there is no murder weapon, no eyewitness, no set of finger-prints, and no confession. The prosecution believes that DNA will convict O. J. Simpson.

> *Because you are not perfect, O. J. is innocent.*
>   —Director MILOŠ FORMAN characterizing the
>   defense's stance that the LA police
>   botched the collection of evidence, at a
>   party at Roddy McDowall's.

By this time, it's hard for me to believe that any of the jurors could accept the defense theory that the Los Angeles Police Department engaged in an elaborate conspiracy to frame O. J. Simpson for the murders of his former wife and her friend Ron Goldman. The constant repetition of the idea of conspiracy – a sort of jury brainwash – had become a tired, worn-out act even before the trial reached a point where the defense could have put it to dramatic effect. It had been so overworked by the time defense lawyer Peter Neufeld stepped up to the lectern that there was a general feeling of 'Oh, that again' every time his voice expressed outrage at the mishandling of blood samples by the police. Probably no one pointed out the absurdity of the conspiracy argument better than Sean Delonas, the cartoonist for 'Page Six' of the *New York Post*, who on April 27 depicted Timothy McVeigh, the alleged Oklahoma City bomber, being visited in his jail cell by Simpson's dream team of Johnnie Cochran, Robert Shapiro, F. Lee Bailey, and Alan Dershowitz. Cochran,

with a comforting arm around the shoulder of the man
thought to be responsible for the deaths of 167 people,
is saying, 'We believe the authorities planted the oily fertil-
izer in your rental truck as you practiced your chip shot
on the front lawn.'

The defense is having credibility problems on their
conspiracy theme with the public, too. In some quarters,
they are even looked upon as villains. Robert Shapiro, an
avid sports enthusiast, who used to be cheered by fans
when he attended events, has recently been heartily booed
at a Lakers game in Los Angeles and at a prizefight in Las
Vegas. In Las Vegas, people also yelled 'Guilty, guilty,
guilty' as he took his seat.

I know for a fact that two members of the defense team
are having conscience problems with their roles in the trial.
Defense DNA expert Barry Scheck told me personally that
he is haunted by the grief-stricken family of Ron Goldman
and can't bring himself to look at them in the courtroom.
'That family could be my family,' he said. If there is anyone
who is totally innocent in this story, it is Ron Goldman, a
young man whose adult life was just beginning. He was
slain in the process of doing a good deed: returning to
Nicole Brown Simpson her mother's lost eyeglasses. If I
were Scheck, I couldn't look at the Goldmans, either.
Several days and several second thoughts later, however,
when Scheck and I happened to meet up in the men's
room, he assured me that he totally and absolutely believed
in the innocence of O. J. Simpson – in case, I suppose, I
had suspected otherwise after our earlier encounter.

Another member of the defense told a lawyer friend

of mine that he despises two fellow members of the team, whom he referred to as 'fucking liars'. That lawyer is known to want to withdraw from the case.

What's more, there are rumors of financial distress in the Simpson camp. 'Nobody's being paid,' a person close to the action told me recently. The same person said that one of the group is 'hurting for money'. But stick together the dream team must. They're in this to win, even if winning means a hung jury at best.

More than Mr Simpson is on trial here. The jury system is on trial. If the Simpson jury is hung, O. J. could be the poster boy for majority jury.

—MIKE REYNOLDS, of Fresno, California, father of a murdered daughter and an activist for 'majority jury', whereby a single person could no longer hang a jury in noncapital cases.

I had dinner at Drai's with Michael Knox and his wife, Beverly. Knox, in case you've forgotten, was on the jury for forty-nine days, but was dismissed after the prosecution complained about his unseemly behavior, such as staring too hard at pictures on the walls of O. J. Simpson's house on Rockingham Avenue during a jury visit. Knox always stood out from other jurors because of his distinctive manner of dress. I once described him wearing a tomato-red suit, red shoes, and a red tie to court. Knox's book, *Diary of an O. J. Juror*, is shortly to be published by Dove Books. He told me that it will include 'an honest assessment of who's who on the jury, giving readers insight into the jurors and the social baggage they bring with them'. He acknowledged to me that there had been racial tensions on the jury, but he said that the tensions were black against white, rather than the other way around, and also black against black. Knox, an African-American, said, 'There will be a verdict that will shock America . . . Justice is going to prevail.'

> *They came on so friendly, so open, so obviously in need of someone to talk about something. I took their mind off things by telling them my life story. They were very sensitive, very warm. There was no hostility between them . . . Everyone reached out and touched the person next to them . . . I was on way over an hour, alone . . . I didn't feel comfortable being campy, but I told a couple of campy jokes about me.*
> —MR BLACKWELL, famous for his annual
> Worst-Dressed Women List, talking about
> his lecture to the O. J. Simpson jurors.

The jury mutiny in April, when the jurors protested the dismissal of three of the deputies guarding them after Tracy Hampton, the African-American flight attendant on the panel, said it was either them or her, seems to have had a healing effect on the troubled group. For the first time since the trial began, I sense a unity among the jury that was not evident before. They are more relaxed, and seem to be enjoying one another's company. During a long sidebar recently, some of us members of the press were staring at the jurors, and they were staring back. Finally, they all began to laugh at the same time, probably at us for staring at them. Just as we have nicknames for them, they most likely have nicknames for all of us regulars in the courtroom. The white female on the panel whom former juror Jeanette Harris said had kicked her seems to have formed a friendly alliance with another African-American woman, who sits in front of her. If there are tensions among the jurors, they are not evident. Larry Flax, the co-founder and co-chairman of California Pizza Kitchen, played host to the jury at his downtown pizza emporium. Flax told me that he reserved a private section with three tables for the group, and that all of them came except for one. He described them as affable, friendly, and funny. He said that although the men sat together at one table, the women seated themselves in a racially mixed manner at the other two, belying the dismal picture of racial conflict presented by Jeanette Harris. Subsequently, thirteen of the seventeen jurors appeared in the court-room one day wearing California Pizza Kitchen T-shirts. On the back of the T-shirts was written, FOURTEEN ETHNI-CALLY DIVERSE CULTURES PEACEFULLY CO-EXISTING ON A THIN DELICIOUS CRUST.

However, all is still not bliss. The alternate juror who took Tracy Hampton's place is a twenty-eight-year-old single Hispanic woman who works as a real-estate appraiser with the Los Angeles County Assessors Office. Tall and slender, she has long black hair that hangs to her shoul-ders, and her extremely pale face is brought to life by her scarlet lipstick. As an alternate, she often read a self-help book called *Six Pillars of Self-Esteem* during sidebars. On the questionnaire she filled out during voir dire, she wrote of Simpson, 'He's the only person who had a visible motive. It was his ex-wife, and she was with another man. It's something most people would have a problem with.' The defense is not pleased with her as a regular on the jury.

Tracy Hampton, whom Judge Ito released on May 1, was the first of the dismissed jurors to have no words to say to assembled reporters when she returned to her parents' home, or any wish to capitalize on the fame that could have been hers. She held her hands up in front of her face so as not to be photographed. The following day, she was rushed to the hospital after reports that she had suffered a violent seizure. Her face and body were covered with a sheet as she was carried on a stretcher to the waiting ambulance. The young woman had obviously been suffering during the last weeks she was on the jury panel. A miasma of dark rumors suggesting particularly disturbing suicide attempts remain unconfirmed.

> *When I come home, I like to know that the trial is on in the kitchen and in the bedroom.*
> —RICHIE BERLIN, O. J.-trial junkie, who never turns off her television sets.

One day shortly before Heidi Fleiss was sentenced to three years for pandering. I had lunch with the famous Hollywood madam in the garden of the Hotel Bel-Air.

You'd never take her for a madam. She arrived in her own style of incognito – an oversize T-shirt, huge sunglasses, and a baseball cap on backward, looking just like the twenty-nine-year-old California girl she is. In one of these columns, I wrote that she would probably do more jail time for her victimless crime than either the Menendez brothers or O. J. Simpson. I meant it cynically, but then again I didn't. Over lunch she was forthright, funny, and frightened. The idea of incarceration panicked her. When the subject of prison came up, her eyes would gaze off into space in a private reverie, as if she were visualizing that which she feared so much. Although she is currently pitching a book on her escapades, she told me that she does not intend to name the celebrated men who were her patrons. I can tell you – and I didn't get this from her – that there are names on that list that would really make you run to your nearest bookstore. I asked her if any of the rich and famous clients who utilized her services had offered to help cover her large legal expenses. With a shake of her head she gave me an are-you-kidding? look. She said she hadn't heard from any of them. Just then, in a complex juxtaposition of the many overlapping worlds of Los Angeles, Nancy Reagan and Betsy Bloomingdale, in very smart suits, arrived to be seated one table over. Heidi Fleiss knew who they were, and they knew who Heidi Fleiss was.

The much-delayed retrial of the Menendez brothers is now scheduled for August 16. But don't count on it. Most of the defense's requests have been denied by Judge Stanley Weisberg. There will be only one trial for the brothers, not separate ones, as requested by the defense. There will be one jury, not a separate jury for each, as there was last time. The trial will take place in Van Nuys, where the last trial took place, not in the Criminal Courts Building in Los Angeles, as the defense requested. The feeling in the air here is that the teary tales of Lyle and Erik Menendez – the 'battered children', as the defense wants to prove – won't work the second time around, and that convictions are almost certain. The imminent publication by Dove Books of *The Private Diary of Lyle Menendez in His Own Words*, Norma Novelli's account of her relationship with Lyle Menendez, including transcripts of revealing tapes of her phone conversations with him in jail, has infuriated the defense, as has a recent ruling by Judge Weisberg that one of the tapes will be admissible during the trial.

> *You have reached Kato Kaelin International, a division of Time Warner and the* Los Angeles Times. *For general information on Kato, press 1. For general information on Kato's hair, press 2. For information on specific upper-body parts of Kato, press 3. For information on Kato dolls, press 4. Kato dogs, press 5. Kato pilots, 6. Kato in Vegas, 7. Kato CD-ROM, 8. Kato condoms, 9. And for information on a Kato time-share, our houseguest-placement office will be with you in just a moment. You may start your message now. Beep . . .*
>
> —Message on the answering machine of
> Hollywood comedy writer BRUCE VILANCH.

Kato Kaelin, O. J.'s onetime houseguest, is continuing to capitalize on his O. J. fame. He has been signed as the opening act for comedian Louie Anderson for a two-week gig at Bally's in Las Vegas. Anderson said about Kato, 'In addition to his acting, I believe Kato is a natural stand-up comedian.' Kaelin appeared at the Kentucky Derby, where he was snubbed by Geraldo Rivera. His burgeoning film career suffered a setback when his highly promoted guest appearance on *Roseanne* was cut before airing.

> *'I noticed that Kato was wearing Charlie's jacket on the stand.'*
> *'How did you know that was Charlie's jacket?'*
> *'It was the one that wasn't Grant's.'*
> —Telephone conversation between TERRY MOORE, mother of Grant Cramer, and JANET SHEEN, mother of Charlie Sheen, about their sons' friend Kato Kaelin.

Detective Mark Fuhrman has filed a $50 million libel suit against writer Jeffrey Toobin and *The New Yorker* magazine for portraying him as a rogue cop who tried to frame Simpson by planting the famous bloody glove on the football hero's estate, in an article that appeared months before the trial. The suit says that the article indicated that Simpson's lawyers hoped to convince jurors that Fuhrman had planted the glove so that he could then find it and become the hero of the case. Fuhrman, who claims that his reputation was ruined by the charges, has also included defense lawyer Robert Shapiro in the suit, alleging that Shapiro either was a source for Toobin's article or was involved in making the information available.

Shapiro has retained Larry Feldman, known as the lawyer to the Simpson team, to represent him in the Fuhrman suit. Feldman was also retained by Johnnie Cochran to represent him in the palimony suit filed by his former longtime mistress, Patricia Cochran, who is the mother of his twenty-two-year-old son. Feldman had previously won a huge settlement for the fourteen-year-old boy who sued Cochran's client Michael Jackson for molestation.

The Goldman family, specifically Fred Goldman and his daughter, Kimberly, have filed a wrongful-death suit against O. J. Simpson, accusing him of killing Ronald Goldman with 'vicious and outrageous savagery'. Kim Goldman said that the suit has 'nothing to do with the money. If we can make him feel a quarter of the pain we feel, it's worth it.'

> *Hey, Gretchen, sweetheart, it's Orenthal James, who is finally at a place in his life where he is, like, totally, totally unattached with everybody. Ha! Haah!*
>
> —Message left by SIMPSON on the answering machine of Gretchen Stockdale, a former Los Angeles Raiders cheerleader and model, at 7:35 P.M. June 12, 1994, the night of the murders.

Mommy, please call me back. I want to know what happened last night.
Why did we have to go to the police station? Please answer, Mommy!
Please answer, Mommy!
Please answer, Mommy!
Please answer . . . Bye.

>—Message left on June 13 on the answering
> machine of Nicole Brown Simpson by
> SYDNEY SIMPSON, unaware that her mother
> was dead.

Benazir Bhutto, the prime minister of Pakistan, was in town for a few days. Asked by her hostess whom she would like to meet at dinner at Jimmy's, the fashionable Beverly Hills restaurant, Bhutto didn't say Brad Pitt and Julia Roberts, or any variation on the movie-star theme. Instead, she asked to meet Marcia Clark and Robert Shapiro. They both accepted, and Clark brought prosecutor Chris Darden with her.

You should have hung out. You should have bailed out. You should have been on the boat by now. You should have called . . . Women, man, women. Unbelievable. Should have just got away.

>—Message left on O. J. Simpson's cell-phone
> voice mail during the week of June 13 by
> former Simpson teammate BOBBY
> CHANDLER, who subsequently died of
> lung cancer.

What's happened to the Browns? They almost never come to court anymore. Occasionally Tanya, Nicole's youngest sister, and her fiancé come by, but the family as a unit has not been seen for weeks in its section of reserved seats. Juditha Brown, Nicole's mother, did appear one day and engaged in deep conversation with Shirley Baker, O. J.'s sister, about pictures in *Life* magazine of Sydney and Justin Simpson. Brown felt that the children had been exploited. When I asked her why she had not been in court, she said, 'This is not my favorite place to be.'

To my way of thinking, it is a mistake for them not to come. The trial is the last business of Nicole's life. It is also important for the jury to see the family sitting there, watching and listening. Victims' families are a constant reminder that loss has occurred and that people are suffering as a result. The Goldman family, particularly Kim, Ron's sister, and Patti, his stepmother, almost never miss a day, and they pay strict attention, even during the boring parts. In many people's minds, Kim Goldman has become the conscience of this trial. On the other side of the aisle, the Simpsons are equally constant in their attendance. You have to say this for the Simpsons: they're a united family in their support of O. J., and they're respected by everyone. When Carmelita Durio, O. J.'s sister, wheeled her mother, Eunice Simpson, who was dressed from head to toe in purple, into the courtroom one day, everyone stepped back to allow them to pass.

The DNA is very pretty.
> —LISA KAHN, DNA expert for the prosecu-
> tion, to Kim Goldman, sister of Ron
> Goldman, in a corridor of the courthouse.

*It's incredibly strong. It can't get any clearer than
it is. I worry whether the jury got it or not.*
> —KIM GOLDMAN re Dr Robin Cotton's DNA
> testimony.

For months the defense has denigrated the work of the
police, the detectives, the criminalists, and the lab tech-
nicians. Certainly few, if any, of the legal pundits moni-
toring the case for all the TV channels are buying the
defense's belabored conspiracy theory, however. One even
said to me, on a guarantee of anonymity, 'I think it will
be seen as a disgrace to have represented O. J.'

Along came Dr Robin Cotton, director of laboratories
for Cellmark Diagnostics in Germantown, Maryland, the
nation's largest private forensic DNA-testing firm, to present the trial's defining moment. Dr Cotton, who holds a
PhD in molecular biology and biochemistry from the
University of California, Irvine, explained the basics of
DNA to the jurors in a prim, precise manner, as a favorite
schoolteacher might, simplifying the complicated material
but never talking down to them. According to Cotton, the
blood found near the victims could have come from only
1 person in 170 million African-Americans and Caucasians.
That blood matched O. J. Simpson's blood. The blood on
the sock in Simpson's bedroom was consistent with that

of only 1 person out of 6.8 billion – more people than there are on earth – and that blood matched the blood of Nicole Brown Simpson.

At one point Deputy District Attorney George Clarke, anticipating the defense's argument that the blood samples could have been contaminated, asked Cotton, 'So this process of degradation, can it change my DNA into looking like your DNA?'

'No,' she replied.

'Or your DNA into looking like the court's DNA?'

'No.'

'Or any members of the jury or the audience?'

'No.'

The courtroom was rapt. The jurors listened attentively. Almost all of them took notes. I saw a few look at one another as Cotton supplied the statistic of 1 in 170 million. When the camera in the courtroom moved away from the defense table toward the bench, Johnnie Cochran, out of range, stretched and yawned expansively while Robert Shapiro, who was sitting next to him, closed his eyes as if he were falling asleep. I took this to be an ostentatious display for the jury, signifying that the breathtaking figures were of no consequence. Indeed, Cochran was quoted the next day in *The New York Times* as saying that he didn't think Cotton's testimony was 'damaging at all'.

The prosecution's contention that Simpson murdered his former wife and Ronald Goldman was further bolstered, however, by evidence offered by Gary Sims, the lead forensic chemist from the California Department of

Justice, who showed that blood in Simpson's Bronco was consistent with the blood of Simpson, Nicole Brown Simpson, and Ronald Goldman. Sims also showed that blood on the glove found at the Rockingham estate before Simpson returned from Chicago contained a mixture of blood types from Simpson and the victims. During this testimony, Simpson, who once announced to the court that he was absolutely, 100 percent not guilty, calmly made notes on his yellow pad.

Deputy District Attorney Brian Kelberg offered the court the most descriptive explanation of how the murders were committed. In a hearing outside the presence of the jury that Simpson himself waived the right to attend, Kelberg suggested that 'the perpetrator, who we contend is the defendant O. J. Simpson,' came up from behind Nicole, placed his foot on her back when she was face-down on the ground, pulled her head back by her hair, and then slashed her throat from ear to ear. Kelberg also said that the knife was drawn against Ron Goldman's throat in one sharp, clean motion.

People are beginning to say that if O. J. Simpson were white, and Nicole Brown Simpson and Ron Goldman had been black, and all the circumstances were the same, this trial would be over by now.

IF THE GLOVES FIT . . .

THE PRESENTATION OF THE DNA evidence has ended, at least for now, and not a moment too soon. Everyone had had enough. Like everything else in this trial, it went on too long, especially the cross-examinations. Defense lawyers Barry Scheck and Peter Neufeld were brilliant, and wonderfully prepared, but they seemed totally unaware that less is more. They didn't understand that asking the same question over and over again ultimately bores people and causes tune-out. Anyone can tell you that a point isn't worth making unless it gets across to the jury. During the DNA material, the jurors' eyes began to glaze over. For at least one of them, Willie Cravin — subsequently dismissed for allegedly intimidating another juror — the DNA evidence apparently proved absolutely nothing. The 170-million-to-1 odds that blood found at the crime scene was O. J. Simpson's didn't convince him. During Cravin's fifteen minutes of fame, spent racing from one television show to another in a chauffeur-driven limousine, he referred to the defendant as 'the Juice'. The fact is, although DNA testing may be as foolproof as fingerprinting, it doesn't cause excitement. It's difficult to respond to. It's like advanced math, brilliant but boring, astonishing but passionless. It made everybody eager to move on to the next phase of the trial, which consisted of the autopsy pictures of Nicole Brown Simpson and Ronald Goldman, the victims of this appalling crime, whose names are so rarely mentioned.

> *The people that like DNA are the police, the victims, the prosecutors who are looking for the truth. The only person that's got to worry about a DNA test being done in a criminal case is the person who committed the crime.*
>
> —Assistant US Attorney JAMES WOOLEY on *60 Minutes.*

In most murder trials, the prosecution and defense fight over the admissibility of autopsy photographs. The defense doesn't want the jury to see them. The prosecution does. Leslie Abramson, Erik Menendez's lawyer, once called autopsy pictures 'a cheap prosecutorial trick'. Pamela Bozanich, the prosecutor in the first Menendez trial, gave the perfect response: 'Those who have committed crimes like these, it ill behooves them to complain of the carnage they leave.' Judge Ito ruled in favor of the prosecution on this point, though he described the pictures in advance of the jurors' seeing them as 'horrible'. Johnnie Cochran prepared the way for O. J. Simpson to leave the court during the viewing of the photographs of his former wife's slashed neck if necessary, but in the end Simpson stayed. The first day the photographs were shown to the jury, he was flanked on his left by Carl Douglas, who kept up a running conversation with him, and on his right by Robert Kardashian, who provided protection from the constant gaze of the television camera. The pictures, which were mounted on large boards placed on an easel, were forbidden territory for both the Court TV crew and still photographers. Simpson rocked back and forth on his chair, occasionally exhaling in loud *whoosh* sounds, and stared straight ahead or up at the ceiling the whole time, particularly during the very graphic reenactments of the murders, with coroner Dr Lakshmanan Sathyavagiswaran playing the perpetrator/narrator and Deputy District Attorney Brian Kelberg the victim. 'Her carotid artery was transected on both sides,' the coroner said. 'It was literally divided in two pieces.' Behind Simpson, his sister Carmelita Durio removed her glasses and wept.

Orenthal James Simpson . . . planned and prepared to assault, batter, and murder Nicole Brown Simpson and did thereafter brutally and with malice afore-thought stalk, attack, and repeatedly stab and beat decedent Nicole Brown Simpson [and] left her on the walkway in front of her residence to die.

> —From the wrongful-death lawsuit against O. J. Simpson filed by the estate of Nicole Brown Simpson.

Probably because of the presence of the Goldman family, seated only a few feet away in the courtroom, the autopsy pictures of Ron Goldman elicited a more emotional reaction from the jury than the equally gruesome pictures of Nicole Brown Simpson. A seventy-two-year-old African-American alternate juror covered his face with a handkerchief and blew his nose, and the male juror sitting next to him asked if he was all right. A female juror, in obvious distress, signaled the bailiff and fled from the courtroom. When she returned ten minutes later, Judge Ito recessed court for the day.

As someone who has seen the photographs of the mutilated bodies close up, I can tell you that they are appalling to behold. We reporters had to hire an attorney to argue our right to view the photographs, and even though the forty-eight of us who were picked to see them displayed on easels had braced ourselves for the viewing, a couple – myself included – got a little faint and had to sit down for a portion of our allotted twenty minutes. What I was not prepared for was that Nicole's and Ron's eyes were open, reminding me that they must have looked upon who it was who was knifing them to death. Nicole's lips were parted. You could see her teeth. Her blond hair was stained dark by the blood that flowed from the knife wounds on her scalp. One of the photos showed the contusion from a blow that was supposed to have knocked her out so that the perpetrator, according to the prosecution's version of the murders, could kill Ron, who had appeared on the scene to deliver Juditha Brown's glasses, then return to Nicole, place his foot on her back, pull her head up by her hair, and slit her throat. She looked so much like her sister Denise in the pictures that they could have been twins. I found myself thinking, Only a monster could have done this to a beautiful young mother of two, with the kids upstairs asleep. To me, Nicole's slashed neck was the worst picture of all to look at, but I couldn't stop looking. I had never seen a slashed neck before, and I hope never to see another. The color was crimson. There were exposed muscles, veins, tendons, and spine, washed free of blood for optimum clarity. Then I moved on to the next easel, to look at what had happened to Ron. God, he looked young. On the front of his neck were some torture cuts, slices made before the killer went in for the lethal strokes. Some of his hair had been shaved away to expose the knife wound on his scalp.

That afternoon, back in Department 103, O. J. made his usual star entrance into the courtroom, beautifully dressed as always. He gave his raised-eyebrow-sad-smile greeting to his sister. I found it hard to look in his direction. That morning, Johnnie Cochran had said on the *Today* show that O. J. was distressed over a new poll which claimed that a majority of Americans believed he was guilty.

I think the jury will do him a favor to convict him.
I don't think it will be safe for him outside.
— Overheard during intermission at Terrence
McNally's new play, *Master Class*, starring
Zoe Caldwell, at the Mark Taper Forum.

A few days later, in what has subsequently become known as the glove debacle, prosecutor Christopher Darden asked defendant Simpson to try on the infamous pair of bloodstained gloves, the left one found at the crime scene at Nicole Simpson's condominium on Bundy and the right one found outside Kato Kaelin's room in the guesthouse of Simpson's estate on Rockingham. In a dazzling bit of showmanship, Simpson seized the moment and ran with it, just as if he had caught a pass and made an eighty-yard touchdown at the height of his athletic power. That the gloves contained the blood of his deceased former wife appeared to be of no consequence to him. Every eye in the courtroom was upon him. Reporters sat half out of their seats as he crossed in front of us on his way to the jury box, surrounded by deputies. Jurors stared up at him, fascinated, and wrote furiously in their notebooks at the same time. 'They don't fit,' Simpson said, holding his hands up in the air, and they didn't. Darden had not established in advance that the gloves could have shrunk from exposure to blood and liquids until they were almost a size smaller than they had been when they were purchased at Bloomingdale's. Exasperated by Simpson's performance, Darden asked Judge Ito, 'Could we ask him to straighten his fingers and put them in the gloves as one would normally put them in the gloves?' But Simpson was like a man fighting for his life, and he may have just saved it. There are some who think he may have won the case.

* * *

WHEN IS MARCIA CLARK returning to center stage? She's been on the back burner far too long, as five or six other prosecutors have moved to the forefront during the long DNA and coroner portions of the trial. The jury must be confused by now as to who's in charge of the prosecution team. A lot of us in the media are. In the beginning, there was the strong duet of William Hodgman and Clark. Then came the interesting duet of Clark and Christopher Darden, with Clark in charge. Lately, it seems like a department store with a lot of specialty boutiques operating independently of one another. Who's calling the shots? Is Bill Hodgman directing the team from the eighteenth floor of the courthouse? Or is it Los Angeles County district attorney Gil Garcetti who's really running the show? The jury needs a strong presence on the team to bond with, and Marcia Clark is the obvious one. Meanwhile, the prosecution began to recoup its losses with the strong testimony of FBI authority William Bodziak on the size-12 Bruno Magli shoe prints at the scene of the crime.

Faye Resnick took a cake at Rodeo last night.
—Overheard at Carrie Fisher's birthday
party for Griffin Dunne, a reference to
Resnick's first-year anniversary in
Alcoholics Anonymous.

There is always a yin and yang to things. Someone I know who has access to defense information told me in the corridor during a break that the defense really believes it's going to win this case. 'They think the autopsy photographs are going to work in their favor,' this person said. 'They're going to bring in expert witnesses who are going to say that this could only be the work of a professional killer from a Colombian drug cartel, not a man like O. J. Simpson.'

I first heard the Colombian-drug-ring idea last July, when I had dinner at '21' in New York with F. Lee Bailey, about six months before the trial began. He described it to me that night as if he were trying out his opening statement before a jury. He said Nicole's slashed voice box was the clue. He described it all wonderfully, very dramatically, but it seemed ludicrous to me then and it continues to seem ludicrous to me now. I believe it is unlikely to sway anyone other than a dedicated pro-defense juror, one who wouldn't convict Simpson even if a videotape of him committing the murders miraculously appeared. Would that I knew a way to contact a high-ranking member of a Colombian drug cartel to see how *they* feel about being accused by some high-priced defense attorneys in Los Angeles of savagely killing two innocent people on Bundy Drive a year ago.

Faye Resnick has been subpoenaed by the defense and, like Kato Kaelin, will surely be declared a hostile witness. She has been told to appear on July 3, which happens to be her birthday, and she is very nervous at the prospect. Evidently the defense is going to try to fit her right into the Colombian-drug-cartel scenario. The defense indicated early in the proceedings that the Colombians were after her, not Nicole.

What surprises one about Faye Resnick is how bright she is. And fearless. I don't think she's going to be the

pushover the defense is expecting. She knows a lot about
O. J. and drugs. She told me that she had taken drugs
with him. She'd think nothing of spilling the beans on
the stand if the defense got rough with her. She knows
full well that Nicole Simpson and Ron Goldman weren't
murdered by a Colombian drug cartel who thought they
were killing her because she owed them money. I've seen
Resnick roar with laughter at that idea.

*I have watched the trial since the very beginning
and I have noticed each week how the lawyers,
witnesses, audience and O. J. have all started playing to the camera. They are obviously aware of
when the camera is on them. They can see the
camera move and even see the lens turn when it is
zooming in to a close-up. As a result, the people in
the courtroom are increasingly performing when
they are on camera.*

*Yesterday Barry Scheck obviously disagreed and
disapproved of your ruling in such an obvious way
that anyone watching television felt that he had
been severely damaged in his defense of O. J. by
this and other rulings.*

—Portion of a letter sent to Judge Ito by
        George Schlatter, producer of *Laugh-In*
        and *Real People*.

I went to my home in Connecticut for the Memorial
Day weekend, my first time back in five months. I wanted
to clear my mind of O. J. for a few days. Barry Scheck

was on the same plane, on his way home for the long weekend with his family in Brooklyn Heights. There was a lot of 'Oh, Mr Scheck' from the moment he stepped aboard, and soon he got upped to first class, into the seat right next to me. Scheck had had a hard day in court, conducting a vigorous cross-examination of Collin Yamauchi, the Los Angeles Police Department criminalist who performed the first DNA tests on evidence found at the crime scene on Bundy and at the Simpson residence on Rockingham Avenue. Scheck and his partner, Peter Neufeld, are masters of the art of belittlement and humiliation. That day Scheck had tried to show that Yamauchi was too inexperienced for the task assigned him, that he had been forced to rush his results, and that his speed in analyzing samples may have resulted in cross-contamination. Yamauchi's dislike of Scheck was obvious.

I didn't think I was going to like Scheck, but I did. Opposites in our beliefs, we conversed nonstop during the flight. He did most of the talking, and since my forte has always been listening, that was OK with me. He spoke of O. J. in glowing terms, as if he were a swell guy it was his honor to serve. Most of the people I spend time with don't think O. J.'s a swell guy at all. More and more I hear people say things like 'If O. J. walks, I'm going to leave the country.' Scheck really believes that the LAPD set up Simpson, or he puts on a good show of believing that. While spreading caviar on toast tips, he posed a hypothetical question, in words to this effect, for I wasn't taking notes: If I could prove to you beyond a shadow of a doubt that the police moved evidence in a conspiracy to frame O. J., could you

as a member of the jury vote to convict O. J.? I don't for
an instant believe that the police moved evidence in order
to frame O. J., but I went along with his premise. Yes, I
said, I could convict, knowing that. If the police had done
what he said they did, then they should be punished, but
I could never believe that the perpetrator of a double
murder should go free because of police obstruction of
justice. Scheck gave me an I-don't-get-you look. I gave him
back an I-don't-get-*you* look.

We went on to other subjects. It interests me how people
respond to fame, and Barry Scheck is now famous. Even
60 Minutes has done a piece on him and Neufeld. He said
he doesn't like being recognized everywhere he goes. He
told me he was upset when a radio personality made fun
of the size of his nose. He thought it was embarrassing
for his children. He seems absolutely crazy about his two
kids and his wife, Didi. When he talked about them, he
was a different person. Nice. He told me he had worshiped
his father, who was a tap dancer, a hoofer, and a friend of
Honi Coles, one of the all-time greats of tap dancing.
Later, he said, his father managed musical acts, including
Bobby Darin, Connie Francis, Mary Wells, and Hazel
Scott, the great jazz pianist, who married Adam Clayton
Powell Jr, the Harlem congressman. When Scheck
described Hazel Scott's funeral to me, which he attended
with his father, I felt as if I were there.

In court the following Tuesday, we reverted to our original roles, with me watching and taking notes and Scheck
up to his old belittlement tricks. 'He was snapping at the
witness, interrupting the witness, pointing his finger,

embarrassing the witness,' said Laurie Levenson, a law professor at Loyola Marymount University. But Yamauchi stood his ground. 'Would you mind not pointing at me like that?' he angrily demanded of his tormentor.

I was bumped from my appearance on the Tom Snyder show when Willie Cravin became available at the last minute.
> —MICHAEL CHABON, author of *Wonder Boys*, at a dinner party given by biographer Scott Berg and studio executive Kevin McCormick.

Everybody in this story wants to write a book about his part in it. That even goes for Ron X, the lookout man for J. R., the drug dealer to the stars who claims to have sold crystal methamphetamine to O. J. Simpson and Kato Kaelin in O. J.'s black Bentley in the parking lot of a Burger King on the night of the murders. Ron X came by to see me one afternoon. It was my first face-to-face with him; we had spoken on the telephone several times, and I was eager to put face to voice. He had told me in advance that he looked like a homeless person. He was not exaggerating. 'Every homeless person smells like urine,' he told me. 'I let my cat pee on me. The police can smell the urine on me and think I'm homeless.'

'Don't sit in that chair,' I replied, pulling out a wooden one from the kitchen.

He's somewhere in his mid to late thirties, with a nice-looking face which he manages to make very difficult to get a good look at. His hair, which is long, curly, and ratty, hangs in front of his eyes, concealing them, and the rest of his face is obscured by his mustache and beard.

The prosecution continues to maintain its distance from these dealers, even though many of the people who traveled in the world of the Simpsons before the murders suspect that O. J. was high at the time of the killings.

When I pointed out to Ron X that there was apparently no trace of drugs in Simpson's blood, he said that crystal meth leaves the bloodstream quickly. He said that the police messed up by not giving him a urine test, because the drug would have shown up in his urine. I suppose nobody had the nerve to ask such a big star to urinate in a bottle. Ron X claimed that a number of criminals in recent news stories were all on crystal meth. He called them tweeker freak-outs, a slang term for habitual users of the drug. He has a book project.

> *I wasn't chewing. I was sucking.*
> —KIMBERLY MAROE, KCAL-TV reporter,
>   telling me what she said to Judge Ito when
>   she was called into his chambers for chew-
>   ing gum.

Judge Ito seems to despise the media, and frequently makes reporters the objects of his wrath. Laughter is now forbidden in the courtroom, even if something funny happens, which is rare. On two recent occasions Judge Ito rebuked the court. After hearing ripples of laughter that were really no more than stress-relieving chortles, he .

said through clenched teeth, 'This is not an audience-participation function.' Another time, after a minor disturbance, he said that if it happened again he would clear the courtroom.

Mr Dunne, I spent an evening with O. J. Simpson. At Mortons. Every beam, shaft, and hint of light bounced off his being. He was a man who shifted the energy in the room . . . Not for a second do I think he'll be convicted, but he'll haunt the lives of those who 'knew' and did nothing about it.
     —Excerpt from a letter from a stranger.

At the party for Richard Pryor's book *Pryor Convictions* at Georgia, a man introduced himself to me as Kato Kaelin's publicist. Kato didn't do his gig in Las Vegas after all, but he's got some TV shows lined up, and he's planning to sue Marc Eliot, his former co-author, for a share in the profits of the book *Kato Kaelin: The Whole Truth*. Fame being as fickle as it is, Kato's not quite as famous this month as he was last. Of course, if Marcia Clark were to put him back on the stand and were able to prove that he lied under oath – his version of things in Marc Eliot's book is different in part from what he said on the stand – he'd be right back in the spotlight again. Also at Richard Pryor's party, I ran into the young lady who had told me at Paul Jasmin's birthday party that her girlfriend had been in a three-way with O. J. 'Thank God you didn't use my name,' she said. 'I would have died. I've got a kid now.'

At Joe Torreneuva's hair salon in Beverly Hills, I was

introduced to Robert Cabral, who used to teach karate to Nicole, Sydney, and Justin Simpson. He told me a fascinating story about O. J.'s not wanting to shake hands with him at Nicole's funeral, and then not looking him in the eye when he finally did. A woman who was watching her four-year-old grandson get a haircut told me that she would introduce me to a friend of hers whom Rosa Lopez used to work for before she went to work at the Salingers' house on Rockingham next door to O. J.'s, where, she claimed on the stand, she saw the white Bronco parked on the night of the murders. Speaking of Rosa Lopez, there's a story going around that she's engaged to be married to a twenty-eight-year-old ventriloquist from Baltimore who saw her testify on television and then followed her to El Salvador, where they met, fell in love, and plan to marry. The only part of the story I don't believe is that Lopez doesn't want to have the wedding until after the trial, because she wants O. J. to give her away. When I told all this to Dan Rather, on whose CBS newscast I appear on Fridays to discuss the Simpson trial, he asked, 'What do you think of that?' I replied, 'It's perfect.' And it is.

> JUDGE: *All right. So we may finish with the pros-*
> *ecution case this month?*
> DARDEN: *We may.*
> JUDGE: *All right. That would thrill me to death.*
> —JUDGE LANCE ITO and prosecutor
> CHRISTOPHER DARDEN discussing the sched-
> uling of remaining prosecution witnesses.

Former attorney general Richard Thornburgh appeared in court one day, as did Roone Arledge, president of the News Division of ABC. Sometimes I forget that there is another world going on here in Los Angeles, where people talk about things other than DNA and slit throats, although all conversation eventually returns to the trial.

The Beverly Hills Hotel, that grande dame of Hollywood life, reopened with a splashy movie-star party. For the purists, the Sultan of Brunei did not overgild the beloved pink birthday cake in his $100 million renovation. The Polo Lounge is as before. Don Loper's banana-leaf wallpaper still covers the halls and the coffee shop. Of course, there are those rather excessive chandeliers that look as if they came straight out of the palace in Brunei, but we'll get used to them in time. In the crush, a woman I had not seen in years told me that Marcus Allen was not going to come back to testify in the O. J. trial. The defense wants Allen to say on the stand that he told O. J. he had had an affair with Nicole and that O. J. still gave him his wedding at the house on Rockingham – all of this to prove that O. J. was not a jealous man. My friend had just talked to Allen that afternoon. He had called to say that he couldn't fly in for her daughter's wedding the following Saturday because he didn't want to come to LA.

Batman Forever opened with an old-fashioned premiere at the Mann's Village Theater in Westwood, complete with screaming fans going mad at the sight of the stars, Val Kilmer, Jim Carrey, and Nicole Kidman with her husband,

Tom Cruise. At a party afterward at the Armand Hammer Museum, I asked a friend of O. J.'s how Simpson's money was holding out, after reports that his legal costs will amount to $6 million by the end of the trial. I was told that O. J. continues to sell memorabilia, that he has received more than seven figures from his book *I Want to Tell You*, that he took out a $3 million line of credit on his house, and that he continues to own equity in HoneyBaked Ham.

And Dennis Hopper, of all people, emerged as the host with the most at his fifty-ninth-birthday party in his art-filled house in Venice, arranged and presided over by the beautiful actress-singer Victoria Duffy. It was what they used to call out here a star-studded evening, with ninety-six guests seated and place-carded, among them, in no particular order, Jack Nicholson, Anjelica Huston, Warren Beatty, Robert De Niro, Uma Thurman, Roddy McDowall, and Sean Penn, as well as such Los Angeles artists as Ed Ruscha, Robert Grant, and Chuck Arnoldi. Jury sequestration, and why it doesn't work, was the main topic of conversation at my table. Ten of the original twenty-four jurors are gone, and not a one because of illness or family hardship, which are the usual reasons for dismissal. Sequestration is an unnatural state, everyone agreed. Does anyone really expect us to believe that information is not whispered into some jurors' ears during the pillow-talk portion of conjugal visits? Shortly thereafter, I heard that a second dismissed juror had been hospitalized following a suicide attempt.

*The case is in the hands of twelve people who didn't
have brains enough to get out of jury duty.*
—MILTON BERLE at a Sunday brunch at
Hillcrest Country Club.

Recently, the *National Enquirer*, which has been right
most of the time in what it has published about the O. J.
Simpson case, reported that there were secret talks of a
plea bargain, that Simpson would claim Nicole attacked
him first and the sentence would be seven years. Johnnie
Cochran vehemently denied this in court, and told the
press that the only thing his client would accept from the
state was an apology. That's what's known as chutzpah.

*Sometimes, I turn around and I look at the
Goldmans, and if you could see the hurt and suffering on their faces. Sometimes, I see them, and
they're smiling, but when they are in the courtroom,
sometimes they are dying inside . . . The victims
just keep mounting up. The Goldmans are victims.
The Browns are victims. The Simpsons are victims.
Sydney and Justin Simpson are victims. We're
victims because the grief and the pain and the
suffering are spread around equally.*
—CHRISTOPHER DARDEN, member of the
prosecution team, in an interview in the
Los Angeles Times.

If gossip is to be believed, another juror is in jeopardy. This news was whispered in my ear at the candlelight

vigil commemorating the first anniversary of Ronald Goldman's death, honoring Ron, Nicole Brown Simpson, and all victims of violent crime. We were in a lovely park in Agoura, about thirty miles north of Los Angeles. (Simultaneously, in Dana Point, ninety miles away, the Brown family was holding a similar candlelight vigil.) A private detective of my acquaintance, who always seems to know a great deal about what is going on in this case before it happens, told me the juror had lied on the voir dire questionnaire, and that – shades of another juror, Jeanette Harris – there was domestic violence in this juror's background which had not been reported. When I passed along this bit of information a few minutes later to a reporter friend of mine, he said he already knew it, and added more to the rumor. 'I heard that [the juror] is supposed to have said that Nicole deserved what she got,' he said. With that, we lit our candles.

It was a beautiful night. If it wasn't a full moon, it was just a night before or a night after one. Hundreds came. They sat or stood on the hillside. There were television cameras from all the local stations. The Goldmans, with their outgoing friendliness, made themselves available to the crowd. It was a gathering of families. People brought their kids. Kim Goldman, twenty-three, a senior at San Francisco State and an employee of Wells Fargo, was the mistress of ceremonies. She has been at the trial every day, a model of perfect behavior. Telling the crowd about Ron, she cried and laughed as she remembered him. 'My brother was only twenty-five, and just on his way to a happy and healthy and prosperous life, but he was literally stopped in his tracks.'

I sat between Rabbi Bernie King, who gave the invocation and closing of the ceremony, and district attorney of the county of Los Angeles Gil Garcetti, who was also a speaker, as was I. During one of the speeches, I stood up to move around and case the crowd. In the dark, as I was talking to Suzanne Childs, communications director of the district attorney's office, a woman came up and introduced herself to me. She was Jill Shively, with her mother and a child in hand. Jill Shively, for those who have forgotten, claimed early on that she had seen O. J. in his white Bronco near Nicole Simpson's condominium on the night of the murders. She lost her value as a prosecution witness because she went on *Hard Copy* and took money for telling what she had seen that night. Inasmuch as everyone else involved in this trial is making a buck off it with their books and television appearances, I never saw what was so wrong with Jill Shively's taking money from *Hard Copy*. I went over to KCBS investigative reporter Harvey Levin, with whom I do a Sunday-night wrap-up about the week at the trial, and said, 'There's Jill Shively. Grab her. I think she wants to talk.' Harvey put his hand up. He was listening to the speech. All around us, candles glowed. 'Not now,' he said. 'This is too moving.'

THE TWO FACES OF O. J.

T HE PROSECUTION HAS RESTED. There was no drama, no swelling crescendo. If you hadn't been waiting for it, you might almost have missed it when Marcia Clark said the words 'The people rest.' But there was a broad smile on the face of juror No. 3, a sixty-year-old white female, indicating that she could now see a light at the end of the tunnel. The most-asked question was: Did the prosecution prove its case beyond a reasonable doubt? Yes, of course it did. Marcia Clark said that never in her career had she seen so much evidence. Over and over, observers repeated that defendants have been sent to death row on much less. But there is still a lingering doubt. Faye Resnick called me in a rage, saying that I shouldn't have said on television that the prosecution hadn't proved its case, but she hadn't listened to my whole sentence. What I said was that if a juror were disinclined to believe that Simpson is guilty, the prosecution did not prove its case beyond a reasonable doubt. We all know that the glove really fit, but the debacle surrounding it provided just what a doubter needed, in the same way that the mathematical error that satistician Dr Bruce Weir owned up to could color *all* the DNA evidence for a doubter who hadn't understood it in the first place or who wanted to believe that a conspiracy had occurred.

> *If the jury takes a look at all of the evidence and then accepts the law, as they must, there is only one conclusion they can reach.*
> —Los Angeles district attorney GIL GARCETTI.

To me, one of the great disappointments of the trial was that the prosecution did not introduce the freeway chase into its case in chief. Flight after murder is generally conceded to be an indication of guilt. When the fleeing murder suspect is carrying a gun, a passport, thousands of dollars in cash, and a fake beard, the guilt factor increases. Since every juror had probably seen the freeway chase on television, along with 90 million other people, it seemed like a missed opportunity. The defense has put a spin on that flight, of course, saying that O. J. was on his way to commit suicide at Nicole's grave. I never believed that, not even before I heard that the man at the wheel, A. C. Cowlings, had driven past the exit for the cemetery, in the direction of Mexico.

A. C. Cowlings, who is called Al by his friends, remains one of the great mystery characters in this story. A former University of Southern California Trojan and National Football League player, Cowlings has been O. J. Simpson's closest friend from their childhood days in the projects in San Francisco. O. J.'s first wife, Marquerite, had been Al's girl first. Some people will tell you that Al's a swell guy; others will tell you just the opposite. When I likened O. J. and Nicole to Othello and Desdemona a few Letters back, after watching Placido Domingo enact the Moor's jealousy and rage in grand opera, several people asked me, 'But who's Iago?' Sometimes I think Al Cowlings fits the part. He was driving his old pal in the white Ford Bronco on the famous June 17 freeway chase, five days after the murders and one day after Nicole's funeral. While crowds on the sidelines cheered for their hero's safe getaway, Cowlings was calling all the shots, with one hand on the wheel and the other on a cellular phone. His best friend was being transformed during that ride from a mere sports star into a dark legend, part of the folklore of America, and Al – always there for O. J. – was helping to make it happen.

Cowlings has been mostly out of the news since a grand jury elected not to indict him for aiding and abetting a fugitive. But when I saw him on July 22 at the Palm restaurant, he was the star celebrity of the evening. In February he made a press appearance to announce his 900 number, where for $2.99 a minute you could get a taped message from him about O. J. He also appeared in court when he was sued by a would-be buyer of the Ford Bronco, which has become a treasured piece of American Pop art; the buyer claimed Cowlings had reneged on the deal and tried to sell it to someone else for more money. In late June, Cowlings surfaced again at the Los Angeles airport, with a garment bag in one hand and an airline ticket in the other. A Chicago-based CBS television reporter named Byron Harlan, who was in Los Angeles to cover the Unabomber's threat to blow up an airplane at LAX, spotted Cowlings and attempted to interview him. The incident that followed was recorded on video by Harlan's cameraman.

'We're from CBS News,' said Harlan, holding out a microphone.

'I don't give a fuck where you're from, CBS News,' said Cowlings.

Harlan politely persisted. Cowlings lunged forward, swung the garment bag at Harlan, and struck him.

'Hey, I'm traveling, man! Get the fuck out of my face,' said Cowlings.

'You shouldn't have hit me, man,' said Harlan.

'No, I should have knocked your fucking head off. That's what I should have done,' Cowlings replied, walking away.

For my money, Al Cowlings, like Kato Kaelin and Robert Kardashian, knows a lot more than he's telling.

Starting this Tuesday, June 6, K-EARTH 101, Oldies Radio, will give viewers of the O. J. Simpson murder trial something to do during the countless sidebars . . . Every time Judge Ito calls for a sidebar, viewers should turn on their radio to K-EARTH 101.1 FM. During the sidebar, we'll play the K-EARTH 101 'O. J. Sidebar' jingle and immediately take the first five callers, who will each win a

special O. J. watch . . . These collectible wrist-
watches depict the infamous white Bronco being
pursued by the California Highway Patrol.
  —Commercial on LA radio station
    K-EARTH 101 FM.

There are moments in the trial that pass without
comment but that could bear closer scrutiny. One such
concerns the golf clubs that Simpson took with him on
the plane to Chicago on the night of the murders. He was
met at O'Hare Airport at 5:34 a.m. by Hertz employee
Jim Merrill, who kept the clubs in the trunk of his car so
that he could deliver them to Simpson at the golf tournament later that day. After Simpson received word of the
murder of his former wife, he made plans to return to
Los Angeles immediately. He contacted Merrill by phone
three times, and apparently was short-tempered and rude.
Merrill was not able to get the clubs to Simpson's plane
in time. Later, Simpson called Merrill from Los Angeles
to apologize for his earlier rudeness. Merrill had the clubs
put on a later plane. In the midst of mourning for his ex-
wife, Simpson himself, accompanied by his friend Robert
Kardashian, went to the airport to claim his golf clubs.
What was so urgent about retrieving the clubs at that
particular time that he himself had to go rather than send
Ron Shipp or Kato Kaelin? Certainly he wasn't going to
play golf at the Riviera Country Club until after the
funeral service. Some of us have wondered if the missing
knife that killed Nicole Simpson and Ron Goldman could
have been stashed in with the golf clubs, thereby escap-

ing discovery by the airport metal detector. Or the Bruno Magli shoes.

> *Although he looked like Tarzan, he was walking more like Tarzan's grandfather.*
> —Defense witness DR ROBERT HUIZENGA,
> bolstering the defense argument that
> Simpson's arthritis was so bad that he
> could not have committed the crime of
> which he is accused.

As the most visible members of the family of the defendant in this horrible crime, O. J.'s sisters, Shirley Baker and Carmelita Durio, are in a difficult position, but they have behaved with such dignity and style that they have won the admiration of all the reporters. They have put their lives on hold until the trial ends. Constantly loyal to their brother, Shirley has a warm smile and sad eyes, and Carmelita, whom I have seen weep, is funny and outgoing. She knows as much of the courtroom and media gossip as any of us, and during the breaks is always the center of a group in the corridor. Shirley remains beside her husband of thirty-three years, Benny Baker, and their daughter Terri is usually with them. The Bakers recently took a few days off from the trial to stay with a baby grandson who had taken a fall and had to go to the hospital in San Francisco. O. J.'s brother, Truman, who has had 'problems', has been in court only once. Their mother, Eunice, to whom they are devoted, comes from time to time in her wheelchair.

At the beginning of the defense case, Johnnie Cochran put all the Simpson ladies on the stand as a way of showing O. J. through the eyes of those who love him. First came Arnelle, Simpson's beautiful twenty-six-year-old daughter from his first marriage, then Carmelita, then Eunice, and then Shirley. On the first day, the Simpson women, including O. J.'s first wife, Marguerite, were all dressed in shades of yellow, which, we were informed, is the color of hope. After months of testimony in which the prosecution had depicted Simpson as a violent wife beater who ultimately grabbed her by the hair and slit her throat, the family presented a different Simpson altogether – a loving father, a loving son, a loving brother. Cochran used them to emphasize two salient points: Simpson's arthritic condition and the drinking problems of his former friend Ron Shipp, who as a witness for the prosecution had stated that O. J. told him on the night after the murders that he had had dreams of killing Nicole.

Arnelle said that owing to rheumatoid arthritis O. J. had had to give up tennis and had been unable to dig a grave for the family's pet dog. Eunice, who also suffers from arthritis, rose from her wheelchair and – with a cane and an assist from defense lawyer Carl Douglas – hobbled to the stand, her body bent over.

The defense image of a limping, pain-racked Simpson, too weak to kill, was later blown out of the water with the introduction of his exercise videotape, made two weeks before the murders.

Each of the Simpson women spoke about Ron Shipp on the evening after the murders in the house on

Rockingham, and by the end of their testimony Shipp came off as a drunk and a liar. Carmelita said she had smelled his breath and realized he was high. She called him glassy-eyed. Eunice said he was spaced. Shirley said that Shipp was never alone with O. J. in his room that night.

'Not so,' Ron Shipp told me the night following her testimony, after Nicole's great friend Cici Shahian had arranged for me to meet him in a Beverly Hills restaurant called On Cañon, downstairs from Dove Books, where Shahian works.

> *I don't think you let the defendant – of all people – be the one to tell you the glove doesn't fit.*
> —Author and former LA deputy district attorney VINCENT BUGLIOSI criticizing the prosecution's glove debacle.

Ron Shipp provided one of the defining moments of the trial. He made all of us realize that we could look at and listen to the same witness on the stand and interpret him differently; black journalists saw Shipp one way and white journalists another, and all felt confident of their take. Shipp, an African-American former LAPD officer, had been one of O. J. Simpson's best friends. I was so impressed by Shipp's testimony and sense of honor that he became for me a figure of nearly heroic proportions, a deeply conflicted man caught between duty and friend-ship, racked by guilt for not doing anything to halt the domestic violence he knew was going on in the lives of his friends Nicole and O. J., a violence he came to believe resulted in murder. Twice he spoke directly to Simpson from the witness stand. The first time he said, 'This is sad, O. J.' The second time he said, 'Tell the truth, O. J.' When I told an African-American reporter my impressions of Shipp, she looked at me as if I were mad. The person she had seen was a sneak, a snake, a most disloyal figure.

'*No one* had a drink on the night of the thirteenth,' Shipp said emphatically, slapping his hand on the table in the restaurant. 'I didn't have a drink all that day.' It was particularly hurtful, he said, that Eunice Simpson had used the word 'spaced' to describe his condition that night. 'Even when I've been drunk, I've never been spaced . . . Someone had to say to her, "Mom, don't you remember when Ron Shipp was spaced?"'

Shipp had admitted on the stand that he had had a drinking problem, and he didn't hesitate to discuss it now. 'I drank quite a bit when I was a cop. I got to the point where I hated the job. I loved the people, but I hated the job.'

'Do you still drink?' I asked.

'A little bit of wine and beer. Not much, but I do. Is that wrong?'

He was still smarting from a television interview with Bryant Gumbel on the *Today* show that morning, during which he had been accused of having called Simpson's mother a liar.

'I got to the house the day after the murders about six or six-thirty. They were already there, both sisters and Mom. I kissed her on the cheek. I'd met her there at big parties and the wedding.'

'The sisters say you were never alone with O. J.,' I said.

He responded very precisely. 'The conversation took place between ten and eleven that night. It was just me and O. J. The girls were downstairs in the kitchen, or in the room outside the kitchen. They never came up when I was there. Shirley said on the stand, "I told Bob Kardashian to go up and take off O. J.'s clothes," or something like that, and Kardashian wasn't even there. He was already gone. He left about a half-hour before I went up there. The girls knew I was upstairs. When I came down, Shirley said to me, "Don't let him fall asleep alone. Stay up there with him."'

Anyone who has been in a household where a murder has occurred can tell you that no one's total time can be accounted for. Shock prevails. People come, people go. They hug. They whisper. They weep. Conversations are going on all over the house – in corners, in hallways, in the kitchen, bedrooms, bathrooms, garage. Secrets are shared. Revelations are made. Speculation is everywhere. News bulletins on the murder are relayed throughout the house by those watching television.

Luke McKissack, the veteran criminal-defense attorney and legal analyst for Fox News, said to me about the different versions of what had transpired that night, 'O. J.'s a guy's guy. If he's going to tell anyone he had a dream about killing Nicole, it's not going to be his mother, or his daughter, or his sisters. It's going to be a guy like Ron Shipp.'

Shipp and I were splitting a pizza. As he picked up a slice, he was thinking back to his lost friend. 'The police loved O. J. I'd take cops by there, and O. J. loved having them over. He knew what I was doing, and he'd do it for me. I'd drive over there without telling the other cops where I was going. Then the cops would walk in and realize where they were. He posed for pictures with them and signed autographs. What is the reason now that the LAPD hate him and want to conspire against him?' He smiled sadly at the absurdity.

'Has this been tough for you?' I asked.

'It's been tough for both Chris Darden and me in the black community, I'll tell you that,' he replied.

As we were leaving, I asked Shipp one last question. 'What was the final thing that set him off? Why do you think the murders happened that night?'

'I feel it was the rejection at the recital,' he answered. 'No seat. No invitation to dinner. O. J.'s a guy who always lived to be loved.'

> *She's a good lawyer, but the word 'finesse' and Marcia Clark should not be used in the same sentence.*
> —HENRY WEINSTEIN of the *Los Angeles Times*, in corridor conversation about Clark's hostile cross-examination of copyright lawyer Mark Partridge, who sat next to O. J. Simpson on the flight home from Chicago the day after the murders and later copyrighted his eight pages of notes about the flight.

Sometimes you have to separate yourself from the trial and go back to real life. I left court fifteen minutes early on July 11 so that I could get to Eva Gabor's funeral on time. It was a 7 p.m. funeral Mass at the Church of the Good Shepherd on Santa Monica Boulevard in Beverly Hills. For years this church has been referred to affectionately by its wealthy parishioners as Our Lady of the Cadillacs. It was my church for years. It was Eva Gabor's church, too. The place was packed. There was a roped-off area toward the front for the swells, and because of my recent 'celebrity' status as a television commentator on the Simpson trial, I was taken in hand by an overzealous usher who asked me about the trial as he led me up the aisle, much too far forward, considering the degree of my friendship with Eva. In fact, to my mortification I was put in the family section, in the same row with former First Lady Nancy Reagan and Merv Griffin, who was for years the very best friend of Eva, and two rows behind Eva's sisters, Zsa Zsa and Magda. The Gabor ladies looked like glamorous grandes dames, dressed in black chiffon with pearls at the neck and pearls at the ears, holding large lace handkerchiefs to weep into. Magda, in a wheelchair, wore a huge black straw hat. On the altar was a large blowup of Eva, framed in pink and red roses. As of that day, the surviving sisters had not told their mother, Jolie, who is said to be 109, that Eva was dead.

Right across the aisle was Eddie Albert, who played Eva's husband on *Green Acres*. Behind him, next to Suzanne Pleshette, sat Mr and Mrs Lew Wasserman – an assurance in the film community that the A group, as it used to be called, had turned out to say farewell to Eva.

On the way out, I dropped behind so as not to look like a member of the Gabor family. 'Do you think he'll

get off?' someone asked me. 'He's going to walk, isn't he?'
'What's Marcia Clark like?' As I was leaving, a very famous
woman whispered in my ear, 'Nick, promise me something. When I die, don't let them put a big photo blowup
of me on the altar.'

> *I liked Marcia Clark better with curly hair.*
> —BETSY BLOOMINGDALE at a lunch party
>   given by Marguerite Littman at Harry's
>   Bar in London.

My telephone rang. It was Michael Fleeman, who is
covering the Simpson trial for the Associated Press. He
was writing a newspaper article about what killers do after
they kill, in anticipation of the defense's plan to bring in
what are called demeanor witnesses, to say that Simpson
had behaved in a perfectly normal manner at the airport
and on the plane the night of the murders, suggesting
that he was not guilty.

'What did the Menendez brothers do after they killed
their parents?' he asked.

'They bought Rolex watches to wear to the funeral,' I
replied without a moment's hesitation.

It's naïve to think that an intelligent killer would behave
in a sinister or suspicious manner after taking a life. On
the contrary: a person who has spent his whole career in
the public eye would certainly be able to sign 'Peace to
you' on two autographs shortly after the killings if he
were called upon to do so, as Simpson was at the airport
and on the plane.

I also had a call from George Schlatter, the television producer, who had had lunch with his old friend Howard Bingham, the photographer. Bingham had been a demeanor witness for the defense, because he was a passenger on the flight from LAX to Chicago that night, and talked briefly with O. J., whom he knew, on the plane before takeoff. It was a 'Hi, Juice', 'Hi, Bingham, how's it going?' sort of conversation – no deeper than that. Bingham, an African-American and a close friend of Muhammad Ali's, brought to court a coffee-table book of his photographs of the prizefighter, which Johnnie Cochran mentioned in order to establish Bingham with the jury. Bingham is a greatly loved figure in the circles in which he moves. A stutterer who treats his affliction with humor, he was a good and likable witness, who provided a few witness-stand laughs. As he described his encounter with O. J., he was eager to establish that he hadn't been in first class, as he normally would be, because he had three seats in coach so that he could sleep during the flight. There was no sense that he was either pro- or anti-defense; he was just a citizen doing his duty. Over lunch several days later, Bingham told Schlatter that he had been contacted by Judge Ito's secretary, asking for a signed copy of his Muhammad Ali book. The following week, Bingham appeared in court with a box of signed books for the jury, to be given to them after the trial. He had an in-chambers meeting with the judge and a courtroom seat for the afternoon session.

It's among the most popular programs we've ever done. It's one of the highest-rated programs ever on

*Sky, consistently every week, even during the DNA
period.*
>   —MIKE BUCKELL, producer for Sky News,
>   London, discussing its coverage of the O.
>   J. Simpson trial in England.

Anita Hill came to court one day. A few weeks earlier,
I had been introduced to her at Drai's, during a dinner
party given by Michael Viner, the CEO of Dove Books,
for Vincent Bugliosi. Hill was at a different table.
Prosecutor Chris Darden was expected at Viner's party,
and the whispered gossip was that there was a match-
making plan afoot to have Darden and Hill meet. The plan
went awry when Darden failed to show up; an hour into
the dinner, a waiter removed his glass and silverware, and
the meeting did not take place. The day Hill appeared in
court – looking extremely handsome and very well dressed
– she was reputed to be a guest of the prosecution, but
it was not clear whether or not she was Darden's guest. I
went over and spoke to her, and she cut me dead. In the
same way she cut a number of people dead, including
author Joseph Bosco, who is writing a book on the case,
when he expressed admiration of her. During breaks, she
did not go into the corridor, as everyone does, but
remained in the courtroom. A few days later, Diane
Sawyer, Geraldo Rivera, and Jackie Mason were all in the
courtroom at the same time, and they all spoke to everybody.

'Are you disappointed?'
'I never get too high on the good days, or too low on the bad days. I take them as they come.'
    —JOHNNIE COCHRAN, in the corridor, after being informed that Judge Ito had curtailed defense efforts to suggest that Faye Resnick was the target of a Colombian drug hit that killed Nicole Simpson by mistake.

I had dinner at Drai's with dismissed juror Tracy Kennedy and his wife, Judy. Kennedy was described at the time of his dismissal as Native American, but his appearance – skin, hair, beard, manner – is whiter than white. As is the fashion these days for dismissed jurors, he is writing a book about his tenure on the panel, and Dove Books is going to publish it. Like another dismissed juror, the flight attendant Tracy Hampton, whom we saw on a stretcher being removed by paramedics from her parents' home with a sheet over her face two days after her dismissal, Kennedy suffered from severe depression both during and after his time on the jury. Although he admits that he did not endear himself to the deputies in charge or to some of the other jurors, he felt an acute sense of failure when he was dismissed by Judge Ito. He felt he had let everyone down. But if he was devastated, he was relieved at the same time. Now anger had set in.

Judy Kennedy's outrage over the horrors of sequestration exceeds that of her husband. 'They discuss sequestration with all these legal minds, but they didn't discuss it with psychologists or psychiatrists to see what the consequences would be.'

'Tell me how the conjugal visits came about,' I said.

'I would drive to a certain place in an underground garage to pick up the van that took the visitors to meet the jurors. They searched you. We were taken to the service elevators of the hotel where they are sequestered. Cameras monitored the halls. You had to stay from 7 P.M. to 12. If you wanted to leave earlier, you couldn't. Then we were taken back on the van to our cars in the underground garage to drive home after midnight. That was scary sometimes.'

'What they're doing to the jury is inhuman,' said Kennedy. 'I predict that there will be psychological fallout. They're in a catatonic state, like a trance. It breaks your spirit after a while.'

'I watched my husband change from week to week,' said Judy Kennedy. 'There was this blank look on his face, when you lose the expression in the eyes. The jurors were losing their identity. They were sitting so close to the families of Nicole and Ron that they could feel their grief. Every week I watched all of them begin to turn inward. Each family member began bringing more food. The food became more elaborate. Food is a comfort.'

She looked at her husband and placed her hand on his as she continued to talk about him. They seemed deeply connected to each other. 'I lost my best friend,' she said. 'He became hyper, agitated.'

'I didn't realize it,' said Kennedy.

'I thought to myself, I don't know this man,' Judy

Kennedy continued. 'After a certain number of weeks, we couldn't talk to each other. They took away his humanity. He didn't want to live anymore.'

'We didn't know that the rooms weren't bugged,' said Kennedy.

'The paranoia is rampant,' his wife explained.

Kennedy nodded in agreement. 'Everyone changed to an unnatural state. The deputies made us feel we were an inconvenience to them. They were awful.' He had a particular loathing for one, whom I happen to have had dealings with myself.

'We call her Big Girl,' I told him.

'We called her Butch,' he replied. Then he laughed, looking over at his wife in a way that indicated they had shared a lot of stories about the deputies.

As we looked at the menu, he recalled the sequestration food with a dismissive gesture. 'The food is employee food. It's cafeteria-style. You go in, stand in line. Plenty of it, all you want, but . . .' He ordered the filet mignon.

'In court, you go up in the elevator to what is called the food room. In the beginning, there were twenty-four of us, twelve jurors and twelve alternates. There were only two sofas and four tables with four chairs per table. Jurors complained that there weren't enough seats during the long waiting periods. A month and a half later, Deputy Jex said, "Well, I got you another table." There still wasn't enough room.'

Judy Kennedy said, 'I think the reason there are so few convictions in Los Angeles is because of the way the deputies treat the jurors. It's as if they're prisoners.'

We discussed which of the remaining jurors would be the foreperson. 'They've taken all the leaders away,' he replied sadly, referring to the dismissed ones. Like Michael Knox, the dismissed juror who published an account of his time on the panel, he predicts that juror No. 1, a black female fifty-year-old vendor, will be the foreperson. Unlike Knox, who believes that Simpson will be convicted, Kennedy believes that there will be a hung jury. About one juror, he said, 'I get the feeling he hates all white people.'

On the Friday before the Memorial Day weekend, nine weeks after Kennedy had been dismissed, he went to see his doctor about his depression, and was put on medication. When he returned to his house, he found a new jury summons in the mail. 'That was the straw that broke the camel's back,' he said.

THE 'N' WORD:
Not Guilty

A REPORTER I KNOW who's a friend of a deputy who's a friend of another deputy who's connected to the jury of the Simpson trial called me early on the morning of October 2, the first day of deliberation, to tell me that some of the jurors had already packed their bags in the Hotel Inter-continental, where they had been sequestered for so long, before leaving for court. At that time, that bit of information seemed too improbable to pay attention to. I had told both Dan Rather and Larry King on television that I believed there would be a hung jury. But some of the jurors *had* packed their bags. They had also apparently already made up their minds. The deputy who told the deputy who told my friend said some of them had made plans for the weekend. The night before, a person I know had visited O. J. in the county jail. He reported him to be upbeat, making plans for his future, looking forward to being with his kids, a man 'with not a negative thought on his mind'. That afternoon, in the courthouse, another journalist went up to turn in his press badge to Deputy Jex, after hearing a court reporter read back to the jury a section of the transcript dealing with the limousine driver Allan Park, who had testified that he had seen an African-American man of six feet and 200 pounds enter the house. The journalist assumed the day was over. 'You better stick around for another hour,' replied Deputy Jex.

In a trial of stunning surprises, nothing was more stunning than the news that the jury had arrived at a verdict in less than four hours of deliberation. Another deputy reported that from the time the jurors received their verdict forms from Judge Ito it took them eight minutes to arrive at their unanimous decision: NOT GUILTY.

What happened happened just as this letter was going to press. Next time, I'll tell you about the closing arguments, the deep dissension in the ranks of the defense team, the three heartbroken families, the plans for the future. And the aftermath. What follows is from my notebooks of the events leading up to O. J. Simpson's walk to freedom and a new life.

'I WANT ALL of the citizens of Los Angeles to remain calm,' said an enraged Johnnie Cochran in a sentence that said one thing but that could be interpreted as meaning another, during a press conference in which he blasted Judge Ito for ruling that only two of the forty-two uses of the word 'nigger' on the Fuhrman tapes could be presented to the jury. 'The cover-up continues,' said

Cochran, suggesting that Judge Ito himself could be part of a conspiracy against Simpson. Many people were shocked by Cochran's statement. Later, in a sidebar in the judge's chambers, Ito told Cochran that he was going to overlook his public outburst.

For a brief time, the anticipation of Mark Fuhrman's second appearance as a witness and then his courtroom presence eclipsed O. J. Simpson at his own trial – a temporary abdication of the spotlight that was probably very welcome to Simpson. Judge Ito interrupted Marcia Clark right in the middle of a sentence when Fuhrman entered the courtroom, surrounded by four tough-guy bodyguards who stayed by the door. You may hate this man with every fiber in you, but he has an aura about him. He knew how to make that entrance. People twisted in their seats to look at him, and for a second he scanned the crowd as if looking for a friendly face. In the back row sat Art Harris of CNN, who – long before the discovery of the Fuhrman tapes – had written and produced a television segment in which Fuhrman was portrayed by two African-American women as a compassionate man in cases in which they had been involved. Passing behind Harris on his way to the stand, Fuhrman squeezed his shoulder. His step was still decisive, as it had been six months earlier, and his TV-star face was still haughty, but there was a deadness in his eyes, as if he knew that people were staring at him with loathing. I kept thinking of his kids. What's it going to be like for them?

The prosecution looked upon him as a betrayer for not having informed them of the infamous tapes before he professed under oath on the stand that he had not said the word 'nigger' in ten years. At the time, I was critical of F. Lee Bailey's cross-examination of Fuhrman, but I watched that segment again recently and in hindsight I see how good Bailey was at entrapping him. It made me wonder if Bailey knew about Laura Hart McKinny's tapes at that time, and was setting Fuhrman up for his eventual fall. Chris Darden shunned Fuhrman by leaving the courtroom before he entered. Marcia Clark did not look at him. Kim Goldman, Ron Goldman's sister, who was sitting next to me, turned her head away.

For the defense, Fuhrman was manna from heaven. Outside the courthouse, an angry throng chanted, 'Give us Fuhrman! Give us Fuhrman!' There was an ominous feeling in the air. No one talked of conviction anymore. For people of the pro-prosecution persuasion, like me, who believe Simpson is guilty of the crimes with which he was charged, a hung jury would have seemed like a triumph at that point. An acquittal seemed more than a possibility. The jury wanted this to be over. They were sick of it. I thought they could arrive at a verdict quickly. In the greatest irony of the many ironies of the trial, Mark Fuhrman, who detests blacks, could end up being responsible for the black defendant's being acquitted of two counts of murder by the mostly black jury. With a victorious air, the entire defense team held a press conference on the first floor of the courthouse in time for the evening news, decrying the scumbag Fuhrman and expressing indignation that their innocent client, as Johnnie Cochran called Simpson, had been in jail for fifteen months. They then made their way out of the front door and up the courthouse stairs to their cars. The triumphant cheers of the African-American crowd outside could be heard for blocks. The underpinning of this whole case – what was propelling it, what it was really about – was race. It was not about the slit throats of Nicole Brown Simpson and Ronald Goldman.

> *This is a trial where neither side can hold their serve.*
>
> —DAVID BEGELMAN, film producer and former head of Columbia Pictures, during lunch at the Regent Beverly Wilshire hotel shortly before his suicide.

Anthony Pellicano, the renowned Los Angeles private detective, who has been acting as Mark Fuhrman's adviser and spokesperson, continues to defend him, although he has admitted in the press that he was as shocked as everyone else by the excessive use of the word 'nigger' on Laura Hart McKinny's tapes. About the rest of the material on the tapes, he said, 'He was trying to impress this McKinny woman. He was trying to be Macho Man and Supercop. At that time of his life – '85, '86 – he hated everybody. He was an equal-opportunity hater.'

I tracked Pellicano down in Chicago, where he was attending a niece's wedding. I've known him for years. I once hired him to follow John Sweeney, the man who killed my daughter, when he was released from prison after serving only two and a half years. 'Fuhrman's had more death threats than anyone in the history of LA,' he said. 'The guy's afraid for his life.'

Fuhrman's transportation from Idaho, where he now lives with his third wife, Caroline, and their two small children, was paid for by O. J. Simpson, as were his hotel bills. Whatever it cost O. J., it was worth it. Fuhrman reportedly spent the first night at the Biltmore in downtown Los Angeles, the second at the New Otani in the same location. He changed hotels every night, managing to escape detection by the media, although Drew Griffin, a reporter from KCBS, acting on a tip from a guest at a Holiday Inn in Burbank, thought he had spotted him there.

'Did Fuhrman have an affair with McKinny?' I asked Pellicano. (McKinny denied this on the stand.)

'Six months. He broke off with her and then married Caroline.'

'Chris Darden said in a sidebar something about love letters.'

'There are love letters. She sent them to Fuhrman.'

I bought a large box of sixty-four Crayolas so I could identify the colors of Johnnie Cochran's suits.
—DAVID MARGOLICK of *The New York
    Times*, at a barbecue given for the media
    by Larry Schiller, co-author with Simpson
    of *I Want to Tell You.*

For all her Botticelli hairdo and martyred expression, there was nothing noble in the motive of Laura Hart

McKinny, who is now described in the media as screen-writer Laura Hart McKinny, although she has never sold a script. In an open letter to McKinny in *Daily Variety*, the editor, Peter Bart, who knows a thing or two about screenwriting, having been the number-two man at Paramount in Hollywood for years, wrote, 'The bottom line, Laura, is that you spent ten years researching and writing a screenplay that understandably no one wants to finance . . . Judging from your script, Laura, your prin-cipal talent lies not in writing but rather in getting into trouble. And for that, we are all paying a price . . . Perhaps instead of teaching a course on screenwriting, you could actually take one.'

When McKinny heard Mark Fuhrman say under oath on the witness stand that he had not used the word 'nigger' in the last ten years, she didn't make any attempt to turn over her mother lode of theretofore worthless tapes – with forty-two sound bites of Fuhrman saying exactly what he swore he had not said – to the prosecution, or even to the defense. Instead, she hired a Los Angeles lawyer, Matthew Schwartz, who had been recommended to her by a teacher at the North Carolina School of the Arts who had gone to UCLA film school with Schwartz. Schwartz's law part-ner, Ron Regwan, admitted they had checked the tabloids to see what the market value of the hate-filled tapes was. McKinny – who in 1993 had left California under a bit of a cloud after filing for bankruptcy to escape $80,000 in debts she and her husband had accumulated – reportedly asked for a half-million dollars from Dove Books for tran-scripts of the tapes, but when Chris Darden put the question to her in court she denied that money was her motive. Personally, I'm sick of people coming out of the woodwork and trying to get rich on the mutilated bodies of Nicole Brown Simpson and Ronald Goldman, the forgotten victims of the Simpson trial.

Pat McKenna, O. J. Simpson's colorful, outspoken private investigator – who performed in the same capacity for William Kennedy Smith at his rape trial in Palm Beach, Florida – acted on a telephone tip, discovered the tapes, and the defense pounced on them. There was jubilation in the defense camp. 'This is a blockbuster. This is a bombshell,' Johnnie Cochran cried out to Judge Ito, with a prance in his step and excitement in his voice. 'This is perhaps the biggest thing that's happened in any case in this country in this decade.'

At that moment the Simpson trial turned into the Mark Fuhrman trial. The fact that the family of one of the victims was in the courtroom made no difference. Fred, Patti, and Kim Goldman were sitting next to me, and I could feel their fury building as the defense team gloated, for the subtext of their remarks was 'Acquittal is in the bag.' That evening, Fred and Kim called a press conference, and the cry of rage emanating from them dominated every newscast. 'This is *not* the Fuhrman trial,' Fred Goldman said. 'This is a trial about the man who murdered my son.'

When Gretchen Stockdale walked off the stand, the defense table rose by six inches.

　　—DAN ABRAMS of Court TV, repeating a
　　courtroom joke about the model O. J.

> Simpson left a romantic message for a few
> hours before the murders, at Larry
> Schiller's barbecue for the media.

From the very beginning, a reporter from *The Philadelphia Inquirer* named Robin Clark won his way into the hearts of all the rest of us covering the trial with his reporting talent, his writing style, and, most of all, his wit. He could do an off-the-top-of-his-head one-liner about any of the players – from Judge Ito to Deputy Jex and all the lawyers in between – that would rock the media room with laughter. One Friday, when we were breaking for the weekend, Robin introduced me to a cousin of his who was visiting from New York with a friend of hers, and said he was going to take them for a spin up the Pacific Coast Highway. An hour and a half later, all three were killed in a collision. Andrea Ford of the *Los Angeles Times* was the first to get the word. She called Shirley Perlman of *New York Newsday*, who called me, as did Joseph Bosco, who's writing a book about the case. For the first time in the long months of this trial, we heard one another cry as word passed from one hotel room to another. It made me realize how close we have all become, sharing this extraordinary experience that the trial has been. The following Monday in court, Judge Ito kept Robin's seat in the courtroom empty, and a deputy hung Robin's press pass on the back of the seat. I missed Robin Clark's memorial service, which was held at the Beverly Hills house that author Joe McGinniss, who is also writing a book about the case, has rented for the length of the trial. My son Alex had been reported missing in the Santa Rita Mountains of Arizona, and I had left for the Nogales home of my former wife, where, with our son Griffin and our granddaughter, Hannah, we waited out the agonizing, nerve-racking days. At the end of day four, I gave up. I said to Griffin, 'He's dead.' Griffin didn't think so. From hanging out at murder trials, as I do, I have grown despondent about the goodness of people. Truth has taken an ignominious decline in importance. Truth is what you get the jury to believe. But I saw and felt goodness again in Nogales. There were volunteers from two counties, K-9 patrols, police, a sheriff, helicopters, and a plane. The telephones never stopped ringing. People from everywhere called to say that they were praying. All those prayers were heard. My son reappeared, having fallen down a ravine and having survived. We experienced joy. Back at the trial the following Monday, Judge Ito began the day by saying, 'Welcome back, Mr Dunne.'

I don't want to hear one word about the O. J. Simpson trial.
        —MRS BILLY WILDER, hands over her ears,
            issuing a command as she seated her
            guests at Mr Chow.

It seems to me that almost everyone in this town has some input into the Simpson case. One night a husband-and-wife private-detective team who had heard me lecture on the case at the Los Angeles Public Library took me for a ride through the backstreets and alleyways of

Brentwood in order to show me that it is possible to make the run between Nicole's condominium on Bundy and O. J.'s mansion on Rockingham in four minutes. If there happens to be no traffic on Sunset – and there probably wasn't at that late hour on the night of the murders – it's quite possible. We did it several times. I hadn't been out to the area for months. There's no prettier part of Los Angeles than Brentwood north of Sunset. The houses are spacious and beautiful. The gardens are impeccably tended. The cars in the driveways are sleek. It's not the flashy-rich part of town; it's the part that has the look of old money. When I drove past the rather stately house where O. J. and Nicole Simpson had lived when the going was good between them, I couldn't help thinking of how perfect it must have looked then to anyone peeking over the wall: the handsome superstar, the beautiful blonde wife, the magnificent kids, the pool, the tennis court, the red-brick mansion. What is amazing is that even now, nearly a year and a half after the murders, crowds of people still come to stare, despite blockades erected to discourage them. The night I was there, gawking just like the sightseers, the cars driving by were old and rattly. Some held six to eight people, a few of them standing on the roofs of the vehicles, trying to see over the wall and focus cameras at the same time. There are guards on duty, and a sound system that starts to blast when anyone gets too close to the wall. 'The longer this goes on, the lower the class of people who come here,' one of the guards said to me. He had other opinions: 'The police did a lousy job. They had a search warrant to look for a sweat suit, a cap, gloves, and a stiletto-type knife. They didn't even search the whole house. They never looked in the wine cellar.'

A week or so later, I found myself back in the same neighborhood. A chance telephone call from the screenwriter Ernest Lehman, who had had dinner with friends of mine the night before, led me to meet Wolfgang and Marta Salinger, O. J. Simpson's next-door neighbors, who are equally well known in the case as the former employers of Rosa Lopez, the maid who provided Simpson with an alibi on the night of the murders but who was subsequently discredited when she lied on the stand and who then flew off to El Salvador. The Salingers have erected a temporary wire fence in front of their property to keep the sightseers off their lawn. It was a Sunday morning. We drank lemonade in a sun-filled book room overlooking a rose garden. Cultivated and shy of publicity, they were amazingly forthright in their conversation. They remembered their one-time neighbor with great affection. 'We liked the man,' said Marta Salinger. 'For seventeen years I had only pleasure from him. He was a wonderful neighbor. We always played on his tennis court.'

Wolfgang Salinger concurred. 'We were at his wedding, and he was at my seventieth birthday. We were at his fortieth birthday. We asked him to my seventy-fifth. He came for a few minutes. He charmed everybody.'

'Justin was a darling boy, and O. J. was wonderful to him,' said Marta. 'He taught him how to play baseball when he was two and a half. His patience was unbelievable.'

We talked about the day they had been in court, when Rosa was on the stand. 'O. J. smiled and waved at us across the courtroom,' said Marta. 'He knew we weren't against him. We are neither for nor against him. When I heard the news, I said a prayer that he had an alibi.'

'O. J. loved the good life,' said Wolfgang. 'That house is what he achieved. Neither wife got it in the divorce. You should have seen him at the Riviera Country Club.' He struck a king-of-the-roost pose.

'I never saw his wife when she was beaten up, but I saw the maid, Michelle, who was beaten up by Nicole,' said Marta. 'That was last year in February. Michelle told me when the Simpsons had this fight and Nicole was injured, Nicole said to Michelle, 'I want you to testify for me,' but Michelle said, 'No, I work for both of you. I didn't see anything.' That was when Nicole fired her. Michelle was a friend of Rosa's. I think Rosa wanted to help O. J. because Michelle had been hit by Nicole.'

The conversation turned to Rosa Lopez. 'I was amused when you quoted someone in *Vanity Fair* as saying, "If Rosa Lopez is as lousy a housekeeper as she is a liar, I'd hate to see the inside of the Salingers' house,"' said Marta. 'So many people sent that to me. Rosa was honest. Nothing was ever missing. But she wasn't a good housekeeper. I never fired her, as she said on the stand.'

'Did Rosa lie?' I asked.

'Of course she lied,' said Marta. 'I've always taken that for granted.'

Her husband said, 'She was here three years. I never was sure if she understood what I said, either in English or Spanish, and I speak Spanish very well. When she spoke, she didn't know the difference between past and present tense.'

'She wanted to be part of it,' said Marta about Rosa's involvement in the case. 'Cochran told her not to talk about it, and she never told us she was in any way connected to the whole thing. The only thing she had ever told us was that Detective Fuhrman came over here to talk to her but that he never came back. I think she went out to O. J.'s office to tape what she said to the investigator. We didn't know anything, because she didn't tell us. They usually can't keep their mouths shut. They usually tell you everything.'

'Do you think she was really out walking the dog that night?' I asked.

'Our dog has a bad allergy,' said Wolfgang, 'and I made it a rule that the dog never go out on the street.'

'Rosa adored Mr Johnnie. She had a new dress every day,' said Marta.

A fence covered by hedges separates the Salinger property from the Simpson property. The Salingers believe that in order for Simpson not to have been seen by the limousine driver that night he would have had to get to his house by coming onto their property and going down their driveway. We walked along the length of the fence. 'My husband thought the only way for him to get over the fence was by this tree,' said Marta. Indeed, there is a tree on the Salinger property with branches that create a ladder which would have made it easy to hop over the fence and come down in the area near the air conditioner outside the room where Kato Kaelin was staying.

They didn't have much time for Kaelin. 'He parked his lousy car outside our house,' said Wolfgang. 'When I complained, he said, "I'm Mr Simpson's houseguest."' They both laughed.

'Did you ever see O. J. play?' asked Marta.

'No,' I replied.

She clapped her hands at the memory of him. 'He was a beautiful runner. He was like a deer.' She shook her head. 'The last time I saw him, I said, "I'm terribly sorry, O. J., that you're splitting up." He said, "Oh, don't take it seriously. She's hot-tempered. She'll come back."'

SPEAKING OF ROSA LOPEZ, here's the latest on her. A few months back, I wrote that she had become engaged to a twenty-eight-year-old ventriloquist from Baltimore named Mike Gabriel, or 'Sensei' Mike Gabriel, as he calls himself, who saw Rosa testifying on television, became smitten, and followed her to El Salvador, where she agreed to accept his hand in marriage. That betrothal has bitten the dust. Gabriel, who is primarily a teacher of cat yoga, recently wrote me a long, chatty letter in which he said that Rosa was allergic to cats and that that had ended the romance. Not to worry. Gabriel's old girlfriend took him back, and they are 'engaged to be engaged'. Her name is Samantha, and she acts in porn. She has just filmed her first anal-sex scene, her fiancé informed me.

*   *   *

NO MATTER WHERE YOU GO, you can't get away from the trial. One night at Drai's, I saw Faye Resnick, Robert Shapiro, and Michael Viner, all at separate tables. Another night I stopped to say hello to a friend and, by accident, bumped into a man seated at the next table. When I turned to apologize, I saw that it was Kato Kaelin. We had seen each other in court but had never spoken. I have written about him several times in a less than flattering way, because I felt that he was keeping secrets that are vital to the story. I have often wondered if he was frightened by someone into withholding what he knew. We stared at each other for an instant, unsure how to play the moment. 'I'm so glad they found your son,' he said, which wasn't at all what I was expecting. 'Would you ever talk to me?' I asked him. He said, 'Sure. Where do I reach you?' I gave him the name of my hotel, but so far I haven't heard from him. There's so much I would like to ask him about the night of the murders. Not that I think he would give me any answers, but I'd still like to ask.

> *How many people do you know who wear cashmere-lined leather gloves and a knit cap on a June night in Los Angeles?*
> —A stranger who came up to me during
>   dinner at the Bistro Garden in Beverly Hills.

Driving down Hollywood Boulevard in the back of a limousine on the way to the premiere of *Waterworld*, a beautiful woman, who must be nameless, told me she knew a man who had been to visit O. J. in jail the day before.

She said that her friend, who had once been very friendly with O. J., asked him if he had done it, and that O. J. replied, 'No way, man. I loved her. Anybody who knows me knows I could never have done it.' Her enactment of her friend's enactment of O. J.'s avowal of his love for Nicole was so convincing that I could visualize him saying it.

'Maybe that's what he'll say if he takes the stand,' I replied.

'My friend's not going back,' she answered.

I don't do windows and I don't do retrials.
—Famed trial reporter THEO WILSON, now
retired, during a media discussion of a
possible Simpson retrial.

A source close to Simpson tells me that he is still paying $10,900 a month for Sydney and Justin, his children by Nicole, which is the same amount he used to give Nicole. The money is paid to the Brown family. Hertz cut him off its payroll after his arrest. A source tells me that NBC continued to pay him for four months and then stopped, although NBC denies this. Money is still coming in, however. Every noon during the lunch break, he sits in the lockup room and signs autographs on football jerseys, football cards, deflated footballs, and photographs – all hot items for collectors, all for sale. So far he has earned $1.3 million, and that's not including what he made on his bestselling book.

He couldn't find a mick in Dublin.
—PAT MCKENNA, defense-team investigator,
refuting District Attorney Gil Garcetti's
claim that the prosecution had discovered
the Fuhrman tapes.

A member of the defense team who doesn't get much
credit these days, and should, is Robert Shapiro, who was
the lead lawyer of Simpson's dream team before, in football jargon, and end run was made around him by the
former running-back defendant, who put Johnnie
Cochran in charge. Some believe Shapiro was brought on
at the recommendation of Simpson's first lawyer, Howard
Weitzman, because of his expertise in plea bargaining,
which may have been a factor sometime early in the case.
At any rate, within days of the murders, Shapiro brought
in two expert witnesses worth their weight in gold who
later performed brilliantly on the stand. One was Michael
Baden, the former New York City coroner, and the other
was Dr Henry Lee from Connecticut, who is invariably
referred to in the press as America's foremost forensic
scientist. Both were present in Robert Kardashian's house
that Friday five days after the murders when Simpson –
instead of turning himself in to the LAPD, as planned
– took off with his friend Al Cowlings in the white Bronco
for the famous freeway chase, leaving Shapiro and
Kardashian behind to read his 'suicide' note to 95 million
viewers. I had not realized that expert witnesses can be
participants in a murder case before the arrest until I was
provided with a photograph of Dr Lee kneeling in front

of a stripped-down Simpson with camera in hand.

Also in the Kardashian house at the time O. J. left for the freeway chase were Shapiro's doctor, Robert Huizenga – who later became a defense witness and suggested on the stand that Simpson was too crippled by arthritis to have committed the crimes – two nurses, psychiatrist Saul Faerstein, and perhaps more. All of them were present in the Kardashian residence because of their professional relationship with O. J., but none of them seems to have seen Simpson and Cowlings leave in the white Bronco. O. J.'s girlfriend Paula Barbieri, who had spent Wednesday and Thursday nights there, and Kardashian's then fiancée, Denice Halicki, left the house before O. J.'s departure.

The mystery of why the prosecution did not bring the freeway chase into the trial is beginning to seep out. Robert Shapiro said to Shirley Perlman of *Newsday*, 'If the prosecution brings in witnesses to the freeway chase, they will regret it.' The story is – and it sounds right to me – that the helicopters hovering over the Bronco picked up and taped O. J.'s many cellular-phone calls. Parts of the transcript of one of them – to his mother, who urges him to turn himself in – have been published in the *National Enquirer*. In other calls, Simpson apparently proclaims that he is innocent and that he is being framed. One could interpret that as meaning that the defense had already come up with its conspiracy theory, before the arrest. For the jury to hear that in O. J.'s voice, probably crying, would be devastating to the prosecution.

Since Shapiro had fostered Lee's involvement in the case, it was considered a slap in Shapiro's face when

Barry Scheck was assigned to take Lee through his direct examination. Although some will tell you it was Cochran's decision to give the gig to Scheck instead of to Shapiro – a source of embarrassment and anger for Shapiro – a person close to the defense told me that it was Simpson's decision and that Cochran was merely the messenger. As of now, Barry Scheck is Simpson's favorite lawyer on the case, and will deliver the closing argument with Cochran. Simpson, by the way, is no passive defendant, complying with everything his lawyers tell him to do. During night strategy sessions in Cochran's office, Simpson, from jail, participates actively by speakerphone.

The infinite charm of Dr Lee is legendary, especially when he talks to juries – beguiling them, amusing them, instructing them, making them feel like mini-authorities on blood spatter and shoe prints. If he suggests to them that there might have been a second set of shoe prints at the crime scene, that's probably what they're going to believe. I have never been one to contribute to the hagiography of Dr Lee, having seen him give a quite similar courtroom performance when he was an expert witness for the defense at the William Kennedy Smith rape trial.

Lee's wit filled the Simpson courtroom with laughter when he misidentified one of the defense lawyers and quipped, 'You people all look alike.' I had a feeling it wasn't the first time he had used that joke, so I called someone I knew in the district attorney's office in Hartford, Connecticut, who laughed and told me it was a staple in Lee's repertoire. Lee said on the stand that 95 percent of the time he is a prosecution witness. The other

5 percent, when he appears for the defense, is usually in high-profile cases. 'I don't know what his motivations are in the Simpson case. He *believes* in DNA,' said the person in the Hartford office.

When Dr Lee finished testifying, he wanted to have his picture taken with prosecutors Marcia Clark and Chris Darden. A person who witnessed this event told me that Hank Goldberg, who had conducted Lee's cross-examination, felt left out, so Barry Scheck turned to Lee and said, 'Don't you want your picture taken with Hank?' A bailiff took the first picture. One of the lawyers took the second.

I don't take that seriously, about Denise. Denise is just a hugging girl. She hugged the wrong man.
> —JUDITHA BROWN, mother of Nicole, after the defense said in court that her daughter Denise had had an affair with mobster and FBI informant Craig 'Tony the Animal' Fiato.

Weariness has set in. The trial has gone on too long. People have cabin fever. Everyone who has been in the courtroom all these months, day in, day out, feels the same claustrophobia. But then we think about the jurors, and they have it worse. We regulars all know one another by now, including the Goldman, Brown, and Simpson families, the judge, the lawyers, the clerks, the court reporters, the deputies, and the media. To my knowledge, no one in the media has spoken with O. J. Simpson, but I understand that O. J. knows who certain reporters are and how we stand on his guilt or innocence. The jury is in a fragile state. They are sick of the trial. This is the longest sequestration of a jury in the history of California law. Some of them are glassy-eyed. They send complaints to the judge, who has been their champion, and many no longer laugh at his jokes. I believe jurors No. 8 and No. 9, two African-American females, have already made up their minds. I think it is possible that No. 3, a Caucasian female of sixty-one, could hang the jury. In mid-September she had financial problems, needed $3,000, and wanted to leave. To keep her, Judge Ito said that he would ask the court for the money. Cochran, speaking for the defense, vehemently objected, arguing that No. 3 would then be beholden to the judge. The defense would love to lose her, fearing that O. J. will never get his acquittal with her on the jury. Subsequently we were told that the problem had been solved, and that LA County funds had not been used.

I think all the jurors know a great deal more about what is going on than they are supposed to know. When Laura Hart McKinny took the stand, I felt that the jurors knew who she was, although they had not heard her name in court before. More goes on during conjugal visits than conjugal things. Cynthia McFadden of ABC said to me at a dinner given by constitutional lawyer Floyd Abrams at Eclipse, 'Remember, the conjugal visits are five hours. That leaves four hours and forty-five minutes for pillow talk.' Even if jurors are openly discussing the case among themselves now, there is little the deputies can do about it. The trial needs the jurors more than the jurors need the trial.

*   *   *

ALTHOUGH THE DEFENSE had not yet rested its case in chief, Marcia Clark got the prosecution's rebuttal under way on a triumphant note, with glove expert Richard Rubin, who said he was 100 percent sure that the gloves Simpson was wearing in videos from his days as a sportscaster were the same style as the bloody pair of gloves found at the crime scene on Bundy and outside Kato Kaelin's room on the Simpson estate. Then FBI special agent William Bodziak, who analyzes shoe prints for the agency's crime lab, attacked the findings of Dr Lee, who had suggested that an imprint found at the crime scene could have belonged to a second killer. Bodziak, with total confidence, said that the imprint was actually tool marks left by workmen who had poured the original concrete on the walkway, thereby boosting the prosecution's claim that there was only one set of shoe prints at the scene, prints made by size-12 Bruno Magli shoes. In his cross-examination of Bodziak, the rarely subdued Barry Scheck expressed dismay at the effrontery of Bodziak to question the findings of the great Dr Lee, but Scheck had finally met his match; Bodziak was not intimidated by him, and held his own, claiming that he was more of an authority on shoe prints than Dr Lee. Meanwhile, back in Connecticut, Lee was so upset by the challenge to his testimony that he called a press conference at the police crime lab in Meriden. He fiercely defended his findings like a man fighting to preserve his reputation, at the same time distancing himself from the defense and praising the FBI. When asked if he would return to the trial for surrebuttal, he replied in the negative. He also said, 'One trial experience is enough. I am not going back for retrial.'

'Are you sorry you got involved in this case?' asked a reporter.

'Yes,' replied Dr Lee.

I don't know how many different ways you can get fucked!
> —BARRY SCHECK, enraged, after he stormed
> out of the courtroom following Judge Ito's
> jury-instruction rulings.

Never underestimate the power of celebrity in Los Angeles. In a dazzling display of showmanship and chutzpah, a carefully rehearsed O. J. Simpson rose to his feet to waive his rights to testify and then electrified the courtroom with an unprecedented speech, stating that he had faith in the jury's integrity and knew they would find he 'did not, could not, and would not have committed this crime', and that he missed his kids. It was hard to know where to look in the shocked courtroom. Judge Ito, who would have cut off any other defendant mid-sentence, merely stared, knowing he had been outfoxed. Marcia Clark fumed. To my left, Simpson's daughter Arnelle sobbed. To my right, Fred Goldman hissed 'murderer, murderer' under his breath. Although the jury was not present, everyone knows by now that the jurors hear what is going on when they're not there. That, of course, was the point. Simpson could say his piece and not be cross-examined. Later, at a press conference, 'coward' was one of the words used by Fred Goldman to describe Simpson.

NICOLE BROWN SIMPSON told every friend she had that O. J. Simpson was going to kill her and get away with it. 'He's going to start his life all over again,' said a joyous Johnnie Cochran in a news conference after the not-guilty verdict. 'I will pursue as my primary goal in life the killer or killers who slaughtered Nicole and Mr Goldman,' Jason Simpson read from a prepared statement by his father.

O. J.'S LIFE SENTENCE

I NEVER THOUGHT it would end like this for O. J. Simpson, winning and losing concurrently, with the loss somehow exceeding the win. I had always thought it would be a hung jury. My jaw dropped – in case anyone didn't notice it on television – when the verdict was read. There were hosannas to my left; there were tears to my right. Simpson was a free man. When he arrived back at the gates of his Brentwood mansion to restart his life, a party was in preparation. His mother, Eunice, arrived in a Rolls-Royce. Limousines pulled up behind her. It was all on television. Women in pink pantsuits waved champagne toasts to the media. Everyone hugged. Al Cowlings was there. Don Ohlmeyer of NBC was there. Robert Kardashian was there. Larry Schiller, Simpson's co-author, was there. Jubilation reigned.

'After the verdict was handed down, the West LAPD – because Rockingham is in our jurisdiction – had to send police units over there to O. J.'s house for crowd control and to protect the estate while they were preparing for a party to celebrate the deaths of two people,' said Detective Paul Bishop when we met for breakfast at Dolores's at Santa Monica Boulevard and Purdue, not far from the station house. His disgust for the assignment sounded in his voice and showed on his face. The police department, which he loves, while acknowledging that there are flaws in it, had been mocked and humiliated by Simpson's legal team. 'Forty crates of champagne were brought in. We sat there and did it. This is our job. We may not like it, but we did it.'

Like his former colleague Detective Mark Fuhrman, Bishop has TV-star looks. He spoke about Fuhrman's arrogance and his my-way-only kind of thinking. Bishop drinks tea, talks straight, and writes books. His second novel, *Twice Dead*, is about to be published by Avon.

'Way back in the beginning, I said to Detective Ron Phillips, "Are we going to win this case?" Ron said, "If we can't convict this guy, we may as well turn in our badges and go home." After the verdict, I walked up to Ron and said, "You're right. We may as well turn in our badges." The next two days you couldn't get through on the phone lines to personnel, because there were so many police and detectives trying to get their paperwork and retire. The ripple effect is going to be unbelievable.'

The elation of the Rockingham party didn't last long. The participants having such a swell time began to get the idea that the city and the country weren't cheering and partying along with them. Simpson's much-heralded pay-per-view TV deal collapsed, and along with it the $20 million he had assumed he would make. ICM, the talent agency that had represented him for twenty years, and Jack Gilardi, his personal agent, dropped him as a client. Polls showed that more than half of the country was outraged by the verdict. Simpson brought new meaning to the phrase 'There goes the neighborhood.' A sign went up on Sunset Boulevard at the entrance to Brentwood saying, WELCOME TO BRENTWOOD. HOME OF THE BRENTWOOD BUTCHER. Another read, MURDERER LOOSE IN BRENTWOOD.

'Does he know?' I asked someone who did know, late one night.

'What?'

'That he is despised?'

'Yes.'

'Does he care?'

'Very much.'

Nicole was right. Everything happened just as she had predicted it would. What Nicole had not anticipated, however, was the rage of the white citizenry across the country over O. J.'s acquittal by a mostly black jury. 'This is what a white riot is,' said the screenwriter and director James Brooks, meaning rage without violence.

Several friends who stood by O. J. during his ordeal – and would have continued to stand by him had he been sent to prison – have distanced themselves from him since his victory party.

> —A source close to the Dream Team who spoke to me on the condition of anonymity.

For a while, Simpson didn't get it. He thought it was going to be like old times. One of his buddies told me that O. J. was livid that District Attorney Gil Garcetti had announced on television that he was closing the case and wasn't going to pursue the 'real killers'. I was also told that O. J. was looking into suing the National Organization for Women (NOW) on the grounds that it was depriving him of his right to earn a living.

Simpson, not satisfied with a mere acquittal, wanted more from us. He wanted our adulation back. Adulation is what he craves. He is addicted to it. By now, however, he knows that he will never have it. When Robert Shapiro was booed at a Lakers game last spring, it was a foretaste of things to come. If Simpson's golfing pals Craig Baumgarten and Don Ohlmeyer remain steadfast in their friendship, they're going to have a hard time finding a golf club to tee off at. The Riviera Country Club, where Simpson is a member, doesn't want him back. One member told me that the explanation it gives is that he is a security risk, which he is – a golf course being an ideal place for an assassin to pick someone off – but there is more. I have spoken with other members of that club who say they will resign in droves if he is allowed back.

Many have speculated that Simpson will flee the country rather than give a deposition in the upcoming wrongful-death suits being brought by the Brown and Goldman families. I questioned a friend of his on the possibility of suicide. There was a long pause. 'He has no life other than an afterlife,' his friend replied. 'It's a tougher sentence than if he'd gone to prison.'

I'm so sorry, kiddo. I did everything I could.
—MARCIA CLARK, crying, to Kim Goldman
after the verdict.

It is hard for Kim Goldman to understand that the life Simpson faces will be painful. She remains unconsoled by the prospect that in many areas he will become a social leper, unwanted, uninvited, barred.

'What does it matter to me if people walk out of a restaurant when he walks in? I won't be there to see it,' she said to me a few nights after the verdict. We were having dinner at Drai's with Cynthia McFadden of ABC and Shoreen Maghame of City News in Los Angeles. Kim hates Simpson with the same passion that her father hates him. 'He's free, and my brother's dead.' She described Simpson in the courtroom seconds after the verdict. 'He leaned over and looked at me and smiled. I said, "Murderer."'

Everyone must boycott his pay-per-view.
—MRS JERRY PERENCHIO, wife of the TV
entrepreneur, at dinner at Betsy
Bloomingdale's on the night of the verdict,
before the pay-per-view deal fell through.

Simpson had to move out of his walled estate on Rockingham. No privacy. Too much media. The day he wanted to see his children for the first time, a diversionary tactic had to be devised so that he could leave the grounds without being detected. As a ruse, a press conference was called. While it was being set up, Simpson sneaked out in a van, one of three cars in a caravan. Once he was gone, the press conference was canceled. The rendezvous with Sydney and Justin, who arrived with an au pair girl in a van reportedly driven by Al Cowlings from Lou and Juditha Brown's home in Dana Point, sixty miles away, took place near Mulholland Drive. 'Sydney was a little on edge at first,' I was told by a witness to the scene, 'but Justin rushed to his father's arms.' Later the same witness said that the children love the Browns, who have taken care of them since the murders, but that 'within them they know they are Simpsons'. Finally Simpson moved into a secluded residence in a canyon near Malibu that had been lent to him. One night he was able to get out and see a film, without being seen. The film he picked was *Showgirls*.

The whole point of security is that nobody knows you have it. It's not to flash it around.
— ROBERT SHAPIRO, with contempt in his
voice, in a private conversation with me in
the courthouse, expressing his rage at
Johnnie Cochran's Nation of Islam guards.

I wish you could have seen Bob Shapiro work the room at the Billy Crystal dinner last night. He never sat down. He kept shaking hands.
— ROB REINER, film director, at a dinner
dance given by Lyn and Norman Lear for
Ben Bradlee and Sally Quinn to celebrate
the publication of Bradlee's autobiography.

Where was the joy of the defense team at the announcement of the not-guilty verdict? Cochran smiled his cat-that-ate-the-canary smile. F. Lee Bailey wore the smirk of victory on his face, and Robert Shapiro, who had already distanced himself from the winning team, made a half-hearted gesture toward Simpson, but the others, particularly Robert Kardashian, looked momentarily dazed, as if the verdict were more than they had expected. The exhilaration that is part and parcel of an acquittal for a wrongly accused person was eerily missing. Barry Scheck and Peter Neufeld had already returned to New York. At the lack-luster press conference in the courtroom following the verdict, there was an absence of euphoria. When Jason Simpson read a message from his about-to-be-set-free father, in which the former defendant said that a priority of his life would be to find the real 'killer or killers', he sat awkwardly, almost hiding his face from us, as if he were ashamed of the message he was reading. In the opinion of many, the lawyers who fought so hard for Simpson's acquittal have become diminished by their association with him. As someone close to the defense team said to me, it was a victory without honor.

You've had a death threat from the LA Crips.
    —A temporary employee at the West Coast
        office of *Vanity Fair*, reading me my
        messages a few days after the acquittal.

Ten days after the verdict, before returning to New York, I dropped by Dove Books in Beverly Hills to say good-bye to Michael Viner and Deborah Raffin. In their office, I ran into three of the Simpson jurors who are appearing in a television documentary on the case which Dove is producing. Two of them shook hands with me. One looked away. All of them had heard me say on television that they hadn't done their jobs. To me, their verdict was a rush to judgment, just as much as Cochran had insisted throughout the trial that Simpson's arrest had been a rush to judgment on the part of the LAPD. A member of the sheriff's department had confirmed that several jurors' bags were packed before deliberations began. A person who works for the British tabloid *News of the World* played me a tape of the daughter of one of the jurors trying to make a deal for her mother and another juror. Three of the jurors left for Las Vegas after the verdict and checked into the Bally hotel, where they had established a line of credit. The lawyer for yet another member of the jury called me at my hotel and asked how much I would pay to interview his client. I said, 'My magazine doesn't pay.' He said in a shocked voice, '*Vanity Fair* doesn't *pay?*' After having heard juror Brenda Moran say on television that domestic violence had nothing to do with the murders and should have been tried in another court, I was no longer interested in what the jurors had to say.

This case was won the day the jury was seated, thanks to the defense's jury consultant, Jo-Ellan Dimitrius. The verdict had very little to do with reason and a great deal to do with race. Months and months ago, I was told in a private conversation that after the jury had been picked

O. J. Simpson said to Johnnie Cochran, 'If this jury convicts me, maybe I did kill Nicole in a blackout.'

> *Some people can't stand the truth.*
> —JOHNNIE COCHRAN, in his closing argument, looking toward the Goldman family.

I and many other people covering the trial believe that if Francine Florio-Bunten had not been dismissed from the jury by Judge Ito there would have been a long deliberation and perhaps a hung jury instead of an acquittal arrived at in three hours. Francine Florio-Bunten was probably the smartest person on the jury, capable of understanding the DNA evidence and explaining it to the others. There was an eagerness on the part of the defense to remove her from the jury, and there is something very smelly about her dismissal. Judge Ito, who seemed to be in the thrall of Johnnie Cochran for much of the trial, received an anonymous letter from a young woman who described herself as a receptionist for a literary agency, paid Ito an unctuous compliment, and reported that Florio-Bunten was in negotiations for a book on the trial:

> *After seeing you last night on the news telling the pain your family went through during the war and what my family in Germany endured, it touched my heart and I felt so grateful to live in a country with very strong civil rights and a strong constitution. I guess that's why I feel so ashamed for the information I have . . .*

I am in a moral dilemma that a 20-year-old receptionist should not be in. I can only identify the juror as female, once an alternate, her husband became ill, about 40 years old, a white woman.

I WAS BROUGHT UP to believe that anonymous letters should be flushed down the toilet, but such thinking did not prevail here. The anonymous letter was taken seriously. Florio-Bunten's lawyer, Rex T. Reeves, has publicly stated, 'That letter is as phony as a three-dollar bill.' Francine Florio-Bunten insists that the information in the letter was false; she had no book deal then, has none now, and does not intend to have one. The reason given for her dismissal at the time was that she had lied about receiving a note from another juror. Even if that were true, how mild a misdemeanor it seems for the punishment Judge Ito gave her. I know a couple of reporters who think they are onto whose handwriting it is in the anonymous letter.

I never saw so many people in dark glasses and very short black dresses.
        —MARGARET WEITZMAN, wife of Simpson's
        first lawyer, Howard Weitzman, describing
        Nicole Brown Simpson's funeral.

Voices heard at parties in Los Angeles: 'I think they should release the autopsy pictures – let everyone see what he did.' 'This is what Nicole always said was going to happen.' 'All Nicole's photo albums were up-to-date.'

'They ought to unseal those papers about what the jail-house guard overheard O. J. say to Rosie Grier.' 'Of *course* I would get up and walk out if he came into this restaurant.' 'It was tacky of them to have a party after the verdict.' 'If he married Paula Barbieri now, it would be like giving the finger to all the blacks who helped him.' 'I bet he skips the country rather than give the deposition.' 'How do we send money to the Goldmans?' 'Ron Goldman and Nicole are the payment of the racial debt.' 'Any girl he hits on now can make herself famous when she sells her story.' 'He's got to look in the mirror every day when he shaves.'

> *You're the first white person to give me money since the verdict.*
> —Black panhandler to a friend of mine who
>   dropped change in his cup.

I wasn't surprised when, at the last minute, Simpson's NBC interview with Tom Brokaw and Katie Couric didn't take place. I had heard the day before that Simpson's friends and advisers were trying to talk him out of it. Then I heard that Johnnie Cochran had arrived at the house and was left alone with him. That did it.

From the beginning, one of the most interesting characters in the many subplots of the Simpson saga has been Don Ohlmeyer, the West Coast president of NBC. A golfing buddy and old-time associate of Simpson's who produced one of Simpson's films, *The Golden Moment: An Olympic Love Story*, Ohlmeyer has been from the time of the murders an outspoken advocate for the innocence of his friend. He was a frequent visitor at the LA County Jail and one of the celebrants at the victory party at the Rockingham house following the verdict. After the pay-per-view deal collapsed, Simpson agreed to have Ohlmeyer set up the interview on NBC. Simpson has only his image to sell. Without it he's nothing, and he knows it; an hour of prime time for him to give his side of the story to Tom Brokaw and Katie Couric was irresistible. It provoked the same urge that had made Simpson want to take the stand during the trial; he is a man who has talked his way out of jams for years, and he thought he could do it again. But along came Johnnie. You had only to look at Cochran's face on the Larry King show the night O. J. phoned in unexpectedly to see just how nervous O. J. makes him when he speaks out extemporaneously. The last-minute cancellation caused embarrassment to Brokaw, Couric, and NBC.

Then came Simpson's subsequent call to Bill Carter, who covers television for *The New York Times*. According to a source, it was Ohlmeyer's idea to call Carter. Ohlmeyer and Carter were known to each other professionally. In fact, it is being told around town that Ohlmeyer dialed the number for Simpson. David Margolick, who had covered the trial from the start for *The New York Times*, was the logical person to call, but he was passed over. 'O. J.'s a coward,' said Loyola law professor and television commentator Laurie Levenson when we met up on a television show that day. 'He only wants to speak in a controlled atmosphere – which *he* controls. He doesn't want to be confronted.'

In his nonconfrontational interview with Carter, Simpson said some curious things, which indicate how near to the surface of his psyche the particulars of the trial reside. In one instance, speaking about prosecutor Marcia Clark, he said that he'd 'like to be able to knock that chip off Marcia's shoulder' – a curious turn of phrase for an acknowledged wife beater. In another, speaking about the NBC interview he had backed out of, he said, 'I heard accounts of things like Tom Brokaw was sharpening knives for the interview' – again, a curious turn of phrase for a man just acquitted of slashing the throats of two people with a sharp knife which has never been recovered.

Simpson needed that $20 million he expected from the pay-per-view deal. The house on Rockingham had been used as collateral for a $3 million line of credit to cover legal fees for the murder trial, some of which have not been paid. There are also the costly civil suits that face him in the near future. Yet he asserted his solvency in *The New York Times*. 'I still have my Ferrari,' he told Carter. 'I still have my Bentley, I still have my home in Brentwood and my apartment in New York.' However, he had already put the apartment up for sale and taken out a $700,000 mortgage on it. Elaine Young, a Beverly Hills real-estate agent, has had an offer in excess of $4 million for the house on Rockingham, but Simpson doesn't want to sell it, even though his neighbors don't want him there anymore.

'How much money is there?' I asked a source.

'I figure he can live in the style in which he is living for another year.'

Meanwhile, people from all over the country are calling in to the Goldman family to offer them money to hire the finest lawyer in the land for their civil suit against Simpson. The Goldmans have chosen Daniel Petrocelli, a partner in the distinguished Los Angeles firm of Mitchell, Silberberg & Knupp.

> *O. J. is entitled to enjoy the fruits of his liberty the way the rest of us are. I think it's unconscionable that people are trying to deny him that.*
>> —Dream Team member PETER NEUFELD, quoted in the *Los Angeles Times*, October 13, 1995.

> *The reaction to his return doesn't seem very American. This is a country that traditionally takes people back who have fallen from grace. Richard Nixon left office in disgrace and was later welcomed at the White House. Spiro Agnew's bust was put in the Capitol this year. There are a lot of examples, including Michael Milken. I don't look for sinister motives, but what is the difference between O. J. and the others?*
>> —JOHNNIE COCHRAN, quoted in the same article.

I said to Robert Shapiro on the next-to-last day of the trial, 'This experience is going to change us all.' He replied, 'You don't know how much.' Now it's time to pack up and leave. What a fascinating and bewildering city Los Angeles is. Heidi Fleiss faces up to eight years in prison, and O. J. Simpson is reportedly cavorting in Beverly Hills with Frederick's of Hollywood model Gretchen Stockdale and openly playing golf in Florida with Paula Barbieri beside him while his daughter Sydney celebrates her tenth birthday with the Brown family. Judge Ito's stepson, Dennis York, thirty-five, the son of Ito's wife, Captain Margaret York, the highest-ranking woman in the LAPD, was arrested on charges of grand theft and operating as a contractor without a license, and the sister-in-law of Johnnie Cochran, Robin Cochran, thirty-nine, was arrested in a crack den and is under investigation for child endangerment for leaving her six-year-old daughter in a car outside.

When I stopped living here in 1979 and moved to New York, I left hating this city. I no longer do. LA is a part of me just as much as New York is. I reunited with old friends here and made many new ones, all of whom I shall miss. I leave with admiration and love for Marcia Clark and Chris Darden, for my friends in the media who have covered the trial every day, and for the Brown and Goldman families. I will never forget Nicole and Ron. The autopsy photographs of their slit throats and open eyes will haunt me forever.

CLOSING ARGUMENTS

FINALLY, THIRTY-TWO MONTHS AFTER the double murders, the Simpson [civil suit] case was over. The truth was outed. Twelve jurors who understood that their responsibility was to justice and not to settling past personal grievances with the Los Angeles Police Department combed through the evidence during their deliberations, discussed it among themselves for five days, asked for read-backs and video playbacks, and came up with the verdict that the evidence has always pointed to: they found Orenthal James Simpson liable for the deaths of his former wife, Nicole Brown Simpson, and Ronald Goldman. They punished him accordingly, to the tune of $33.5 million in damages. It happened not a moment too soon. The saturation point with O. J. Simpson had been reached.

Right up to the end, when his world came crashing down around him, the sheer stardom of Simpson prevailed. It didn't seem to matter if he was being cheered or jeered as he arrived at the courthouse each day in a

black Chevy Suburban with tinted windows and a bodyguard who looked just like Sylvester Stallone, complete
with attitude. Simpson's ever loyal sister Shirley Baker
and her husband, Benny, would precede him. He was
always in character, demanding our attention, sometimes
waving, sometimes not, sometimes limping, sometimes
not, knowing exactly how much of himself to share with
the public on any given day.

National interest in the outcome of the civil trial was
so intense that Simpson very nearly upstaged the president of the United States on the occasion of his State of
the Union address. When that night is written about in
years to come, it will be Simpson's verdict, not President
Clinton's words, that will be remembered – the picture of
Simpson leaving the courthouse with head held at a defiant angle as people screamed 'Killer!' at him.

The person who certainly *was* upstaged that night was
Republican congressman J. C. Watts Jr of Oklahoma, who
gave his party's reply to the president's speech. The event
should have forged his political career in the national spotlight. Instead, it turned into an ironic moment of
Americana: an African-American Republican representative, associate pastor, and former college athlete, at the
top of his form, competing for airtime with an African-
American former sports star, at the bottom of his form,
having just been branded a killer by a civil jury. In Santa
Monica, there were shouts of joy and roars of anger as
the cast of characters that has held our country enthralled
for almost three years – the Goldmans, the Browns, and
the Simpsons – left the courthouse.

There is a messenger in this case you cannot trust,
and that is O. J. Simpson. He has lied and lied and
lied about every important fact of this case.
    —Plaintiff's attorney DANIEL PETROCELLI in
        his closing rebuttal argument.

I never thought that the Menendez brothers, Lyle and
Erik, who are currently doing life without parole at two
different California penal institutions, could be beat as
world-class liars, but I must tip my hat to O. J. Simpson
for besting even them in that department. He lied like a
man who was used to lying and having his lies accepted
as truth. He may have been a lousy actor in films, but he's
a brilliant one in life. He's bad at learned lines, however.
He sounded very unconvincing when he said he was
'Absolutely 100 percent not guilty' during the criminal
trial. That line was given to Simpson by his lawyer Johnnie
Cochran, which explains the awkwardness of his delivery.
On his own in the civil trial, lying from his heart, he was
altogether different. 'He'd rather lie than eat,' wrote Steve
Dunleavy in the *New York Post*. Sitting in the courtroom
watching him lie hour after hour was an experience I won't
forget. Not an iota of shame or embarrassment emanated
from him. As Daniel Petrocelli pounded away at him with
his questions, sometimes standing only inches from his
face, Simpson maintained confidence, assurance, even
dignity during a cross-examination that would have felled
a lesser mortal. Even in the face of irrefutable proof that
he was lying, such as thirty-one photographs of him wearing the Bruno Magli shoes that he had sworn he never

owned, he continued to lie with his kind of total conviction, as if it were his God-given right to get away with murder.

In the criminal trial, Simpson's Dream Team had made much of his demeanor during the flight to Chicago on the night of the murders – signing autographs with the word 'Peace', being charming – as if that were an indication of his innocence. But that's exactly what he's so good at. Of course he didn't look suspicious to those who encountered him that night. Of course he wasn't giving off signals that he had just slit the throats of two people. He has been a public personality for most of his life. He is used to being stared at, and he knows how to present his public persona no matter what is going on in his private life. Image is a thing he understands perfectly.

In the corridor outside the courtroom during a break, Petrocelli said to me, 'Look what they did to Mark Fuhrman for denying he said the n-word ten years ago. He's a felon for life. He can't ever be a cop again. He can't ever get a permit for a gun. Now look at *this* guy. I'm showing him thirty photographs of him wearing the Bruno Magli shoes, one of which was published six months before the murders, and he says they're not his. You know what that's like? That's like saying you're not standing here talking to me. He's denying the undeniable.'

Simpson had won an acquittal in the criminal trial. He had won his children back in the custody trial. But his luck finally ran out in the civil trial. To a man, the jury didn't buy his lies and denials. One juror said to Larry King after the verdict, 'O. J. insulted us on the stand.'

There's nothing a lawyer hates more than being made to look like a liar in front of the jury.
— JEFFREY TOOBIN, author of *The Run of His Life*, commenting on a coolness between defense attorney Robert Baker and O. J. Simpson after the photographs of Simpson wearing the Bruno Magli shoes turned up.

To my way of thinking, one of the worst things a defense attorney can do is mock the dead victim his client is on trial for killing. Simpson's lead defense attorney, Robert Baker, whom I always thought of as a class act in what has become an unclassy trade, shocked me utterly with the cruelty of his remark about Ron Goldman, who had fought with Simpson for his life and – as Dan Petrocelli pointed out in his eloquent closing argument – had died trying to help Nicole, the mother of Simpson's two children. In attempting to minimize Ron Goldman's ambition of one day owning a restaurant, Baker said, 'Let's examine reality. Ron Goldman wouldn't have a restaurant now. He would be lucky to have a credit card.' The tone of his voice matched the ugliness of his words. A chill went through the courtroom, and groans indicating a low blow went through the hearing room, where reporters and journalists who didn't have courtroom seats listened to the trial.

Stranger bedfellows I cannot imagine than O. J. Simpson and Robert Baker. Surprisingly, Baker was recommended for the job by Johnnie Cochran. The Waspy, witty, and very skillful Baker moves in high social circles in Los Angeles and belongs to the exclusive Los Angeles Country Club, where show folk, even those of a conservative nature, need not apply. So deep are the feelings of some members against O. J. Simpson that Baker and his wife have faced certain social penalties for their legal association with him, as has their son, Phillip, twenty-eight, who was also a member of the Simpson defense team. I do not know if Baker and Simpson had any sort of personal camaraderie outside the courtroom. Inside, the relationship of Baker's team with Simpson was very different from that in the criminal trial, where Simpson was constantly coddled and comforted by Cochran's team. In the civil trial no one seemed to jump to every time Simpson spoke. As for those times during the trial when Baker hit below the belt – when he denigrated Nicole and said she hung out with prostitutes, or when he minimized what the future might have been for Ron Goldman – a person who knew Simpson very well told me, 'I bet O. J. insisted he say that.'

EACH TIME SIMPSON left the stand, there was no sense that he was ready to collapse into his lawyers' arms for solace, like a fighter at the end of a round, needing pats on his back and water on his face until he can regain himself. He stopped to speak to this person and that person, smiling, jovial, seemingly carefree. Then he spotted me. I was a latecomer to the civil trial. It was the first time we had seen each other eyeball-to-eyeball since the day of the verdict in the criminal trial. Quite rightly, Simpson is not fond of me. I have never made any bones about my feelings regarding his guilt, either in print or on television, and he in turn has let me have it on several occasions.

'Ohhhh,' he said now, breaking into a dazzling smile and putting me on, 'look, Dominick's here.' He raised his hands in an exaggerated gesture, walked toward me with a big smile on his face, and began to raise his hand to shake mine. The power of his charisma is so overwhelming that for an instant I feared I would actually shake his hand. But in a hundredth of a second I remembered that the blood of Ronald Goldman and Nicole Brown Simpson had been on his hands. I put mine behind my back. Undeterred by this snub, he came right up to me, still with a smile on his face, and said, 'Well, Dominick, at least you can't say I didn't say hello to you.' Then he moved on to join his lawyers before returning calmly to the stand to take more pummeling from Petrocelli.

I want you to meet this comedy-writer friend of mine. He's the guy who wrote the original line – 'If the glove don't fit, you must acquit' – for Johnnie Cochran.

> —A stranger at the opening of painter
> Sacha Newley's star-studded vernissage in
> the lobby of the Chateau Marmont, given
> by his mother, the actress Joan Collins.

The revelation of Simpson's civil trial was the emergence of lead plaintiff attorney Daniel Petrocelli, of the firm Mitchell, Silberberg & Knupp in Los Angeles, into the big time. Articulate, passionate, and very tough, he was nothing short of magnificent. I happened to be in the lobby of the Doubletree hotel talking to Petrocelli after his closing argument when the renowned defense attorney Gerry Spence came up and said, 'You have brought honor back to the profession, sir,' and shook his hand. It was a very moving moment between two men – one famous, one about to be. Petrocelli took the trial back to what it was really about: two murders. Johnnie Cochran, who ran Judge Ito's courtroom in the criminal trial, did what a lawyer does when he knows his client is guilty. He veered the focus away from the defendant. He put Detective Mark Fuhrman on trial. He made it appear that saying the n-word was a worse offense than killing two people. In his rabble-rousing closing argument, he exhorted the twelve jurors he understood so well to give a message to the Los Angeles Police Department. They did what he told them to do. The killer walked, and Johnnie Cochran got his own television show and moved to New York.

Dan Petrocelli is not looking for a television show. He loves the law. Petrocelli was a match for Simpson in a way that Marcia Clark and Chris Darden never were. Simpson was contemptuous of Darden, and he didn't fear Marcia Clark. Too many of her mistakes had been pointed out to him. Once, during the criminal trial, I discussed the defense strategy with Larry Schiller, author of *American Tragedy*, the bestselling book about Simpson. 'Very simple,' Schiller explained. 'The defense strategy is Marcia's mistakes.' Petrocelli did not treat Simpson with kid gloves as some sort of fallen hero because of his celebrity. He treated him as if he were just another defendant on trial for a couple of murders. He called him a liar over and over again. As he pointed a finger at him, he said to the jury, 'There is a killer in this courtroom.'

You ain't gonna get a dime!
—A heckler screaming at Fred Goldman outside the courthouse the day before the verdict in the civil trial.

GO FOR MAMA'S CONDO!
—A sign carried by a woman outside the courthouse, referring to the condominium in San Francisco that Simpson had bought for his mother, which is listed as one of his assets.

Paula Barbieri, Simpson's erstwhile girlfriend, has reportedly signed a $3 million book deal with Little, Brown. Since Barbieri never achieved the star status of Cindy Crawford or Naomi Campbell in the modeling profession, it seems highly unlikely that any publisher would pay such a sum for her life story unless there were a clear understanding that she had something very salable to write, or have written for her, about her former lover. Their sexual union was said to be extraordinary. The sounds of their love-making in Robert Kardashian's house on the night before Nicole's funeral, according to an inside source, woke up the household. Barbieri's real value to the overall story, however, is that she knows what Simpson thought and said about Nicole in the weeks and days before he killed her. Just the night before, they went to a black-tie party in Bel Air together. She broke up with him the next morning, the day of the murders, and went to Las Vegas, as a guest of the singer Michael Bolton. But after the news of the murders, she returned immediately and stayed in Kardashian's house with O. J. She was present during the crucial four days between the murders and the freeway chase.

> *I can understand Paula getting that kind of money.*
> *She's got all the sex to talk about, which sells, and*
> *she was there when the lawyers talked to O. J., both*
> *at the house and in jail. She was always reading*
> *the Bible or writing her Christmas cards – and*
> *listening. She knows a lot, and she's not bound by*
> *the attorney-client privilege.*
> —LARRY SCHILLER, writer.

Larry Schiller, who was a rather mysterious character during the criminal trial, when he seemed to be part of the defense team following the publication of Simpson's book, *I Want to Tell You*, which he co-wrote, emerged as the visionary of the civil trial. The enormous success of *American Tragedy* turned him into a talk-show personality and trial historian. Of all the books about this case, his was the one that gave information no one else had access to. With the help of Simpson's former close friend Robert Kardashian, who will always be remembered as the man who carried the Louis Vuitton bag away from the Rockingham estate, Schiller told for the first time the story of what went on in Simpson's life in the days after the murders and up to the freeway chase, as well as fascinating backstage tales about the defense team.

Hardly a day went by during the criminal trial when Johnnie Cochran didn't say to Judge Ito, 'Your Honor, this trial is a search for truth.' In a recent newspaper interview for his new Court TV show, *Cochran & Grace*, on which he partners with prosecutor Nancy Grace, Cochran was quoted as saying, 'Justice must be served.' Was justice being served when Cochran's team – as described in Schiller's book – altered Simpson's house before the jury was taken through it by removing pictures of white people and replacing them with pictures of black people, and by hanging a Norman Rockwell poster of a black child entering a no-longer-segregated school which had hung in Cochran's office at the top of Simpson's staircase? Cochran has dismissed this as 'an absolute lie'. I can understand replacing a nude photograph of Paula Barbieri with a photograph of O. J.'s mother on the table next to his bed for propriety's sake, but the rest of the redress of the house seems to be pure deceit.

Day after day, Schiller would sit in the corridor outside the Santa Monica courtroom in an overcoat with a fur collar, receiving people, looking like a cardinal hearing confessions as he dispensed the latest news and gossip of the trial. In the dining room of the Doubletree Guest Suites Hotel, next to the courthouse, where all the important people connected to the trial went to lunch – lawyers, reporters, and sometimes Simpson himself – Schiller's table was the one to be asked to sit at. Greta Van Susteren of CNN's *Burden of Proof*, Gerry Spence, and former LA district attorney Ira Reiner were often guests at the table. Schiller is generous with his information, but he qualifies how you can use it. 'You can use this in *Vanity Fair*, or in your book,' he'd say to me, 'but you *can't* use it on Larry King tonight, because it would be traced to me.'

> *Five of the guards O. J. had in the county jail come to visit him in the house on Rockingham. They're so at home in his house that, if they're hungry, they go in the kitchen and make themselves a sandwich.*
>   —LARRY SCHILLER during a lunch break at the Doubletree.

In the course of my career, I have appeared in public with many famous people, including movie stars, but I have rarely been with one who drew more attention than the former LAPD detective Mark Fuhrman, who is invariably referred to in print as 'racist cop', when I took him and his agent, Lucienne Goldberg, to lunch in the Grill Room of the Four Seasons, that noontime bastion of the movers and shakers of New York. The kind of people who normally don't stare were leaning out of their banquettes to get a better look at him.

Fuhrman walked into the restaurant the way he had walked into court the first time he took the stand, looking like the lead in a TV series. Good blazer, good flannels, good-looking. Not a sign of I'm-from-Idaho-visiting-the-big-city.

'Are you aware you're causing a bit of a commotion?' I asked.

He shrugged and smiled; he has become used to that by now. He was in New York making preparations for the publication of his book, *Murder in Brentwood*. He had met with Geraldo Rivera, who had flown him to New York in a private plane so that he could avoid airport hassles. He was going to be interviewed for a second time by Diane Sawyer. Larry King and Oprah had also lined him up for interviews. He speaks in a very low voice; you have to lean forward to hear everything he says. His conversation is riveting, particularly about Judge Ito's wife, Captain Margaret York, the highest-ranking woman in the LAPD. He suggested in no uncertain terms that if the truth about his volatile past relations with her in the police department had come out, Ito would have had to recuse himself from the Simpson murder trial. (Captain York declined to comment.)

Fuhrman claimed to have had a 'casual' sexual relationship with Laura Hart McKinny, who provided the defense with the tapes on which he says the n-word forty-one times after he had testified on the stand that he had not said the word in the last ten years. 'I'm sorry I said that word. I'm sorry I lied about saying it,' he told me. As he pointed out, though, it had nothing to do with the murders. No one in the courtroom, after all, screamed 'Racist!' when Robert Shapiro did a Charlie Chan imitation of criminalist Dennis Fung as he held out a box of fortune cookies, or when Johnnie Cochran skipped down the corridor to the men's room singing 'We're having Fung' during the time Fung was on the stand.

Fuhrman is harsh in his criticism of prosecutor Marcia Clark and Detective Phil Vanatter. 'I am a great detective; Vanatter's only a good one,' he said at one point. He said that he had told Clark he found an empty Swiss Army knife box in Simpson's bathroom on the night of the murders. For reasons unknown, this was ignored by the prosecution in the criminal trial and never brought into evidence – along with the freeway chase, the suicide note, and the taped police interview with Simpson.

Cochran had a very narrow and clear agenda. He was going to get his client off no matter what it took, no matter who he hurt or even ruined, no matter how far he had to twist or even disregard the truth.

—MARK FUHRMAN in his book, *Murder in Brentwood.*

'It's like rubbing salt in the wound to see certain people attain great success following the greatest debacle in the history of the world,' said reporter Betsy Streisand of *US News & World Report* in the courthouse corridor. She was referring to those in the legal profession at the criminal trial who have now given up law, or put it on a back burner for a while, to go into show business. Johnnie Cochran has his Court TV show. Marcia Clark, who received a bonus from Los Angeles district attorney Gil Garcetti after losing the criminal case, has left the office and is about to appear on her new syndicated television show, *LadyLaw*. Chris Darden has also left the district attorney's office, to teach; during the Simpson civil trial, he was a regular legal commentator, along with Alan Dershowitz, of Simpson's Dream Team, on *Rivera Live*. And there's Greta Van Susteren, and Roger Cossack, and on and on.

LESLIE ABRAMSON HAS a book out. Outside of a small group in Los Angeles legal circles, Abramson was relatively unknown until I began writing about her for this magazine during my coverage of the Menendez brothers' first trial, in which she defended Erik, and which ended, triumphantly for her, with a hung jury. Because of her bombastic personality, the presence of a television camera in the courtroom, and her zealous affection for her killer client, she caught on with the public as the judicial version of Alexis Carrington, the character played by Joan Collins on *Dynasty* – a woman you loved to hate, because she would stop at nothing to get what she wanted. Following the current trend of Los Angeles lawyers preferring to be in show business, she was a regular with Ted Koppel on *Nightline* during the Simpson trial. Wanting to have her own chat show, she made a half-hour pilot, and then she made another one. Neither sold. 'She's a five-minute segment, she's not half an hour,' a famous lady of television said to me about her. One Saturday morning, I happened to run into one of her producers on the escalator at Neiman Marcus in Beverly Hills. 'What happened?'

I asked. 'Let's just say she wasn't camera-friendly,' he replied, stepping by me.

During the penalty phase of the second Menendez brothers trial, which she lost hands down, her own expert witness, psychiatrist William Vicary, testified on the stand in the presence of the jury and media that he had changed his notes on Erik at her request. Abramson became front-page news when she took the Fifth Amendment twice. In February, her book came out. When the deal for it was made, after the first trial, for a reported $500,000, the title was *My Life in Crime*, but the book was released as *The Defense Is Ready: Life in the Trenches of Criminal Law*, and the planned initial printing was slenderized. In it, she deals with me in a lengthy but not unexpected manner, while she dismisses taking the Fifth, usually a refuge for gangsters and the guilty, in a few paragraphs, as if it were of no moment. But it is. As Harvey Levin, the television reporter for KCBS in Los Angeles, said, 'No one's ever going to be afraid of Leslie anymore.'

The only breaking-news anecdote in her book concerns her participation in the previously unreported wedding ceremony of Lyle Menendez – who was still in the Los Angeles County Jail, as was Erik, before they were shipped off to separate prisons for life – and Anna Eriksson, who had once posed nude for *Playboy*. The wedding was performed on a three-way conference call. Lyle was on the telephone in the jail. Erik, who was best man, was on a telephone in a different part of the jail. The bride and the performing judge, Nancy Brown, were on a speaker-phone in Abramson's office. Abramson acted as surrogate groom and placed the ring on the bride's finger. Then Lyle and the bride made kissing sounds. Personally, I would be too embarrassed to admit that I had participated in such a charade, but the story was clearly meant to move readers with the beauty of the moment. Hello? In the California prison system, murderers serving life without parole are not allowed conjugal visits.

STAR JONES, a former homicide prosecutor in the Brooklyn district attorney's office who is now senior correspondent and chief legal analyst for the tabloid TV show *Inside Edition*, emerged as a media star during the Simpson civil trial. Jones, a rather exotic African-American woman, wears inch-long false eyelashes and dresses in a theatrical manner. 'This is my Audrey Hepburn look. Audrey Hepburn was my favorite actress,' she said to me one day when I sat next to her in court and commented on her hairstyle. She seemed to have closer access to Simpson than any other journalist. During breaks, she was often in conversation with him, and she was a guest in his house the night the custody case was won, celebrating the happy turn of events along with Greta Van Susteren and Linda Deutsch of the Associated Press. 'I'm plugged in, I'll tell you that,' Jones told me.

ONE OF THE LEAST WRITTEN about but major background figures in the Simpson saga is Don Ohlmeyer, the president of NBC West Coast. A longtime friend of Simpson's, he has been an outspoken advocate for him almost from the day following the murders. He was a constant visitor at the Los Angeles County Jail from the time of Simpson's incarceration after the freeway chase until his acquittal. He attended the much-criticized champagne victory party at Simpson's house on Rockingham following the acquittal. Shortly thereafter, as journalists camped outside the house on Rockingham reported that Simpson was a virtual prisoner inside, Simpson wasn't even there. He had been spirited away to Don Ohlmeyer's house off Benedict Canyon in Beverly Hills, which, incidentally, Ohlmeyer had purchased from Simpson's former great friend Robert Kardashian only three weeks before the murders.

One of the most engrossing tales of the days following the acquittal was that a makeup artist who had worked with Simpson several times went to Ohlmeyer's house and gave Simpson a new look. She cut and shaped his mustache and goatee on his face and taught him how to apply it. The wife of one of his New York golfing friends, who had flown out to Los Angeles the day after the acquittal, selected a pair of glasses for him in Beverly Hills. So convincing and distinguished was the new look the makeup artist gave Simpson that he became unrecognizable in it. A person who saw the transformation described him to me as looking like a Cuban diplomat. Within days of his acquittal, he dined, unrecognized, with his New York friends at the Palm, a popular steak-and-lobster house catering to the sports and movie crowd. One day he drove himself in this disguise to the Beverly Hills Hotel to meet up with his friend Bobby Bender, a New York garment-industry figure. When he stopped at the light on Sunset Boulevard before making the turn into the hotel's driveway, a car pulled up beside him in the next lane. In the car was Kim Goldman, the sister of the man he had just been acquitted of killing. Their eyes met, and he, of course, recognized her, but she did not recognize him. At the time, Simpson told the story to several people. When I heard it, I told it to Kim Goldman during lunch one day at the Doubletree. She stared at me, aghast, and realized for the first time that it had been he.

Following the first trial, Ohlmeyer hired Jason Simpson, Simpson's son by his first marriage, to be the chef in his home. Before that, Jason had been the sous-chef at Jackson's restaurant on Beverly Drive.

Subsequently, Ohlmeyer, in his role of advocate, caused a bit of an industry stir when he departed from his prepared text at the Radio-Television News Director Association Conference and, in an emotional outburst, chastised his own network for what he felt was unfair coverage of the Simpson trial. People I know who were present and heard the speech were dumbfounded. Although the incident was reported, it was handled gently because of Ohlmeyer's position of power. Sometime after the speech, his network announced that he had entered the Betty Ford Clinic in Palm Springs for the requisite twenty-eight-day stay.

That sort of symbolizes the defense right now.
  —LAURIE LEVENSON, CBS trial commentator
  who teaches law at Loyola, remarking on

the arrival at the courthouse of Simpson
defense attorney Robert Blasier in a
wheelchair, in obvious pain from a recent
disc operation, being pushed through
security by his wife.

Running concurrently with O. J. Simpson's civil trial
was the custody trial over his and Nicole's children,
Sydney, eleven, and Justin, eight, who had been living with
their grandparents Juditha and Lou Brown since
Simpson's incarceration in 1994. The custody trial was
closed to the public, and rumors flew that ugly personal
charges were made by both sides in the fight for the children. Simpson juggled the two trials, moving back and
forth between them. As predicted by all the legal pundits,
the children were awarded to their biological father by
Judge Nancy Weiben Stock, who announced the verdict
while the civil trial was still going on. During his closing
argument, Robert Baker reminded the jury that Simpson
had been given custody of his children.

The children were returned to their father's house on
Rockingham from their grandparents' house in Dana Point,
ninety miles away in Orange County. They were enrolled
in new schools. For reasons of economy, two of their father's
defense lawyers were being billeted on the property. Dan
Leonard, from F. Lee Bailey's office in Florida, was living
in Kato Kaelin's old room, and Robert Blasier and his wife
were in Simpson's daughter Arnelle's old room.

What must the atmosphere in the house have been like
for the children on the night after Petrocelli's closing

argument, or after Petrocelli's rebuttal, when every lie Simpson had told and every character flaw he possessed were pointed out to the jury? What must it have been like after the verdict, when the jury found Simpson liable for the death of their mother? What must it have been like for them on those days in school, where they were still the new kids? 'Sydney has a computer. She's on-line,' a person close to the family told me. 'She spends hours talking to people around the world. They're her friends.'

Judge Weiben Stock has been criticized for her decision in the Simpson case, as well as for an earlier judgment, in 1991, when she gave custody of two young children to their biological mother, even though the woman had battered her husband. At the time, the judge noted that there was no evidence that the mother had abused the children. This past January, that mother shot and killed the two children, her lover, and herself. What ever happened to common sense, Judge Weiben Stock?

Although the Brown family continues to seek custody, the chances are slim that Sydney and Justin will be returned to them.

You must send him a message as loud as humanly possible, so he can hear it on whatever golf course he is hiding out on right now . . . You cannot kill two people and get away with it, no matter how much money you have, no matter how many lies you tell.

> —DANIEL PETROCELLI in his closing argument for punitive damages.

Disgraced and defeated, O. J. Simpson watched the penalty verdict while eating a chiliburger in the clubhouse of a public golf course. The next day he issued a defiant statement. 'This is far from over.'

Will this be the end? Of course not. The trials are over, but O. J. Simpson will be among us forever. He's way up there now, in another category of fame. This man is not going quietly into the night. He's going to be making news for as long as he's around. Only days after the verdict, he was caught on videotape swinging two golf clubs like a baseball bat in the direction of an *Inside Edition* cameraman named Dan Hardy. 'I looked into his eyes, and the look I saw scared the holy shit out of me,' said Hardy, who has since brought charges. 'It was like looking into the eyes of a killer.'

IN COLD, BLUE BLOOD

O N AUGUST 2, 1998, a woman of no importance
was beaten and strangled to death in a cheap motel
in Las Vegas, Nevada, that rents rooms on an
hourly basis to prostitutes, drug addicts, perverts, and, on
this occasion, a trio of alleged murderers for hire. Across
the country in a grand mansion at the end of a quarter-
mile-long driveway in the rolling hills of Delaware, an
heiress from one of America's most prominent families
and her third husband were making plans for the opening of an exclusive new golf club that he would manage
on land that she had inherited. The two stories are closely
related.

THE DEL MAR RESORT MOTEL, at the wrong end of Las
Vegas Boulevard, is a few motels away from the one where
the television star David Strickland committed suicide in
March of this year by hanging himself with a bedsheet.
The room where that happened is in great demand by the

sort of people who rent rooms by the hour, as is Room No. 6 at the Del Mar, where the murder under consideration took place. Anything goes in these places. No questions asked. A fifteen-year-old girl testified in court recently that she and her probation officer had engaged in sex at the Del Mar on two occasions when she was fourteen.

Outside is a red neon sign that says, ADULT MOVIES. The dirty movies are included in the cost of a room, which is $30 for three hours. On August 2, 1998, a woman named Diana Hironaga checked into Room No. 6 under her own name, along with two accomplices and the woman who would allegedly become their victim. Diana Hironaga was a fading porn star. She had appeared in sixteen films, of the variety in which no orifice is off-limits. She hung around slot machines in hotel lobbies, which is how she met a man named Christopher Moseley, from Greenville, Delaware, who was throwing around money as if he were rich, which he was not. But his wife was, and like a lot of rich women with poor husbands, she called the shots where money was concerned, both for her husband and for her son from her first marriage, who had formed a romantic alliance with a woman she considered utterly unsuitable. Her son's name was Dean MacGuigan. He had been born Dean Chandor, the son of E. Haring Chandor of New York, but when he was still young his mother had had his last name changed to that of her second husband, Dr John MacGuigan.

None of the three alleged killers felt any animosity toward the woman they were about to murder. According to police, for them it was a job. A rich guy from Delaware was paying the trio for their efforts, and they all needed the money. The victim's name was Pati Margello. She was from South Philadelphia, and by all reports she was a very nice person. The people I have spoken to all had good things to say about her, even as a mother. Her son loved her. Yes, she was a scam artist and a drug addict. Yes, she reportedly had AIDS. Yes, she was an occasional hooker, which meant that she did it only for drug money, and then gave only hand jobs and blow jobs, or so Dean MacGuigan told the police about the woman he loved. But there was something very likable about her, even though she tended to get rambunctious after a few Bacardis. People said she had once been beautiful, but drugs put an end to that. Further, her teeth had been knocked out in an altercation with a drug dealer she had tried to scam, according to neighborhood gossip. She was in love with Dean MacGuigan, who was waiting for her back at the Las Vegas Hilton, but she had been promised $2,000 for a night out on the town with a couple of high rollers, and she and Dean needed the money.

Dean MacGuigan, forty-two, was in Las Vegas to establish a six-week residency so that he could divorce his wife, Linda, whom he had walked out on almost two years earlier. He had then moved in with Pati Margello at her house in South Philadelphia, which acquaintances described as a filthy-dirty drug addict's dump, with dog shit everywhere. Like Pati, Dean was a drug addict reportedly with AIDS. Dean's mother, Lisa, seventy, was the wife of Christopher Moseley, the man who hired Diana

Hironaga to arrange the murder of Pati Margello. She was also a member of the du Pont family.

> *I did, um, in whatever state, uh, ultimately ask for, for, um, Pati to be killed. And, um, then I did in fact pay for it.*
>> —CHRISTOPHER MOSELEY to Detective David Mesinar and FBI special agent Brett Shields prior to his arrest on September 17, 1998, at the Fieldstone Club, a state-of-the-art private golf club in Greenville, Delaware, which he was going to manage.

Although Diana Hironaga used the stage name of Kiane Lee when she was performing in porn films or meeting strangers in hotel lobbies, she checked into the Del Mar motel that night under her own name. According to prosecutors, after having arranged how he would pay Hironaga for her services, Christopher Moseley had returned to Serendip, his wife's estate in Greenville, to prepare for the Fieldstone Club's launch party and to await word that the murder was a *fait accompli*. Before giving the order to have Pati killed, Moseley had tried to buy her off, but Pati wasn't one to be bought off easily when it came to Dean MacGuigan. She had taken money and promised to leave Dean before, only to party with the money and stay right where she was. Most recently there had been an ugly scene in Moseley's suite at the Las Vegas Hilton, where Dean and Pati were also staying. Diana Hironaga was present. 'Don't try and buy me off, you son of a bitch,' Pati screamed at Moseley, Dean later recalled. 'Take your money and shove it up your ass!' Moseley told her, 'You better watch yourself, young lady, or I'll take you out.' Then he called hotel security and had her removed from his suite. 'She was out of control,' he said. Shortly after that scene, Moseley gave Hironaga the go-ahead for the murder. Moseley paid her a retainer fee of $5,000 up front, 'because she was behind in her parole payments'. (Hironaga maintains the money was for secretarial work.) Although it is understandable that any mother, let alone one as grand as Lisa Dean Chandor MacGuigan Moseley, would object to a woman like Pati Margello as a life partner for her son, surely there were better solutions to the family problem than the one Moseley chose.

According to police, Hironaga hired two accomplices, whom Moseley met before he left town. One was Ricardo Murillo, a tough, forty-year-old alleged drug dealer who knew his way around the low-life sector of Las Vegas. The other, Joseph Balignasa, twenty-seven, was an unemployed Filipino dishwasher whose connection to Murillo was drugs. Hironaga then lured Pati out for what she promised would be a night on the town with two big spenders, and she said there wouldn't have to be sex. In his statement to the police, Dean MacGuigan later said, 'They were contacts of [Diana Hironaga] from out of town, quote high rollers, coming in wanting to go out, have a good time, make a lot of money in the casinos and just have some fun.' Compensation of $2,000 was a major score for someone like no-longer-young, no-longer-beautiful Pati

Margello. Dean saw her and Diana off about midnight in the bar of the Hilton and told her he would be waiting for her in their room. Pati had been fitted with dentures, but that night she was wearing only the upper plate, and it was broken because Dean had sat on it. 'I sit on them all the time,' Dean later told the police. 'I see her take them out every day.'

Pati dressed smartly for her $2,000 score and her night on the town. 'She was in black,' Dean told the police. 'She had a jacket that may have had some white on it, black pumps, black bag, orangish lipstick.' He said that he had bought her some nylons, dark tan in color. From the beginning, Pati Margello must have sensed that something was wrong. It would not have been out of line for her to expect to arrive at the MGM Grand or Caesars Palace in a limousine or a town car. Instead, the group met up shortly after midnight at the San Francisco Bay Club, not one of the classier nightspots in town. Hironaga made the introductions. Pati had reason to be distrustful of Hironaga, whom she knew to be associated with Christopher Moseley, who was determined to break up her romance with Dean MacGuigan. Hironaga had been in Moseley's bedroom when he threatened to have Pati taken out. Moreover, Pati had been around enough in her forty-five years to realize that there was no way Ricardo Murillo and Joseph Balignasa could ever be mistaken for high rollers. They just didn't have the right look, even though Balignasa was wearing a Calvin Klein belt with CK on the buckle. Pati was paired off with Balignasa, who was about five feet four. The one thing all four had in common was a fondness for drugs, and that night, according to Balignasa, they were on methamphetamine, which is called crystal meth in drug parlance and is said to give the highest of highs. From the San Francisco Bay Club the quartet drove to the Del Mar motel in Murillo's girlfriend's nondescript white car, and Hironaga booked a room. The wonder is that Pati didn't make a run for it then and there, but she didn't. She went along with the three of them to Room No. 6.

I HAPPEN TO have been in that room in May of this year, during Joseph Balignasa's trial. (Balignasa was tried separately in Las Vegas because he was the only one of the accused killers who didn't subsequently cross state lines, and his first trial ended with a mistrial. Along with Murillo and Moseley, he is pleading not guilty.) On a visit to the crime scene with the trial historian Judy Spreckels, I went up to the front desk, asked to rent Room No. 6, and handed over $30 in cash. The manager spotted us for the media types we were and wasn't about to let us in, but then he recognized me from the O. J. Simpson trial. He asked me if I thought that O. J. was really guilty, and I said yes. He said he was in total agreement, and introduced himself as Rodger O'Neill. He said the room was currently occupied, but if we came back at the same time the next day, he'd show it to us and we wouldn't have to pay. He told me Room No. 6 was very popular. 'A lot of sickos come here and want to take the room where the girl was murdered,' he said.

No set designer could have come up with anything grimmer, or grimier, for a hooker to be murdered in. The curtains, closed tight, looked as if they hadn't been opened in years. A large mirror was tilted out from one wall so that customers could watch themselves take drugs and have sex while dirty movies played on the television set. It occurred to me that ejaculations in the low thousands had taken place in that bed. As if reading my thoughts, Rodger O'Neill said, 'We change the sheets after each customer.'

On the night of the murder, Balignasa says, the quartet took drugs. They didn't have sex or watch dirty movies. They were there for another purpose. There weren't enough chairs for all of them, so at least some of them must have sat on the bed with its well-worn spread. At some point Pati clearly began to feel uncomfortable. About 2:30 she used the telephone several times, speaking in a low voice so that the others couldn't hear. She called Dean at the Las Vegas Hilton. He wasn't in, so she left a message. MacGuigan later told the police she said, 'Deanie, I think I need you, baby. This is really weird.' He added, 'I'd gone out to take a walk because I was going stir crazy in the room, and I wasn't going to gamble and had broken up, uh, a fight.' Pati then called a friend named Jimmy Facenta, but he wasn't in, either, and she left a message saying that she was at the Del Mar. Then she called Dean again, and this time he answered. She told him that she didn't feel right about where she was, and she asked him to come and get her. He said he didn't have any money and couldn't afford a taxi. He told *her* to take a taxi and come back to the Hilton. Perhaps he did not comprehend the seriousness of her call. He also told her that he had been in an altercation outside and had stopped a fight between a Hispanic man and a woman, and that he had gotten his nose broken. (When his wife, Linda, whom he was in Las Vegas to divorce, heard this later, she said that Dean had once told her the exact same story, about having his nose broken while he was coming to the aid of a woman who was being beaten up by a Hispanic man.) By the time Pati spoke to Dean that night, she sensed that she was in real danger, and she suspected that Christopher Moseley was involved. She asked Dean if he thought Moseley had set her up. Dean said no. Then she asked him if he was in on this with his stepfather. Dean denied that he was, but he didn't go to help her, even though the Hilton was only a mile from the Del Mar. Instead, he went to sleep and didn't wake up until eleven o'clock in the morning.

After Dean let her down, Pati must have realized that she was on her own. She excused herself and went to the bathroom, hoping perhaps that she could climb out the window, but there was no window. According to Balignasa, when Pati was in the bathroom, Hironaga said to her accomplices, in what sounds like a line from a Gloria Grahame movie, 'Are you guys going to do this or not?,' as if to indicate that she was sick of waiting. Standing in that dreadful, creepy room afterward, I could imagine the toilet flushing, the sound of water running. I could almost see the door opening and Pati coming out of the bathroom, facing the three people who are accused of killing her. Murillo, the thug of the bunch, grabbed her and started to choke her, according to Balignasa. As rotten as Pati's life was, she still wanted it, and she fought hard to save it. Both Hironaga and Balignasa claim that Murillo forced her down onto the bed, then onto the floor, and started beating her. The porn star and the unemployed dishwasher have implicated each other in helping Murillo as he held a pillow over her face to muffle her screams. She still wouldn't die. Murillo said to Balignasa, 'Give me your belt.' Balignasa pulled off his belt with the CK on the buckle and handed it to him. Hironaga and Balignasa say Murillo pulled the belt tight around Pati's neck and finished her off. He stuffed the buckle in her mouth with her broken upper denture. It had taken the three of them fifteen minutes to kill her.

'Do you think Dean had something to do with this murder, or is he capable of that?,' FBI special agent Brett Shields asked Christopher Moseley.

'I don't think he did. I think he really cared for this woman, and I think he still does,' Moseley replied.

Diana Hironaga's plan for the murder, which Christopher Moseley, in military fashion, named Operation Dean, hadn't gone much beyond the murder itself. No one had given any thought, for example, to disposing of the body. It was now 3:30 in the morning. The three-hour rental of the room was up. Hironaga went to the desk and took the room for another three hours, then went back to sit with Pati's body while Murillo and Balignasa drove in

Murillo's girlfriend's car to a Walgreen's drugstore three blocks north of the Del Mar. This was like the gang that couldn't shoot straight. They didn't consider that Walgreen's, which is open twenty-four hours a day, might have thirty surveillance cameras. In a video that was shown at the Balignasa trial, one camera picks up the two alleged killers deciding which plastic garbage bags and tape to buy to hide the body of the dead woman, while another shows them up at the cash register dutifully paying for those items, along with some cans of 7-Up and Coke.

As emaciated and ravaged by drugs as Pati Margello had become, she was still too big to fit into a garbage bag, so, according to police, they folded her body in two, breaking fifteen of her ribs in the process, nine on one side and six on the other. Then the killers tied her in that position with the jumper cables from Murillo's girlfriend's car and television cable wire. There was blood, so they wrapped the body in a bedsheet before stuffing it into the garbage bag. They removed the grate from the air-conditioning unit on the wall, shoved the wrapped body through the ten-inch opening into the space behind, and replaced the grate. They wiped for fingerprints. They put Pati's shoes and purse into a plastic bag together with some of the towels they had used to wipe up the blood. Then they left the Del Mar. They stopped at the same Walgreen's drugstore so that Hironaga could buy some Band-Aids and cigarettes. Balignasa put the bag with Pati's shoes and purse into a trash bin behind the store. Then they dropped Hironaga off at the Hilton, where she was also staying. Before she fell asleep, she telephoned Christopher Moseley at Serendip. It was now 6:30 in the morning in Las Vegas, 9:30 in Greenville. She notified him that Pati Margello would no longer be a problem. Two days later, on August 4, Hironaga and Murillo flew first-class to the Philadelphia airport, which also serves Greenville. There a chauffeur sent by Moseley gave them a packet containing $15,000. They did not see Moseley. They returned on the next plane to Las Vegas.

IN APRIL OF THIS YEAR, several weeks before flying to Las Vegas for the Balignasa trial, I went to family court in Wilmington, where Linda MacGuigan, the forty-five-year-old wife of Dean MacGuigan, made a plea for increased financial support. Since Dean did not stay in Las Vegas long enough to establish residency to divorce her, the couple is still married. Linda, who suffers from the muscular disease fibromyalgia syndrome, lives in Phoenix, Arizona, and for several years she has been virtually destitute. We dined together at the Du Pont Hotel the night before the hearing, and she told me stories of the family life at Serendip and Louviers, the marital home where she and Dean had lived. For a year after leaving Louviers, she said, she was on welfare, but in February 1998, at a family-court hearing, she was awarded $4,000 a month from Dean's $2 million trust fund. She told me that she prefers to be called Rags, a nickname she acquired because of her fondness for reggae music. That night she was with a California friend named Pauline Miller, who had been a friend of Dean and Linda's when they were together.

The next morning, as we waited for the hearing to begin, Linda and Dean MacGuigan, who had not seen each other for two years, did not speak. It was the first of my two encounters with Dean, both in courtrooms. For a crack addict allegedly suffering from AIDS, he looked surprisingly healthy to me. The signs of addiction and illness were not visible in his face, as they had been in photographs I had seen of him. He had obviously been in rehab after leaving Las Vegas, where he had cooperated with the police and the FBI in setting up his stepfather, Christopher Moseley, for his arrest at the launch of the Fieldstone Club. From all reports, his mother, who remains loyal to Moseley, no longer speaks to him. I had expected to encounter a scumbag, but his looks were distinctly at odds with his reputation. There is a slightly snobby cast to his face, and his class shines through his scruffy clothes. His tweed jacket was shabby and needed to go to the cleaners, but it was well cut. As for voice, manners, style – they're all there. His nose is aristocratic, very like his mother's. 'It's the du Pont nose,' whispered Linda MacGuigan. The du Pont nose, I noted, didn't have the look of a nose that had been broken in the last year.

Dean came over to Pauline Miller and hugged her warmly. He asked her about her husband, whom he called by name, and about her dog, whose name he remembered. Pauline said the dog had died, and they shared a moment of mourning for the animal. Linda looked straight ahead during this conversation.

Dean now lives in Manassas, Virginia. That day he was

with his divorce lawyer and a woman named Janet Oddonino, an airline employee, at whose house he is currently living. She heard me remark to Dean's lawyer, Gary Lance Smith, 'Who's the lady in the palazzo pajamas?' When I saw her several weeks later at the Balignasa trial in Las Vegas, where Dean was a witness, she said, 'I'm the one who was in the palazzo pajamas.' At the hearing, Dean told the judge that he was currently employed as a waiter at a TGI Friday's, where he was paid $2.10 an hour and tips. The court's judgment came down against Linda. Instead of getting an increase in support, she learned that what she had been receiving would be cut in half. Wilmington is probably not the ideal place to take on a du Pont.

If she knew I was speaking to you, she'd never
speak to me again. I don't know anything, really.
    —A friend of Lisa Moseley's who asked to
    remain anonymous.

Back in the '50s in New York, I used to stare at elegant folks such as Ann and Bill Woodward and think how wonderful their lives must be. Then Ann killed Bill. I was not part of the high life back then, merely a fringe character standing in the stage line at dances. There was a girl named Lisa Dean from Wilmington, Delaware, who fascinated me. I knew who she was, but she didn't know me. What she had that other postdebs of her era didn't have was a strain of the exotic about her, passed down from a Lebanese great-grandmother. She made me think of what

Rebecca de Winter in Hitchcock's *Rebecca* must have looked like as she danced past stag lines, roaring with laughter, madly popular. Like all really stylish women, Lisa Dean found her look early and never changed it. 'Sleek' and 'glamorous' were the adjectives that applied to her. She looked rich, even before you knew she was. When people talked about her, and they often did, someone in the group would invariably say, 'She's a du Pont', and images of privilege would fill the air. Her mother, Paulina du Pont Dean, was the daughter of William K. du Pont, whose great-grandfather founded DuPont in 1802. Today, DuPont is the largest chemical company in America.

In 1953, Lisa Dean married a popular but controversial figure in New York society named E. Haring 'Red' Chandor. Chandor was the first of Lisa's three husbands, and Lisa was the third of Red's five wives. Chandor, a raconteur and wit who is now seventy-eight, had a reputation in those days as a charming rascal and prankster, whose rich-boy mischief was a staple of society columns, including Cholly Knickerbocker's in the *New York Journal-American*. In all three of her marriages, Lisa was the one with the money, an advantage which tends to guarantee the leading role in any partnership. But there are du Ponts and du Ponts, and some are richer than others. Chandor once referred to Lisa as a 'pauper du Pont'. However, her reported $25 million fortune – measly compared with the fortunes of some of her relatives – was ample enough for her to be able recently to offer to put up $4 million, and later $8 million, in bail for her incarcerated current husband, who is in the North Las Vegas Detention Center awaiting trial. Bail was denied in each case. Nevada considers Christopher Moseley a flight risk.

By all accounts, the young Chandors were briefly happy and very much a part of the New York social scene. Wherever it was fashionable to be, they were. Lisa was photographed by Richard Avedon for *Harper's Bazaar*. The society painter René Bouché painted her portrait. In 1955, dressed as a Lebanese slave girl, she won first prize for best costume at socialite Fernanda Wanamaker Leas's 'A Night in Baghdad' party in Southampton, and pictures of her with Gary Cooper, dressed as a Foreign Legionnaire, who won for best men's costume, appeared in the New York tabloids. They lived on the Upper East Side and soon had two sons, Peter and Dean. The marriage looked perfect.

Even the obstetrician who delivered Lisa's second son, Dean, was the fashionable obstetrician of the day. His name was Dr John MacGuigan. '*Everyone* went to Dr MacGuigan,' said a New York hostess when I told her this story. The Chandor marriage came apart when Lisa fell in love with MacGuigan, who was also her gynecologist. MacGuigan, too, was married at the time. Lisa moved into a new apartment at 765 Park Avenue, and MacGuigan followed. Chandor served Lisa with papers for divorce on the ground of adultery, but the suit was dropped in 1959 when Chandor, in a feat of derring-do, absconded with his older son, Peter. The headline on the New York *Daily News* read, NY SOCIALITE SEIZES SON, 5, IN FLA., FLEES

LAW. Chandor took his son to Venezuela and Brazil and then to Cap d'Antibes in the South of France. The 'kidnapping' was New York society's favorite fun read for months. Chandor was caught four months later at the airport in Nice, and Peter was returned to his mother. Lisa was quoted in Cholly Knickerbocker's column as saying about Chandor, 'He deserves a good long jail sentence, and I'm not going to let him off the hook.' Chandor was sentenced to 120 days for contempt of court. He served 80 days and got two years' probation. Such untoward behavior got the couple kicked out of the *Social Register*, which was still a big deal in New York in the '50s, when people in their set used the *Social Register* as their telephone book. Lisa and MacGuigan married, and the last name of the two Chandor sons was changed to MacGuigan, engendering a bitterness on Chandor's part that persists to this day.

LISA MACGUIGAN MOVED back to Delaware with her husband and two sons. Greenville, where most of the rich of Wilmington live, including many members of the du Pont family, has rolling hills, ducal gates, long driveways, and stately mansions. The area is sometimes referred to as 'château country'. There, Peter and Dean MacGuigan lived on their mother's estate, Serendip. Having left behind her front-page social life in New York, Lisa settled into country life, developing passions for gardening and golf. Her gardens at Serendip are renowned. For years busloads of tourists would arrive to admire them. She was already a golf champion at Shinnecock in Southampton. Back home she belonged to Bidermann, the golf club favored by members of the du Pont clan and named after the husband of one of them, which is considered more exclusive by far than the Wilmington Country Club, nearby.

Chandor swears that MacGuigan was abusive to his sons and that both boys hated him. (Dean's attorney says that Dean 'had great love and respect' for his adoptive father.) Even before they left New York, Peter had been kicked out of more than one school. By the time he was fourteen or fifteen, he had a $100-a-day drug habit. Dean went to Lawrenceville, a prep school in New Jersey, and to the University of Virginia, where, according to Chandor, he was known as the coke king of the campus. He was arrested twice for dealing drugs, Chandor says, and could have received fifteen years on each charge, but after his mother appeared on his behalf, he wound up serving less than a year. Dean had a brief career on Wall Street at PaineWebber. There are varying stories about his ethics and capabilities in the job. His wife, Linda, is quite blunt on the subject of his career in finance. 'He was fired for bilking clients,' she told me. (Dean's attorney says that Dean was a top broker at PaineWebber, did nothing illegal, and left the company to pursue real-estate investments.) Dean MacGuigan's life has seemingly been distinguished only by the multiplicity of his failures.

In 1985, John MacGuigan died of a heart attack. From all reports, Lisa was devastated by his death. Three years later, she placed an ad in the newspaper for a groundskeeper, and a man named Christopher Moseley applied and got the job. 'Groundskeeper' is a high-class word for gardener. At Serendip it also meant chauffeur.

NOT LONG INTO his employment, love bloomed. Moseley, who is eleven years younger than Lisa, is said to have declared his love when the two of them were planting a tree. He soon moved from the gardener's cottage to the main house. They married in 1989. Moseley had two previous wives and four children, but they play no part in this story. Rags MacGuigan said about Moseley, 'Peter and Dean just hated Christopher. Dean's goal was to screw up Christopher. Once, Dean ordered a gun, because he said he was going to kill Christopher, but he never got around to picking up the gun. Finally, Christopher picked up the gun. There was no way something wasn't going to happen. It was all fueled by drugs and booze.' (According to his lawyer, 'Dean describes himself as a gentleman and basically a pacifist. He says that murder is not a component of his makeup.') Dean said on the stand at the Balignasa trial about his stepfather, 'Over the years, we got along well and horribly. When he was drinking, he would do maliciously nasty things to me.'

Although there are those who refer to Lisa as Lady Chatterley for having dallied with her gardener, the circumstances of the gardener's life are so atypical as to be worth noting. Moseley comes from a socially registered family on Long Island. His late father, Frederick Moseley Jr, was captain of the Harvard football and hockey teams and later a prominent figure on Wall Street, where he was an executive vice president of J. P. Morgan & Co. Christopher was considered a hell-raiser and a bit of a family disappointment. He attended an exclusive New England prep school, although he did not graduate. Two weeks after his eighteenth birthday he joined the army, where he served for a total of twenty-five years as a communications expert. He was honorably discharged as a first sergeant in 1985. As with most of the people in this story, ambition did not play a big part in his life. When his father died, he returned home. He asked if he had been left anything in the will, and his stepmother replied, 'Yes, debts.' Relatives and people who knew him say he would tell fanciful tales of his exploits in espionage and secret government work during his army years, but his military records reportedly do not support his claims. No one ever believed him, anyway. 'He always told stories,' a stepsibling of his confided to me. J. Simpson Dean, Lisa's brother, was quoted in a Wilmington paper as saying about him after his arrest, 'To be perfectly honest with you, I never paid any attention to [his stories].'

I heard that Moseley doesn't really mind being in jail. It reminds him of the army.
    —Another friend of Lisa Moseley's who wishes to remain anonymous.

In 1991, Dean met Linda Youngstrom Plescia at a nightclub in Palm Springs, California. Linda had been a bookkeeper for a television production company in

Hollywood. She had been married previously and had a son. Linda and Dean fell in love. But Lisa was a hard mother to please when it came to the women in Dean's life. She never liked Linda, and the feeling became mutual. 'She never spoke to me,' says Rags. Dean and Linda were married at Serendip in 1992. The wedding was a preview of the marriage ahead. Rags recalls that at the bridal dinner the night before the wedding, at the house where Lisa had grown up, Peter MacGuigan, who was to be the best man for Dean, was drunk on alcohol and codeine cough medicine. He behaved appallingly. His mother had already banned him from staying in the house. He went to a local bar, but he was so crazed that the bartender refused to serve him. After everyone had gone to bed, he climbed up to Dean's room, smashed in the window with a tire iron, and got into a fistfight with his brother. Peter was disinvited to the wedding by his mother, and the best-man duties were taken over by another guest. According to Rags, Dean was unwell at the time of their marriage, perhaps with AIDS.

Dean's lawyer denies that Dean has AIDS, and insists that Pati had been given a clean bill of health shortly before her death. However, after the murder Pati's son, Eric Howarth, discovered a handwritten letter from Dean to Pati in which he wrote, 'You may never see your Grandchildren because of me. I should have told you I had Aids + not waited 6 mos. You have been showing signs of it . . . I've had it for 10 years . . . I feel like a murderer.'

When Linda walked into the front hall of Serendip on her wedding day, one and a half hours early so that she could change into her wedding dress, her about-to-be mother-in-law said to her, 'What the hell are you doing here?' Linda and Dean were married by the same female Presbyterian minister who had married Lisa and Moseley. Dean built a house in La Quinta, California, but it soon went into foreclosure. They returned to Delaware and moved into a lovely estate called Louviers, a du Pont house which Lisa rented for them for $2,500 a month. The house is painted ocher and has white pillars. The halls and rooms are graceful in proportion, but it was never a happy house. 'We weren't invited to her dinner parties,' says Rags. 'We weren't introduced to anybody.'

In 1995, Dean's brother, Peter, died of a heroin overdose in Boulder, Colorado. At his mother's request, there was no obituary in the papers. Lisa, who doesn't attend funerals, did not attend Peter's, just as she had not attended her husband John MacGuigan's. Dean, increasingly drugged, was discontented at Louviers. Rags claims that he was abusive to her. Previously, she says, he had dragged her by her hair and hit her. (Dean's lawyer vehemently denies that Dean ever abused her.)

Dean reportedly met Pati Margello at a drug rehab, although Linda disputes this. Pati was forty-two. He was thirty-nine. 'We fell in love and were soul mates for two years approximately, ending with her death,' Dean testified at the Balignasa trial.

Meanwhile, at Louviers, Rags had a call from Moseley, asking if she would allow Lisa to come over and collect some heirlooms she had given Dean. 'Christopher always remained the hired help, but with bedroom privileges,' says Rags. Lisa arrived, clipboard in hand, with Moseley and Lesley Davis, the new groundskeeper. 'She wanted me to go through every room at Louviers,' says Rags. 'She had Lesley pack up things and put them in the trunk. The rent had been paid to the end of the lease, but she had said, "I want you out of here as soon as possible. Whatever arrangement you make with Chris is all right with me." Then she said I could only communicate with the family by fax. I was told not to call.'

Rags was fired, like a maid. Adequate provision was not made for her, she says, nor were her possessions ever returned. In a letter she wrote to her lawyer, she said, 'In my meeting with Chris [Moseley] at Louviers on 3/26/97, at which Chris requested that my mother be present as witness, he pulled a gun from the waistband of his pants, put it on the kitchen table, and told us he always "packed heat" and that he "knew how to get things done".'

DEAN'S LIAISON WITH Pati was anathema to his mother, particularly during a brief period when Pati moved into Louviers with Dean, after Rags had left. Their drugged behavior was unacceptable to the family, and they abused the house. The feces their dogs left on the floors seemed not to offend them. When they were moving out, Dean reported to the police that $15,000 worth of computer equipment and jewelry had been stolen from the house, but the police found the equipment in the back of the car Pati was driving, and she and Dean were fined for falsely reporting an incident. 'My mother didn't like Pati,'

Dean said on the stand. Lisa cut Dean's money off, and he moved out of Louviers into Pati's mother's house at 1320 Moore Street in South Philadelphia. It is a low-income neighborhood, but the antics of the addicts were as unpopular there as they had been in château country. Curiously, Dean seemed to prefer low life to high life.

When I went to look at the house in May, it was boarded up and I was not able to enter, but people told me that it was beyond slovenly; it was filthy. Dean and Pati had no money, not even for food. At the Saint Nicholas of Tolentine Church, in South Philadelphia, the poor could obtain food donated by parishioners. Pati, who was a member of the parish and had gone to parochial school there, started appearing every two weeks, and soon every week. She wanted only soup or pasta. 'She didn't take vegetables, because of her teeth. She couldn't chew,' said Mary De Gregorio, who oversees the program at Saint Nicholas. 'One time she called me and said, "Can my boyfriend pick up the food?" After that, Dean started to come.'

'What were they like?' I asked.

'Her arm was wrapped up once. She told me various stories about how it happened. She said her dog bit her. She said she was hit by a car. I felt sorry for her. I was tempted to give her some soap along with the food, they were so dirty,' replied De Gregorio.

The pristine nature of the property was preserved to provide members and their guests with an

unparalleled golf experience . . . Most simply put,
Fieldstone is pure golf for the golf enthusiast.
        —From the brochure describing Fieldstone
        Golf Club.

At the heart of this story is a 184-acre tract of rolling
piedmont and woodland only ten minutes from downtown
Wilmington. Lisa inherited the land from her maternal
grandmother, and she and Moseley were developing it into
the Fieldstone Club, designed to be the finest eighteen-
hole golf course in Delaware. At one time the land was
to have gone to Peter and Dean. After Peter's death, it
was to have gone to Dean, who had the idea for a top-of-
the-line golf course. After Dean became ill, Lisa deeded
the land to Moseley. At the family-court hearing in
Wilmington in May at which Rags MacGuigan pleaded
that she was destitute, Dean told the judge that he had
turned over his interest in the land to his stepfather without being paid, 'because I love my mother and she
requested it. I did what she wanted.' In truth, he was very
unhappy to have part of his inheritance in the hands of
a stepfather he disliked intensely.

Moseley, along with two partners, hired Hurdzan/Fry
Golf Design to construct Fieldstone. He was no longer
the sergeant, no longer the gardener. The club became his
passion, but he had the Pati Margello problem to deal with
first.

In July 1998, Dean was sent to Las Vegas to establish
a six-week residency so that he could divorce Rags.
Christopher Moseley went along to find a lawyer for Dean,

get him a job, keep him off drugs, and dole out money to him. In Dean's first days in Las Vegas, according to Moseley, he managed to go through $7,000, mostly on gambling and drugs. He spent part of the money on a plane ticket for Pati so that she could come out and join him. That infuriated Moseley.

> *[Pati and I] had a rocky tumultuous relationship, which was one that was just our style. Usually when the police were called to our house, it was to save me. Chris thought she wasn't good enough for me, that, uh, she was a risk. Everything with Chris is missions, operatives. He was in the military many years.*
>
> —Dean MacGuigan *at his police interrogation in Las Vegas.*

When Dean woke up at 11 A.M. in the Las Vegas Hilton on August 2, 1998, Pati wasn't there. Later he told the police he hadn't known what to think about her absence. 'Pati is, was, a very compulsive, energetic girl,' he said. 'She would go off, you know, eighteen hours, and just be having fun.' At about eleven o'clock that night, he called Diana Hironaga in her room and said, 'What the hell happened to Pati last night? She never showed up.' Hironaga said she had dropped her off in the lobby that morning. 'Don't worry about it, Dean. You know these high rollers. She probably just got a better offer.'

Dean said he thought she might have flown back to Philadelphia. 'Her house was in some danger of getting a city sticker on it [indicating that it was a "vacant public nuisance"], and her dog had died, and she was very upset about things.' The next day he made a few calls to his stepfather at Serendip, asking if he knew of Pati's whereabouts. Moseley said he didn't, but he assured Dean that everything was all right.

Two days later, Dean wrote out a report, which began, 'There is a missing person, my girlfriend, Pati Margello. She is about 5' 5" tall, Black hair, and is missing half of her middle finger on one hand.' Before he turned it in to the police, he saw on television that the body of an unidentified woman had been found inside an air-conditioning duct at the Del Mar motel, where Pati had been when she called him. A maid had complained of an unpleasant odor, and the motel handyman discovered the body. The Del Mar had to have the room cleaned professionally several times in order to get rid of the stench of Pati Margello's decomposing body.

DEAN WENT TO THE POLICE the following day and said that he believed the woman in his report and the unidentified woman found at the Del Mar motel were the same. If Diana Hironaga had checked into the Del Mar under her stage name of Kiane Lee, she might not have been found so quickly and informed on her alleged accomplices. By then, Joseph Balignasa had already been arrested on a drug charge and was in jail. Dean cooperated with the police and allowed them to record several conversations he had with Moseley. I do not have transcripts of those conversations, but something sufficiently incriminating was said by Moseley to cause homicide detective David Mesinar of the Las Vegas Metropolitan Police and FBI special agent Brett Shields to fly east and interview him.

Moseley didn't know they were coming, and they didn't realize that their visit would coincide with the launch party for the Fieldstone Club. The golf course, which is still under construction, is spectacular. The clubhouse will be at the crest of the highest hill on the huge property. There, under a yellow-and-white-striped tent, the party was about to begin. Waiters were setting up drink tables and carrying out glasses and ice. Moseley had not yet arrived. Mesinar and Shields told a person at the desk of a construction-site office that they wanted to speak with him, and a call was made to Moseley, who showed up twenty minutes later. He immediately called Lisa and told her to get an attorney, but he spoke to the detectives without one. The questioning took place in the temporary office on the Fieldstone grounds. Moseley began by telling the police, 'I was pretty well drunk most of the time I was in Las Vegas.'

'Do you have access to all of your wife's money?'
FBI agent Brett Shields asked Christopher Moseley.
'No, I don't have access to the money. We have a very tight marital agreement. She occasionally floats me a loan . . .'
'Did she know Pati?'
'She has seen her or met her, I think, once and just basically refuses to have anything to do with her . . .'

    'How did you tell your wife? I mean, how did
the conversation come up?'
    'I just, like, said that Pati was no longer with
us . . .'
    'What was her response when you told her that?'
    'Her response was basically a little disbelief that
I would take that drastic a measure.'

Mesinar and Shields questioned Moseley for an hour
and a quarter. It was reported in the Wilmington paper
that some people cried when the police led Moseley away
in handcuffs. They took him to the FBI office in
Wilmington, where he was booked. After his arrest,
Moseley resigned his position at the Fieldstone Club, but
the scandal seems not to have affected business. When I
visited the club in early June, I learned that the initiation
fee is $45,000.

    Lisa, who had been forewarned by her husband, did
not appear at the launch party. She was at Serendip when
the call came from Detective Mesinar telling her that her
husband was in jail, charged with murder. Mesinar said
that he and Shields wanted to come by and talk with her.
'I can hardly wait,' she replied, in what Mesinar says was
a sarcastic voice.

    Serendip is a grandly proportioned and elegant house
at the end of a long drive. Lisa opened the door herself.
This is a house with servants, but there were no servants
around. She was alone. She led the police upstairs to a
second-floor library, and they sat down. The detectives
told her what had happened. She listened, but didn't say

much, except to tell them that she had no information. She said that she had not cared for Pati and had not approved of her relationship with Dean. When Mesinar asked her what she thought of Pati's death, she replied, 'Well, I can't honestly tell you I'm sorry.'

After they left, Mesinar realized that he had forgotten his briefcase, and he had to go back. Lisa opened the door and let him go upstairs to get it. When I met Detective Mesinar at the Las Vegas courthouse during the Balignasa trial, he recalled that the smell of tobacco smoke from Lisa's and Moseley's chain-smoking permeated the upholstered furniture and cushions of the grand house. As I listened to him, I recalled a story in Ralph Cipriano's article on this case in *Philadelphia Magazine*. Cipriano wrote that once, according to Moseley, when he had quit smoking for three weeks, Lisa insisted that if he didn't start up again she would divorce him. She said she didn't want anyone to kiss her whose breath wasn't as bad as her own.

> *'The problem I have here is if you're willing to take Dean down with you and you're willing to take your wife down with you, because this money is going to be traced back to your wife,' FBI agent Brett Shields told Christopher Moseley in questioning him.*
>
> *'I don't want to take either one of them down with me,' said Moseley . . .*
>
> *'This is the problem I'm having, 'cause Kiane [Diana Hironaga] is telling us there's a voice mail*

*that explicitly says that Pati's no longer a problem,
mission complete, Step 5, she's no longer with us.
Now, if you didn't pick up that voice message, that
means your wife picked up that voice message,
'cause what you've said is that only you and your
wife are present here, and that's leading me to
believe that maybe you confided some of these
things in your wife . . .'*

*'She knew after the fact. She had nothin' to do
with it. The money was not in any way, shape,
manner or form given to me to do what I did,'*
Moseley replied.

When prosecutor William Koot handed Dean
MacGuigan a photograph of Pati Margello for identification at the Balignasa trial, Dean responded, with emotion,
'That's my Pati.' As he left the stand that day he appeared
upset. Janet Oddonino followed him out the door of the
courtroom. I went out into the corridor in time to see
Dean and Janet, arms around each other, running down
the long hallway to the stairwell, laughing. They looked,
inappropriately, carefree.

The person I most wanted to talk to while I was in Las
Vegas for the Balignasa trial was Christopher Moseley, who
has been sitting in the North Las Vegas Detention Center
for nearly a year waiting for his trial to begin this October.
I wrote him a letter and told him I was going to be writing about his case. I told him that I knew one of his step-
siblings and that I used to know his wife, sort of. I said
that the kind of people he and Lisa were accustomed to

having dinner with were starting to tell stories. I asked him if he would care to make a statement. He didn't reply to my letter, but he gave copies of it to his Las Vegas lawyer, John Fadgen, and to Lisa. I had also written to Lisa, but she had not answered. Casino owner Steve Wynn, one of the major figures in Las Vegas, made a call to an FBI agent to see if he could get me into the jail to meet with Moseley. The next day the FBI agent said, 'His lawyer would be a fool to let you in there.' I knew that, but it was worth a try.

I did get in to meet John Fadgen, a jovial fellow of sixty or so with snow-white hair. He has a bungalow-type office within walking distance of the courthouse where the Balignasa trial was taking place. The story goes that Moseley got Fadgen's name from a prisoner in the next cell who was doing time for a Mob offense. Fadgen and I had a big laugh over the stupidity of Diana Hironaga's signing in at the Del Mar motel under her own name. 'If she'd taken an ad out in the *Las Vegas Sun* it wouldn't have been more obvious,' he said. He was then deeply immersed in the murder trial of a Las Vegas Mob figure named Herbert 'Fat Herbie' Blitzstein, a lieutenant of slain mobster Anthony 'Tony the Ant' Spilatro, which he would later win. He spoke glowingly of Lisa, with whom he was in regular communication. He said that Lisa and Moseley talked on the telephone every day, that they were very close.

THE FUTURE LOOKS BLEAK for Christopher Moseley. In all probability he will never set eyes on Serendip again, or play a round of golf at the Fieldstone Club, which he so wanted to manage. The likelihood is that he will receive at least twenty-five years. For a man of sixty, which he will be on his next birthday, that's the same thing as a life sentence. His case wasn't helped when the lawyer for Diana Hironaga, about whom nobody had given a thought since the murder, except to joke about how stupid she was, provided new information that adds a further twist to this twisted plot. Hironaga pleaded guilty to a federal conspiracy charge, but, in hopes of receiving something less than a life sentence, she claimed that Moseley had hired her to kill Dean MacGuigan as well as Pati – a charge that Fadgen says is 'absolutely untrue'. Her sentencing is set for December. It was at this point that Lisa made a second bail offer, of $8 million, along with a promise to have Moseley wear a surveillance ankle bracelet and have police live at Serendip in order to ensure that he would not make a run for it. No way, Jose, was the court's response.

AFTER THE MURDER, Dean returned briefly to South Philadelphia. Unknown people had been in Pati's house and ripped open her furniture, looking for drugs. A friend of hers told me, 'Pati was adept at hiding drugs.' Dean paid a visit to Saint Nicholas of Tolentine Church, where he and Pati used to go for free food. He told Mary De Gregorio that he wanted to have a memorial service for Pati. He didn't tell her that Pati had been murdered; he said she had been killed in a 'bad accident'. He said that he wanted to leave a donation. De Gregorio, who still thought he was a street person, said he didn't have to leave any money. Dean said he could afford it and, taking out a wad of bills, handed her a twenty. De Gregorio told me, 'I thought he should keep it. Then I read in the paper that he was a du Pont.'

IN MAY, WHEN I WENT to South Philadelphia to see where Pati and Dean had lived, I dropped in on a man named Bob Santoro, who had been a close friend of Pati Margello's for years. Because of her drug addiction, Santoro once stopped speaking to her for three years, but he remains loyal to her and her memory. 'Pati never put a needle in her arm,' he insisted. 'And the only person Pati ever hurt was herself.' Through a fluke of timing, Pati's son from an early marriage, Eric Howarth, happened to be in Santoro's house that day, out of sight upstairs, reluctant to see me. I could hear him say, 'I don't want to talk to anybody from the media.' Ralph Cipriano, who first wrote about this story in *Philadelphia Magazine*, talked him into coming down. Eric, thirty, is a credit to his mother. A guitarist of talent, he is a musician by trade. 'When this is all over,' he said, 'I'm going away with my guitar and my music.' He told me how hurtful it had been for him to have his mother portrayed in the press only as a prostitute and a drug addict. His memories of her are filled with affection. 'Even when she was bad on drugs, and I went to her, she was always there for me,' he said.

Dean wanted to have Pati's body shipped east and buried in Philadelphia. In Moseley's statement to the police, he said he gave Dean money to pay for the funeral of the woman he had paid to have killed. But Eric Howarth would have none of the family's largesse. 'I didn't want them to have anything to do with my mother's funeral,' he said. 'I hate those rich people.' In the end, Bob Santoro helped out with Pati's funeral.

I recently heard that Eric is considering filing a civil suit against Lisa Moseley after the criminal trials – of Christopher Moseley, Ricardo Murillo, and Joseph Balignasa, whose first trial ended in a mistrial – are finished. That may depend on two things: at what point Lisa Moseley knew of the alleged plot to murder Pati, and whether it was her money that paid for the disastrous Operation Dean.

DEAN MACGUIGAN HAS RECENTLY filed suit for divorce from Linda 'Rags' MacGuigan in Manassas, Virginia, where he is living in the home of Janet Oddonino, who accompanied him to family court in Wilmington and to the Balignasa criminal trial in Las Vegas. Dean will be a witness for the prosecution at his stepfather's trial in Las Vegas. Recently I asked Gary Lance Smith, Dean MacGuigan's lawyer, whether Dean and his mother were still not speaking. He declined to answer. He did say that Dean is astonished that his mother continues to believe in Moseley's lies, and in Moseley. Dean, it seems, is interested in writing a book in order to tell his side of the story.

Meanwhile, Lisa Dean Moseley, the mystery figure of the story, remains secluded at Serendip. She has made no statement. She rarely appears in public. Her friends are worried about her. 'Beyond anorexic, weighs zero,' said one. 'She's very frail,' said another, whom I had asked to intercede. 'She's being very, very strong about everything, strong in that sense, but frail. She'll never talk to you. She's a very private person. She talks about the case all the time. She's very loyal to Christopher. I suppose they'll move him to a prison in Delaware so that she can visit him.' Then the friend said, 'What do you suppose was in Christopher's *mind* when he did such a thing? Of course he was drunk.' I asked if Lisa would be going to the trial in October. 'Oh, yes, Lisa's going to the trial.'

THE GIGOLO, THE HEIRESS, AND THE CANDLESTICK

Throughout the pattern of the Lonergan murder case are woven the deep purple threads of whispered vices whose details are unprintable and whose character is generally unknown to or misunderstood by the average normal person.

—*New York Journal-American*, October 29, 1943

SEXUALLY, THE BEAUTIFUL COUPLE in this story were way ahead of their time, decades ahead, and they were only in their twenties. Wayne Lonergan eloped with Patricia Burton in 1941, when she was nineteen, and he killed her in 1943, when she was only twenty-two. From the very beginning, it was a stormy marriage. After the murder, the newspapers quoted their friends as saying that the two had 'fought like cats and dogs', even on their honeymoon. She was spoiled and said to be a screamer. On one occasion, after a bitter public argument, she jeered at him, 'I suppose that's to be expected when a girl marries beneath her!' He took her verbal abuse. As so often happens in arrangements involving an heiress and a fortune hunter, she soon got sick of keeping him. She told friends she was tired of paying his bills, particularly since he was anything but attentive to his marriage vows. Like a lot of men who marry for money, he always had a little action on the side, and work never took up much of his time. But he played cards well and was a good dancer. The Lonergans were often seen at the Stork Club and El Morocco, the two most famous New York nightclubs back then, and their names appeared in the gossip columns from time to time. They were fringe, but they were pretty, and she was rich, and the fact that it was common knowledge that her husband had once been her father's boyfriend gave them a sort of celebrity status in the café-society set in which they moved.

Wayne Lonergan came from a middle-class family outside of Toronto. He attended St Peter's Roman Catholic Church and was taught by nuns at the parochial school. He had a sister and a brother, and his mother was four times a patient in the Ontario Mental Hospital in Toronto. His aunt, who spoke for the family after the murder, said that Wayne had always been a fine boy but that he fell into bad and fast company after he went to New York in 1938. She said, 'We told him that crowd and all that New York running around would only result in trouble,' but he wouldn't listen. She referred to his wife as 'that rich girl he married'. None of the family, she said, had known that Wayne 'lived a bisexual life'.

Lonergan worked as a chair pusher at the New York

World's Fair in 1939. Off-season, when the fair closed down for the winter, he sold ties at Abercrombie & Fitch. He was one of those young men in New York who like to be taken care of, and he had the kind of looks, swagger, and charm that could ensure that he was. 'Charm' is the key word here. There is not a person who remembers him who does not speak of his charm. He had an innate ability to make himself agreeable. He liked girls and he liked guys. Rich girls and rich guys. And he was available, under the right circumstances. At the world's fair he met William O. Burton, whom he pushed around the grounds in a rented rattan chair on wheels. Chair pushers were picked for their looks, just as waiters at charity balls are picked today. Lonergan was six feet three, with a handsome face and a lifeguard's body. His work uniform consisted of khaki shorts, a white shirt rolled up over the elbows, and a pith helmet. The look was not lost on William O. Burton.

Burton, whose family had changed its name from Bernheimer in 1917 because of its 'Teutonic' sound, was the heir to a $7 million brewing fortune. In today's economy, that would be somewhere in the $70 million range. Certainly it was more than enough for the Burtons to live abroad as expatriates, maintaining an impressive villa in the South of France – W. Somerset Maugham was a neighbor – and a yacht big enough to be able to cross the Atlantic. For diversion, Burton painted portraits of smart people in idle poses, but painting was not his passion. People like Wayne Lonergan were. After the murder, one newspaper described Burton as a 'gay artist'. He was dead by then, and the word 'gay' in those days meant one thing only: joyous, lively, merry — all of which he apparently was. Yet somehow the paper managed to convey the more recent meaning of the word as well.

NOT LONG AFTER they made contact at the fair, Lonergan became Burton's companion, the polite word for a kept man at the time, and he was often at the Ritz Tower on Park Avenue and 57th Street, where Burton maintained a suite during the early years of World War II. Burton's wife, Lucille, who was known as Lou, divorced him, charging cruelty. In her suit she said her husband had hurled a suitcase at her in San Sebastián, thrown her down a staircase in Paris, and knocked her against a stone wall in Biarritz. After the war started, Burton sent his yacht back to the United States, loaded down with family possessions, which included a prized collection of gold chalices. When the yacht arrived in New York, the Corsican crew stole the chalices and bolted with them. Burton couldn't even report the theft to the police, because he had been trying to sneak the chalices past customs without declaring them.

The Burtons' daughter, Patricia, who was sometimes called Patsy, hadn't lived in the villa with her parents. She and her nanny lived in the guesthouse, which had been done over especially for her. A Palm Beach society lady, who wishes not to be named, remembers Patsy from those childhood days in the South of France. 'We lived in Cannes, and the Burtons lived in Mougins. The Burtons were out so much. Never home. You probably heard the father was gay. Patsy and I were about the same age, and we used to play together. She was an only child. She was very nice but extremely spoiled. One time she showed me her jewelry. She was about twelve or thirteen at the time. It was incredible that a child should have that much jewelry.' Patricia loved jewelry right up until the end. Lying about in the room where she was murdered were fourteen rings set with emeralds, jade, rubies, and diamonds, seven bracelets, seven dress pins, seven pairs of earrings, and two strings of large pearls. That was why the police were certain from the start that robbery was not the motive.

When the family returned to New York, Lucille Burton played cards in the afternoons with Ruby Schinasi, a well-known social figure of the period. Ruby's daughter, who was then called Bubbles Schinasi and is now Leonora Hornblow, the widow of film producer Arthur Hornblow, still remembers Patricia vividly and fondly. They played together in New York and did glamorous things for people so young. 'We knew we were different from other little girls,' Mrs Hornblow told me recently.

Burton died before his boyfriend married his daughter, but he had already broken off with him, and in all probability he would have disapproved of the union. His aspirations for his daughter and only heir were aimed far higher than Wayne Lonergan, although it had been Burton himself who brought the young people together, at a dinner party he gave in a hotel dining room, where he seated them next to each other. Patricia was still in her late teens, but quite sophisticated. Having grown up seeing her father in the company of handsome young men, she totally accepted the situation. That night at dinner, she confessed to Lonergan that she had always longed to go to the Stork Club. Society people and movie stars went there, and celebrities such as Joseph P. Kennedy, J. Edgar Hoover, and Billy Rose. It was written up almost daily by Walter Winchell, Dorothy Kilgallen, and Cholly Knickerbocker in their gossip columns. There were balloon nights at the Stork, and Sherman Billingsley, who owned it, gave bottles of Sortilège perfume to his favorite debutantes. Patricia Burton wanted to be a part of that scene.

Finally her father had agreed to take her there, she said, and for the occasion he had overdressed in white tie and tails. The haughty maître d', who decided who got past the gold chain and who didn't, turned them away. That mortifying experience still embarrassed her, she told Lonergan, and he was touched by her story. Right then and there, he led her out of her father's party and took her to the Stork Club, where the maître d' said, 'Good evening, Mr Lonergan,' and opened the gold chain. They had a drink. They had a dance. Then they returned to her father's party. As grand gestures go, this was a pretty good one, guaranteed to make an impression on a worldly young lady.

WAYNE LONERGAN DID NOT confine his social climbing to the Burtons. Like the character Matt Damon plays in *The Talented Mr Ripley*, Lonergan had a deep yearning to be accepted by people on a higher social plane than his. Also like Ripley, he could go either way, and did. What is amazing about him is how quickly he managed to ingratiate himself with so many of the groups that made up New York society. He went to opening nights on Broadway and to dinners at '21' with Lucius Beebe, the preeminent social observer of his day. He played squash at the Princeton Club. He moved between café society and the highest reaches of the American aristocracy.

One problem with writing about the very rich or the truly swell is that they never want their names used, as the lady in the following story doesn't. She happens to be a member of what is arguably America's grandest family, whose ancestors were the kind of people Edith Wharton wrote novels about. But you'd have to know that about her. She wouldn't bring it up. Too classy. We met at her apartment on Fifth Avenue, where an enormous John Singer Sargent-style portrait of one of those ancestors hangs in the front hall. We had tea and cookies served by a maid. My hostess has about her an old-fashioned elegance that has gone out of style but is still very stylish. I could hardly believe that she had ever been acquainted with Wayne Lonergan.

'Is it true that you knew him?' I asked.

'Darling, I went to bed with him,' she replied forthrightly, and most unexpectedly. 'I knew him in the biblical sense.'

When we stopped laughing, she gave me some details. She had been only fourteen and a student at Brearley, the private school in New York for girls of the highest caliber. On several occasions she invited him out to her family's estate on Long Island, where they had picnics on the beach and took long buggy rides. 'I remember making the fire, and the fireflies, and my brother – whom I called to say I was meeting with you – reminded me that he'd cooked the steaks on a grill. Wayne was easy to be with and so sophisticated. The word for him is "smooth". He took me to the Stork Club, and he was such a good dancer. All those teenage boys I knew were so boring and terrible and only talked about ice hockey at St Paul's. Wayne was playful and fun.'

'How would a person from such a rarefied world as you grew up in ever get to meet a person like Wayne Lonergan?' I asked.

'I met him through Henry Barclay, an older man,' she replied. 'I haven't a clue what happened to Henry. Probably dead. If he's alive, he'd be very old now. After the murder, my father was absolutely disgusted that I knew Wayne Lonergan. He was told that I'd better be taken out of the state during the trial, or I might be called as a witness. I was whisked out of Brearley and sent to Sea Island, Georgia, during the trial.'

'What was Wayne like in bed?' I asked, expecting to be shown the door, but the lady was not affronted.

'Oh, goodness, I hardly remember,' she replied, smiling. 'I think we only did it once. I think he probably liked it better the other way.'

LUCILLE BURTON DIDN'T APPROVE of her daughter's infatuation with Lonergan. She disliked her late ex-husband's boyfriend, and didn't want her daughter to have anything to do with him. She wanted Patsy to have a society debut in New York, so she took her out to Santa Barbara, California, in order to break up the romance and in the hope that there she would meet an eligible young man from her own background. Lonergan followed them, and on July 30, 1941, the lovers eloped to Las Vegas. When the news was printed in the New York *Daily News*, Wayne's last name was misspelled as Larnagan. Patricia, who had a trust of $200,000 and was in line to inherit the $7 million Bernheimer brewing fortune after the death of her grandmother, didn't care that her husband had been her father's boyfriend. On the contrary. In fact, she was widely quoted as saying, 'If he was good enough for my father, he's good enough for me.' During the murder trial, that line was repeated over and over.

The Lonergans rented an apartment at 983 Park Avenue. They had a butler, a cook, and a laundress, and soon they had a baby named Wayne Lonergan Jr. The infant was an incidental part of their life, cared for mostly by a nurse named Elizabeth Black while they nightclubbed until closing time.

In those days society people played cards in the afternoon and after dinner – bridge and gin rummy. Lonergan was good at both, and therefore in demand. Displeased as she was with her daughter's marriage, Lucille Burton nevertheless sometimes pulled her son-in-law in when she needed a fourth for her afternoon bridge games with Somerset Maugham, with whom she had often played bridge when they were Riviera neighbors. The famous

British novelist was now sitting out the war in a suite at
the Ritz Hotel when he wasn't at the Long Island guesthouse or the South Carolina plantation of his publisher
Nelson Doubleday.

THERE ARE STILL a few people around New York who
remember Lonergan from before the murder, when he and
his wife moved about in café society. The socialite producer
Billy Livingston is now a man of a certain age and very
much a gentleman of the old school. For years he was identified in the social and theatrical press as a favorite beau
of Brenda Frazier, probably the most famous of all
American debutantes, a picture of whom in her 1938
coming-out year was on the cover of *Life*. Frazier's every
move was documented in the press, and Billy Livingston
was always at her side, until she ran off and married John
'Shipwreck' Kelly, the great New York Giants halfback.
Billy Livingston knew Wayne and Patsy Lonergan briefly.
He now lives only a block from the brownstone at 313 East
51st Street in Manhattan where Patsy took an elegant
triplex apartment after she moved from 983 Park Avenue.
The neighbors at 983 had complained about the Lonergans'
fights, and Patsy also needed more room for the baby and
his nurse. It was in this apartment, in the section of New
York known as Beekman Hill, that Wayne Lonergan killed
Patsy. Livingston was a paratrooper, serving in New
Guinea, at the time of the murder, but Dorothy Kilgallen,
who covered the trial for the *New York Journal-American*,
kept him informed.

These days Livingston rarely leaves his cozy East Side apartment, with its French chairs, multitudes of plants, and two yapping dachshunds, which kept interrupting his stories the day I visited him. He is a great raconteur of society and theater tales from the '30s, '40s, and '50s, and in me he had a rapt audience. He told how he had to costume Myrna Loy in long dresses to conceal her unfortunate legs when she appeared in his revival of Clare Boothe's *The Women*. He described Brenda Frazier's breakup with Shipwreck Kelly, and he told a hilarious story about a blow job involving Jimmy Donahue, the playboy Woolworth heir, and the Duchess of Windsor. Then we got to the Lonergans.

He had met them playing gin rummy in the penthouse of the late actor Kurt Kasznar and his very rich first wife, Cornelia, in the Westbury Hotel. Livingston recalled Wayne as having great charm, but he remembered Patsy less fondly. He said she nagged and nagged Wayne during the game, ruining it for everyone, and these were people who took cards very seriously. 'She was pathetic. I mean, if Wayne hadn't killed her, I could have,' he said, not meaning it literally, merely as a way of expressing his exasperation at how spoiled she was. 'Wayne was having dalliances during the marriage,' he added.

SOMEONE ELSE WHO remembers Wayne Lonergan is John Galliher, known as Johnny, who is now and has been for decades one of the most popular men in New York society. He also met the Lonergans as a couple during the war, when he was an ensign on a ship dry-docked at the Brooklyn Navy Yard. Even back then, Galliher knew all the right people. A grand English lady named Doris Castlerosse, who was a viscountess, invited him to a dinner party at Le Pavillon, the finest and most expensive restaurant in New York at that time and for many years afterward. It was the Christmas season. The host was a man named John Harjes, a member of an international banking family, whose social lineage was impeccable. There was a family home in Tuxedo Park, an exclusive enclave not far from the city. 'His mother was Mrs Seton Porter,' said a lady I know, as if that should explain everything about his background. 'The scandal was the talk of Tuxedo.'

John Harjes had a great affection for Wayne Lonergan, who had been an usher at his wedding. Harjes's marriage had turned out to be of short duration. Wayne and Patricia were guests at the Pavillon dinner. Galliher had been kept late at the navy yard that night and did not arrive at the restaurant until the party was having dessert. When he bent down to kiss his English lady friend, he accidentally knocked over a glass of red wine onto the tablecloth, whereupon Harjes said petulantly to the viscountess, 'Your friend is not only late, but clumsy.' It was an embarrassing moment for Galliher, who did not know Harjes. Doris Castlerosse rose with a glass of crème de menthe, said, 'Merry Christmas, everybody', and poured the green liqueur over the spilled red wine, thereby turning the awkward moment into a joke. Meanwhile, a young man across the table from Galliher leaned over, squeezed his shoulder, and handed him a glass of cognac, as if to say,

'Don't mind about our host.' The young man was, of course, Wayne Lonergan, in a typical moment. 'He was intent to charm,' said Galliher to me recently. In Harjes's *placement*, Galliher was seated next to Patricia Lonergan. Continuing her habit of sharing intimacies with dinner partners she'd never met, Patricia told Galliher that their host liked her husband very much and gave him very expensive presents. But she didn't seem to mind. In fact, she told Galliher that Harjes always gave her smaller presents at the same time, which she loved.

At the end of the dinner, Galliher remembered, Harjes had called his butler at home and told him to bring Harjes's dogs down to the restaurant so that he could walk them. In time, this same butler, whose name was Emill Peters, would become an important witness in the murder case, when he exposed as a lie Wayne Lonergan's shocking alibi of what he had been doing in Harjes's apartment at the time the crime was committed.

AT THE HEIGHT of the war, when every fit male was proudly going into the service to fight the Germans and the Japanese, it was an embarrassment not to be in uniform. Lonergan was called up twice for the American army but was turned down each time because of his homosexuality, a fact that came out before his trial.

The Lonergan marriage was doomed from the start, but Wayne didn't want it to end. He certainly didn't want to give up someone who was due to inherit $7 million at some time in the future. He knew enough about odds to realize that such an opportunity would not come his way again. Although Patricia said she wanted a divorce, he was not agreeable to the idea. They separated in July 1943.

Patsy had become socially aggressive. She wanted her datebook to be filled with engagements. She liked going out every night and was always happy in nightclubs. She knew how to wangle invitations to parties to which she hadn't been asked. She had what was known in those days as a hollow leg, meaning she was able to drink prodigious amounts of liquor without getting drunk, or so she thought. The tennis pro at her club said she sometimes didn't wear panties under her tennis dress.

Figuring that she would be less likely to divorce him if he was in uniform, Wayne returned to Toronto and joined the Royal Canadian Air Force as a cadet, neither asking nor telling, that time around, about the other part of his life. Patricia agreed to postpone the divorce until after the war, and in the meantime they were both free to go out with other people. However, rich girl that she was, she immediately changed her will, in which Wayne was a beneficiary. In the new will, Wayne was removed and their year-old son was named as her heir.

PATRICIA STARTED GOING OUT with an Italian count named Mario Enzo Gabellini. After the murder, Gabellini, who was an early suspect, described himself to the press as a decorator, although he was not listed in the membership of the Association of Interior Decorators. Twenty years older than Patricia, the count had been divorced twice, and he didn't have any money. Their little romance could be seen as a preview of what her life might have turned out to be as the prey of a string of fortune hunters.

Patricia flirted on the dance floor at El Morocco one night with a handsome Marine officer named Peter Elser, and later danced with him when he cut in on an angry Gabellini. Elser had been a Harvard football star, and was considered a great catch in New York, the kind of man her parents would have approved of wholeheartedly. Patricia made a date with him for dinner on the following Sunday night, which turned out to be the night of the day of her murder.

On Saturday, October 23, the last night of her life, she went out to dinner with Count Gabellini and another couple and then made the rounds of the nightclubs, ending up at the Stork Club, where they stayed until four in the morning, closing time. Gabellini later said they had danced at the Stork 'until the last drop of music'. He told the papers Patricia had been in a very gay mood, and friends of his hinted that the two of them had been engaged, which they had not. Even after the club closed, they were still not ready to call it a night. They went on to someone's apartment for more drinks. Gabellini then dropped Patricia off at her apartment at 6:30 A.M. She went straight to her bedroom, where she took off her mink jacket and string of pearls and black dress and girdle and bra and shoes and stockings and fell naked on top of the covers of her oversize Second Empire-style bed. She didn't check on her son, who was asleep in the next room with his nanny, Elizabeth Black. Black was a wonderful nanny, apparently, but she happened to be hard of hearing, so she was unaware of the violent scene in Patricia's room a few hours later.

WAYNE LONERGAN WAS in New York, in his RCAF uniform, that weekend on a forty-eight-hour pass. Patricia knew he was coming, but she had made no plans to see him. He reportedly knew that she had cut him out of her will. On Saturday he went to FAO Schwarz and bought a toy elephant for his son. He had arranged to spend the night at the apartment of his friend John Harjes. Harjes was away in the country for the weekend, but his butler, Emill Peters, was on duty. Saturday night, while Patricia was doing the town with Count Gabellini, Lonergan attended the Broadway musical hit of the season, *One Touch of Venus* – by Kurt Weill, S. J. Perelman, and Ogden Nash, and starring Mary Martin – in the company of a recently separated stage actress named Jean Murphy Jaburg, who was a friend of Harjes's and lived in the same building. Jean Murphy went backstage to see a girlfriend who was in the production. Later, Lonergan was quoted as saying that the show wasn't as good as the critics had said it was. After the theater, they had supper at the '21' Club, and then they went to the Blue Angel for more drinks. He had three scotch and sodas at '21' and three more at the Blue Angel. It is a matter of record that Lonergan took Mrs Jaburg back to her apartment at 4 a.m. He told the police that he had kissed her good night and made a date to have lunch the next day at the Plaza hotel.

Six hours later he called for Emill Peters to bring him some scrambled eggs – obviously in order to establish that he had spent the night in the Harjes apartment. The butler told the police that he had demanded his breakfast in a loud voice and 'was very nasty'. Lonergan didn't eat the eggs. He wrapped them in a napkin and hid them in a bureau drawer, where they were later found. He took a gray suit from Harjes's closet and left a note:

John: Thank you so much for the use of your flat. Due to a slight case of mistaken trust, I lost my uniform and borrowed a jacket and trousers from you. I will return it on my arrival in Toronto. I'll call you up and tell you about it. Yours, Wayne

Lonergan cut his bloodstained uniform into small pieces with a pair of scissors and stuffed them into his powder-blue RCAF duffel bag, which he weighted down with one of the dumbbells Harjes used for exercising. The butler saw him leave the apartment with the bundle. Lonergan walked to the East River and dumped the duffel bag in it. At some point he bought Max Factor foundation makeup from Max Levinson, a druggist, on First Avenue, presumably to cover scratches on his face. He kept his lunch date at the Plaza with Jean Murphy Jaburg, who brought along her nine-year-old child. She recalled later that Wayne had not been in uniform at lunch. She did not remember seeing scratches on his face and neck. Early that evening, still wearing Harjes's suit, Lonergan took a plane to Toronto, where he went to the apartment of a friend.

*   *   *

PATRICIA LONERGAN LED the kind of life where she sometimes stayed out all night and slept all day, so it did not
seem unusual to the nanny or to Lucille Burton that she
did not emerge from her room all day Sunday. That night
she had a dinner date with Peter Elser, the Marine captain
she had flirted with at El Morocco. Late that day, Lucille
Burton spoke with Elser from Patsy's apartment and asked
him to come over. Elser removed the hinges from the door
of Patricia's bedroom, which was locked. Sprawled on the
bed was her naked body. There were signs of a terrific
struggle in the blood-spattered room, and a trail of blood
marked the path the murderer had taken through the other
door out into the hall. Two bloody candlesticks were found
on the bed. Bits of human flesh were found under
Patricia's long, well-manicured fingernails, apparently
scratched from her attacker's body as she fought for her
life.

Soon the place was swarming with detectives. It was
immediately clear that the murder had all the elements
of a big newspaper story. Rich. Young. Beautiful. Nude.
Patricia's address book had 300 names in it, and her datebook was filled with her social engagements. The police
found Count Gabellini in short order. He had been the
last one to see her alive, when he brought her home from
the clubs at 6:30 A.M. They put him in jail, and he didn't
have bail money. Luckily for him, he had told the taxi
driver to wait when he delivered Patricia to her house.
She had made it clear there was to be no sex that morn-

ing, so he simply dropped her off at the door and then hopped back into the cab. He even treated the cabdriver to a cup of coffee in an all-night diner across from his apartment. The driver promptly came forward to his rescue.

Every paper carried a picture of the count looking grief-stricken, and he played his big moment to the hilt. He said that he knew Wayne Lonergan and that the three of them had gone out to the clubs together a few weeks previously, when Wayne was in New York on a pass. He said, 'Wayne does a better rhumba than I do, and I dance a better tango.'

There may have been a war raging in Europe and the Pacific, but for days the Lonergan case hogged the front pages. Money, looks, and sex had the same mesmerizing effect on the public fifty years ago as they do today. I was a teenager in boarding school at the time, and I remember risking expulsion every afternoon by sneaking into the town of New Milford, Connecticut, during sports period to read the latest accounts in the New York *Daily Mirror* and the *New York Journal-American* at the local drugstore. Lonergan was taken into custody by the Toronto police the day after his wife's body was found. A Detective Captain Mulholland was quoted as saying, 'We picked up Lonergan in the apartment of a friend on Bloor Street. He admitted being in New York Sunday and said he took the 7:30 plane out, arriving back in Toronto at 11:30. He had scratches on his face and neck. It looked as if he had been in some kind of a scrape.'

'Isn't it a fact that both you and your wife have been living abnormal lives and that you had a violent disagreement?'

'We never had a violent disagreement.'

'Do you always take everything in such a cold manner?'

'I suppose so.'

—DETECTIVE SERGEANT HARRIS of the
Toronto police, questioning Lonergan.

Lonergan was held in the Toronto jail for fifty-five hours before being turned over to New York assistant district attorney John Loehr and a couple of detectives for the journey back. He was taken off the train in Fort Erie for failure to have proper papers to cross the border. The group then flew from Buffalo to New York City.

'I had nothing to do with Pat's murder, absolutely nothing,' Lonergan declared on his arrival in New York, smiling and waving to the photographers. 'I want to be at her funeral, and I want to see our baby.'

He didn't get to her funeral. His wife had already been buried by her mother in a private ceremony. Lucille Burton didn't need to wait for a jury to tell her that her son-in-law was her daughter's murderer. He did not get to see his baby either. The child was put in the custody of his grandmother, and in time his name was changed legally from Wayne Lonergan Jr to William Anthony Burton.

*   *   *

LONERGAN LIED INVENTIVELY, apparently without embarrassment. The alibi he gave for his whereabouts at the time of his wife's murder was so audacious that the Toronto police at first believed him. 'A guilty man would never offer an alibi so degrading,' one officer said to the press. In New York, even the most hardened cops were shocked by his salacious story; they passed it on to the reporters of the tabloid papers, who ran with the lurid lies, keeping the story on the front pages. Syd Boehm, a reporter for the *New York Journal-American*, wrote, 'He's lying. The only bit of truth in the whole story is that he admits that he is a degenerate.' Other newspapers described him as 'depraved' and 'sex-twisted', and one said that he gave 'boastful descriptions of his degeneracy'.

Lonergan said that he had picked up an American soldier on the street at four o'clock in the morning and taken him to the Upper East Side apartment of John Harjes. He explained away the scratches on his face and neck by saying that they had been inflicted in a fight when the soldier tried to rob him, even though the clawlike traces could have been made only by long pointed fingernails. He stated that the soldier's name was Maurice Worcester, and that he had awakened to see him stealing his RCAF uniform and $100 in cash. It wasn't smart of Lonergan to be rude to the butler that morning, or to have made up the name Maurice Worcester, for there happened to be such a person. The butler denied that there had been any American soldier spending the night at the Harjes apartment, and an indignant man named Maurice Worcester, recently honorably discharged from the service, appeared from Bridgeport, Connecticut, with proof that he had not been in New York at the time of the murder and that he had never seen or heard of Wayne Lonergan, about whom he went on to speak with contempt to the press.

THE NEW YORK POLICE grilled Lonergan relentlessly for twenty-three hours, with only short breaks and not much food. For a long time he stuck to his lies, but once his alibi was exposed as fraudulent and the police confronted him with fingerprints taken from the bloody candlesticks in the bedroom where his wife's body had been discovered, he broke down and confessed in great detail. He said that he had gone to Patricia's apartment at 8:45 on that Sunday morning. He knocked on her bedroom door, and she let him in. Then she returned to her bed. In a statement leaked to the press – which did not quite match Lonergan's confession as it was read at the trial months later – he reported their conversation in a faux Somerset Maugham manner.

> LONERGAN: *I understand you're the belle of El Morocco.*
> PATRICIA: *Your behavior hasn't been so good either.*
> LONERGAN: *Where's the baby?*
> PATRICIA: *The baby's in bed, and don't disturb him. You'll have to come back later.*
> LONERGAN: *I can't come back later. I have a lunch date with a girl.*

PATRICIA: *Why don't you have lunch with me?*
LONERGAN: *I can't. This is a previous date, and I
        must keep it.*
PATRICIA: *You know, I'm amazed. I can't control my
        men friends anymore.*

As he turned away to get his overseas cap from the dresser, he said, Patricia told him, 'You're not going to see the baby again, ever.'

'I lost my head,' Lonergan said. His baby was his only link to the fortune that was eluding him. He picked up a brass-and-onyx candlestick from the dresser and struck Patricia on the head with it. It broke, and he picked up the other of the pair and struck her again. She managed to get out of bed, fighting and kicking for her life. He grabbed her and choked her as she clawed at his face. He said he figured that it had taken 'several minutes, about three minutes', for her to die. He said he was horrified by the blood from her head all over the place and on his gloves and the front of his uniform. Later, he would say that the confession had been coerced out of him, but it did not sound that way from the transcript.

WAYNE LONERGAN WAS probably the best-looking degenerate ever to go on trial for murder in the history of the New York court system. People couldn't get enough of him. They lined up each day of the trial to catch a glimpse of him when he arrived from his cell in the New York jail known as the Tombs. His calm demeanor was constantly remarked upon in the press. Judge John J. Freschi deplored the 'morbid curiosity' the case was attracting. Dorothy Kilgallen, who would become nationally famous a decade later when she was a panelist on the hugely successful television game show *What's My Line?*, was not only one of the great gossip columnists of her era but also a noted crime and trial reporter, as her father had been before her. She wrote in her column just before the trial began that Lonergan's lawyer, the prominent defense attorney Edward V. Broderick, intended 'to unfold the whole unsavory past of Bill Burton, the slain girl's father', meaning that he was going to spill the beans on how a nice young man from Toronto had been seduced and debauched by a rich dirty old man who happened to be the victim's father. Of Lonergan himself, Kilgallen wrote: 'Roman even profile, big shoulders, long white beautiful hands. He looks like a college boy, probably a football player . . . He looks as little like a murderer as anyone in the court room.'

But no one doubted that those long white beautiful hands had killed Patricia Lonergan. Pleading poverty, at first the former café-society figure was assigned three charity lawyers, but he soon fired two of them when a mysterious male benefactor offered to pay for the services of the third, Edward Broderick. Broderick was like a bulldog defending his client. Loud and obnoxious, he was soon threatened with contempt of court. In his opening statement, he said that he would prove that Lonergan had been 'the victim of double dealing, double crossing, and double talk'. He suggested that Mrs Lonergan's death had been caused by a whiskey bottle in a nightclub fifteen hours earlier. He called her a drunk.

Lonergan listened without flinching as the prosecutor described the bloody crime scene to the jury. When he was handed a picture of his dead wife with her arms upraised 'as if to ward off the blows that were wrenching the breath of life from her body', he stared at it long and hard, but not a flicker of emotion showed on his face. Syd Boehm wrote in the *New York Journal-American* that Lonergan was dressed in a conservatively tailored blue suit, double-breasted with a quiet pinstripe, a blue polka-dot tie, and polished black shoes. Ever since his brief stint at Abercrombie & Fitch, Lonergan had always known the right thing to wear for every occasion. 'He looked like the young man-about-town, accustomed to the stimuli of the nourishing juices of Café Society life,' according to Boehm.

BRODERICK PORTRAYED LONERGAN as the victim rather than the offender in a tragedy of love and frustration, and insisted that Lonergan's confession had been obtained by methods that included 'allowing the defendant to go hungry for a lengthy period, plying him with brandy, and pyramiding a series of petty discomforts'. He fought hard to keep the confession from being read to the jury, but he lost. He tried to put the blame on Count Gabellini, to no avail. He tried to keep the jury from considering first- and second-degree-murder charges, and lost again. Lonergan did not take the stand – it was his right not to – and one alternate juror thought that that had reflected badly on him. When Jean Murphy Jaburg appeared as a witness for the defense, she complained to the press that the publicity associating her with Lonergan had ruined her stage career. She said she had been up for three parts on Broadway, and they all fell through.

The trial lasted ten days. In his closing argument, Broderick described Lonergan as a simple country boy whose confession had been wrung from him after he had been made drunk and was worn out with fatigue. He even picked up a candlestick and struck himself on the head with it to show its ineffectiveness as a murder weapon. He said that four people connected with the trial should be sent to prison, and he named the district attorney, two assistant district attorneys, and the detective who had questioned Lonergan during the confession. It was the closing argument of a defense attorney who realizes he is going to lose his case.

In the prosecution's closing argument, Assistant District Attorney Jacob Grumet called Lonergan a 'brutal cold-blooded killer' who should die in the electric chair for the 'deliberate and premeditated' murder of his wife. He reminded the jury that while Lonergan's wife's battered dead body lay in her apartment, he was having lunch at the Plaza with Jean Murphy Jaburg. He called him a parasite who 'lied and lied and lied . . . He stooped to the lowest depths of degradation in telling his lies.' During the closing arguments, Lonergan sat completely immobile in his chair, arms crossed on his chest in 'yogi-like rigidity', as one reporter wrote. The extent of his muscular control fascinated spectators in the courtroom.

* * *

OVER THE YEARS, the Lonergan case has attracted a cult following, and the lascivious tales that have always been a part of the saga are still repeated in graphic detail. One of the great disappointments in writing about Lonergan today has been the discovery that the most persistent and erotic part of the murder legend turns out not to be true. It was invariably told that Lonergan had maintained that Patsy, while performing a final act of fellatio on him, had almost bitten his penis off, which had caused him to grab the candlestick and strike her. Billy Livingston told me he knew someone who claimed to have seen a photograph of Lonergan's injured member, but he had not seen it himself. There was certainly nothing in the photographs of him after his arrest in Toronto, smiling and waving to the cameras, to suggest that he was in excruciating pain down below. But as defenses go, it could have been a brilliant one. Years later Count Gabellini told Hamilton Darby Perry for his book *A Chair for Wayne Lonergan* that he thought Lonergan was already in the apartment when he delivered Patsy home at 6:30 in the morning. There is no record of Lonergan's movements from the time he dropped off Jean Murphy Jaburg at 4 a.m. until he called John Harjes's butler and ordered scrambled eggs at 10 a.m. Gabellini told Perry that Patsy had shooed him away abruptly, as if she knew someone was inside.

The bitten-penis story had a certain plausibility. Patsy was nude and drunk after twelve hours of drinking at the clubs, and Wayne, in his RCAF uniform, was half-drunk, ready to settle some scores but also ready, as usual, for a little action. We know he didn't fully undress, because

Patsy's blood splattered over his uniform when he struck her with the candlestick. It certainly wasn't the kind of story Lonergan would have been too embarrassed to tell about himself, and Broderick would hardly have been shy about using it. If it had been true, Lonergan could very easily have been found not guilty by the all-male jury, but the fellatio version appeared neither in the confession nor in the court transcript.

On March 31, 1944, after deliberating nine hours and thirty-nine minutes, the jury returned a verdict of guilty of murder in the second degree. 'There is no question that Lonergan murdered his wife,' an alternate juror told reporters. 'But I think it is obvious that he did not premeditate it. I don't think he went to see his wife for the purpose of murdering her. I think he went to have an understanding with her. They got into an argument, and he simply lost his head.'

Lonergan was sentenced to thirty-five years to life in prison, and a crowd of between 400 and 500 people gathered to see him get into the car that took him from the Tombs to Sing Sing. The Stork Club and El Morocco were forever behind him. He told a probation officer, 'I did not murder my wife. I am innocent. The so-called confession was false.' At Sing Sing, he was assigned a cell in the lifers' block. His mother-in-law, Lucille Burton, who announced that she would legally adopt the twenty-two-month-old Lonergan baby, made it known that she considered the verdict too lenient. 'I thought it would be murder in the first degree,' she said to the papers. In other words, she had wanted him to get the chair.

*   *   *

IN PRISON, Lonergan enjoyed the sort of celebrity certain high-profile killers achieve among the other inmates. The glamour attached to the case and the enormous amount of publicity he had received preceded him and lingered on. His charm worked for him in prison just as it had in life. He was spared the hard labor that was the lot of ordinary prisoners and got relatively cushy desk jobs in the purchasing office and the mailroom. There is very little information about him during the years he spent in prison, but by all accounts he was a model prisoner. He was always aware that his thirty-five-year sentence could be reduced to twenty-two years on the grounds of good behavior, and he behaved. Eventually he was transferred from Sing Sing to Clinton Prison in Dannemora, New York. Through it all, he continued to proclaim his innocence to anyone who would listen.

In the exercise yard at Dannemora, he ran into a 300-pound con man known as Big Mizo, whom he had known briefly when they were both in the Tombs in New York during the trial. Big Mizo believed his story, or said he did. They both realized that if the verdict could be appealed and his innocence proved, he would be eligible for one-third of his slain wife's fortune, for they had still been husband and wife at the time of the murder. The fact that Patricia had specifically disinherited him seemed not to be a factor. Big Mizo, who got out of prison before Lonergan did, set about acting as his representative in establishing a claim on Patricia's estate. Calling himself a confidential law clerk, he enlisted the aid of a female lawyer named Frances Kahn, who tried to persuade the courts to throw out Lonergan's confession and conviction, and who demanded Lonergan's one-third share of the estate. But nothing ever happened. Lonergan didn't win an appeal, and he never got any money.

ON DECEMBER 2, 1965, after twenty-two years in prison, Wayne Lonergan was released from Dannemora for good behavior. He was given a prison-issue suit and a fedora and was deported to Canada with the stipulation that he never return to the United States, except with the permission of US authorities in connection with legal appeals. By the time of his release, his son, who was then twenty-three, had long been the possessor of a new name, had graduated from a tony prep school and Harvard University, and had come into the Bernheimer brewery fortune, which had increased in value from $7 million to $15 million since his mother's death.

Lonergan was quite up-to-date on his rich son. He told Ron Lowman of *The Toronto Star* at the time of his release, 'I know where my son is, but I'd rather not say. He's had enough to put up with. No one ever hears of him, or where he's living, and he has a bodyguard to keep it that way.' When Lowman asked Lonergan what his son worked at for a living, the ex-convict grinned and said, 'He doesn't have to.' Living well and not having to work for it was Wayne Lonergan's idea of an ideal life.

After the immigration officers left him at the Canadian

border, he dramatically threw his prison-issue fedora into the Richelieu River and said he wanted to visit a decent tailor. In prison Lonergan had started to lose his looks, but there was enough left of the old sex appeal, charm, and swagger to attract a couple of formidable ladies in Toronto's artistic circles. He soon discovered that his days as an object of sexual desire were not necessarily behind him. People turned to look, and they would until he died, but now they were looking at a celebrity who had been convicted of murdering his heiress wife, just as people in future periods would turn to look at Ann Woodward, after she shot her socialite husband, and at Claus von Bülow and O. J. Simpson, after their highly publicized acquittals.

One of the first things Lonergan did following his return to Toronto was call his son, who was still living in his grandmother's apartment on Park Avenue. Their conversation lasted for some time. According to reports, the son was neither warm nor distant. Lonergan explained that under the terms of his parole he could not go to New York, but he invited his son to visit him in Toronto. The son didn't go. There was a second telephone call, and Lonergan repeated the invitation. Soon after that, Lonergan received a letter from an attorney in New York threatening him with legal action if he ever tried to get in touch with his son again. The young man later left New York and moved out West. There was never any further contact.

*   *   *

I RECENTLY MET Hamilton Darby Perry, the author of *A Chair for Wayne Lonergan*. He had once been a crime reporter for *The Florida Times-Union* in Jacksonville, and claims he had met Lonergan at a few New York cocktail parties before the murder. He saw Lonergan in Canada on only three occasions, after which they did not meet again. 'He always dressed well after prison,' Perry said, 'but he was really strange. He would only meet and talk to me in a place where there were other people. He always wanted to have someone there when we talked. He loved hanging around crime reporters, and he loved being a celebrity, but he was a spooky guy. He would talk a lot, and then he would back off. When he was talking to me, I could never tell if he was telling me the straight story or leading me down a path.'

Although the 1972 book is overtly favorable to Lonergan, it was my impression that Perry had subsequently come to feel that it was pretty obvious that Lonergan was guilty. The book is Lonergan's version of the events, dealing mostly with how his richly detailed confession was coerced out of him by the police and with his trial. Some of his revisionist history is risible. For example, Lonergan claimed that when he made the extraordinary admission to the police that on the night of the murder he had picked up a soldier on the street about four o'clock in the morning and taken him to the Harjes apartment for sex, he was actually doing the gentlemanly thing and protecting the name of a prominent society woman, who was the person he had in fact taken back to the apartment. Now that I think of it, the winning story

I told earlier about Lonergan's taking the teenage Patricia Burton to the Stork Club on the night they met was also told to Perry by Lonergan. We mustn't forget that he was a world-class liar.

AS EX-CONS' LIVES after years in prison go, Lonergan's went remarkably well, even without the fortune he had hoped to receive from his murdered wife's estate. From his early days at the world's fair on, he was the kind of guy people provided for. Back in Toronto, he forsook his bisexual practices and concentrated on the ladies. In his first week out of prison he met a woman executive, and he soon moved in with her. 'He needed a nest, and she provided it,' says a friend of theirs. Although the woman loved him, she could be verbally abusive to him when she was drunk. Lonergan always maintained that he had not killed his wife, on the rare occasions when the subject came up. After one such denial, the same friend remembers, the woman responded, '"I know you did it, you fucking murderer, you son of a bitch." And he just took it.' Nevertheless, the lady was 'hurt, angry, furious, enraged', in the words of the friend, when a well-loved character actress named Barbara Hamilton, often called the funniest woman in Canada, took Lonergan away from her and moved him up to a better nest in a ritzy part of Toronto.

Hamilton came from a distinguished Canadian family prominent in Toronto society. She had been educated fashionably in private schools and caused her father some distress when she took up a life on the stage. She was a

large, heavy, jovial woman with a double chin, who was
fondly remembered by all who knew her as both a gifted
comedienne and the life of the party. Donald Harron, a
Canadian writer and performer who adapted the novel and
wrote the lyrics for the musical *Anne of Green Gables*,
which has been playing on and off in Canada for thirty-
six years, says Hamilton was the original and best of all
the Marillas in the show. An all-around good egg, Hamilton
left some of her gowns to Harron for his Dame Edna-type
drag act.

Hamilton loved Lonergan madly for the fourteen years
of their romance, although she too, on occasion, could
abuse him in public, especially when she was drunk. He
took it. He always took it from the people who kept him.
Hamilton would even introduce him to friends as 'the lady-
killer', and sometimes she called him Lil, short for Live-
In Lover.

According to Jocko Thomas, a retired and celebrated
crime reporter for *The Toronto Star*, Lonergan traveled
in the best circles in the city with Hamilton, and they
were very much a couple. 'He was very attentive and
charming to her publicly,' says the actor Tom Kneebone.
'They were out socially a great deal – parties, openings,
that sort of thing. I was disarmed by him. He was a well-
mannered, gracious gentleman, the epitome of charm and
elegance, and he was enormously literate. He was up on
everything. He read voraciously. And I never saw a second
of his bisexuality.'

*   *   *

ANOTHER FRIEND WHO KNEW Lonergan with both women had mixed feelings about him. 'He was debonair, bright, smart, and fun to be with,' she says. 'They used to say about him that he had read the encyclopedia all the way through several times. He would talk about the Stork Club as if it had happened yesterday, and he would talk about what happened two weeks ago, but he never referred to anything that happened in prison. When he came back to Canada, he was a star. He had a tall, commanding presence. People showed him off a bit, and he put out at dinner parties. He knew he was the entertainment. He sang for his supper. But my cat hated him. He once hurt my cat when he was on his lap. Another time, swimming in the lake at my farm, he grabbed the tail of my blind Labrador to pull him. I was furious. When he grabbed your shoulder or arm, it was always a little too hard.'

'The term "big blonde" really applied to Barbara,' says Brian Linehan, the David Frost of Canadian television, who knew her and Lonergan. Linehan remembers her at parties, the center of attention, roaring with laughter, with a cigarette in one hand and a drink in the other. In their social life, Hamilton was the dominant one. 'They were a great pair. Wayne was unusually tall, very much a physical presence. I couldn't associate his past with the man I met,' says Linehan. 'He always deferred to her. He seemed so quietly reserved.'

Barbara Hamilton made it a condition of any interview she gave that Wayne Lonergan's name would not be brought up. She was very protective of him. When he got cancer, she took care of him, and when he died in 1986, she was devastated. Nevertheless, she took a business call from her agent about a new part immediately after covering Lonergan with a sheet, and she didn't say that he had just died.

'Oh, he was handsome as a prince,' she was quoted as saying after his death. 'He was the most kind, gentle, and wonderful person I have ever known.'

Somewhere, Wayne Lonergan's son may be reading this article. He was a year and a half old when his father killed his mother in 1943, so he would be fifty-eight today. I didn't try to track him down. Children of a parent who kills their other parent lead dreadful lives. Every day someone points at them and says, 'Their mother killed their father', which the sons of Ann Woodward had to endure, or 'Their father killed their mother', which the children of O. J. Simpson have had and will have to bear. Ultimately the tragic Woodward sons committed suicide – both by defenestration – and the Simpson children, in sharing their father's pariah existence, have lost out on their childhood. Wayne Lonergan's son escaped that fate. His grandmother did a first-rate job of keeping him out of the public eye. If his name had not appeared in his father's obituary in *The New York Times* on January 3, 1986, he would have remained totally forgotten. I think he made a very wise decision when he declined to meet his father after he was released from prison. A life without memories is not such a bad thing, when the alternative could have been a litany of denials of guilt and requests for money.

DEATH IN MONACO

ON DECEMBER 3, 1999, in Monte Carlo, Monaco, the multibillionaire banker Edmond J. Safra, along with one of his nurses, died of asphyxiation in a locked, bunker-like bathroom in a conflagration that engulfed his magnificent duplex penthouse, atop a building housing the Republic National Bank of New York, which he had made final arrangements to sell a few days previously. Early accounts said that two hooded intruders had penetrated the apartment, which was as solid as a fortress, and stabbed a male nurse. The bizarre death made headlines everywhere and sent shock waves through the banking community, as well as through the principality of Monaco, probably the safest, most tightly controlled tax haven in the world for the very rich. There is one policeman for every 100 of its 30,000 inhabitants. You can barely take a step in Monte Carlo without being monitored by closed-circuit cameras, which are on the streets, in underpasses, in the halls of hotels, and in the casino. Three days after Safra's death, Daniel Serdet, the attorney general and chief prosecutor of Monaco, announced that a male nurse named Ted Maher, from Stormville, New York, had confessed to setting the blaze that killed his employer in order to win favor with the banker. Serdet said that Maher had started a fire in a wastebasket in an effort to draw attention to himself. 'He wanted to be a hero,' Serdet said. There were no hooded intruders, and the stab wounds in Maher's abdomen and thigh were self-inflicted. Serdet released a statement to the press about Maher, saying that at the time of the fire he was highly agitated, 'psychologically fragile and under the influence of medication'. Serdet concluded, 'From this moment on we can exclude with certainty all [conjectures] of any international conspiracy.' Marc Bonnant, the lawyer for Safra's widow, announced in *Time* magazine, 'The fact that Maher is unstable became apparent to us only after the accident.' The damnation of Ted Maher, the low man on the nursing staff's totem pole, had begun. In no time the case had been all tied up with a neat bow: the guilty party was in custody, and the principality of Monaco was safe again.

From the beginning, very few people believed that the story was as simple as that. It seemed too pat, too quickly resolved. 'Monaco wants it all hushed up,' observers said. 'The Russian Mafia,' some suggested. Others whispered, 'Palestinian terrorists.' Although the Safra name is little known to the public at large, it is very prominent in the worlds of international banking, philanthropy, and society. Several financiers have described Safra to me as the most brilliant banker of his time. At any moment during the catastrophe he might have saved himself, but he was reportedly so fearful of being murdered by the intruders he had been told were in his house that he refused to come out of the locked bathroom, in spite of the pleas of firemen and police. He put wet towels along the bottom of the bathroom door, but to no avail. When rescuers finally got into the bathroom two hours later, they found the billionaire dead, his body blackened with soot, his skin incinerated. His eyes had popped out of his head. Nearby was a cell phone, on which several calls had been made. Dead along with Safra was one of his eight nurses, Vivian Torrente, an American of Philippine origin. She also had a cell phone, which Ted Maher had given her to call for help. So far it has not been reported that Torrente's neck was allegedly crushed.

One thing is certain: Edmond Safra, whose specialty was private banking for wealthy clients and who was said to know 'all the secrets of the financial planet', had his enemies. Although he pursued an image of great respectability among the very wealthy and powerful, a taint of scandal and suspicion dogged him. He was accused of having laundered money for Panamanian dictator Manuel Noriega, as well as for the Colombian drug cartels. And both his bank and his private jet were alleged to have been pressed into service to move money and personnel during the Iran-contra scandal. The rumors of Safra's involvement were found to have been part of a smear campaign by American Express, and Safra ultimately won a public apology and an $8 million settlement, which he donated to charity. Nevertheless, his closest friend in New York has been quoted as saying, 'Edmond was no choirboy.'

ANOTHER CERTAINTY IS that Safra was obsessed with security. It was widely reported that he felt menaced, and considered himself a hunted man. Even before collaborating with the FBI in 1998 and 1999 to expose the Russian Mafia's international money-laundering operation, he was apprehensive for his safety. He spent millions each year on security for himself and his wife, her children, and her grandchildren. At each of his many residences he lived virtually surrounded by a private army. The penthouse over his bank had been rebuilt to accommodate the latest surveillance cameras and security devices. He had eleven bodyguards with machine guns, many of them veterans of the Mossad in Israel, who worked in shifts and were always with him, often to the consternation of friends who disliked being surrounded by armed men every time they arrived for a visit. One of the great mysteries of the case is that not one of the guards was on duty the night Safra died. They had been dispatched to La Leopolda, the Safra estate at Villefranche-sur-Mer, twenty minutes from Monte Carlo, one of the great showplaces on the Riviera. The unanswered, or inadequately answered, question is: *Why* weren't any guards in the penthouse at the time of Safra's death, doing what they were trained to do, protecting the life of one of the world's wealthiest men?

Conflicting stories of Safra's last days circulated in the European press. The Italian newspaper *La Stampa* reported that he had been seen at Cap d'Antibes with Boris Berezovsky, the Russian oligarch implicated in the 1999 Aeroflot scandal, in which tens of millions of dollars were alleged to have been diverted from the state-controlled airline. *La Stampa* reported that Safra was also seen at the restaurant of the Hotel Martinez in Cannes in the company of two other Russians, with whom he had quarreled before leaving angrily. People close to Safra dismiss such stories out of hand, saying that he was too ill and too medicated to have been at either place. The sixty-seven-year-old Safra suffered from an advanced case of Parkinson's disease – he had donated $50 million to create a new foundation for medical research on it. In the last year of his life, several of his visitors remarked to me, he was often paranoid and delirious, which they attributed to his heavy medication. In addition to eight nurses, including Ted Maher, four doctors were on call around the clock. By the time of the fire, Maher had been in Safra's employ for just under four months. The French magazine *Le Nouvel Observateur* quoted an anonymous Monegasque attorney as saying, 'Safra denounced the Russian Mafia, and some of his clients who were concerned by that could have become afraid and used Maher . . . It wouldn't be the first time a poor soul was used in the service of a grand criminal scheme.'

IN STORMVILLE, NEW YORK, which is a two-hour drive from my house in northeastern Connecticut, I meet up with Ted Maher's wife, Heidi, who is thirty and also a nurse, currently working overtime to support their three children. Without Ted's income, she has had to give up their house and move in with her mother and father. 'The kids miss that house,' Ted's sister, Tammy, tells me when she drives me by the place, which is comfortable-looking and sits in a sylvan glade. Heidi's parents' house is small and a little crowded, what with four extra people living in it, and with Ted's sister and Heidi's brother stopping by all the time to find out the latest about Ted, whom they all love. Heidi's mother, Joan Wustrau, looks after the kids when Heidi is working. The strain Heidi is under shows on her face as she pulls pictures and letters out of a large box to show me.

'Ted wasn't supposed to be on duty that night,' she says. 'Someone changed the schedule at the last minute, and they put Ted on.' She tells me that Ted was about to resign from his job with Safra so that he could return to his family in Stormville and his job at Columbia Presbyterian Medical Center. She says she heard the news from Tammy (who had heard it on television) that Edmond Safra and a nurse had died in a fire in Monte Carlo. Heidi at first assumed that the dead nurse was Ted.

Spotless & Brite, Inc., an employment service which tended to the affairs of the nurses and guards in the Safra employ, located in the Republic Bank Building at 452 Fifth Avenue in New York, provided Heidi and her brother with round-trip tickets to Nice and a car and driver to Monte Carlo. Heidi says a woman at Spotless & Brite described Ted as a hero and told her he had been stabbed trying to save Mr Safra. Heidi thought she was going to see her husband in Princess Grace Hospital, where his wounds were being treated, but by the time she arrived in Monaco, Ted had been arrested, and she was taken to the police station instead. The return part of her plane ticket was canceled. She shows me records from Princess Grace Hospital proving that, contrary to Daniel Serdet's assertions, Ted had no alcohol or drugs in his system. She was not allowed to see her husband.

The story that Heidi Maher tells about Ted's 'confession' is quite different from the one coming out of Monaco. She tells me her passport was taken from her by three policemen and shown to Ted. She says the confession was forced out of him in the hospital, and that during his first two days there, Ted was told that Edmond Safra was still alive. She says Ted lit the fire in a wastebasket to set off the fire alarm. Then she shows me a letter that Sue Kelly, a member of the US House of Representatives from New York, wrote to His Serene Highness Prince Rainier III:

> *. . . We believe that the international human rights and civil liberties of this American citizen and his family have clearly been violated. After being bound hand and foot, catheterized, isolated, interrogated, and kept awake for three days, Ted Maher was forced to sign a confession written in French with no English translation. His wife, Heidi, was also interrogated for several days and kept under police surveillance . . . She was grabbed off the street, thrown into a car by three unknown people*

wearing black, and taken to her hotel where her
room and luggage were ransacked and her passport
was taken. Ted was then shown his wife's passport
and threatened that she would not be able to return
to their three children unless he signed the docu-
ment confessing to the crime.

'The confession's in French and Ted doesn't speak
French?' I ask Heidi.

'He doesn't speak French,' Heidi replies.

'What about the videotapes in the surveillance
cameras?' I say. 'They don't show any intruders.'

'The tapes have vanished,' she says. 'The judge was
given a blank tape and an old tape showing guests arriving at a party.'

Subsequently, one of the original tapes has been discovered, but the authorities will not reveal what is on it.

THE SAGA OF Ted Maher, the forty-two-year-old male nurse
who now sits in the Monaco prison on a charge of 'voluntary fire setting leading to the death of two people', is an
interesting and serendipitous one. For ten years he was a
highly regarded neonatology nurse at Babies & Children's
Hospital, part of New York's Columbia Presbyterian
Medical Center. Then, in a life-changing moment, he
found an expensive camera that had been left behind by
a patient who had been discharged. A source I talked to
in Monaco who is familiar with the case said rather dramatically, 'He was unable to read the sign of his own destiny.'

Instead of turning the camera in to his superior or to the lost-and-found department, he removed the film and had it developed. He recognized the patient, a woman who had recently had twins. Her husband had taken the pictures of her and the babies. Through the hospital's records, Maher was able to get the address of the couple, and he returned the camera and photos to them.

Their names were Harry and Laura Slatkin, and they were charmed and touched by Maher's good deed. Their great friend Adriana Elia, who is the daughter of Lily Safra, Edmond's widow, by her first husband, Mario Cohen, was also impressed by Maher. Harry Slatkin is the brother of Howard Slatkin, a New York decorator of palace-like interiors, who happens to be the favorite decorator of Lily Safra. On the side, Howard Slatkin has a successful scented-candle business, which Laura Slatkin runs. Howard Slatkin names his scented candles after various society ladies, such as Deeda Blair and C. Z. Guest.

It occurred to Adriana Elia that Ted Maher would make a perfect nurse for her stepfather. Maher was interviewed by a member of Safra's staff, who offered him a salary of $600 a day, more money than he had ever earned. The nurses' union at Columbia Presbyterian was about to go out on strike, which would have left Maher without an income. Moreover, he had incurred $60,000 in legal bills obtaining custody of a son by his first marriage. So he went on unpaid leave from the hospital and took the job Safra was offering. He had misgivings about moving to Monte Carlo, since he had a wife and three children, whom he hated to leave. Heidi Maher was briefly considered for a job on Safra's nursing staff as well, but once it was discovered that the couple had three children, Heidi's job offer was rescinded. In the end Ted went alone.

In the nearly four months he worked for Safra, Maher reportedly developed a hearty dislike for the chief nurse on Safra's staff, Sonia Casiano. After having been a well-respected employee at Columbia Presbyterian, he was suddenly the most junior member of the team. He found himself having to take orders from people whose credentials were less impressive than his. And there was definitely a growing strain between Maher and Casiano. However, Safra was fond of Maher, and Maher was fond of Safra. Maher had scored extra points with both Edmond and his wife, Lily, by fixing an air conditioner, and the fact that Maher had been a Green Beret also impressed Edmond. A lot of people in the banking world were suspicious of Safra, but he had warm and affectionate relations with those who attended to him – assistants, servants, nurses, guards. These staff members had less affection for Safra's wife, who disliked having so many nurses and guards underfoot all the time. The fire Maher allegedly started in the wastebasket was lit with one of Howard Slatkin's scented candles. Heidi Maher told me there were always scented candles around Safra, because he was sometimes incontinent and had chronic diarrhea. Two nurses had to help him from his bed to the bathroom, which had been designed like a bunker so that the family could escape there in case of an attack. In the long run, its perfection as a refuge is what killed him.

As prisons go, the one in Monaco is pretty deluxe, from

what I hear. I was not allowed to visit Ted Maher when I was there in July, but I was told he has a nice view. He can watch the boat traffic on the Mediterranean, and on clear nights the reflection of the moon ripples on the water. Below him are well-tended gardens. There are forty-one cells, and in July there were twenty-two prisoners. Most of them were in for drug crimes.

THE JET-SET GOSSIP started the day after the funeral. *Le Monde* reported that two Arab guests at the Hôtel Hermitage, which abuts Safra's penthouse, had been questioned 'because of their criminal histories', but had been released and were no longer under suspicion. The deep hatred that had long existed between Lily Safra and the brothers of her late husband, Joseph and Moise Safra, who live in Brazil, came to the surface for all to see. The once very close Safra brothers – Syrian Jews born in Lebanon, where their father, Jacob, had established a bank – were not close at the time Edmond died, and Joseph and Moise blamed Lily for that. According to sources close to the family, the brothers claimed that Lily kept Edmond isolated from them as his condition worsened, and that their telephone calls were not relayed to Edmond by secretaries. By the time Joseph and Moise arrived in Monte Carlo from Brazil, the casket had been sealed and they were not able to see their brother's body.

Lily Safra further outraged the siblings by changing the burial site from Mount Herzl, in Israel, where a space had been reserved, to the Veyrier Jewish cemetery just outside Geneva, Switzerland, where Edmond and Lily had another home. So bitter was the feeling between the widow and her brothers-in-law that she did not want them to be present at the Hekhall Haness synagogue for the religious service. The synagogue was placed under strict police surveillance, and armed officers prevented journalists and photographers from getting near the funeral. The guest list and seating for the service were prepared by Lily. Seven hundred attended – or a thousand, depending on which paper you read – including such celebrated names as Nobel Prize winner Elie Wiesel, who gave one of the eulogies, Prince Sadruddin Aga Khan, former UN secretary-general Javier Pérez de Cuéllar, and Hubert de Givenchy, the French couturier, who had been Lily Safra's favorite designer until his retirement. No member of Monaco's ruling family attended, a fact that was remarked on by many people, since Safra was considered the most important person in Monte Carlo after Prince Rainier.

I KNOW SEVERAL PEOPLE who attended the service, and heard their stories afterward. The Safra brothers could not be turned away at the synagogue, and security guards carried chairs to the front for them, seating them prominently for all to see. 'It was like a wall of ice,' one person said to me, describing the feeling in the air. The main eulogy was given by Sir John Bond, the group chairman of HSBC Holdings, the bank that had bought Safra's Republic New York Corporation, who had met Safra only a limited number of times, in connection with the sale.

At the end of the service Joseph and Moise elbowed their way in among the pallbearers and helped carry the coffin to the hearse. They made no attempt to attend the reception held later by Lily. Not everyone asked to the funeral was asked to the house afterward.

Several weeks later, a memorial service for Safra was held in New York at the Spanish and Portuguese Synagogue, on Central Park West at 70th Street. Again it was by invitation only, and again not everyone was asked back to the Safra apartment on Fifth Avenue, a fact that miffed several grand ladies of the city. Among the speakers at the service were Paul Volcker, former chairman of the Federal Reserve; James Wolfensohn, head of the World Bank; Neil Rudenstine, president of Harvard University; and Shimon Peres, former prime minister of Israel. Lily read a letter written to Edmond by her granddaughter, which was very moving. By sheer happenstance, I attended a dinner that night at Swifty's restaurant on the Upper East Side, and five of the twelve guests arrived there after having attended the memorial service. For two hours they talked of nothing else: 'Lily said she gave the key to her chief of security at La Leopolda, but the Monaco police put him in handcuffs.' 'Lily said she had Edmond's body placed on her bed afterward, and his face was black with soot.' 'Lily said that the male nurse gambled.' 'Lily said there were two fires.'

That was the first time I heard that there had been two fires, though since then I have heard it often. And therein, at least in my opinion, lies the second big question in this mystery: Who might have lit a second fire? A lady I know in Paris, who used to be a great friend of Lily Safra's, told me at the Café Flore that an incendiary object had been thrown into the penthouse. Even if that was only her surmise, it might explain the raging inferno that erupted.

LILY SAFRA, a Brazilian of Russian Jewish heritage, is by far the most colorful figure in this story. Now in her mid-sixties, she has had a fascinating and eventful life, rife with both splendor and tragedy. She is these days one of the richest women in the world. She came into $3 billion after Edmond's death, and she had possessed a fortune before their marriage, courtesy of her second husband. She has suffered greatly in her personal life. Before the most recent tragedy, she had lost both her son Claudio and her three-year-old grandson in an automobile accident.

I had never met either of the Safras, but I had seen them on certain grand occasions in New York at the Metropolitan Museum and the Metropolitan Opera. Their wealth floated like an aura around them. Edmond Safra was a dignified, bald man of stocky build and medium height, more at ease in conferences about financial matters with world leaders than at society functions, where his glamorous wife was the attention grabber. With her slightly foreign manner, her marvelous clothes from the couture in Paris, and her spectacular jewels, Lily Safra has the presence and personality of a diva. One account I read of her youth said that her father was a British railroad worker named Watkins, who immigrated to Brazil, where Lily was born. Her first husband, Mario Cohen, was an Argentinian multimillionaire manufacturer of nylon stockings, whom she married when she was nineteen, and with whom she had three children – a daughter, Adriana, and two sons, Edouardo and Claudio. During the marriage they lived part of the time in Uruguay. After their divorce she married a Brazilian, Alfredo 'Freddy' Greenberg – he later changed the name to Monteverde – who had fallen madly in love with her. Monteverde was the very rich owner of a chain of electronics stores. There is an adopted son from that marriage, named Carlos Monteverde, who seems not to participate in family matters. After Monteverde's surprising suicide, Lily inherited a fortune estimated at $230 million, which she put into the hands of Edmond Safra, head of Banco Safra in Brazil but already destined for bigger things on an international scale.

SAFRA, THEN IN HIS EARLY FORTIES, had never married. His brothers often urged him to take a wife and have children so that the family could carry out its dream of having a bank that would last a thousand years. Safra always said he was worried that a woman would marry him only for his money. Lily Monteverde, however, had a fortune of her own, which set her apart. A family friend told me, 'Joseph begged Edmond not to marry Lily.' Lily Monteverde was definitely not the woman Joseph and Moise had in mind for their beloved brother. The suicide of her second husband had been investigated twice by police, although nothing untoward was discovered. It also bothered the brothers that Lily was past the age of childbearing and would bring with her children of her own. They succeeded in talking Edmond out of the marriage, and that was the beginning of the enmity between Lily and Edmond's brothers.

Edmond Safra returned to New York, where he had an apartment over his New York bank. Jeffrey Keil, who worked for him for twenty-six years, told me Edmond was brokenhearted to have lost Lily. He said Safra almost never left the building where he lived and worked. Then, in another dramatic episode unknown to most of her friends, Lily married her third husband in Acapulco in January 1972 and separated from him two months later. He was a thirty-five-year-old Moroccan-born English businessman named Samuel H. Bendahan. The marriage surfaced when she applied for Monegasque citizenship; all past marriages had to be listed. If, as some think, Lily hoped the marriage would make Edmond realize what he had lost, it had the desired effect. He was soon begging her to marry him, and a year later she divorced Bendahan. Bendahan brought a suit against her and Safra, claiming that she had reneged on an agreement to pay him $250,000, but the suit was thrown out of court. The newspapers referred to her as the heiress to a chain of discount stores. Lily in turn charged Bendahan with extortion, but that case was dismissed as well.

The marriage of Edmond and Lily Safra took place in 1976. A Brazilian friend who knew both parties described the union to me as 'the irresistible combination of a lady with a past and a man with a future'. A 600-page prenuptial agreement was reportedly drawn up – one colleague jokingly called it a merger – but the marriage turned out to be a successful one. It is an interesting fact that Edmond and Lily Safra's Monegasque citizenship papers came through the day before he was killed. The sale of his Republic New York Corporation and Safra Republic Holdings had been approved by shareholders just days before that. Edmond had been so eager for the approval of the sale to go through that at the last minute he lowered the price by $450 million, a totally uncharacteristic thing for him to do, according to the European press. The *New York Post* reported in its financial pages: 'The merger – originally worth $10.3 billion, now valued at $9.9 billion – had been delayed by allegations that a major client of Republic's securities division committed a $1 billion fraud.' It broke Safra's heart to sell his bank. He had wanted it to last for a millennium, but he was ill, and his brother Joseph, who had his own bank in Brazil, had declined to take it over. Safra's great disappointment was that he had never had children of his own to whom he could hand over the reins.

THERE ARE PROBABLY NOT 200 people in the world today who live at such a level of grandeur as the Safras did over the last twenty years. They had a vast apartment in one of the finest buildings on Fifth Avenue in New York, as well as a spare apartment in the Pierre Hotel, staffed and exquisitely decorated, for visiting friends to use. There were also homes in London, Paris, and Geneva, as well as the duplex penthouse over the bank in Monte Carlo and

– the jewel in the crown – La Leopolda, one of the two most fabled houses on the French Riviera. I wrote about the other, La Fiorentina – which was built by the frequently widowed Lady Kenmare, whom Noël Coward nicknamed Lady Killmore – in *Vanity Fair* in March 1991. La Leopolda was planned at the turn of the century by the King of Belgium for his mistress, and was built by architect Ogden Codman Jr, who was for a time the best friend and collaborator of Edith Wharton. More recently, La Leopolda was owned by the legendary jet-set figure and auto tycoon Gianni Agnelli, who, for a time, shared the villa with Pamela Digby Churchill Hayward Harriman during their sexy romance. The Safras added a landing pad for their helicopter and quarters for their Mossad guards. They reportedly also constructed an enormous underground habitable bunker that could serve as a bomb shelter. Everyone who has dined and danced at the villa raves about its beauty.

The Safras' first foray into the big league of international society was their famous ball at La Leopolda in 1988, which was attended by such members of the crème de la crème as Prince Rainier and Princess Caroline of Monaco, Princess Firyal of Jordan, Christina Onassis, and a lot of Rothschilds. People I have spoken to who were at the ball get misty-eyed at the memory of its perfection. There was one gaffe, however. The name of Lily's great friend Jerome Zipkin, the late famous walker of such important ladies as Nancy Reagan and Betsy Bloomingdale, who had helped put Lily across in New York, was inadvertently left off the guest list, and he made such a scene with the

guards at the gates of La Leopolda that Rolls-Royces and
limousines were backed up for miles on the Moyenne
Corniche.

THE NOTORIOUSLY SNOBBISH SOCIAL CRITIC John Fairchild,
for years the publisher of *W* and *Women's Wear Daily*,
wrote about what he called 'the Safras' meteoric rise to
social power. They have taken the Riviera, Southampton,
New York, the Metropolitan Opera, Geneva – all in a space
of five years. What's next?'

Lily Safra knows about eighteenth-century French
furniture the way Candy Spelling knows about diamonds.
So abundant is her collection of the finest of this furniture that a warehouse is necessary to hold the overflow
from her many residences. Edmond Safra was once quoted
as saying, 'If instead of furniture I had bought paintings
of the same quality, I would have made a more consider-
able fortune.' It has been sworn to me by a reliable source
that Howard Slatkin's re-decoration of Lily's bedroom at
La Leopolda – not including the eighteenth-century
French furniture, which she already possessed – cost $2
million.

Lily Safra is famous for the extravagant gifts she gives.
One year she sent Manolo Blahnik shoes to all her friends,
after having a secretary call to get their sizes. Eleanor
Lambert, the nonagenarian doyenne of American fashion,
told me, 'Lily sent me a shahtoosh before anyone ever had
one.' Doctors who arrived from New York to treat Edmond
in Monte Carlo or at La Leopolda always flew home with

large gift packages. When her friend Zipkin stayed with
her at the Safras' Grosvenor Square apartment in London,
a green Rolls-Royce and chauffeur were at his beck and
call full-time. He visited so often that the guest towels in
his bathroom were monogrammed with his initials, JRZ.
Lily Safra's extravagance earned her the nickname the
Gilded Lily, a phrase that has been picked up by the
European press.

ON JULY 5, a little more than a week before I was to leave
for Monte Carlo, I was at my house in Connecticut writing an article about the Skakel–Moxley case when the telephone rang. 'Mr Dunne?' Yes. 'This is Lily Safra.'

You can imagine my surprise. I had never dreamed
that she would talk to me. She said she was calling from
London and was on her way to Paris. She said we had a
mutual friend in Nancy – no last name, but I knew she
meant Nancy Reagan. She speaks with an accent, probably Brazilian, since she spent much of her life in Brazil,
up through her first two marriages. Her voice was deep
and friendly, with a slight sound of widowhood in it.
Then she got to the point of the call. She said she had
heard I was writing about her husband. I said that was
true. I told her I was sorry for the tragedy that had
befallen her. She thanked me. Then she said some very
nice things about my books and articles. I knew I was
being charmed, but, quite honestly, she charmed charm-
ingly. She said, 'I have never given an interview, in all the
years, but I would talk with you.' I was absolutely dumb-

founded. She asked where I would be staying. The Hôtel
Hermitage, I said. I had picked it because it is adjacent
to the building where Edmond Safra died. Debris from
the conflagration fell on the terrace of the Hermitage.
She asked for the date of my arrival and gave me her telephone number at La Leopolda. She said I should call her
and we would meet. I was thrilled. I wanted to hear about
the fire from her point of view – what it was like for her
that morning, how she heard, whom she called, how she
escaped.

Then she must have called her lawyer, Marc Bonnant,
and told him she had spoken with me. I can only imagine that he must have flipped out, because he was not in
a good mood when he phoned me from his office in Geneva
the next day. By coincidence, I had met him a few weeks
earlier at the Carlyle Hotel in New York in connection
with another case, involving the very complicated circumstances surrounding the suicide of the daughter of the
Baron and Baroness Lambert of Geneva. This time he
announced himself as the lawyer for Lily Safra, and his
heavily accented voice conveyed deep annoyance. He
happens to be one of Europe's finest lawyers. He represented Edmond Safra in several libel suits connected to
the smear campaign initiated by American Express against
the billionaire. 'What is this about an interview? It's
impossible. She can't do an interview. What did you want
to talk to her about?' I said I wanted to talk about the
fire. 'But that's *exactly* what she *can't* talk about, with
the upcoming trial,' he said, his voice growing sharper. I
reminded him that I had not called Mrs Safra and

requested an interview, that she had called me and offered one. Then he told me that I should send him a list of my questions, that he would decide which of them I could ask, and that he would be present at the interview.

I LET SIX DAYS PASS and then sent him a fax stating that his terms were unacceptable. I said that Edmond Safra's death was a major story, and that he was not going to be able to control the press. I said that Mrs Safra had talked openly to many of her friends about the fire, and that her remarks had been repeated with great regularity at dinner parties. I gave him some examples of things she had said to mutual friends about the death of her husband, without revealing who had told them to me. I said I was aware of the hatred that existed between Mrs Safra and Edmond's two brothers. I suggested that Mrs Safra and I meet at La Leopolda for tea, just to meet, and said that I would not ask her about the fire. I ended my letter, 'Quite honestly, I wish I weren't staying in Monaco. People tell me that my phone will be tapped and that I will be followed, all of which is quite nervous making, but good copy once I get home.'

BONNANT DID NOT REPLY to my fax, but the next day I received a second call from Lily Safra. She said she was very sorry about the call from her lawyer and said that, yes, of course we could meet, but she would prefer doing it in Paris rather than at La Leopolda. She set a time for

two days earlier than we had originally planned to meet.
I was to call her on my arrival in Paris.

The night before I left for Monte Carlo, I had a telephone call from David Patrick Columbia, a New York society columnist with great connections in the social world.
He had just had a call from a prominent resident of the
principality who had heard I was coming to cover the Safra
story. 'Tell Dominick there were two bullets in Edmond's
body,' the Monegasque citizen had said.

After arriving in Monte Carlo, I checked in at the
Hermitage. The first thing I did was walk out on the terrace
and look up at where the fire had been. Reconstruction
work was in progress. Workmen on ladders were installing
a bright new mansard roof. After making myself known
in the hotel, I asked one of the concierges if he had been
on duty at the time of the fire. He had. He told me fire
hoses had been dragged through the lobby of the hotel
and out to the terrace to combat the flames. It took three
hours to put the fire out. He said the lobby had been filled
with Monaco police dressed in riot gear with masks, holding machine guns, because they believed that a terrorist
attack was under way. He said there was utter confusion,
with people running to and fro but accomplishing very
little. Later, when I asked him his name for this article, he
blanched. 'No, no, Mr Dunne,' he said, 'please don't use
my name.' He drew a finger across his throat.

THE FEAR OF INCURRING the displeasure of Prince Rainier
is rampant among the citizenry. A young woman who is

a resident of Monaco and whose mother is a friend of mine had agreed to work as my translator while I was there. On my arrival, she told me she had decided not to take the job. She said she thought it might not be wise for her to be seen with me, since the renewal of her residence papers was coming up. Although I had been warned that I would be followed, I don't believe I was, but I did have one slightly unsettling experience. I was out walking one Sunday morning when two men in gray suits approached me. I had an odd feeling and immediately said I was looking for the Catholic church to attend Mass. One of them courteously pointed it out to me. I went to Mass and stayed to the end. Later, I saw the same two men in the lobby of my hotel.

The rumor of the two bullets in Safra's body was a constant in conversations among the fashionable element of the town, although it was spoken of in hushed tones and with caution. The fact that no such thing appeared in the autopsy report did not diminish the rumor's popularity, for a very highly placed person was named as the source. People with whom I dined in public stopped talking whenever a waiter put a dish down or took one away, saying that you never knew who might report you. Furthermore, by then the word was out that members of the Safras' nursing staff, as well as butlers, secretaries, and assistants, had been asked to sign confidentiality oaths. Certain of them received as much as $100,000 for not speaking to journalists or outsiders.

*   *   *

W. SOMERSET MAUGHAM, the late British novelist who spent most of his life on the Riviera, once described Monte Carlo as 'a sunny place for shady people'. There are no bums, no panhandlers, and no homeless people sleeping on the street. 'I feel perfectly safe wearing my jewels out at night here,' a lady said to me at Le Grill, a restaurant on the roof of the Hôtel de Paris. But the fatal attack on Safra threw into question, in the words of *Le Journal du Dimanche*, 'the legendary inviolability of the ultrapro-tected State'. It seems absurd that Edmond Safra was not rescued, with all that manpower running around the prem-ises for two hours. One of the most intriguing examples of the botched police work was that, when Lily Safra's chief of security, Samuel Cohen, finally arrived at the scene, she gave him a key that would have unlocked the door to the bunker bathroom, where Safra and Vivian Torrente were inhaling the fumes that were going to kill them. But the Monaco police seized the security chief and put handcuffs on him. It doesn't seem unreasonable to me that someone in that battalion of rescuers could have informed the police that the man they were holding in handcuffs possessed the key to the locked bathroom, and that two people were dying as a result.

Safra's death has come at a particularly bad time for the principality. France has recently accused Monaco of being a major center for money-laundering. Prince Rainier, seventy-seven, who enjoys the status of supreme authority as monarch, has been in ill health and has recently undergone three operations. His heir, Prince Albert, forty-two, has shown no sign of marrying and carrying on the 700-year-old Grimaldi line. Princess Stephanie's unfortunate romantic alliances and inappropriate marriage have dominated the trash media and become a family embarrassment, and the beloved Princess Caroline's third husband, Prince Ernst of Hanover, is proving unpopular with the populace for his unseemly behavior while intoxicated, for example beating up a cameraman and urinating on the Turkish pavilion at the Hanover World's Fair, a prank that nearly caused an international incident. To get the Safra mystery solved and out of the papers as quickly as possible is obviously highly desirable.

THERE WAS NO WAY that I could see Ted Maher in the Monte Carlo prison, and his lawyers, George Blot, who is a citizen of Monaco, and Donald Manasse, an American who lives there, would not be interviewed. From what I gather through friends in Monaco and Ted Maher's family, the lawyers' line is the party line. It occurs to me that Ted Maher needs an Alan Dershowitz to come to his rescue.

One night I went to a birthday party at the Villefranche-sur-Mer villa of Mr and Mrs Oscar Wyatt of Houston, Texas, who have summered on the Riviera for years. The villa, which is pretty special, looks right down on La Leopolda, which is utterly magnificent. Grace Kelly and Cary Grant shot *To Catch a Thief* in the Safra house, when it belonged to other people. I was hoping that Lily Safra would be at Lynn Wyatt's birthday party, but she did not attend. Prince Albert appeared briefly before dinner, dressed in black-tie for a concert that was being held in the palace that night. We were not introduced. Subsequently I heard an unconfirmed report that Prince Albert had been helicoptered out of Monte Carlo on the night of the fire because his father believed that a terrorist attack was under way.

Lynn Wyatt said she had seen Lily Safra at La Leopolda the week before, at a small lunch party for the art dealer William Acquavella and his wife. She said that Lily was in a black T-shirt and black pants, and wearing no jewelry, and that she was staying in the guesthouse because the big house was so lonely without Edmond.

'I'm going to see her in Paris on Thursday,' I told her.

WHEN I FLEW TO PARIS and checked in at the Ritz Hotel, however, I was handed a fax from Lily Safra canceling the interview. Although the fax bore her signature, there was a social faux pas in the letterhead that made me realize it was a legal letter faked as a personal one. Someone as socially adroit as she would never have a letterhead that read 'Mrs Lily Safra'. It would be either just plain Lily Safra or Mrs Edmond Safra. 'Mrs Lily Safra' is the letterhead of a divorced woman, and Lily Safra has ascended in the ranks of the wealthy as possibly the richest widow in the world.

'Dear Mr Dunne,' the fax read. 'On reflection, it is my view that the privacy of my family and that of my husband's family is so precious that it would be inappropriate for me to meet with you at this time. This is particularly so because my husband only died recently.' What didn't ring true to me was the line about the precious privacy of her husband's family, since I had been hearing from all sides for nearly a year stories of their mutual hatred. There were even rumors that the Safra brothers were going to contest Edmond's will, which had been changed in Lily's favor in the months prior to his death.

In Paris, Lily Safra's great friend Hubert de Givenchy declined by fax to meet with me. But the crowd in that city that goes out to dinner every night had a lot of versions of what had happened on the fateful morning of December 3, 1999, when two people died who could very easily have lived. Everyone thought the story was more complicated than the official version – which was that the male nurse did it. 'Sure, sure, he'll do four years, and there'll be $4 million waiting for him,' one man said to me. His wife didn't agree with him. 'You wait. He'll conveniently die in prison in a few years of pneumonia or something.' A more conservative friend of the Safras said to me in Paris, 'Among friends, we avoid talking about it. It might not be what it is.'

THE WELL-KNOWN New York public-relations figure Howard Rubenstein called the editor of this magazine to say that he was Lily Safra's new press representative and that he wanted to set up a meeting for himself and her lawyer, the notoriously tough Stanley Arkin, who had been one of Edmond Safra's lawyers in his case against

American Express. The editor said that he would not meet with the lawyer, and the get-together did not take place. But the point had been made that Lily Safra was distressed that an article was being written about her husband's death.

I was then asked to have lunch with Jeffrey Keil at the headquarters of his business, International Real Returns (IRR), on Wooster Street in the SoHo section of New York.

Keil, who is fifty-seven, left Edmond Safra to start his own financial-advisory firm. He remained very close friends with Lily Safra, and was the first person to arrive in Monte Carlo from the United States after Edmond's death. According to informed sources, he helped Lily make up the guest list for the funeral in Geneva, arrange the seating in the synagogue, and decide which guests would be asked to the reception at the house after the service. He later performed the same function for the memorial service in New York.

THE FLOOR-THROUGH HEADQUARTERS of IRR are wonderfully stylish, in a spare, black-and-white way. Keil's secretary took me into a conference room, where two places had been set at the table. Then Keil came in from another room, where a meeting was going on. He was carrying two presents wrapped in shiny white paper. He said that he had read several of my books and articles in the past weeks and felt he knew enough about me from the way I wrote to know the kind of books I would like. He gave me two beautifully preserved first editions from decades earlier, the memoirs of the Duchess of Windsor, entitled *The Heart Has Its Reasons*, and one called *HRH*, a character study of the Prince of Wales, published in a limited edition in 1926. He also knew that I preferred Perrier to wine.

I'd done my homework, too. I knew that he lived in a beautiful house in Brooklyn Heights. I knew that he'd once gone out with Bianca Jagger and also with Joan Juliet Buck, now the editor of French *Vogue*. His cook had come from his home to prepare our vegetarian meal. The lunch was interesting in a chess-match sort of way. When the social conversation lapsed, we still didn't get to the point of the lunch, which I suppose was to find out what I knew. There was a long power silence, which I hear is supposed to make you nervous, but we both sat it out quite calmly. What he wanted to talk about was how Lily Safra was going to be portrayed in this article. I took out my leather notebook and pen and made no secret of writing down what he said. 'It is important in this part of her life that she be well thought of. It would be devastating for her to be treated unfairly in New York, as she was in the French press. She should be thought of more as, say, Mrs Astor than Mrs Grenville – I mean the younger Mrs Grenville.' I looked at him. I could hardly believe what he had said. Years ago I wrote a popular novel called *The Two Mrs Grenvilles*, based on a tragic death in the Woodward family. In my novel, the younger Mrs Grenville shoots and kills her husband. He must not have finished the book, I thought, remembering that he had just said he had read my books in the past few weeks.

I asked him why there were no guards on duty that night. 'The thought was to reduce the show,' he said. 'It is Monte Carlo, after all, with all its security, so all the armed guards weren't needed.'

I was touched by his very sincere love and respect for Edmond Safra. He told me Edmond loved Lily's grandchildren as if they were his own. He also said that Safra was sensitive about the effects of his disease. He worried that his saliva would drip, and he patted his mouth with a handkerchief constantly. Further, he would leave a room when he anticipated that he was going to shake so that people would not see him.

When I had to leave for another appointment, Keil went down in the elevator with me. I felt as if something had been left unsaid.

'You should really see her,' he said.

'Did you know we were supposed to meet twice, and each time it was canceled?'

He knew. I showed him the fax I had received at the Ritz in Paris. 'She never wrote this,' he said instantly.

'But she signed it,' I said.

He told me Mrs Safra was in New York for the Jewish holidays, which I knew. I said I would be delighted to see her. It never happened.

I KEEP IN CONSTANT TOUCH with Ted Maher's family in Stormville. Heidi Maher and Tammy, her sister-in-law, E-mail me all the updates on Ted's case. Things are not harmonious between Maher's family and the lawyers representing him. When Heidi requested a translation in English of the French fire report, she was told by the lawyers that it would cost $1,000, which she does not have. *Dateline* is preparing a segment on the case. 'Ted wasn't supposed to be on duty that night,' Heidi Maher tells me again and again. 'They put him and Vivian on at the last minute.'

IN HER WIDOWHOOD, Lily Safra has remained mostly out of sight, although she is frequently discussed. A friend of mine and her husband dined at La Leopolda late last summer. My friend told me that their chauffeur-driven car had to be cleared by the guards at the outside gates, and as soon as they entered the grounds they were surrounded by four more guards, carrying machine guns, who escorted the car to the house. My friend described the experience as 'unnerving'. In all probability, La Leopolda will be put up for sale. It's too vast for one person, too lonely. A fascinating rumor made the rounds that Bill Gates had bought it for $90 million. Although there was no follow-up to that story, real estate has definitely been on Lily Safra's mind of late.

She bought a second apartment in her Fifth Avenue building for her daughter, Adriana. A well-known real-estate broker told me that Lily was annoyed that the financial terms of the transaction had been printed in the New York papers. She has also bought a mansion on Eaton Square in London, where they say she will be spending more time. In late August she donated a spectacular fountain and garden for Somerset House, which is being restored in the manner that Jacob Rothschild restored Spencer House. Lily Safra and Lord Rothschild gave a very grand dinner with an international guest list to dedicate the fountain and garden in Edmond Safra's name. The fountain has fifty-five jets of water shooting into the air. Five was Edmond's lucky number. He believed it warded off evil spirits.

EARLY IN OCTOBER, I was dining at La Grenouille, one of the swellest restaurants in New York, with three friends. The ladies sat side by side on the banquette. The other man and I sat on chairs opposite them, our backs to the room, so I didn't have an opportunity to case the joint, which I usually do. When the six people at the table directly behind us got up to leave, I noticed them for the first time. I recognized the banker Ezra Zilkha and his wife, Cecile, prominent citizens in the business, social, and cultural worlds of New York, whom I know. Among their guests was the heiress Amalita Fortabat, who is always described in the society columns as the richest woman in Argentina. The Zilkhas' closest friends for years had been Edmond and Lily Safra. Then I found myself looking directly into the face of the elusive Lily Safra, who had been seated directly behind me for two hours, at the same time that I was talking about her at my table. We recognized each other. I could see it on her face. I could feel it on mine. She bowed her head slightly in a very elegant manner, more of a European gesture than an

American one. I rose to my feet and put out my hand. 'Good evening, Mrs Safra,' I said.

She gave me her hand, replying, 'Good evening, Mr Dunne.'

She was all in black. With her left hand she tossed her shawl over her right shoulder and walked on to join the Zilkhas at the door. They looked so privileged. But I had heard from Heidi Maher earlier that day that there was going to be a re-enactment of the night of the deaths of Edmond Safra and Vivian Torrente for the Monegasque judge handling the case and that Lily had been ordered to be present. Donald Manasse, Ted Maher's lawyer, told me over the phone, 'We hope and expect that the charges will be reduced at the end of the investigation.'

THE RE-ENACTMENT TOOK PLACE on October 20, in great secrecy, at 10:30 at night. It was held in the penthouse, over which a new roof had been built, but which otherwise is as it was on the night of the fire. Everyone involved during the hours of the conflagration was there. It was the first time since Edmond Safra's death that Lily Safra, who had been in her bedroom at the other end of the house when she was awakened by the report of the fire, was in the presence of Ted Maher. She was accompanied by three lawyers, and Ted Maher was under guard, wearing handcuffs and a bullet-proof vest. A source who was present told me they were 'terrified of seeing each other'. Ted went through a re-creation of lighting a toilet-paper fire in a wastebasket with a Howard Slatkin scented candle. The re-enactment lasted until five o'clock in the morning.

Maher has now been in prison for eleven months. He gets to talk to his wife once a week for twenty minutes, and their conversations are monitored and taped. Once, according to Heidi, when Ted brought up the name Lily Safra, the connection between Monaco and Stormville was cut off.

TRAIL OF GUILT

They were careless people . . . they smashed up things and creatures and then retreated back into their money or their vast carelessness, or whatever it was that kept them together, and let other people clean up the mess they had made.
—F. SCOTT FITZGERALD, *The Great Gatsby.*

ON OCTOBER 30, 1975, a fifteen-year-old girl named Martha Moxley was viciously bludgeoned to death in the most exclusive part of Greenwich, Connecticut, one of the most exclusive communities in the United States, where rich people live in grand mansions on lush grounds and go to country clubs and yacht clubs and always feel perfectly safe. The girl's body was dragged sixty or eighty feet and left under a pine tree near her parents' house, where it was discovered the following day by a schoolmate.

The only thing that said Greenwich about the crime was that the murder weapon was a No. 6 Toney Penna golf club. Martha was struck so hard that the shaft broke into four pieces, only three of which were discovered at the scene of the crime. The grip part, which might have had fingerprints of the perpetrator on it, has never been found. The killer used one of the pieces, which had a sharp point, as a dagger and stabbed Martha Moxley through her neck.

For a lot of people in Greenwich, it was inconceivable that one of their own kind could have committed such a heinous crime. They talked about how some awful transient must have come in from Interstate 95 and killed the poor girl. Behind closed doors, however, a lot of people in Belle Haven, as the exclusive enclave is called, firmly believed that the perpetrator was most likely one of the brothers who lived in the beautiful residence of Rushton Skakel, a widower with six unruly sons and a daughter and a staff consisting of a tutor, a nanny, a cook, and a gardener. Tommy Skakel, then seventeen, was the last person to be seen with Martha, and they were rough-housing. Rushton Skakel's very rich family had been residents of Greenwich for three generations. Martha's parents had been residents for only a little over a year. For a quarter of a century, the murder has gone unsolved. This is not a step-by-step account of the case. This is a mini-memoir of my part in this story many years later.

In 1991, when I was covering the William Kennedy Smith rape trial in West Palm Beach for *Vanity Fair*, a rumor circulated around the courthouse that Willie Smith had been an overnight guest at the Rushton Skakel house in Greenwich the night Martha Moxley was killed. Although Tommy Skakel, the second son, had been considered a suspect for years, no charges had ever been brought, and the case was at a standstill. In the end the rumor turned out to be bogus; Willie Smith had not been in the Skakel house that night. But my curiosity had been aroused. 'What ever happened to that case?' I asked someone I knew in Greenwich. 'Nothing,' I was told. At that point, sixteen years had gone by since the murder. 'Remind me of exactly what happened,' I said.

A young girl was beaten to death with a golf club that belonged to a set of clubs in the Skakel house. The Skakels had always enjoyed a bad reputation, and Tommy was thought to have been involved. 'What happened to the family of the dead girl?' I asked. They moved away. Then the father died. 'Where's the mother?' Annapolis, Maryland, was the answer. Her name was Dorthy Moxley. Somehow I felt drawn to this woman. I wrote her and asked if I could come and see her. I said I wanted to talk about her daughter's murder. In those days she was media-shy. She did not ask me to her house. Instead we met at a coffee shop in the Baltimore/Washington airport. I asked her why she had moved away from Greenwich, since that meant there was no one there to keep the case alive. She said she could not bear to look out her windows at the Skakel house. As she described it, I called it a house of secrets. She said she didn't know who had killed her daughter, but she was sure that someone in that house either had done it or knew who had. She told me that the day after the murder there were limousines with out-of-state license plates parked in the Skakel driveway. In 1988 she and her husband, David, who was then head of the New York office of Touche Ross, moved with their son, John, to New York. After her husband died and her son married, Dorthy Moxley moved to a condominium in Annapolis.

I had just written three bestselling novels in a row, and they had all been made into TV mini-series. I told Mrs Moxley that I thought I could write another based loosely on her daughter's murder, since no facts were known publicly at the time, and it might turn a spotlight on the long-dormant case. She said she wasn't sure. Then I told her that I too was the parent of a murdered daughter. Our daughters had been born a year apart, and each was viciously attacked by a man she knew on October 30, although in different years. That moment marked the beginning of our friendship. She said OK, I could write the book.

I changed the murder weapon to a baseball bat, because I didn't want to be sued by the Skakels. I also changed the family makeup a bit and gave some Kennedy touches to the Skakels, whom I called the Bradleys. I threw in a little of my own large Irish Catholic family, too. All of this was for libel reasons. *A Season in Purgatory* came out in 1993, and it made the bestseller lists. The *CBS Evening News* did a long segment on how the book had helped to revive interest in a 1975 murder case in Greenwich, Connecticut. Martha Moxley was soon back in the news, and I was on television quite often talking about her murder. I learned that in certain houses in Greenwich the subject was being discussed again for the first time in years. But no one came forward.

* * *

DURING MY BOOK TOUR for *A Season in Purgatory*, a tall, handsome, well-dressed African-American woman came up to me in the Tattered Cover bookstore in Denver and said that she had information about the Moxley case. We met later at the Brown Palace Hotel. She was a forensic psychologist, and early on she had been hired by the Greenwich police to work on the case. For some reason, which she did not explain, she either left or was let go. She had with her the autopsy pictures of Martha Moxley's body, which no one but the police had ever seen. They were large photographs, about 11 by 14 inches, and simply awful to behold. It is one thing to discuss being bludgeoned by a golf club; it is quite another to see the effects of such an attack. One of the blows had taken off a portion of the right side of Martha's scalp, which was hanging by a piece of skin down over her face. You could see the wound where a short, pointed piece of the shaft had been stabbed into the side of her neck. In one full shot you could see that her jeans had been pulled down. I felt faint. 'He had to have been drunk, or stoned, to have done that to her,' I said, not wanting to see any more. I felt that this woman, whose name I did not write in my notebook – at her request – and which I subsequently forgot, knew more than she was telling me. But I liked her. I trusted her. As she was leaving, she said, 'It wasn't Tommy.' She repeated it. Up till then, Tommy Skakel had been the major suspect in the case. I was convinced that he had done it, and had said so on television. Her words haunted me.

Back home at my house in Connecticut after the book

tour, I was visited by several members of the police team involved in the Moxley case, including Frank Garr, who had played a major part in the investigation from the beginning. They brought me a Connecticut Division of Criminal Justice coffee mug, a Connecticut State Police plaque for my wall, and a Connecticut State Police T-shirt. They asked me to stop criticizing the police work on the case, which I agreed to do. They said it wasn't helping in their ongoing investigation. In the pleasant conversation that ensued, I happened to mention that I had seen photographs of the autopsy. They looked stunned. I said someone had shown them to me in Denver. I saw them look at one another, very upset. 'She stole those pictures,' one said to another. I do not know the mystery behind that story, but there certainly is one. All my attempts to track down my informant have come to naught.

In May 1996, an excellent mini-series of *A Season in Purgatory*, produced by Aaron Spelling, David Brown, and Buzz Berger, was telecast on CBS. The network publicized the show every day for a week before it went on, saying it was based on an actual crime in Greenwich, Connecticut. Newspaper stories talked about the real murder in relation to the mini-series. People were soon discussing the case regularly and openly, but there never seemed to be any progress in solving it.

SEVEN MONTHS AFTER the mini-series aired, an extraordinary thing happened. I had a call at my New York apartment from Bernice Ellis, the receptionist at *Vanity Fair,* who, along with her other duties, monitors calls that come in for the magazine's writers. She knows how to separate the wheat from the chaff. 'It's about the Moxley case,' she said. 'I think you should talk to this guy.'

I did, and we made a lunch date for the next day at Patroon, a restaurant on East 46th Street. Carrying a manila envelope, he came into the restaurant wearing jeans and a T-shirt. That wasn't quite the dress code for Patroon, but they let him in. I hadn't imagined, talking to him on the phone, how young he was going to be. He was twenty-four, but could easily have passed for seventeen. A recent university graduate and fledgling author, he had already had an article published in a national magazine. This is the story he told me.

In 1991, Rushton Skakel, wanting to take the spotlight of suspicion off his sons, had hired a private-detective service in New York called Sullon Associates to investigate Martha Moxley's murder. The agents, who were all former detectives or police officers, signed confidentiality agreements never to reveal anything they learned in the course of their investigation. They were given access to the seven Skakel children and were guaranteed cooperation in a way that the Greenwich police never had been. During the process, Michael Skakel, who had never been a suspect, because he had an alibi that he had been at a cousin's house watching a Monty Python movie at the time of the murder, changed his story completely. He told the detectives that he had climbed a tree outside Martha's bedroom window and masturbated. The agency worked for nearly three years on the assignment. My source told me that the bill for the private investigation was $750,000, and I have subsequently heard a figure even higher than that. When it came time to give the results to Skakel, the agency knew it had to put all its findings into a cohesive report that he could read and digest. Through a friend, the young recent graduate got the job of putting the detectives' findings – from psychiatric reports to interviews – into a narrative form, with a time line and profiles of Skakel family members.

When the report was presented to Rushton Skakel, it indicated that Tommy had not killed Martha Moxley. Michael, the fourth Skakel son, who had never been a suspect, had in all probability killed her. The report suggested that Tommy may have helped his brother move the body. Michael and Tommy were very competitive and fought constantly. Michael had a crush on Martha, so Tommy moved in on his territory. That was the way they behaved. Rushton Skakel, an acknowledged alcoholic, was presumably undone by the findings. He paid the agency, and the report was stashed away, never to see the light of day. But the young man with whom I was having lunch had become emotionally involved in the story he was hired to put together. It was my perception that he had developed an enormous sympathy for Martha Moxley and her mother, and that he was outraged that justice would not be done, that money could make a difference even in a case of murder. Because he was hired several years after the private detectives, no one had thought to have him sign the confidentiality oath. He had read my book and seen me on television, so he secretly appropriated the report and called *Vanity Fair*. Sitting there in Patroon, he handed me the Sutton report.

He was deeply frightened that something bad could happen to him, he said, and he had reason to be. I promised that I would never reveal his name. My plan was to take the report to my house in Connecticut and read it slowly over the next few days before deciding how to deal with the amazing information it contained. But I didn't keep my word. Before I left for the country, hoping to buoy up Dorthy Moxley's spirits, I told her I was in possession of some incredible news. I learned from this experience that everyone tells a secret to at least one person, and Dorthy, in her excitement, did just that. The person she told, apparently jealous of my stash, called Sutton Associates and said that some kid who worked for them had given Dominick Dunne the Skakel report. Confronted, the young man felt betrayed and frightened. I felt awful for having caused him so much anxiety.

RUSHTON SKAKEL HAD ATTENDED Canterbury, the Catholic boarding school in New Milford, Connecticut, which was then for boys only. I also attended Canterbury. Rushton, or Rush, as he was called, was a few years ahead of me, although I did not know him or even remember him until I saw him at Robert Kennedy and Ethel Skakel's wedding in Greenwich, Connecticut, on June 17, 1950. I was there not on a direct invitation from the Skakels but as the date of my then girlfriend, Barbara Cahill, who had been a classmate of Ethel's at Manhattanville College of the

Sacred Heart, the school of choice for proper Catholic girls from rich families. We arrived from New York by yacht for the wedding and reception. I remember being dazzled by the beauty of the Skakel estate, on Lake Avenue. The bridesmaids were Skakel sisters and Kennedy sisters and a cousin of Ethel's. It was the first time I ever saw Rose Kennedy, the wife of the former ambassador to the Court of St James's. She wore a silk dress from Paris and carried a parasol of the same material. She was the absolute queen of Irish Catholic society, and people stepped back as she made her way through the nearly 2,000 guests, greeting friends and meeting strangers. Jack and Bobby Kennedy, the best man and groom, in cutaways, already possessed the glamour and looks that were shortly to fascinate the nation. From every point of view, it was a marriage made in heaven, except that, even then, there was backstage trouble between the Skakel and Kennedy families, which exists to this day.

The Skakel money was from Great Lakes Carbon, once one of the largest privately held companies in the world. The Kennedy fortune came primarily from liquor. By some reports, the Skakels were even richer than the Kennedys. Ethel's father, George Skakel, despised Bobby's father, Joe Kennedy. In his book *The Other Mrs Kennedy*, Jerry Oppenheimer quotes Skakel referring to Joe Kennedy as 'low-life, Irish trash'. This love-hate relationship between the families is also mentioned in a book proposal that Michael Skakel wrote in 1998, almost two years before he was indicted for the murder of Martha Moxley. He writes that his maternal grandfather 'was betrayed, slandered, and vilified' by Joseph Kennedy.

The Skakels are right up there with the Kennedys in the tragedy department. Ethel and Rushton's parents were killed in a private-plane crash in 1955. Their brother George was also killed in a plane crash, and his wife choked to death on a piece of meat at a small dinner party. Rushton's son Tommy, the longtime suspect, was thrown from a moving car when he was four and sustained severe head injuries. Rushton's wife, Ann Reynolds Skakel, died an agonizing death from cancer in 1973, leaving him to raise his unruly tribe of six sons and a daughter. One of Ann Skakel's golf clubs was the weapon that killed Martha Moxley.

A lot of people wanted to get their hands on the Sutton report, but I wasn't willing to share it until the right person came along. My assistant, Arthur Gorton, hid the report so that even I wouldn't know where it was in the event that a wrong person would come after it. In time I gave a copy to Greenwich detective Frank Garr, because he asked for it. It surprised me that I never heard a word from him after that. It's not the sort of report you read and dismiss. Despite some of the startling information in it, nothing advanced the case as a result of Garr's having it. Eventually I came to the conclusion that nothing ever would.

THEN ANOTHER EXTRAORDINARY thing happened. I received a telephone call from Lucianne Goldberg, who was then a literary agent and whom I had known since I covered the 1984 trial of Claus von Bülow for the attempted murder of his wife, Sunny, in Providence, Rhode Island, for *Vanity Fair*. The call came several months prior to the arrival in Goldberg's life of Linda Tripp, with her salacious tales of Monica Lewinsky, blow jobs in the Oval Office, and a semen-stained dress that almost changed the course of American history. Goldberg had become the literary agent of Mark Fuhrman. After he exited from the O. J. Simpson trial in disgrace, Fuhrman had written a book called *Murder in Brentwood*, a fascinating account of the Simpson case from a detective's point of view, which had become a bestseller. Fuhrman will always be a controversial character, but he also happens to be one of America's great detectives. Goldberg said she was looking for an unsolved murder on which Fuhrman could next turn his detective skills for another book. It was a magic moment. 'The Moxley case,' I said excitedly. 'I have some incredible information that I will give him.'

In some accounts of this story it has been said that I became friends with Mark Fuhrman during the Simpson trial. That is not true. Although I was present in the courtroom each time he appeared on the witness stand, I never spoke a word to him. In fact, I had the same hostile feelings toward him back then that everyone who didn't want to see race brought into that case had. I met him for the first time through Lucianne Goldberg. I took him to lunch at the Four Seasons restaurant in New York, and people practically fell off their banquettes trying to get a look at him. He came up to my house in Connecticut, where I gave him the Sutton report, and we talked through the case. I called Dorthy Moxley, who agreed to meet with him. He was excited about the story and eager to go to Greenwich and check things out.

I gave a cocktail party for him. I've always admired cops, and I hate to see the way they are treated on the stand by defense attorneys at murder trials. I invited several of the local cops and their wives, as well as some O. J. junkies among the weekenders who wanted to meet the famous – or infamous – Mark Fuhrman. I also called to invite Frank Garr, thinking he would be thrilled that another book on the case was in the works. He wasn't thrilled at all. He declined to come to the party and said he was writing his own book on the case. I was surprised at that, considering that nothing had been accomplished in twenty-two years. Garr now claims that he was not invited to the party and that he never planned to write a book about the case. What I realized from that call, however, was that Fuhrman was going to get a hard time from the Greenwich police.

I HAVE NEVER REGRETTED giving the Sutton report to Mark Fuhrman, even though it bothered some people greatly. I knew that he would be able to run with the powerful material in the report. Fuhrman is an attention-getter, and people have strong feelings about him. A lot of people hate him, but plenty of others admire him. He was a ruined man after the O. J. Simpson trial, while the man I believe to be the killer of two people walked free. In that courtroom, the charismatic lawyer Johnnie Cochran mesmerized people into believing that to say the n-word was a worse crime than to slit the throats of two people. To me, the two things don't compare in any way, and I knew for sure that the n-word would never pass Mark Fuhrman's lips again. Extremely articulate, he knows how to handle himself on television. Nothing throws him. One of television's great nights was when Fuhrman took on F. Lee Bailey, his tormentor at the Simpson trial, on Larry King's show. He wiped the floor with Bailey, who had done jail time since the Simpson trial, and who had been taken off after his arrest in leg-irons. I knew that Fuhrman would get on all the television shows and make the name Martha Moxley known throughout the land. He so pissed off the Greenwich police that they virtually kicked him out of town. Everything he did was in the news. He was fearless in his statements about Michael Skakel's being the killer. And I firmly believe that his book *Murder in Greenwich*, for which I wrote the introduction, is what caused a grand jury to be called after twenty-five years.

Stephen Carroll, a detective present at the murder scene in 1975, is one of the heroes of this story. Now retired, he has had an enduring passion to see Martha Moxley's killer brought to justice. Carroll was one of the few members of the Greenwich police – perhaps the only one – to understand that Fuhrman had the power to make something happen after all those years. Other police officers stopped speaking to Carroll, and he failed to get a seat at the hearings in Stamford this past June, possibly on the grounds that he would be a witness at the trial.

Among the guests at the cocktail party I gave for Mark Fuhrman was a friend of mine, Connecticut state trooper Conrad Winalski, who appears as a character in my novel *Another City, Not My Own*. Like a great many cops, he is an admirer of Fuhrman's, and he was up on the details of the Moxley case. Months later, on May 2, 1998, Winalski was on desk duty at the police station in Westbrook, Connecticut, when a man came in carrying a woman's pocketbook he had picked up on the side of the road along Interstate 95 in nearby Groton. There was a name and telephone number in the bag, and when Winalski called, the owner was thrilled that her bag had been found. For some reason she had placed it on the roof of her truck, and it had blown off when she drove away. Winalski thanked the man who had turned in the pocketbook and asked for his name so that he could enter it into the field notebook. His name was Michael Skakel.

Winalski, shocked, looked at him. 'Do you know who I am?' asked Skakel. Winalski said yes, he had read a book about the case. 'By that fucking asshole Dominick Dunne?' asked Skakel. He also had some choice names for Fuhrman. Winalski did not tell him that he knew us both. He later quoted Skakel as saying, 'If I had time, I'd tell you exactly what happened. You'll find out. I'm writing a book about it. It'll come out in eight or nine months.' He was in an amiable, chatty mood, according to Winalski, and he went on to say that he was clean and dry. Winalski said Skakel then said, 'Better than anyone, Dunne should know. He's an alcoholic. He goes to meetings. He understands.' Skakel told Winalski, 'People thought I was retarded when I was younger. I went to thirteen schools. Finally they found out I was dyslexic.'

THE NIGHT BEFORE Michael Skakel was indicted, I had a call from Dorthy Moxley. Over the years, since our first meeting at the Baltimore/Washington airport, she and I have become friends. My admiration for her strength and sense of purpose in seeking justice in her daughter's murder is limitless. She said that she had never thought this day would come. 'You started it, and I'll never forget,' she said. We had a little cry over our murdered daughters. She told me I was one of her 'angels'. Other of her angels include Inspector Frank Garr, Mark Fuhrman, and *Newsday* reporter Len Levitt, who has pursued the story with fierce determination from the start. Once friendly, he and I had a falling-out over the fact that I gave the Sutton report to Fuhrman, but we are on the same side and always have been. Our friendship was restored during the hearings on the case in Stamford in June. One day I needed a ride to the railroad station, and he offered to drive me. He lives in Stamford and was on his way to watch his son play in a baseball game. I told him a story about my granddaughter, and soon all was right again.

The night before the indictment, I also talked with Fuhrman, who was in New York to appear on *Good Morning America* and Geraldo Rivera's show. He said that the great irony was that the Sutton report, for which Rushton Skakel had paid so much money in order to have his son Tommy's name cleared, was the very thing that had brought about Michael's indictment. Without it, the case would have been whispered about but ultimately forgotten, as it almost was back in 1991, when I first went to see Dorthy Moxley. A few days later, *Good Morning America* hired Fuhrman to be a commentator at the upcoming trial and announced it in the papers. A few days after that, ABC fired him. I knew from Fuhrman's writing partner, Steve Weeks, that he was devastated. He returned to his home in Idaho.

When the hearings were under way, I saw Charlie Gibson, the co-host with Diane Sawyer of *Good Morning America*, at show-business reporter Claudia Cohen's farewell party for Kathie Lee Gifford at Swifty's restaurant. Several of the ABC hierarchy were there. During dinner, Gibson asked me across the table if Mark Fuhrman was at the hearings. I said no. 'Was it because of us?' he asked. 'I think so,' I replied. He said the reason the show had let Fuhrman go was that there had been complaints from minority members in the news department. He said the situation had been badly handled – things should have been checked out before Fuhrman was offered the job. Although Fuhrman's extraordinary work on the Moxley–Skakel case has brought about a redemption in his life, there will always be some who can never forgive him.

Fuhrman's mention of the Sutton report, the night before Michael Skakel's indictment, made me remember the young man who had removed it from Sutton Associates and given it to me four years earlier. I had never heard from him again, or ever revealed his name, although another writer petulantly did in a book he wrote on the case. I was not sure if he still lived in New York. I dialed the number I had in my notes and recognized his voice on the answering machine. Calling him by his first name, I left a message saying, in effect, 'Michael Skakel is going to be indicted tomorrow in Stamford. I want you to know that I consider you the hero of this story. You're the one who made it happen. What you did was very brave.' About a week later, he left a message on my machine thanking me.

A FASCINATING AND TRAGIC SIDE FIGURE in this story is a man named Ken Littleton. In 1975 he was a twenty-three-year-old graduate of Williams College who taught science and coached sports at the exclusive Brunswick School, which three of the Skakel boys attended. He was hired by Rushton Skakel to be a live-in tutor for his sons and help curb their wild ways. His first night on the job turned out to be the night of the murder.

Early that evening, he took some of the Skakel children to the Belle Haven Club for dinner, since their father was away on a hunting holiday. A few of them, including Tommy and Michael, drank considerably, although they were only teenagers. There is no indication that either Littleton or the club objected. It was the night before Halloween, called 'mischief night'. About a dozen friends, including Martha Moxley, went to the Skakel house after dinner. Some of the Skakel boys went over to the house of their cousins the Terriens. No one bothered to check with Ken Littleton whether that was all right, so clearly he was not emerging as an authority figure in the minds of the Skakel brothers. After the body of Martha Moxley was discovered the next day, Littleton became a prime suspect. Nearly a year later he left the house after a falling-out with Rushton, and over the years he was interrogated again and again.

It would have been a great convenience for everyone to blame the murder on the tutor; indeed, the mother of one girl present that evening later went as far as to suggest to the police that Littleton had done it. The experience of that night virtually ruined Littleton's life. Subsequently he was arrested in Nantucket for grand larceny, breaking and entering, and burglary. He became alcoholic. It is possible that Littleton knew more than he told the police. But there's one thing I'm sure he didn't do: he did not kill Martha Moxley.

THE WOMAN WHO POINTED the finger at Ken Littleton as Martha Moxley's killer went to visit Dorthy Moxley at her current home in New Jersey after Mark Fuhrman's book came out but before Michael Skakel was indicted. She took along her daughter, who had been at the Skakel house the night Martha was murdered. The two women had not seen each other in years. During lunch, the visitor asked Dorthy Moxley, whose friend she had once been, to give up pursuing the case. So much time had gone by, she argued. What good would it do? Hadn't the Skakels suffered enough? Dorthy Moxley said, 'Would you ask that if it was *your* daughter?' Then the visitors left.

I believe that many people who lived in Belle Haven back then know things about the murder that they haven't told. I got a call last year from a distraught woman who had just attended her twenty-fifth reunion at the Convent of the Sacred Heart in Greenwich. She was horrified that several of the girls who had been at the Skakels' house on mischief night in 1975 were talking openly about it, telling what they knew and what their parents had known. But none of them wanted to come forward. Best not to get involved, they all agreed.

Last winter I was stopped on the street on the Upper East Side by a man who told me he used to be a good friend of Michael Skakel's. 'Michael told me he was so drunk he didn't remember whether he did it or not,' the man said. When I asked him what his name was, he walked away. There was no way I could evaluate his statement, even though it would turn out to be consistent with some testimony given at the trial.

This past July, I was browsing in the Northshire bookshop in Manchester, Vermont. A very good-looking woman came up to me and told me she was from Greenwich. 'I read Mark Fuhrman's book and agree with every word,' she said. 'My first husband lived very near the Skakels.' It turned out that I had gone to school with her first husband's brother. 'Do you think they're going to get this guy?' she wanted to know. At the time, the judge's ruling on whether the case would go to trial had still not come down. Then she said the most startling thing: 'I know where the grip part of the golf club is.' 'You do?' I asked, stunned. 'A lot of people in Greenwich know,' she said. 'Are you going to tell me? It's very important,' I said. 'No,' she replied and left the store.

THREE DAYS AFTER Michael Skakel was indicted, Robert Kennedy Jr was quoted in *The New York Times* as saying that I had a vendetta and that Mark Fuhrman was in this for the money. The next day a reporter from the *Times* came to interview me for the 'Public Lives' column. She asked if it was true that I had a vendetta. I do have a vendetta against people who get away with rape and murder, although I knew that was not what Kennedy meant. The reporter had just called Robert Kennedy Jr, she said, and he had told her his cousin was *not* guilty. My feeling was that Kennedy had brought her around to the same opinion, but I do not know that. She said she had never heard anyone speak as badly about another person as Kennedy had spoken about me. That startled me, because to the best of my knowledge I have never met him, although he has ample reason to dislike me because of my coverage of the William Kennedy Smith rape trial and the many Kennedyesque touches in my book *A Season in Purgatory*. A Hudson River environmentalist, he is often photographed walking about with a falcon on his forefinger. I asked the reporter what Kennedy had said about me, but she declined to tell me, saying it was off the record.

Robert Kennedy's defense of his cousin surprised me, as did his subsequent appearance on Skakel's behalf at the hearings in Stamford. In Michael Skakel's book proposal, which had leaked into the hands of certain members of the press, myself included, he quotes Robert Kennedy as saying about his brother Michael Kennedy, 'Oh, my God, he's just like Willie,' meaning their cousin William Kennedy Smith. Skakel continues: 'Questioned further, he tells me that William Kennedy Smith was guilty of rape, that his acquittal was the result of Kennedy power.' (Robert Kennedy denies having made these remarks.) At times, Skakel's depiction of the family of Ethel and Robert Kennedy is absolutely lethal, although he is admiring of Robert junior's return to sobriety, which they did together. The much-gossiped-about book proposal had two titles. One version was called *Dead Man Talking: A Kennedy Cousin Comes Clean*. The second, toned-down version bore the title *The Obvious*. The proposal, which was submitted to five publishers before Skakel's indictment, has been scrapped. The book will probably never be written.

When Congressman Joseph Kennedy was planning to run for the governorship of Massachusetts in 1998, he wanted his brother Michael to be his campaign manager. Michael Kennedy ran Citizens Energy Corporation, a nonprofit fund based in Boston which provides heat and fuel for the poor. In Michael Kennedy's absence, they brought in their cousin Michael Skakel to mind the store. Somewhere along the line, there was a disagreement between the cousins, and Michael Kennedy dismissed Michael Skakel. It is generally agreed that it was Michael Skakel who, in revenge, leaked to the papers that Michael

Kennedy was having an affair with a teenage baby-sitter. The news was devastating to the Kennedy family. John Kennedy Jr, then the editor of *George* magazine, described his cousins as poster boys for bad behavior. Michael Kennedy and his wife, Victoria Gifford Kennedy, the daughter of Frank Gifford, filed for divorce. The father of the baby-sitter, who was a family friend and contributor to the Democratic Party, threatened to sue Kennedy. In 1997, Michael Kennedy was killed in an accident in Aspen while playing football on skis. Joe Kennedy dropped out of the gubernatorial race and later left Congress. 'I am a member of a family sick unto death with generations of secrets,' Michael Skakel writes in his proposal.

AT A PARTY in New York, I heard from a renowned author with close ties to the Kennedy family that the Kennedys were distressed that Michael Skakel was constantly identified in the press as the nephew of Ethel and Robert Kennedy, because it dragged the Kennedy name into a murder case in which they had no involvement whatsoever. The fact of the matter is, had it not been for the Kennedy connection, this story would not have aroused nearly so much interest. The same person told me that the Kennedys were pressing for a plea bargain so that the case would not go to trial, but that there was a reluctance on the part of Michael Skakel and his lawyer, Mickey Sherman, who seemed sure that Michael would be acquitted. Since my informant had not spoken off the record, I repeated the remarks to several people, and eventually an item appeared in Liz Smith's column. Sherman called Smith to deny absolutely that there had ever been talk of a plea bargain, which she dutifully printed.

When I arrived at the courthouse in Stamford at 8:30 A.M. on June 28, the word had already been spread to the press by Mickey Sherman that Robert Kennedy Jr might be attending the session that day. 'Maybe even Ethel, I heard,' one journalist said to me, but Ethel was a no-show. Then along came Robert Kennedy Jr and his brother Douglas. Robert made a forceful statement to the media that his cousin was *not* guilty. He said, 'It is a horrible, unspeakable tragedy, but it only compounds it to blame Michael, who is innocent.'

Kennedy was newsworthy himself that week, because eight of his board members at Riverkeeper, the environmental group he heads, resigned in protest after he secretly rehired a fired board member who had smuggled rare cockatoo eggs into the United States to be hatched and sold as pets. Kennedy sat with the Skakel family during the morning session, gave Michael an in-full-view bear hug at the lunch break, but did not return for the afternoon session. It reminded me of John Kennedy Jr's courtesy visit to the William Kennedy Smith trial in West Palm Beach, where he posed for pictures and left, never to return.

LORRAINE MURPHY, the trial-court administrator who had the terrible job of trying to satisfy the seating demands of the press in the very small courtroom in Stamford, was extremely good to me, and I was well seated for the whole enchilada, never having to share my seat with anyone. Two of my pals from the O. J. Simpson trial were also there. Jeffrey Toobin, who wrote a bestseller about that trial and another about the Clinton impeachment, was covering the hearings for ABC News and *The New Yorker*. Dan Abrams, who has become a star legal reporter since the Simpson trial, was covering them for NBC News.

For me, one of the most interesting things to observe in a courtroom is the interplay between the families of the victim and the defendant. Dorthy Moxley, her son, John, and daughter-in-law, Cara, her late husband's sister, Mary Jo Rahatz, the *Newsday* reporter Len Levitt, and an advocate for Victims Rights sat in the row in front of me. Over the years Dorthy has become very media-savvy, and she is extremely popular with the press. Across the aisle, directly behind Michael Skakel at the defense table, sat the Skakels. Although the Skakel family is famously dysfunctional, four of Michael's five brothers, his sister, and his brother-in-law gave the appearance of a united family. Tommy Skakel, the longtime suspect, was not present, although his lawyer, Manny Margolis, who has represented him for almost twenty-five years, was. Michael's wife was not present. Nor was his father, Rushton Skakel. Rushton, who now lives in Hobe Sound, Florida, with his second wife, did everything possible, including having his lawyers declare him mentally unstable, to avoid testifying before the grand jury. In his book proposal, Michael calls his father an alcoholic and reveals an abiding hatred of him. Curiously, Michael and his wife, the niece of another

Skakel lawyer, lived in the same condominium complex in Hobe Sound as Michael's father, but they have recently purchased a house in Windham, New York, where the Skakel family had a weekend house at the time of the murder.

Because this was a probable-cause hearing, not a trial, there was no jury. It would later be up to the judge, Maureen Dennis, a former public defender, to decide whether there was sufficient evidence to go to trial and, if so, whether the defendant should be tried as a juvenile or as an adult. Skakel was fifteen in 1975; he is now thirty-nine.

THE PROSECUTION CALLED in three former acquaintances from the Elan School in Poland Springs, Maine, who say they heard Skakel confess to the crime. The school, which has a current tuition of nearly $50,000 a year, is, or was, a reform school for the children of the rich. It was a place to send troubled, drunk, drugged kids whose families had given up on them. In addition to whatever else Michael Skakel was, he was a drunk and a drugger when Rushton Skakel sent him there sometime after the murder. When he ran away from Elan, and he did several times, he was always caught and sent back. In his book proposal, Michael Skakel describes Elan as a concentration camp for kids, 'where I was subjected to a level of torture deemed unacceptable even for prisoners of war'.

During the hearings, I watched Joe Ricci, the headmaster of Elan, on the Geraldo Rivera show. No tweed sport coat and gray flannels in the New England prep-school tradition for Ricci: he had a shaved head, wore a black shirt and jacket, and sweated noticeably as he answered questions and decried former students of the school who had taken the stand to testify against Skakel. He appeared to be reading his answers off file cards. 'I bet Mickey Sherman gave him those answers he's reading,' said a lady I know, who happens to know Sherman very well. 'Doesn't it sound like Mickey?' Sherman denies having coached Joe Ricci.

John Higgins, who is now thirty-seven, described the school as 'a place to hide your kids if they bothered you . . . It was a place for my stepdad to keep me at bay.' After Higgins had been at the school for six months or so, he made the acquaintance of Michael Skakel. They met in their dual roles as 'night owls', guards who kept watch on other students to prevent them from running away. 'He related to me he had been involved with a murder,' said Higgins. He said they had talked for a couple of hours. He said that Michael had told him he took a golf club out of a bag and was running through the woods and had a black-out. 'He said he didn't know if he did it. He couldn't remember if he did it.'

In the jury box, which was in front of me, I could see two sketch artists, who had the best view of Michael, begin excitedly drawing tears on his face. I looked over at him, and although his face was turned away, I could see that he was crying. Soon everyone was staring at him. It was close to lunchtime, and Judge Dennis called a break. As the courtroom began to clear, Michael Skakel stood up and turned to his siblings, his face drenched with tears. His four brothers and his brother-in-law all crowded around him and hugged him. His sister, Julie, who became the mother in the family after their mother's death, was crying as she kissed Michael on the cheek. Still wrapped together as one, the seven of them moved slowly out of the courtroom into the corridor.

MOST PEOPLE HAD LEFT the building for lunch. Michael moved away from his siblings, and his face had the look of a man in psychic pain. He leaned forward until he was almost doubled in two, and sobbed uncontrollably. For a moment I thought he might confess. Only once before had I seen a man cry with such utter hopelessness. Jason Simpson, the son of O. J. Simpson from his first marriage, sobbed in that manner on the floor of the courtroom, unable to be comforted by his mother, his sister, or his aunts, on the morning before his father's acquittal was announced. Later, when my eyes met with Michael Skakel's, he looked defeated to me. Meanwhile, outside in front of the cameras, Mickey Sherman, in a supremely unclassy moment, with a sneer on his face and a note of contempt in his voice, referred to John Higgins as a moron.

Then a second Elan alumnus, Gregory Coleman, who at the time was in a maximum-security prison in Rochester, New York, for criminal trespassing on his former wife's house, took the stand. He had been sent to Elan after stealing a television set. He was one of many students who participated in punishing a female student for some infraction he could not remember by beating her with wooden paddles and their hands. 'She went into shock . . . urinated on herself [and] defecated on herself,' said Coleman, who was put in charge of guarding Michael Skakel after he ran away. He said Skakel had special privileges – he had a stereo and could listen to music. Coleman once said, 'This guy can get away with murder.' He said that Skakel replied, 'I'm going to get away with murder. I'm a Kennedy.' Using a golf term, Coleman testified, Skakel said he 'drove her skull' after she resisted his advances. On a later occasion, Coleman said, Michael told him that he had masturbated on Martha's body. During a primal-scream session, Michael Skakel was told to scream, 'I'm sorry. I'm sorry.'

Coleman's testimony was another setback for Michael Skakel. Mickey Sherman told the television reporters outside the courthouse that Michael was crying because he couldn't bear hearing the witnesses lie.

THERE IS SOMETHING very likable about Mickey Sherman. I have known him, though not well, since 1994, and we have been on *Burden of Proof* and other talk shows together. He is fun to be with. He's a regular at Elaine's, the Upper East Side hangout for the literary set and reporters, and he loves media attention. What Robert Shapiro was to the Simpson trial in matters of publicity, Mickey Sherman is to the Skakel case. One of his close friends is the singer Michael Bolton. In fact, Bolton's very tall bodyguard served as Michael Skakel's bodyguard during the hearings in Stamford. The first time I telephoned Sherman, it was to check out a story I'd heard – that he and the model Paula Barbieri were lying side by side on lounge chairs at the swimming pool of the Mirage Hotel in Las Vegas, where both were the guests of Michael Bolton, when Paula got the telephone call informing her that Nicole Brown Simpson, her boyfriend O. J. Simpson's wife, and a man named Ronald Goldman had been murdered the night before. Yes, it was true, Sherman said, but he asked me not to use it. He wanted to be a talking head on television during the Simpson trial, and the public association with Barbieri, whom he had seen only that once, might inhibit that. I didn't use the information, but now it doesn't matter. On one of the television shows on which we appeared, he kept saying that the Sutton report was 'stolen', but he made it sound as if stealing it were a worse crime than the murder of Martha Moxley.

I was surprised to run into Sherman in Los Angeles during the Academy Awards festivities this past March. I was having lunch in the coffee shop of the Beverly Hills Hotel with the playwright Mart Crowley when Sherman walked in. We greeted each other, and he sat on the stool next to me. He said he was surprised that I hadn't been at Michael Skakel's arraignment, which had taken place a week or two previously. I hadn't been able to attend. 'What did you think of what Michael said to Mrs Moxley?' he asked proudly. (Skakel had gone up to Dorthy Moxley at the courthouse and told her she had the wrong guy, and his remark made all the papers and newscasts.) I told Sherman what I thought of it. I said, 'I thought it was fake and staged, and I'll bet that you wrote the line for him to say. It was like Johnnie Cochran giving the "absolutely 100 percent not guilty" line to O. J. Simpson. Would you like to hear what Dorthy Moxley thought about that stunt? She was deeply offended. She said to me on the telephone, "How dare he come into my space? I haven't seen him for twenty-five years, and he's on trial for killing my daughter. How *dare* he call me Dorthy?"' You can say things like that to Mickey Sherman, and he doesn't get mad.

I PREDICTED, quite incorrectly, that Judge Dennis's ruling as to whether to proceed to trial or not would come down quickly. I felt that *I* could have arrived at the correct ruling in less time than it took the O. J. Simpson jury to arrive at its acquittal. But the judge took her own sweet time. After two weeks with no word, I went off to Monte Carlo to work on another story of death and mystery. I returned after ten days. I called my friends in the press. I called the district attorney's office. There had still not been a peep from the judge.

Then on August 17, nearly six weeks after the conclusion of the hearings, Judge Dennis released her ruling. She wrote about John Higgins and Gregory Coleman, Skakel's schoolmates at Elan, whose testimony had made him cry in the courtroom, 'having observed the conduct, demeanor and attitudes of these witnesses, the court finds them each to be credible'. She said in her thirteen-page statement, 'The court finds that the specific element of intent to cause death has been proven well beyond a mere suspicion.' Mickey Sherman, who happened to be appearing on Court TV on another case at the time the judge's ruling came over the wire, professed on television not to be surprised. Judge Dennis delayed her decision as to whether Skakel should be tried as a juvenile or an adult. If he is tried as a juvenile and found guilty, he could possibly receive four years at most. If he is tried as an adult, he could receive sixty-five years, or so Mickey Sherman told Katie Couric on the *Today* show the next morning. I called Dorthy Moxley for her reaction. 'I've been patient for twenty-five years,' she said.

The conclusion of this sad story has yet to be reached, as this book goes to press. But much has happened in the intervening times. Judge Maureen Dennis, in one of the slowest decisions on record, ruled quite correctly, that Michael Skakel, now forty and fat, would be tried as an adult, although as of now, no date has been set for the trial. There have been backstage dramas that have kept the story in the news. Michael Skakel's wife, Margo Sheridan Skakel, left him, taking their child with her, and threatening, according to the tabloids, to write a tell-all book about Michael. Margo is the niece of the first lawyer hired by Rushton Skakel after the murder twenty-five years ago, so she has literally grown up with the story. It amazed me that family pressures weren't put on her to stay in the marriage until after the trial. It's also just come to light that the Greenwich police questioned the Skakel gardener-chauffeur in 1978, three years after the murder, about an incident where Michael pulled a knife on the driver as he was being driven to his psychiatrist in New York, saying, 'Shut up and drive, or I'll stab you,' after having had a fight with his father, Rushton. Michael also tried to commit suicide twice that day by jumping out of the car and trying to jump off the Triborough Bridge. Way back then, the police also knew about the confessions at the Elan School, the elite reform school in Maine where Rushton Skakel sent Michael. If everyone had acted honestly all those years ago – family, friends, police, and priests – the juvenile perpetrator would long have been out of prison by now.

Time Warner Paperbacks now offers an exciting range of quality titles by both established and new authors. All of the books in this series are available from:

TIME WARNER PAPERBACKS
PO Box 121, Kettering, Northants NN14 4ZQ
Tel: 01832 737525. Fax: 01832 733076
Email: aspenhouse@FSBDial.co.uk

POST AND PACKING:
Payments can be made as follows: cheque, postal order (payable to Time Warner Books UK) or by credit cards, Visa/Access. Do not send cash or currency.

All UK orders	**FREE OF CHARGE**
EC and Overseas	25% of order value

Name (BLOCK LETTERS) ....

Address ....

....

....

Post/zip code: ....

☐ I enclose my remittance £ ....

☐ I wish to pay by Visa/Access/Mastercard/Eurocard

Card Expiry Date
